When There is No FEMA

Survival for Normal People in (Very) Abnormal Times

by Richard B. Bryant

Nov 6, 2013

Published by Dread Moon Enterprises, LLC
Tampa, Florida USA
www.dreadmoon.com

Dread Moon Enterprises LLC has endeavored to provide proper trademark information about all companies and products referenced in this book through the appropriate use of capitalization, however we cannot guarantee the accuracy of this information.

Published by:
  Dread Moon Enterprises, LLC
  5470 E. Busch Blvd, Suite #174
  Tampa, FL 33617

International Standard Book Number (ISBN): 978-0-9898194-0-4

First Printing: Oct. 2013

Printed in the United States of America by CreateSpace - an Amazon Company *(www.createspace.com)*.

IMPORTANT NOTE TO THE READER:
Some aspects of disaster preparedness involve various degrees of risk. While every effort has been made in the compilation of this book to be as accurate and complete as possible, the author and publisher assume no liability or responsibility for errors, omissions or any misuse of the information contained herein which might result, either directly or indirectly, in physical or financial damages or other losses.

*This book is dedicated to
those with busy hands
and watchful eyes
who work diligently
to protect the ones they love.*

Acknowledgements

This work is truly a multi-generational family effort that could not have been realized without the contributions of some treasured family members, and I must take this opportunity to acknowledge those contributions and convey my unending gratitude. My oldest son, Richard L. Bryant, served as the editor and carefully reviewed the manuscript (in some cases multiple times) from cover-to-cover for proper organization and clear content. Without his truly erudite insights and contributions the quality of this work would have suffered greatly.

My dear mother, Willazene Bryant, who throughout my life has been a true stickler for grammar and language (a true defender of the King's English) provided a final 'polishing' proofread (I found a way to put her undying affection for words and language to good, and less vexing, use!).

I must also acknowledge the contributions of my father, Mr. Dick Bryant, who in fact contributed unknowingly. It was he who introduced me to hunting, fishing and camping; and put me to work on the family farm in my younger years. As I became a prepper all of the knowledge gained from these experiences came flooding back through time and space to help add much-needed substance to key sections of this book. Without these core contributions I'm sure the content between these covers would be so dry that the pages would simply crumble and blow away like so much dust in the wind.

Words do me poor service in thanking these wonderful people so profoundly for helping to breathe life into this work.

Richard B. Bryant
Tampa, Florida

Contents

Contents

Contents

Contents

Contents

List of Tables

List of Tables

Author's Preface

NOTE: *If you are opening this book to deal with a major disaster that is already taking place (or which is imminent) then please begin immediately with chapter 14 on page 391 ('Forming a Disaster Community'), and bring that chapter to the immediate attention of influential members of your community. If you are not well-prepared, then the guidance provided in that chapter may make the difference between life and death for many people!*

In the presentations I have been privileged, over the years, to provide on the subject of disaster preparedness I have always started with an apology; an apology that I would also like to offer here to you. I would like to apologize that in the discipline of disaster preparedness I cannot point to a university sheepskin on the wall that conveys to me The System's 'seal of approval' indicating that I have formally achieved some well-recognized, standard milestone in the subject domain.

Certainly there are many classes that are taught on survival and disaster management, however by definition all classes that are part of *"The System"* inevitably assume that *"The System"* will always exist, and that *"The System"* is part of the solution rather than being part of the problem. Even military survival courses assume that the soldier-on-the-run is being backed up by a literal army.

These are **NOT** the types of disasters that I am anticipating as I write this book. This book anticipates disasters on the order of magnitude of *Hurricane Katrina* and *Superstorm Sandy* when *"The System"* broke down and the calvary did not come charging over the hill in time to save lives and property. In fact, **this book anticipates disasters that will make Hurricane Katrina and Superstorm Sandy look like a walk in the park.**

There are no diplomas given for preparing for the end of a system that produces diplomas. There are, however, endless nights of painstaking research spent chasing down elusive facts, distilling them, and framing the results of that effort into proper context. The ultimate result of those endless nights is the book you now hold in your hands. To understand some measure of the effort involved I would invite you to peruse the bibliography. I cannot point to a sheepskin, however I can point to this work, which I humbly pray will provide its own testament.

My own interest in disaster preparedness started with the advent of the global financial crisis of 2007 (a crisis which continues to this day). Since that time financial disasters have erupted across the world, and nothing in the news has done anything to allay my concerns. The political situation in the US since that time has also deteriorated to the point that, at times, it seems our society is ready to come apart at the seams. With regard to politics, I did not get far into prepping before I dropped all concern with finger-pointing. If there is a finger to be pointed it ultimately must be pointed at a great many of us who have allowed our society to degenerate over many, many years. To prepare for that which looms ahead very few of us have time or energy for finger-pointing (myself included!).

Over the years that followed I started a local prepper group that has met semi-regularly since. Through that diverse group I gained new insights and enlightenment, and my thought processes began to evolve significantly. While I started, as many preppers do, in contemplating a post-disaster world as what I like to refer to as an 'extended camping trip', I quickly came to realize that the reality facing us is not nearly so kind, and infinitely more dangerous. I came to understand the value of community, and the need to not just put back supplies, but to develop new skills for a very different future economy. I came to understand that the most important preparation is maximizing one's health **TODAY**! And, ultimately, I became aware of the critical importance of the spiritual side of prepping, and how it can enrich one's life in amazing ways.

As I continued to study the topic of preparedness I also became aware of other serious threats that I had never considered - threats which merit every bit as much concern as any economic disaster. As I read about the *Spanish Flu* outbreak of 1918 I realized how, in today's world of global travel and high population density, a recurrence would be profoundly devastating. I learned that the New Madrid fault in the southeastern US, which is overdue for a serious earthquake, could make the damage of Hurricane Katrina seem a child's temper tantrum. I learned how a very possible recurrence of the 1859 *Carrington Event* - which is entirely possible - could instantly plunge much of the world into total, decades-long chaos and anarchy. And since that time I've seen major disasters around the world only validate my concerns.

In addition to becoming aware of these other very real and serious threats I also came to believe that our society has evolved into a real 'house of cards'; that our systems are so inter-dependant that if one goes down for any significant time the other systems will follow. For example, if electricity becomes unavailable then fuel pumps stop working; if fuel pumps stop working then transportation systems stop; if transportation systems stop then the shelves of grocery stores quickly become empty; and if grocery shelves go empty it suddenly becomes too dangerous for anyone to venture forth to repair any of the aforementioned critical systems. History (even modern history) is dotted with the ruins of nations that descended from the lap of luxury into clusters of vacant buildings pock-marked with holes left by bullets and artillery shells.

Please do not misinterpret my concerns as being any sort of panic, because that is far from the truth. Rather, I have simply come to realize that I have not, over the years, performed appropriate due diligence to prepare for the types of major disasters for which there is ample historical precedent, and that as a result I must now diligently and methodically work to correct that oversight. Having met many other preppers over these recent years I can tell you that, unlike those depicted in the mass media, the great majority of preppers share my own long-term view and commitment. We realize that even if we were fortunate enough to avoid a major disaster in our lifetimes (not likely, unfortunately), our children very well may not. And, if they are to be ready is it incumbent on our generation to set the example by leaving a legacy of preparedness.

Decades ago, before I was an "urban professional" (read "yuppie"), I was a small town farm boy growing up in the bottom lands of West Tennessee. While in later years I would be mesmerized by the nicest car or the fastest computer, in those early days I was equally transfixed by the best fishing tackle and the best ammunition for my .22 caliber Remington Nylon 66 rifle (which, by the way, would be a **TREMENDOUS** prepper gun today if you can find one in good condition!). As I became a prepper I became re-acquainted with that earlier version of myself, and that experience alone has been worth everything I've invested into my own preparedness.

Purpose and Scope

Unlike many books that seek to cover the topic of contemporary survivalism, you will find very little discussion of *'zombies'* within these pages, nor will you read anything of a paramilitary nature. I will leave it to other authors to appeal to the emotional side of prepping while I seek to inform those with a more pragmatic (and realistic) streak. As the title suggests, the information distilled for you here is intended to address the needs of the common person who wishes to perform the due diligence required to have best chances of surviving a large and widespread disruption to normal life. Between these covers you'll dive into deep detail about many aspects of modern survival - **details that are intended to save lives!** For those new to prepping, this book is also intended to accelerate the evolution of your own survival-related thought processes in such a way that you'll be able to make the best, most practical decisions on how to prepare with the resources you have available.

I have been tempted to describe this book as *"part tutorial, part reference"*, however also dispersed within are important "nuggets of gold" that were born from dogged research and countless into-the-night discussions with other expert preppers. (In one case in particular that involved describing the safe handling and use of certain possibly-dangerous substances, multiple days of research were necessary before I felt comfortable composing a single para-graph.) This painstaking process resulted in a work that is more than reference or tutorial - it has resulted in a book containing insights that should serve to help the prepper (partic-ularly those new to prepping) to *'keep their heads on straight'* about prepping.

This book seeks to cover every major aspect of disaster preparedness with sufficient detail that the reader has a 'fighting chance' to survive under the harshest conditions. The reader is encouraged to compliment this material with other high-quality references that drill down into even more detail on those relevant topics which apply most to their specific situation. I've identified some additional highly-recommended sources of information in section 15.9 in the final chapter of this book.

About Using this Book

It is not necessarily intended that the reader will, as with many books, ingest the full contents from cover-to-cover and then place it on a shelf to collect dust. Rather, I envision the reader being like a bee hovering from flower to flower in no particular sequence and collecting whatever nectar of information suits the needs of the moment. It is also my intent that when the bee does settle on a flower (or, in this case, the reader's attention does settle on a chapter or section of this book) that their needs be satisified to the fullest. So, please accept this invitation to peruse the contents, find a topic that has particular appeal, and dig in!

Thoughts for Those Who Feel 'Overwhelmed'

In speaking before many groups on the subject of preparedness I have been deeply affected by the concerns expressed by those who sense danger ahead but feel that they are not physically and/or financially able to adequately prepare. Before plunging into the facts and figures of preparedness I want to share a message of hope with those who have this feeling of helplessness.

For those who have some financial means but have physical limitations I would suggest working to team up in advance with those who are physically capable but have no financial resources. In building such relationships you must be **EXCEEDINGLY** careful. Don't trust anyone just because you are related to them, and don't trust someone in this role just because you 'like' them. Also, you should disqualify anyone who has any strong fondness for **any** narcotic or intoxicant. Age should not be a strong factor if they bring the physical ability to the table (I have known as many people of high character who were young as who were older). A potential partner's or employee's political beliefs should not be a factor (once again, I've known as many people who would quality for total trust who were liberal as were conservative). As an example, if you know someone you can implicitly trust who has a strong interest in working on cars but cannot afford tools or advertising, then you might team with them to start an auto repair business (even if it's just a 'shade tree mechanic' business that places free ads on The Internet).

For those who have physical limitations and have little or no financial means let me assure you that there is one service you can offer for sale (or with which you can barter) that will be in great demand. That service is 'security'. **Even if you are in a wheelchair you can hold a gun in your lap and watch a door.**

For the types of disasters potentially facing us today I will assure you that a single bucket of food and a single round of ammunition can, under the right circumstances, be well worth ten times its weight in gold. A simple bar of soap, roll of bathroom tissue or tube of antibiotic ointment would have tremendous value. Those little flattened, dehydrated sponges that take up almost zero space until water is added will likewise be worth a king's ransom (you'll understand why when the bathroom tissue runs out!).

In addition to doing what you can to prepare, the most important thing you can do has absolutely zero cost - and that is to become a little more physically fit every week. If your mind is becoming stronger, and your body is becoming stronger, then your perspective will begin to improve and that feeling of being a victim will be replaced with a positive feeling of empowerment and self-determination.

1. Introduction

"And God said unto Noah,
The end of all flesh is come before me;
for the earth is filled with violence through them;
and, behold, I will destroy them with the earth."

Genesis 6:13-14

Recent news and events, such as the devastating earthquakes in Haiti, Chile and Japan, as well as international unrest associated with the world economic turmoil that began in 2007, have caused many people to start to give serious consideration to getting prepared for disasters that, in previous years, would have been unthinkable.

While the subject of disaster preparedness is sufficiently broad and deep that no single book can cover the topic completely, this was written to be the book you would want to have if you could 'only take one book with you'. Even the bright red cover was intentionally designed to make it stand out on a crowded bookshelf - ready to grab-and-go at a moment's notice!

In recent months the popular term *'prepping'* has been coined to describe this process and those involved in prepping are often referred to as *'preppers'*. In years past the term *'survivalist'* has been used to describe those actively involved in disaster preparedness, however with the passage of time this term has, rightly or wrongly, come to be associated with militant and/or anti-social behavior. Throughout this book I will use the words *'prepper'* and *'survivalist'* interchangeably.

Most modern-day preppers are neither militant nor anti-social, and they are as focused on planning, provisioning and gaining new skills as they are on security and defense. This is the audience for whom this book is primarily intended.

Within the United States the governmental agency *FEMA* (the Federal Emergency Management Agency) is tasked with responding to major disasters. However, it is conceivable that FEMA will not be available in all cases. In fact, there are already plenty of examples of major disasters that have profoundly affected the lives of Americans to which FEMA has either not responded, or not responded in a manner that addressed the full needs of all victims. This book is intended to provide information and inspiration to people (of all nations) who wish to be prepared to cope with disasters without necessarily relying on governmental assistance.

Chapter two identifies those things that the beginning prepper can do immediately even before diving headlong into the remainder of the book. This chapter was motivated by the belief that, as it is human nature to procrastinate, many readers will be anxious to get started. While presenting the reader with a condensed action list, much of the underlying rationale for those recommendations is deferred to subsequent chapters that provide detailed information.

The Prepper Mindset

Over time the prepper's concept of potential disaster scenarios evolves. Consequently, new preppers often make less-than-optimal decisions with regard to how to expend their limited time and budget. By understanding the more evolved mindset of experienced preppers the new prepper gets a stronger start and will make informed decisions.

Key elements of the prepper mindset include:

- Working under the assumption that government agencies will not be available to assist (or even assuming that they may actually work against the best interest of survivors). In recent years there has been plenty of experience to suggest that the government is not capable of addressing all emergency needs in a timely manner.

- Regularly creating and reviewing plans and lists. - The prepper has plans and lists for every contingency.

- Thinking in 3-month intervals - Many preppers tend to think in terms of preparing first for a 3-month disaster. Once that is achieved then the goal is moved out in successive 3-month intervals. This mindset allows the prepper to keep bounds on their activities so that the entire process remains manageable.

- Considering all perspectives of all disaster scenarios. - The prepper strives to be able to address any challenge posed by a disaster scenario (e.g. medical, self-defense, food, water, fuel, power, etc.).

- Constantly expanding and evolving their prepping-related thought processes.

- Understanding and appreciating the value of community. - The prepper understands and appreciates the principle of *'strength in numbers'*.

- Making the most efficient use of resources. - The prepper realizes that every resource in his or her possession can eventually be consumed, and so sets a priority on conserving those resources to the greatest extent possible and practical.

- Planning for all stages of disaster. - The prepper is always thinking forward to (and planning for) all stages of any expected disaster.

- Constantly giving consideration to operational security (*OPSEC*). - The prepper does not overly advertise the things they are doing or the current status of their preparations. Otherwise, in the event of disaster, it is very possible that what resources they have been able to accumulate could become "community property".

- Building bonds with like-minded individuals. - It is natural for preppers to communicate with other preppers to exchange ideas and opinions. This process naturally leads to building up a trusted base of friends and associates.

- Thinking like a Boy Scout. - Preppers often discover that the new knowledge they gain in the course of preparing is empowering. This rewarding sense of empowerment has a self-reinforcing effect with regard to gaining new skills, knowledge and capabilities. It is not a coincidence that the Boy Scouts' motto is *'Be Prepared!'*.

NOTE: *Be aware that all individuals engaged in prepping do not have a true prepping agenda or prepper mindset. Some attempt to join prepper communities to cultivate commercial opportunities while others use prepping as an excuse to pursue personal interests such as gun collecting or hunting. You can generally recognize such* posers *by the fact that they will overly emphasize one aspect of prepping while paying very little attention to others.*

Commonly Encountered Preparedness Terminology

Certain terms and acronyms have been adopted as common jargon within the disaster preparedness community. Some of the terms most often encountered include:

- *BB&B* - "beans, bullets and band-aids" - often used to refer to the most basic disaster preparedness provisions.

- *Bug Out* - To evacuate when faced with imminent disaster.

- *Bug In* - To elect to remain in place when faced with imminent disaster.

1. *Introduction*

- *Bugout Bag* - A bag or other container that has been pre-loaded with provisions to "grab and go" when bugging out.

- *Cache* - As a verb this refers to the act of hiding away emergency food and gear. As a noun this refers to a location where emergency food and gear are concealed (often buried) for access in the event of some future disaster.

- *COMSEC* - an acronym for "communications security", which refers to taking measures to preserve the confidentiality of your communications (which could include the use of encryption or pre-defined "code words").

- *OPSEC* - an acronym for "operational security", which refers to keeping information about your prepping activities "close to the vest".

- *Every Day Carry (EDC)* - refers to items that a person carries on a daily basis in order to have some minimal degree of readiness at all times. Some EDC items may be as innocuous as a wrist watch or an ink pen.

- *Get Home Bag (GHB)* - refers to a bag that is often kept in an individual's vehicle that has been packed with items that better enable the driver to return home under disaster conditions that could disrupt routine travel. By definition all GHBs should, at a minimum, contain maps of local road systems and terrain.

- *GOOD bag* - "GOOD" is an acronym for "get out of Dodge". A "GOOD bag" is another term for "Bugout bag" (see above).

- *Gray Man* - refers to an individual who dresses and otherwise presents themself in such as way as to not stand out in a crowd.

- *Grid* - originally *'the grid'* referred to the electrical grid. More recently, however, the term applies to the flow of both electricity and information (for example, credit card transactions result in information flowing across *'the grid'*).

- *Grid-down* - refers to a situation in which the normal flow of electricity and information is disrupted.

- *LEO* - an acronym for "law enforcement officer".

- *LP/OP* - a military acronym for "listening post/observation post", which is a location that has been specially prepared for keeping watch.

- *MAG* - an acronym for "mutual assistance group" - a group of individuals that have have banded together to form a survival community (note: this group, especially pre-disaster, may not necessarily be living together in a common location.).

- *MRE* - an acronym for "meals, ready-to-eat", which refers to pre-prepared packages containing ready-to-eat meals that typically have a storage shelf-life of several years.

- *Normalcy Bias* - the natural tendency for an individual to believe that their current reality will not be subject to dramatic change - particularly as the result of a major disaster.

- *Off-grid* - refers to a location or situation in which electrical power and the electronic flow of information is unavailable or disrupted.

- *Prepper* - a modern-day survivalist who is actively preparing to survive major disasters.

- *Prep* - an abbreviation of the word *'preparations'* (sample usage: *"These are my food preps."*).

- *SERE* - a military acronym that, in the US, means "Survival, Evasion, Resistance and Escape" and in the UK means "Survive, Evade, Resist, Extract".

- *Sheep* - refers to individuals who passively follow orders and accept assurances of safety from those in positions of power.

- *SHTF* - a prepper acronym for "shit hits the fan" - the time when major disaster strikes.

- *Situational Awareness* - refers to maintaining a keen awareness of things that are transpiring in your immediate environment.

- *Survivalist* - someone who is intensely involved in attaining a state of complete self-sufficiency (a.k.a. "a prepper on steroids").

- *TEOTWAWKI* - an acronym for "the end of the world as we know it".

- *WROL* - an acronym for "without rule of law" - a situation of lawlessness.

- *Zombies* - refers to desperate and dangerous refugees who would appear in the aftermath of a major disaster.

Most chapters of this book start with a *'Straight Thinking'* box that summarizes the most important takeaways from that chapter. I would recommend you start by visiting each chapter and reading that little summary. In this way you're starting with the "big picture". I would then recommend that you identify specific chapters that you feel are most important to your situation and dive into those chapters individually.

It is expected that some chapters will be of more universal interest. The *'Planning'* chapter is a good example **(also, this is one of the best disaster planning references available in the Author's not-so-humble opinion)**.

Other chapters, such as the first aid chapter, have some content that will be of greater interest when actually needed. For example, the procedures for treating various forms of trauma will be most helpful when facing those situations (although the lists of recommended medical supplies in that same chapter should be of immediate interest).

The bottom line is that this book is intended to serve as both a general learning tool as well as a reference guide. As such, **it is expected that the reader will skim some content while focusing intently on other content.** When faced with an actual disaster, however, every word contained in these pages will be golden!

Of Most Immediate Interest

While all of the information presented in this book is intended to fill important needs during time of crisis, the great majority of it also applies to the 'here-and-now'. Areas of particular interest in a pre-disaster context include:

- Chapter 2 *('Getting a Quick Start')* - identifies actions the prepper can and should consider taking immediately.

- Chapter 3 *('Bugging In, Bugging Out and Disaster Planning')* along with companion Appendices A and B - provides a detailed road map for single- and multi- site disaster planning.

- Chapter 4 *('Emergency Drinking Water')* - helps the prepper to identify water purification supplies and equipment that will be needed.

- Chapter 5 *('Emergency Food')* - describes the preparation and proper storage and use of emergency food supplies.

- Chapter 6 *('Disaster Communications')* - identifies communications equipment that the prepper should consider adding to their emergency inventory.

- Chapter 7 *('Emergency Fuel and Power')* - discusses fuel storage and usage strategies.

- Chapter 9 *('Hygiene and Sanitation')* - identifies supplies and equipment that should be stockpiled before disaster strikes.

- Chapter 10 *('First Aid')* - identifies first aid equipment that should be stockpiled (some sections of this chapter, such as those describing first aid procedures, may be of greater interest in a post-disaster scenario as they are needed).

- Chapter 12 *('Home and Community Defense')* - identifies defensive measures and strategies that that apply at the household and community levels.

- Chapter 13 *('Survival Farming - Achieving Self-Sufficiency')* - provides detailed instructions for raising crops and small livestock.

- Chapter 15 *('Next Steps')* - identifies follow-on actions that can be taken and supplies that should be stockpiled by the serious prepper.

- Appendix C *('Acquiring Precious Metals as a Preparedness Strategy')* - describes how some preppers might benefit from storing some precious metals for post-disaster use.

- Appendix D *('Guns and Ammunition - 101')* - provides a good introduction to the selection, use and maintenance of guns.

2. Getting a Quick Start

"I've got to start i've got to go
there is something i have to do
not sure what awaites me
eyes wide open i will see
into the darkness or into the light
the rainbow warrier will start his fight"

'Getting Started' by David Alexander Findlay

Given the condition of the world and the news of the day it is completely understandable that anyone interested in preparedness might feel a need to start **doing something** as quickly as possible. This chapter is intended to give those new to prepping a good, strong start. As you read and begin to act on some or all of the recommendations made in this chapter you can continue into this book while taking comfort in the knowledge that many of the bases are already being covered.

> **NOTE:** *The recommendations made for the basic preparedness steps in this chapter represent several years of study and analysis. While conforming to these recommendations will carry some cost, these are basic 'starter preps' and the costs should be more than offset by your own time savings. Once these steps are taken you will be be in a* **much** *stronger position to deal with any disaster.*

Before taking any steps, determine the number of people that you intend to provide for and the time period, in days, for which you are preparing (your *'planning period'*). For many preppers a 90 day planning period is a reasonable fit, with the understanding that additional provisions can be secured later to extend that period. Multiply the number of people times the number of days in your planning period to calculate the number of 'PersonDays' that will be referenced throughout this chapter.

The quantities of dried beans and rice described below are based on a beans-and-rice meal consisting of three ounces of dried beans and three ounces of dried rice (the proportions of beans to rice for many beans and rice recipes is one-to-one). The calculations also assume that two meals each day will have beans-and-rice as the main meal constituent (beans and rice provide a good, although not perfect, balance of proteins and carbohydrates).

The following sections are organized into areas in which you can begin to work immediately, with suggested preparations for each area.

2.1. Initial Food Preps

- Make sure your pantry is filled with canned and dried foods that have a shelf life of at least 6 months and which will be palatable to everyone in your group. If possible identify and/or install additional shelves to extend your pantry storage.

- Purchase and store large containers of your preferred peanut butter, as well as a good quantity of raw, unfiltered honey. Store a supply of crackers with the peanut butter.

> **AUTHOR'S NOTE:** *I recommend peanut butter for several reasons. It packs a good combination of energy, fats and proteins into a small space, it is palatable to most people (except, of course, those with peanut allergies!) and it can add much-needed variety to the survival diet. I have recently consumed my own emergency store of peanut butter 18 months after storage and it was as satisfying as if it had come right off the shelf at the store.*
>
> *Raw, unfiltered honey is recommended because it packs a lot of food value into a small space, has an almost-indefinite shelf life, and has successfully been used as a topical antibiotic for centuries[373] ('Manuka Honey' from New Zealand has a particularly good reputation for its antibiotic properties[376]).*

- Acquire and store a large container of multi-vitamins, and a large container of high quality protein powder. Also consider storing a supply of candy bars, which might provide a source of quick energy or which might be used as a treat to provide some psychological uplift during stressful times.

- If you are considering the option of evacuating to another location (a.k.a. *'bugging out'*) then obtain a sufficient quantity of MREs to provide food for everyone in your group while they are in transit.

- Dried beans and dried white rice, vacuum-packed in mylar bags, are a cost-effective source of important proteins, carbohydrates and other nutrients. When properly packed these foods can store at room temperature for as long as 25 years. If you plan on dry-packing beans and rice in this way then you can start by doing the following:

  - Acquire a *'food saver'* with a vacuum tube attachment and at least one vacuum-sealed jar (for storing oxygen absorbers between uses).

  - Acquire dried white rice and dried beans (black beans and pinto beans are good candidates, and often available in larger-size bags at wholesale food sources). The number of pounds of each can be calculated by multiplying 0.375 times the value for "PersonDays" you have already determined.

NOTE: *With the exception of long-term food packed in mylar you will actually be consuming your food stores over time. This allows you to adapt to your emergency foods, and even more importantly enables you to replenish your food supplies before they approach their expiration date. If the economy happens to be inflationary (when it is **not** inflationary?) then storing back food supplies in advance will actually **save** you money.*

Even stored vitamins and protein powder should be consumed regularly and replenished.

  - Acquire or order food-quality plastic buckets and mylar bags (4.5 - 7 mils in thickness) for long-term food storage (see section 5.2). The minimum number of 5-gallon buckets and 5- or 6- gallon sized mylar bags to obtain can be calculated as the number of pounds of dried beans and rice combined divided by 10.

    Also acquire a quantity of 3-gallon food-grade plastic buckets to store smaller quantities of other recipe ingredients such as sugar, salt, bullion and spices. Ordering one 3-gallon food-grade bucket for every three 5-gallon buckets should be sufficient. Section 5.2 provides instructions for dry-packing dried beans and dried white rice in mylar bags and plastic buckets.

  - Obtain a clothes iron and any solid object with a flat surface that is about 1/4 inch thick and about 12 inches long for heat-sealing mylar bags after they have been filled with food. (The edge of a half-inch-thick wooden board works just fine as a backing to iron against to seal the bags).

    − Obtain 1 or 2 pounds of food-grade diatomaceous earth powder (1 tablespoon of *'DE powder'*, sprinkled over food before sealing, can provide further protection against insects).

2.2. Initial Water Preps

It is conceivable that in a major disaster normal water supplies may become unavailable and/or contaminated. Because humans can only live a few days without water it is critical to take steps to ensure that drinking water remains available. The most spartan estimates strongly recommend that a ration of 3 gallons of water per day be planned for each individual in your group. Those 3 gallons break down roughly into 1 gallon for drinking, 1 gallon for cooking and 1 gallon for sanitation purposes. The following measures will enable you to begin to meet, and possibly exceed, these minimum needs:

- Obtain a high quality *'gravity-fed'* water filter that has a *'pore size'* no larger than .1 micron and which is labeled as a *'water purifier'*. It is strongly recommended that you read chapter 4 before making your purchase decision. In addition to obtaining the water filter, obtain a sufficient quantity of spare filter elements to process 3 gallons per day for each individual in your group for your planning period.

- Obtain several large food-rated bottles for storing filtered water. The plastic bottles used by many water coolers are ideal for this purpose, however thoroughly-cleaned plastic milk jugs will also work.

- Keep one gallon of regular household bleach (without additives) stored at all times, being sure to rotate through it once per year.

- Consider purchasing and storing at least 1 pound of granular calcium hypochlorite, being sure to store it in a proper container and away from food (see sections 4.10.1 and 4.10.2 for important information about storing and using this potent chemical for water purification).

- Obtain one or more water barrels that are made of food-grade material and which have not been used to store anything other than foods. Obtain at least 225 square feet of heavy plastic sheeting to be available for rain water collection. (Depending on the weather at your location and the size of your group these may not be sufficient to meet your needs. Refer to section 4.13 for instructions for better calculating your specific needs.)

2.3. Initial Defensive Preps

History (especially recent history) has demonstrated repeatedly that in the wake of disaster there are those individuals who are willing to do anything necessary to obtain the items they need to survive. As a consequence it is necessary to plan to defend yourself and your property. Such measures might include:

- If you do not already have a gun for home defense, acquire one, along with at least 100 rounds of ammunition. Appendix D provides information to help you make informed gun and ammunition decisions.

- For any guns you may already own, confirm you have at least 100 rounds of ammunition. For handgun cartridges, the ammunition used for actual defense should be *'hollow-point'* or *'soft-tip'* ammunition, rather than *'ball ammo'*. For shotguns confirm that you have at least 100 birdshot and/or buckshot shells.

- Consider having one or more dogs of a breed that has a good reputation as a home-defender (see section 12.6). (This will, of course, commit you to storing food for the dogs, just as you would for any other members of your group.)

- Consider installing a home alarm system (although good home defense dogs should be considered preferable, as they function as both a deterrent and a detector, and because they do not require electricity).

- Obtain spools of medium gauge wire, numerous eye bolt screws, a number of small bells and some wire cutters. These can be used to erect 'webs' of trip wires known as *'tanglefoot'* [426], which can serve to both detect and impede intruders. (**CAUTION:** an obstacle such as tanglefoot has the potential to cause serious injury, and should be put into place only under dire circumstances.)

- Obtain a number of strongly-worded warning signs that you can post around your property to dissuade intruders.

2.4. Initial Communications Preps

With good communications you can gain advance notice of the security situation within your area and adjust your own actions and plans accordingly. There will also be a need for regional and local news. Even if the phone system is still functioning, person-to-person communications will almost certainly not be a good way to gather timely information. When traveling good communications can often enable you to avoid impassable or insecure routes. The following measures will address many of these security needs:

- Obtain an emergency radio receiver that can accept regular or rechargeable batteries and obtain several sets of extra batteries for the radio.

- Strongly consider installing a CB radio in all vehicles that may be used during the disaster or during the recovery period. (See section 6.4.6 for a discussion of the advantages of CB radios and their significant usefulness during disaster.)

- Consider obtaining a police-band scanner.

- Consider obtaining a number of small, handheld 'FRS' or 'GMRS' two-way radios for use around or near the property. (Refer to chapter 6 for details about the various handheld radio devices that are available.)

2.5. Initial Sanitation Preps

In the aftermath of the recent major earthquake in Haiti thousands of people died due to poor sanitation. Proper sanitation is as critical to survival as having good sources of food and water. The following measures will allow you to address many of your sanitation needs in a post-disaster scenario:

- Store a good supply of bathroom tissue and other consumable personal hygiene items. Also purchase a good supply of dehydrated sponges in a variety of sizes (when the aforementioned supply of bathroom tissue is exhausted the usefulness of these sponges will make itself known!).

- Obtain and store one or more 40- or 50-pound bags of dry lime power that can be used to help sanitize human waste if there is a disruption of utilities (consider each bag to be sufficient for 250 person-days).

- Obtain some sort of emergency toilet, which may be as simple as a 5- or 6-gallon plastic bucket with a special lid that allows a person to sit over the bucket and use it as a toilet.

- Obtain a shovel that can be used to bury any biological hazards, including covering human waste.

- Obtain and store large containers of regular and anti-bacterial liquid hand soap with dispensers for each.

2.6. Initial Medical and First Aid Preps

While a good first aid kit contains much more (see chapter 10), obtaining the following items will allow you to deal with the great majority of common first aid needs:

- Tubes of antibiotic ointment (to extend shelf-life store refrigerated - but not frozen - if possible)

- Elastic bandages for sprained ankles, etc.

- A good quantity of medical gauze

- Sterile bandages

- Adhesive bandages for minor cuts and abrasions

- Tweezers for removing splinters

- Medical tape

- Rubbing alcohol, hydrogen peroxide and Betadine

- Epinephrine

- Safety pins

- Aspirin

- Cotton swabs

The quantity of the above items obtained should be consistent with the size of your group.

2.7. Initial Fuel and Energy Preps

Even a modest supply of fuel and other energy stores can make a critical difference in a post-disaster scenario. If, for example, you have sufficient batteries to power your radio for 2 weeks, and during those 2 weeks that radio provides you critical instructions for obtaining much-needed assistance, then obviously those few batteries made all the difference.

> **AUTHOR'S NOTE:** *I am stating this rather obvious example of the importance of even limited resources because for some reason, when it comes to disaster preparedness, it seems that many people have a tendency to resign themselves to becoming victims simply because they cannot afford to put in place perfect preparations that guarantee their survival under all circumstances. (In the 1960's this is what was referred to as a 'cop-out'.)*

The following measures will allow you to meet some important basic needs for a few days to give you time to adapt or for other opportunities for relief to make themselves known:

- Obtain spare tanks of propane for any propane-fueled cooking grills you may have.

- Obtain spare batteries for all emergency radios, flashlights and other battery-powered electronic devices you may use during the disaster and recovery period.

- Strongly consider obtaining a one-room portable air conditioner, a generator that is capable of powering it and a heavy electrical cord (or cords) to connect the generator (which will be be outdoors) to the air conditioner. Obtain fuel containers for fuel to power the generator and *'fuel stabilizer'* additives to extend the storage life of the fuel (see chapter 7 for more details on this topic). This air conditioner and generator may only be sufficient to provide cooling for a couple of hours each day for several days, however that will buy you time to become better acclimated and perhaps make other arrangements to cope with heat. You may also want a power strip to enable you to plug in other devices in addition to the air conditioner (your generator may also require a special power strip).

  During the hot summer months, and particularly in the cases of those who are infirm due to age or medical conditions, this measure may make the difference between life and death.

In addition to the above tasks there are some procedures that need to be initiated. One procedure alluded to in the above lists is the regular consumption of stored foods such that newer foods are regularly being restocked. Another procedure that needs to be initiated is a practical diet and exercise program.

As a prepper, because you don't want to risk injury unnecessarily, you should develop a different concept of exercise. This new concept is to push yourself each week to become just a little more capable than you were the week before. See Chapter 11 for ideas on diet and exercise that you may be able to incorporate into your own personal fitness plan.

> **AUTHOR'S NOTE:** *Living in the state of Florida, and in a modern home that is not designed for natural ventilation, I have experienced summertime air conditioner outages that rendered our home virtually uninhabitable within a mere 2 hours.*
>
> *After these incidents I became a little introspective and realized that this was not entirely the fault of my home's design. Had I been in better physical condition I could have toughed it out overnight and saved myself some hotel expenses.*
>
> *Since that epiphany I initiated the first truly serious diet of my life. That was nearly a year and 85 pounds ago, and every day I become stronger and better able to endure the hardships that I am increasingly certain lie ahead.*

As a final step in getting a quick start as a prepper you should begin to develop your disaster plans. You can start this process by doing the following:

- Identify and document the *'chain of command'*.

- List any bugout destinations and criteria for bugging out.

- Identify all locations to be covered by your plan (e.g. your home, bugout destinations, locations where other group members reside, etc.).

- Identify emergency provisions to be kept at each location.

- Develop a pre-bugout checklist of things to do prior to bugging out from any location.

- Describe preferred travel routes between all locations.

These steps will provide you with a simple disaster plan. Please refer to chapter 3 for instructions on developing a much more comprehensive plan.

This chapter has provided suggestions for first steps that you can take on your path to preparing for a worst case scenario. The intent has been to enable you to begin ramping up quickly. The remainder of this book will provide additional background on the rationale behind these suggestions, as well as numerous additional preparedness recommendations and a wealth of information on virtually every aspect of prepping.

3. Bugging In, Bugging Out and Disaster Planning

*"Let our advance worrying
become advance thinking and planning."*

Winston Churchill

AUTHOR'S NOTE: *I must confess that the task of family disaster planning has been one of the aspects of preparedness in which I have procrastinated the most. The process of putting together a plan just seemed a little overwhelming. The information contained in this chapter should provide any prepper with all the information needed to put together a practical disaster plan.*

Originally it had been my intent to cover the topics of bugging in and bugging out in separate, dedicated chapters. However, as I began to work and re-work the concept of disaster planning, I became aware that bugging in and bugging out are fundamental strategies, and as such they are inseparable from planning. You can't realistically bug out unless you have identified a destination, and having a destination implies that you are executing a plan. Similarly, you can't stay put without having made plans for dealing with the challenges presented by that decision.

I concluded that a proper treatment of the topics of bugging in and bugging out required that they be covered as an integral part of disaster planning.

3.1. Contemplating the Future

It is not possible to predict the future with any degree of certainty, however everything we have seen and heard in the news for years suggests that "green shoots" are not around the corner. Indeed, it seems that our level of civilization retreats noticeably with each passing day.

In other words, things may very well not get better before they become far worse! In one scenario the developed nations may gradually devolve to something resembling Mexico, and in worse scenarios one could find oneself in the midst of a total social breakdown. It's easy to imagine that our complex and interconnected society might be a house of cards ready to tumble at any time.

In reality, the precedent for a major national disaster already exists. The Great Depression in the US provides a look at how modern societies can fall into very hard times. The first half of the classic American novel and movie 'The Grapes of Wrath' provides a realistic view of American life during the Great Depression. The more recent movie "Cinderella Man" provides a possibly even better representation in that it depicts the affects on the affluent as well as the less privileged. It would be supremely arrogant for anyone to believe that what happened to that generation cannot happen today, and it would be equally arrogant to think that God is any more predisposed to alleviate our suffering than He would have been to have alleviated the suffering of the victims of earlier disasters.

Considering that today our society is far less moral and far more violent than it was going into the Great Depression, imagine how very dangerous the future can and will be! One has only to look at the past (or at Mexico today, where drug cartels control much of the nation) to have some grasp at the future for which one should prepare.

NOTE: *Let me somewhat ameliorate this picture of doom and gloom with a couple of important counter points. We humans have built within us a wonderful ability to adapt. When faced with challenging times we can, with sufficient opportunity, adapt and overcome. It has been experimentally demonstrated that animals living under harsh and deprived conditions can become leaner, healthier and have longer life spans.[2]*

*Prepping is all about **buying time to adapt to a new reality**. Prepping is about surviving the 'forest fire' so that, after it burns past, you can emerge into a new world that you may eventually find more to your liking than the old one. What is critical is that you give yourself the opportunity to adapt.*

3.2. To Stay or to Go

One of the more frequently discussed topics among preppers and survivalists is the merits of staying put vs. evacuating in response to disaster. For many preppers the conversation is moot simply because they do not have a realistic *bugout destination* or because they already live in areas that many would consider ideal bugout locations.

NOTE: *There is a special word in the English language for someone who decides to bug out without a clear destination in mind - that word is* 'refugee'. *Virtually all preppers and survivalists can agree that you want to absolutely avoid becoming a refugee.*

If you live in an urban area then you should justifiably feel that you'll be in a dangerous situation in the event of a disaster that disrupts law enforcement and other social services. However, all disasters will not be totally disruptive. Regardless of your location, if you can manage to survive for several weeks you should see levels of disorder decrease everywhere as the finite supply of energy (and ammunition!) within the community is exhausted.

There are no guarantees in the survival business - one simply does the best one can with the resources available. In doing so one greatly increases the probability that they and those they love will survive.

It should also be mentioned that bugging in and bugging out are not mutually exclusive strategies. You may very well have a plan that involves staying put as you assess the situation, and then bugging out if and when certain criteria are met (e.g. the first time you hear gunshots).

3.3. Bugging In

If you are committed to digging in your heels and 'staying put' in the face of any and all disasters then you can at least take some comfort in the knowledge that your planning needs are a bit less complex. You might consider using the disaster planning guidelines and examples presented in this book as a blueprint for your own. You might still have both a General Disaster Plan ('GDP') (minus the 'Travel' sections) as well as a Site Plan for your location (see section 3.6 for a descriptions of GDPs and Site Plans).

Before you start your plan give some thoughts as to how you expect to be dealing with others during the disaster. You should have *'rules of engagement'* in your mind for friends, relatives, neighbors, law enforcement and other governmental personnel, as well as for complete strangers.

Also, just because you plan on weathering the storm at home does not necessarily mean that you should plan to be a hermit. Give consideration to how you might work with others in the aftermath of the disaster. Consider ...

- getting to know other preppers and/or survivalists in your area.

- (carefully) discussing your concerns with friends and neighbors who might also share those concerns, with thoughts towards forming a *mutual assistance group ("MAG")*.

- getting involved with a local church (many churches are already well-equipped with infrastructure that could make a big difference during a disaster).

You should try to anticipate the communications needs that will present themselves during a period of social disruption. Would it be useful to be able to provide walkie-talkies and defensive weapons of some sort to neighbors? Would it be helpful to have a police-band radio scanner to be aware of things happening locally? Certainly it would be advisable to have a standard emergency radio. Also, CB radios could be extremely helpful if you must travel the roads by car or truck. (See chapter 6 for detailed information on various communications technologies that are available.)

In summary, by taking some time to simply envision likely disaster scenarios you will develop a mindset that will be conducive to producing better, more realistic and more effective disaster plans.

3.4. Bugging Out ('Evacuation')

If you intend to have the option of evacuating in the event of disaster then you need to have site plans for each location, including your bugout location. Since your bugout location will almost certainly be in a different type of environment (e.g. relocating from an urban center to a small town or rural area) the plans may vary substantially.

The common wisdom within the survival community is that a bugout destination should be as far removed as possible from major population centers. Ideally it should also be a location that has a large population that is largely self-sufficient. However, there are other factors that should also be considered. For example, a small group may not be in sufficient numbers to meet their own basic security needs while also performing those tasks that are necessary to day-to-day life. A small group is also limited with regard to the size of the geographic area that it can control. If the area controlled by the group happens to be smaller in size than the range of a good hunting rifle then the group could be setting itself up for difficulties down the road.

Conversely, a small community may be able to preserve critical infrastructure such as municipal water supplies and sewage systems while at the same time being able to hold a large geographic area. Those living within the community might then be living under much less stressful circumstances and have more time and resources to allocate to growing and raising food and other vital tasks. This larger controlled area would almost certainly include other infrastructure that could form the basis of a new economy.

Ultimately your choice of a bugout destination is specific to your own unique situation and assessment of the future. Regardless of the destination you choose, you should have plans in place not only in support of that location but for travelling to the location as well. Among other things these plans should define the criteria under which you will begin the evacuation, travel routes between locations, and the various resources that may be available long the way (food and rest stops, lodging, etc.). By following the disaster plan guidelines presented in this chapter you can be certain that you cover these and other important planning needs.

Other important rules regarding bugging out include:

- Have food, equipment and other supplies you plan on taking packed and pre-positioned in advance.

- Perform occasional full or partial bugout drills.

- Try to scout out and take notes about all the routes between your location and the bugout destination.

- Have a pre-bugout checklist of activities to perform before bugging out, including communicating your plans to any other interested parties.

- Try to develop relationships with the inhabitants near your bugout destination in advance.

- If possible, consider permanently relocating to your bugout destination before disaster strikes.

- Visit your bugout destination in advance and pre-position supplies and food if possible. Also develop detailed maps and drawings of the site for additional planning.

- Identify or consider installing defensive features in advance.

3.5. Survival Bunkers

A small percentage of preppers are 'going the extra yard' and building survival bunkers to which they intend to relocate in the event of a major disaster. These bunkers are typically underground living quarters that are designed to meet all the basic needs of life. Some of these bunkers are specially built for this purpose, and others are refurbished facilities such as nuclear missile silos that are relics from the Cold War. Those that are custom-built tend to either be full-featured long term living quarters or smaller *'urban foxholes'* that are intended to provide storage and shelter on an as-needed basis. These urban foxholes are often small underground rooms that have been excavated under the floor of a garage, while the full-featured bunkers are often underground living units that have been strategically located in sparsely-populated areas.

> **NOTE:** *During World War II the citizens of England converted narrow, external below-ground-level stairwells into bomb shelters by covering them with arched, corrugated steel plates and 1 to 2 feet of earth.[516] These impromptu bunkers were credited with saving many lives.*

The following issues and features should be considered when planning a bunker or urban foxhole:

- Local Construction Ordinances - Many jurisdictions have regulations that do not permit the construction of fortified buildings. Be aware of how any such ordinances may affect you before you begin designing and constructing any bunker.

- Depth underground - In order to provide reasonable protection from the radiation associated with nuclear fallout, any underground bunker should be buried at least 36 inches below the surface.[517]

- Local Geography and Drainage - The underground structure must be designed such that water is not allowed to accumulate during rains or floods. Also, the probability of earthquake should be considered, with adjustments made to the design accordingly.

- Building Materials Used - Any structure buried underground may be subject to rust and other forms of corrosion and should be painted or otherwise treated before being installed.

- Structural Reenforcement - Any structure that is going to be located underground must have the structural strength to support the weight of the earth surrounding it. Domed or arched roofs can support greater weight than flat roofs, and metal columns or beams can also be used to provide needed reinforcement.

- Size of group - The maximum size of the group to be using the facility should be determined in advance to provide the assurance that the facility will have sufficient capacity with regard to space and ventilation.

- Food and water storage - Space should be allocated for the storage of food and water.

- Ventilation - The bunker should have provisions for circulating fresh air from the outside. Such provisions should include air filtration as well as screening and 'U-bends' in pipes and ducts to prevent infiltration by insects and rodents. Consideration should also be given to having the ability to positively pressurize the atmosphere in the bunker so that airborne contaminants will not enter through any exposed openings. An effective air filter should make use of an *NBC filter* that incorporates HEPA-certified filter elements. NBC filters are filters that are designed to filter out nuclear, biological and chemical contaminants. HEPA filter elements are filter component types that have been certified as meeting certain very strict filtering criteria, and are often used for filtering air in such sensitive environments as surgical operating rooms.

- Sanitation - Provisions must be made for the capture and disposal of human waste within the bunker, as well as for personal hygiene. Ideally the bunker would have its own septic tank, however if this is not possible provisions should be made for the temporary containment and treatment of human waste within the bunker.

- Security - The bunker should be designed with security as a primary consideration. Measures taken should include the installation of heavy, sealed doors that open inwards (so that they cannot be blocked from opening by debris). Also, the doorways should be at a 90 degree angle to the approach to the doorway such that multiple individuals do not have space to easily work together to breach the door. The door should feature multiple deadbolts on both the side and top and/or bottom of the door, with hinges mounted on the inside of the door. Other more offensive security protections may also be put into place around the door to disable or dissuade any potential intruders.

- Communications and Intelligence - There should, at a minimum, be some way to receive radio signals from within the bunker. Additionally, it is important to have some means of viewing and/or communicating with those on the outside of the bunker (for example to determine friend-or-foe before allowing entry).

- Alternate Escape Route - Hidden escape doors may provide a last chance for survival in the event that the bunker comes under attack. One common method of creating such doorways is to fill the escape hatch with sand such that it can be emptied into the bunker to provide a clear exit.

- Energy - Plans should be made for the use of batteries and/or external generators (and associated fuel storage). Some source of energy will be needed in all cases, even if only to provide for lighting and radio communications.

- Redundancy - If possible all bunker-related issues and features listed here should be addressed through multiple measures.

Shipping Containers as Survival Bunkers

Many preppers and survivalists advocate the use of new or slightly used shipping containers for the construction of survival bunkers. These containers are attractive because they are sturdy, pre-fabricated and can be purchased for reasonable costs compared to the cost of other bunker options. Shipping containers are typically either 20 or 40 feet in length and 8 feet wide. The 20-foot containers are 8 1/2 feet in height, while the 40 foot containers can be 8 1/2 or 9 1/2 feet in height. With proper reinforcement multiple containers can be linked and structurally reinforced to provide larger usable space (or multiple containers may simply be used individually).

Due to the space constraints imposed by shipping containers it is common to install fold-down bunk beds along the inner walls of containers that are intended to serve as sleeping quarters. This allows the sleeping space to be used for other purposes during non-sleep times, and also provides additional seating and storage options when the beds are not needed for human occupancy.

AUTHOR'S NOTE: *There are many excellent companies that manufacture and install survival bunkers.*

While planning for a bunker I recommend that you consider the possibility that attackers might be able to overcome a bunker's defenses by compromising the ventilation system (essentially 'smoking you out').

When planning to hunker down in a bunker for an extended period, you should anticipate how the social structure in your area may change while you are sheltered. If you have not participated in building the new community then you may find yourself pretty low on the totem pole when you emerge!

3.6. Disaster Planning

Imagine for a moment that you have just turned on your television and learned that a major national disaster is underway. The nature of this disaster is of such severity that you immediately realize there is real potential for social breakdown and violence (let's face it, in today's world even the results of a sporting event can result in violent riots in the streets, so imagine what is possible in the event of a major disaster!).

Under these circumstances even the most hardened, well-prepared person or group can and will feel that urge to panic. These are ***NOT*** the circumstances under which anyone has the ability to plan. However these are ***EXACTLY*** the circumstances under which everyone would greatly benefit from having a pre-defined plan outlining exactly those tasks they need to be performing. If you have a plan, then that nervous energy can be put to good use. If you don't have a plan then your chances of survival are greatly diminished.

Those having a plan to execute in the event of a disaster are not the ones who are going to be greeted by empty supermarket shelves.

The following sections, along with companion appendices A and B, will provide you with all the information and examples you'll need to develop an effective disaster plan for yourself and/or your family or *mutual assistance group ("MAG")*.

A good disaster plan should guide the actions of your group from the instant that a disaster is declared until final recovery. The time between disaster declaration and recovery may be only days, or it may persist for months or even years. During that time it may become necessary to adjust and adapt the plan, but it should nevertheless provide a strong framework for the group throughout that period.

The General Disaster Plan and Site Plans

To be comprehensive there should a separate *General Disaster Plan ('GDP')* that covers all sites where members of your group reside in addition to a Site Plan that is specific to each site. Of course if you are only concerned with a single site then the GDP can just be incorporated into the Site Plan however, if there is the potential for the plan to be expanded in the future to cover other sites, then it is advisable to keep the GDP as a separate document.

The GDP includes:

- A list or table of all alert levels and the criteria for declaring each alert level.

- A list of roles and responsibilities (especially identifying the "chain of command", with only the available person highest up the chain being able to declare disaster levels).

- General guidelines for travel.

- General guidelines for communications (radio frequencies and channels, best communication times, code words, etc.).

3. Bugging In, Bugging Out and Disaster Planning

NOTE: *A NOTE ABOUT 'PROCUREMENT':*

An unfortunate reality is that most people are unable to obtain, in a timely fashion, all the supplies that they believe might be needed to deal with a major, long-term disaster. However, what everyone **CAN** *do is to plan on obtaining those supplies should the sense of urgency increase. They can also develop plans for tasks to carry out if and when normal life is disrupted.*

While you may not be realistically able to have a henhouse in your back yard right now, you can **PLAN** *to obtain the materials to construct one, and you can have instructions for assembling it printed and available. In this way you give yourself a fighting chance to act quickly at the onset of disaster (maybe before most people in your area even begin to understand what has happened).*

Of course you want to be ready to move quickly when disaster strikes - this is why the plan is critical. As you read on you'll come to understand that one important aspect of the disaster plan is procurement *(obtaining needed supplies). If there are supplies that you need to obtain at the last minute then you need to have pre-defined where you are going to go to obtain them and the order in which you can most efficiently visit those locations. Additionally, you may plan for multiple procurement trips to take place concurrently and specify the individuals in your group who will be making each trip.*

In some cases it may make sense to pre-identify call-ahead numbers and shopping lists so that items may be waiting for you at the checkout counter when you arrive. At this point you should be starting to understand the **TREMENDOUS** *advantage of a disaster plan - it allows you to live more comfortably with the knowledge that while you won't necessarily have all the supplies you would ideally want to have, you at least have a plan in place for quickly obtaining them.*

- A full list of contacts, including names, addresses, phone numbers and any special notes.

- A list of basic emergency supplies and equipment that should be kept on hand at each site.

- Travel maps between all sites with routes and travel resources (fuel stops, food stops, rest stops, lodging, etc.) labeled and highlighted, and a table that provides additional information for each such resource labeled on each map.

NOTE: *Appendix A provides a sample of a GDP for a hypothetical family living in Tampa, Florida with one college-aged family member residing in Tallahassee and with a family bugout retreat located in Ocala (Ocala is a good example of a mid-sized city that has an industrial infrastructure that may enable the area to recover from disaster faster than other more densely-populated and urbanized areas).*

Each Site Plan should contain the following sections:

- *Inventory List* - a list of items, in addition to the inventory items listed in the GDP, that need to be pre-procured and readily available for this specific location.

- *Procurement Plan* - defines pre- and post- procurement activities, and organizes procurement destinations into individual 'shopping trips' (allowing multiple shopping trips to be performed concurrently). The Procurement Plan breaks down into the following sub-sections:

  - *Pre-procurement Tasks* - a list of things to do before the procurement trips commence. One example might be to fax a shopping list to a local store that is willing to pre-gather the items for quick checkout when you arrive. Another example might be to fill up the gas tanks in vehicles before commencing the shopping trips.

  - *Procurement* - includes a of list procurement trips and associated waypoints, and for each waypoint a list of items to be acquired. To minimize time at each waypoint these items should be listed in the order in which they should be gathered. Developing this list may require you to make some notes about the layout of each destination.

  - *Post-procurement Tasks* - a list of tasks to perform after procurement trips have been completed (e.g. **build** the henhouse now that you have acquired the requisite tools and supplies).

> **NOTE:** *Each trip, procurement destination and procured item may be qualified by criteria indicating under what circumstances it is to be procured. Most commonly this criteria will be the alert level. This means that the destinations you visit and the supplies you procure may vary based on the specific circumstances. See Appendix B for an example of a disaster plan with these types of conditional criteria.*

- *Defense Plan* - identifies all defensive measures and strategies to be used to defend the site. This can include alarm systems, guard and watch dogs, weapons, identification of defensive locations, a discussion of tactics and schedules and activities for defensive drills. This plan should cover the following topics:

  - *Layered Defenses* - how multiple protections are to be implemented.

  - *Deterrence* - how potential intruders are to be discouraged.

  - *Intrusion Detection* - how intruders will be detected and rules of engagement.

  - *Use of Deception* - how deception will be employed.

  - *Intelligence Gathering and Communications* - how defense-related information will be obtained, stored and communicated.

  - *Fixed Fortifications and Defenses* - discusses defensive barriers and how they will be used.

  - *Response* - discusses responses to intrusion attempts, including the use of concealment, tactics, communication and strategies.

  - *Community Defense* - discusses how the group will contribute to the defense of the surrounding community.

- *Energy Plan* - identifies power sources that will be available at the site and the policies for regulating energy usage.

- *Food Plan* - identifies how food is to be rationed, as well as how food is to be grown, raised or otherwise obtained.

- *Water Plan* - identifies how water is to be collected and rationed.

- *Sanitation Plan* - identifies hygienic practices and policies as well as how human waste is to be managed and disposed of.

- *Daily Activity Plan* - identifies tasks that are to be performed on a regular basis. This should include provisions for all members of the group to get a reasonable amount of regular exercise.

- *Medical Plan* - identifies plans for dealing with disease and injuries within the group (including quarantine policies for anyone joining the group).

- *Commerce Plan* - identifies plans for exchanging goods and services with others in the aftermath of a major disaster.

- *Evacuation Plan (a.k.a. "Bugout Plan")* - this section of the plan exists to facilitate any strategic relocations. The evacuation plan breaks down into the following subsections:

    - *Pre-departure Checklist* - this is similar to the checklist an aircraft pilot reviews before takeoff. It is a list of things to be certain to have on hand, or tasks to complete, prior to evacuation.

    - *Evacuation Routes* - identifies the routes that might be taken to reach the pre-defined evacuation site(s). Multiple routes are necessary as, depending on the nature and scale of the disaster, some routes may become 'problematic'.

    - *Evacuation Arrival Checklist* - lists the tasks to be performed immediately after arriving at the destination, and may optionally assign specific tasks to specific individuals or groups.

NOTE: *Everyone covered by the disaster plan should be provided a full copy of the General Disaster Plan in addition to* **all Site Plans**. *In this way everyone is better prepared to render assistance to other group members who may experience problems in transit.*

Please refer to Appendices A and B for examples of a General Disaster Plan and Site Plan for the hypothetical family discussed previously.

4. Emergency Drinking Water

"Water, water, everywhere, Nor any drop to drink."

from *The Rime of the Ancyent Marinere*
by Samuel Taylor Coleridge

STRAIGHT THINKING: *The most important aspect of emergency water management is obtaining a good and trusted water source, and water from the most pristine-looking stream may not necessarily be a trustworthy source (Does that stream run past a farm that sprays pesticides? Is there a carcass of a dead animal upstream for your location? Is the upstream water contaminated by animal feces?). These concerns should cause any prepper to give serious consideration to the use of rain water, or water drawn from springs or underground wells.*

While all water sources may not be trustworthy, many water sources are very treatable.

During a disaster the water supply is often one of the first casualties. Consequently, making preparations to have adequate safe drinking water must be a top priority. Because a person can only live a very few days without water, the availability of good drinking water should be of paramount importance to anyone who is serious about surviving a major disaster.[7]

In modern times it is not uncommon to hear of cities issuing "boil water notices" to entire areas when certain parts of the utility infrastructure experience an outage. Notice that they never issue a warning to "boil the water or use your water filter". The reason is because **all water filters are not equal**. In fact, they are FAR from equal.

The typical store-bought water filter is designed with the assumption that it will be filtering public tap water and only removing certain trace minerals that affect the taste of the water.

In the event of a disaster those 'lightweight' water filters will be **totally inadequate** to protect you from the virtual flood of bacteria, viruses and harmful chemicals that may very well find their way into the water supply.

There are, of course, some excellent, high-quality water filters that are available for purchase (and many at reasonable cost). This chapter will not only provide you with the information needed to make informed water filter choices but also with critical information on effectively managing your water supply during a crisis.

4.1. Water Contaminants

Water purification is concerned with removing 3 types of contamination:

- *Particulate Contaminants* - any matter suspended in a water supply (debris, rust, mud, silt, etc)

- *Biological Contamination* - harmful microorganisms

- *Chemical Contamination* - harmful chemicals

4.1.1. Particulate Contaminants

Particles and debris can be removed from water by even the least sophisticated water filters. See section 4.2.6 for a discussion of *pre-filtering* water to remove many such contaminants to preserve the useful life of your water filters and filter elements.

4.1.2. Biological Contaminants

Biological contaminants present a grave threat to everyone in a disaster scenario. Introduced to the human body in drinking water, microbes can cause illness that can incapacitate a person for weeks (or even result in dehydration and possible death). Biological contaminants include:

- *Protozoa* - single-celled organisms that can cause serious disease in humans. The protozoa of most common concern in drinking water supplies are *Giardia Lamblia* & *Cryptosporidium* (also known as *'giardia'* and *'crypto'*, respectively).

- *Bacteria* - a special class of single-celled organisms that are smaller than protozoa and which can also cause serious disease in humans.

- *Bacteria Spores* - the 'seeds of bacteria' that are smaller and more difficult to filter or kill than the bacteria themselves, and which eventually develop into bacteria.

- *Cysts* - microscopic protective *cocoons* that contain parasitic microorganisms.

- *Viruses* - extremely small particles of disease-causing organic matter (viruses are orders of magnitude smaller than bacteria).

The risks posed by these biological contaminants is addressed through several means:

- Mechanically blocking them through filtering.

- Killing them with chemical agents such as bleach or iodine.

- Killing them with sunlight.

- Killing them with ultraviolet light.

- Killing them by boiling the water.

- Removing and killing them through distillation.

The full range of possible contaminants cannot be addressed by any single preventive measure. For example, bacteria spores may survive boiling, however they can be filtered out by a filter with a pore size of .45 microns or smaller. Any truly safe and effective water treatment system will incorporate multiple approaches (e.g. filtering and boiling).

This chapter describes several methods that can be applied to greatly reduce the the risks posed by contaminated water.

4.1.3. Chemical Contaminants

Harmful chemicals in a water supply can present every bit as serious a health hazard as biological contaminants (and can be more difficult to filter). In general these chemical contaminants consist of:

- *Heavy Metals* - heavy metals such as mercury and lead typically enter the water supply from vehicle emissions combining with ground water or from runoff from mining operations.

- *Organic chemicals such as pesticides* - water runoff from agricultural operations may result in pesticides and other *volatile organic compounds* (VOCs) finding their way into the water supply.

- *Pharmaceutical chemicals* - antibiotics and other pharmaceutical substances may find their way into drinking water when they are discarded improperly by households or businesses.

- *Salt* - salt may be introduced into a water supply primarily through mixing with seawater.

Heavy metals, pharmaceuticals and salt can be removed from water through distillation and reverse osmosis filtering (see section 4.8). Organic chemicals can largely be scrubbed from water by passing the water through a filtration layer of activated charcoal.

4.2. Water Treatment Concepts

4.2.1. Filter Elements

Water filter elements are the the removable/replaceable parts of a water filter (the *'cartridges'*) that are responsible for actually processing the water. In a disaster situation you should probably replace the filter elements when you notice any type of odor from the water, or when the rate at which the filter produces drinkable water is noticeably reduced. You might also consider replacing an element when it is 1 year beyond its labeled life expectancy (or maybe a little more). Even then, in a true disaster scenario, you should save old filter elements in case you find that you need to cycle through them again.

Some water filters allow for multiple filter elements to be installed, and you only need to install more elements if you need to produce drinkable water at a faster rate. Some filters may only remove bacteria and cysts, while others may block viruses and harmful chemicals as well. Some water filter elements are designed to be cleaned and re-used multiple times, so be sure to read the instructions that accompany your filter or filter elements.

4.2.2. Filter 'Pore Size'

All water filters are rated in terms of their *'pore size'*. A filter's documentation may refer to both *nominal* and *absolute* pore size - it is the absolute pore size that is important.[19] The absolute pore size, most often expressed in microns, is the size of a microorganism which has been shown to be blocked by the filter under strict, industry-standard test conditions.[19]

The Giardia and Cryptosporidium protozoa are 4 microns and larger in size. Harmful bacteria range between 1.5 and 3 microns in size, and viruses range between 0.004 and 0.03 microns in size.[17] So, any filter with an absolute pore size rating of 1 micron or smaller should be considered to be a reasonable filter to use in a disaster scenario.

NOTE: *Water filter elements may feature both ceramic and activated charcoal filtering stages. While this is attractive from a functional perspective it is important to note that the life expectancy of activated charcoal sections tends to be significantly less than the life expectancy for the other filtering materials. As a result, these (more costly) filter elements must be changed more frequently.*

It may be wise to consider having separate activated charcoal filtering equipment, rather than to select an all-in-one solution. Or, if you are certain that your emergency water supply will not contain VOCs, you might not include an activated charcoal filtering stage in your water processing at all (keep in mind that the most common source of VOCs in water supplies is water runoff from agricultural areas).

4.2.3. Bridging

A water filter element with a particular pore size can actually block the passage of contaminants that are smaller than the pore through a process known as *bridging*. Bridging refers to the case in which the bacteria and other contaminants that are stopped on the surface of the filter element begin to overlap in such as way as to block the passage of smaller objects (much like a log jam in a stream might block the passage of objects which are smaller than the logs themselves). It is this bridging phenomena that causes the rate of water flow through a filter to become reduced over time, often requiring reusable elements to be scrubbed with a mild abrasive, or non-reusable elements to be replaced.

NOTE: *Note that even filters with small pore sizes will still pass viruses (with the notable exception of reverse osmosis filters, which have molecular-sized pores). Viruses are not common in most water sources, so they are a lesser concern. However, this does highlight the need to chemically purify water after it has been filtered.*

4.2.4. Filtering vs. Purifying Water

Filtering water simply involves passing the water through some material that blocks the passage of some (but not all) contaminants.

Purifying water goes beyond filtering and is a very specific industry term that indicates that the water produced is safe to drink without additional processing. For example, some filters with very small absolute pore sizes are able to be labeled as water purifiers. In the US and other developed nations a water treatment device cannot legally identify itself as a 'purifier' without passing rigorous industry-standard tests.

4.2.5. Gravity-Fed Water Filters

Some type of force is required to cause water to flow through a water filter. This force may be from an electric, motor-driven or human-powered pump, or it may be simply the force of gravity. Even municipal utility services install water towers to use the force of gravity to provide water pressure. Gravity-fed water filters are filters that are specifically designed to exclusively employ the force of gravity to force water through the filter elements. Because they require no external energy sources, anyone preparing to survive a major disaster should acquire a high quality gravity-fed water filtration system.

4.2.6. Pre-filtering Water

In order to extend the life expectancy of water filter elements it is often a good idea to pre-filter water before processing it through a filter. Such pre-filtering may be as simple as straining the water through a clean t-shirt or other material.

4.3. Water Filtering Basics

The process of filtering water should remove unwanted particulate matter as well as scrub the water of many unwanted chemical contaminants, and some microorganisms. Most often filtering alone is not sufficient to deal with all harmful microorganisms (particularly viruses), hence an additional purification step is highly desirable.

Filters with an absolute pore size of 1 micron or smaller can filter out harmful protozoa such as giardia and crypto. Filters with an absolute pore size of .1 micron or smaller can filter out bacteria, and filters with an absolute pore size of .01 micron or smaller can filter out viruses.[18] (Even if a filter has a pore size that is larger than a particular microbe it may still effectively filter it due to the *bridging effect*. See section 4.2.3 for a description of the bridging effect.)

> **NOTE:** *Coffee filters have a pore size that ranges from 50 to 100 microns[16], and so should not be considered to be adequate for filtering water for human consumption in a disaster scenario (they may, however, be very suitable for pre-filtering water).*

Activated charcoal is often incorporated into water filter elements as a means of removing many harmful chemicals (particularly chemicals such as pesticides originating from agricultural sources).

One pollutant that, if present, may pass through most water filters is *arsenic*. Arsenic is a dangerous pollutant that has been classified as carcinogenic (cancer-causing). Arsenic contamination is most often the result of mining operations or runoff from agricultural areas that make use of chemicals that contain arsenic.

The best way to remove arsenic is through distillation. This highlights the fact that properly captured rain water should be considered one of the most trustworthy sources of water during a disaster (since rain water is essentially distilled).

4.4. Methods of Removing Contaminants from Water

Water filters may remove contaminants through any of the following processes:[22]

- *Filtration* - physically blocking the flow of undesired objects or substances.

- *Sedimentation* - allowing gravity to separate heavier waterborne contaminants from the water. A special (and exotic) case of sedimentation would be the use of a centrifuge to accelerate the separation process.

- *Distillation* - heating the water until it becomes a vapor, collecting the vapor and condensing it back into liquid form in a different container.

> **NOTE:** *While most preppers are concerned with water filtration, sedimentation can also play an important role. By simply locating the spigot of a rain barrel 1 or 2 inches above the bottom of the barrel, for example, unwanted heavier-than-water contaminants can sink below the spigot and be significantly eliminated from the water produced.*

4.5. Trusted Water Sources

Needless to say, the better the quality of your water source the less risk of exposure to waterborne disease. In today's modern, highly-developed world pristine sources of water are very rare. Even the most natural looking streams and rivers can flow past agricultural or industrial sites and pick up all manner of toxic contents. In fact, you could trek to the most remote wilderness area and still encounter water sources that have been contaminated by animal waste or perhaps the bacteria-infested corpse of dead wildlife.

> **NOTE:** *In addition to being less likely to cause health issues, using sources of the purest possible water will inevitably extend the usable life of your water filter elements.*

4.5.1. Rain Water

While it is advisable to have a healthy skepticism regarding any water source, some sources can be trusted more than others. One of the more common trusted sources is rain water. Having passed through nature's own time-proven distillation process, properly collected and stored rain water should be quite pure. (Of course there is always the potential for water to draw contaminants from the atmosphere itself, however this is the same atmosphere you take into your body with each breath.) If the rain flowed over a contaminated path while being collected, or was contaminated by bird droppings en route to your rain collection system then it could still be contaminated. Also, shingles made from composite materials such as asphalt contain toxins that can leach into water flowing over, hence roofs covered with such shingles should not be used to collect drinking water.

To play it safe with rainwater it is advisable that, if possible, it either be purified through filtering, boiling or chemical treatment.

4.5.2. Well Water

Wells that have historically provided good drinking water are another good source that can be considered highly trustworthy. As with rain water, if possible water from wells should also be purified before drinking (especially in the aftermath of a flood or earthquake and if you have no provisions for testing the water).

Depth of Water	Diameter of Well					
	0.5 foot	1 foot	2 feet	3 feet	4 feet	5 feet
10 feet	1/2 cup	1-3/4 cups	7 cups	1 gal	1-3/4 gal	2-3/4 gal
20 feet	1 cup	3-1/2 cups	14 cups	2 gal	3-1/2 gal	5-1/2 gal
30 feet	1-1/2 cups	5-1/4 cups	1-1/4 gal	3 gal	5-1/4 gal	8-1/4 gal
40 feet	2 cups	7 cups	1-3/4 gal	4 gal	7 gal	11 gal
50 feet	2-1/2 cups	8-3/4 cups	2-1/4 gal	5 gal	8-3/4 gal	13-3/4 gal

Notes:

- Use only unscented household liquid chlorine bleach.
- Bleach concentrations can vary between 5% and 6%.
- Quantities given in this table are approximate and are rounded to the nearest practical measurement. Amounts given are calculated in accordance with reaching a chlorine concentration of 100 mg/L

Key:

- gal: gallon
- 1 cup = 8 fluid ounces
- 1 gallon = 16 cups

Figure 4.1.: Quantities of Bleach Required to Disinfect a Bored or Dug Well.[14]

Types of Wells

Wells can be constructed in a few ways. They may simply be holes that are dug or bored out until the water table is reached, or they may be created by drilling or driving a narrow rod into the earth until water is reached. The former are referred to as 'bored' or 'dug' wells, and the latter are referred to as 'drilled' or 'driven' wells.

Things to Look for in a Trustworthy Well

The inner lining of a well is known as he well 'casing'. The material of the casing depends on the type of well. In the case of bored or dug wells the casing might consist of a stone or concrete wall, while in the case of a drilled or driven well the casing is the material of the pipe that has been driven into the ground and through which the water flows. Important things to confirm are:

- The well casing extends higher above the ground than any anticipated flood waters might reach.[13]
- There are no holes or cavities where the earth meets the casing.[14]
- The earth around the casing forms a mound so that if rain falls around the casing it naturally flows away from the well.[13]

- The top of the well is covered with a valve or, in the case of a dug or bored well, there is some structure (e.g. a roof) that prevents contaminants (think 'bird droppings') from falling into the well.

Best Practices for Well Management

Best practices for maintaining a well include:

- Ideally a well should be at least 50 feet deep to provide the assurance that the water has been adequately filtered through the earth.[12]

- There are no chemicals stored near the well, nor any areas frequented by livestock located near the well.[13]

- In addition to any electrical pumping features, the well should also feature a hand pump for those circumstances when electricity is not available.

- Before any anticipated flooding, for any drilled or driven well, the well cap should be put into place with any vent holes plugged.[13]

- If flooding is expected and any above-ground piping exists that transports water from the well, consider using sandbags to shield the piping from the flood waters.[13]

Assessing the Quality of Well Water

Even under normal circumstances the water taken from a well should be periodically tested for chemical and biological contaminants. In the aftermath of a disaster (and periodically thereafter) it becomes much more critical to test the water drawn from a well - particularly if the disaster involved any flooding or an earthquake.[12]

The first and easiest way to assess the quality of well water is to simply smell the water. The 'smell test' may indicate the presence of any fuel in the water (a common source of well contamination). Additionally, the water should be tested with a water testing kit (or sent to a certified outside agency for professional testing). For any well that you are not familiar with, or for **ANY** well in the aftermath of a flood or earthquake, you should not drink or bathe in the water produced until it has been successfully tested.

Disinfecting Wells

If testing indicates that a well has been contaminated then it must be decontaminated before any water it produces can be considered safe for drinking or bathing. If the contamination is chemical in nature (e.g. contamination with fuel) then the procedure for decontamination is to draw water from the well, sampling occasionally until the level of contamination is within acceptable levels (it may prove to be impossible or impractical to decontaminate wells that

Depth of Water	Diameter of Well Casing						
	2 inches	4 inches	6 inches	8 inches	10 inches	24 inches	36 inches
10 feet	3/4 tbsp	3-1/4 tbsp	1/2 cup	3/4 cup	1-1/4 cups	7 cups	1 gal
20 feet	1-1/2 tbsp	6-1/2 tbsp	1 cup	1-1/2 cups	2-1/2 cups	14 cups	2 gal
30 feet	2-1/4 tbsp	9-3/4 tbsp	1-1/2 cups	2-1/4 cups	3-3/4 cups	1-1/4 gal	3 gal
40 feet	3 tbsp	13 tbsp	2 cups	3 cups	5 cups	1-3/4 gal	4 gal
50 feet	3-3/4 tbsp	1 cup	2-1/2 cups	3-3/4 cups	6-1/4 cups	2-1/4 gal	5 gal
100 feet	7-1/2 tbsp	2 cups	5 cups	7-1/2 cups	12-1/2 cups	4-1/2 gal	10 gal

Notes:

- Use only unscented household liquid chlorine bleach.
- Bleach concentrations can vary between 5% and 6%.
- Quantities given in this table are approximate and are rounded to the nearest practical measurement. Amounts given are calculated in accordance with reaching a chlorine concentration of 100 mg/L.

Key:

- tbsp: tablespoon
- gal: gallon
- 1 cup = 8 fluid ounces = 16 tablespoons
- 1 gallon = 16 cups

Figure 4.2.: Quantities of Bleach Required to Disinfect a Drilled or Driven Well.[15]

have been subject to chemical contamination - especially if the source of the contamination originates from the ground itself).

If a well is contaminated by microorganisms (bacteria, viruses, cysts or protozoa) then the procedure for decontamination is:[14][15]

- Obtain bleach that is between 5% and 6% chlorine, a 5 gallon plastic bucket and, if disinfecting a drilled or driven well, a funnel to facilitate the pouring of a disinfectant solution into the well.

- Make sure the area around the well is well-ventilated.

- Use breakers to deactivate all electricity in the vicinity of the well, and clear any debris or chemicals that may be near the well.

- Run or draw water from the well until the water is clear.

- Put on protective eyewear and rubber gloves in preparation for working with bleach.

- If working on a bored or dug well, do not enter the well pit itself as it may contain harmful gasses or vapors.

- Based on the size and depth of your well, reference figure 4.1 to determine the amount of bleach that you need to mix with water for a bored or dug well, and figure 4.2 to determine the amount of bleach that you need to mix with water for a drilled or driven well.

- Pour the bleach mixture into the well (using a funnel for the narrow casing of a drilled or driven well).

- Run water through all faucets connected to the well until the odor of bleach is being emitted from all faucets.

- Turn off all faucets and allow the water to sit undisturbed for 12 or more hours.[14]

- After the 12 or more hours have elapsed, turn on all faucets and allow the water to flow until it no longer smells like chlorine.[14]

- Re-test the well and repeat the process as needed.

After disinfecting a well the water produced should still be separately purified by boiling or with chemicals for 7 to 10 days, after which the well should be re-tested. If the results of the testing have not grown substantially worse since the well was disinfected then the contamination can be considered to have been mitigated. After that first re-testing, the well should also be re-tested 2 to 4 weeks later, and re-tested once again 3 to 4 months after that.

4.5.3. Swimming Pools as a Source of Drinking Water

Collectively the swimming pools in America contain a sufficient quantity of water to meet the drinking needs of every family in America for about one year[9] and it is possible that, if necessary, water from many of these pools may be made safe for human consumption.

The water contaminants of concern that may be present in swimming pools are:

- *Bacteria and Viruses* - This is no different than dealing with these contaminants from other water sources, and can be similarly treated with boiling, filtering, chlorine, iodine and distillation.

- *Chlorine* - The chlorine levels recommended for swimming pools is just slightly higher than the recommended range for drinking water[9], and chlorine quickly breaks down into harmless forms with the passage of time and exposure to sunlight. As a result, the presence of chlorine in typical swimming pool water is a minor concern.

- *Non-chlorine Chemicals* - Non-chlorine disinfectants, algaecides and fragrances added to a pool may pose a significant health risk. Any such chemicals added to pool water should be fully understood before deciding to use water from a swimming pool water for human consumption.

- *Sunscreens, Sun Blockers and other Oils* - Most modern sunscreens and sun blockers are formulated to not be harmful if ingested. Since these oils tend to float on the surface, one way to minimize ingestion of these substances is to collect water at a depth of a few inches below the surface. Additionally, a tennis ball can be tossed into a pool to absorb many such oils.[10] Some sun blockers do contain zinc oxide which some studies have indicated may be carcinogenic. Because zinc oxide has a molecular weight that is over 4 times that of water, any collection of zinc oxide can be reduced by not collecting water near the bottom of a pool that has not been agitated. Also, zinc oxide can be extracted from water by simply passing the water through a good water filter (even a coffee filter will do.[11]).

If you decide to make use of a swimming pool for drinking purposes it is advisable that the pool be covered and protected from sunlight as soon as possible to slow down the breakdown of chlorine in order to keep microbes from beginning to proliferate. **You should also obtain a pool chlorine testing kit to determine if the chlorine level has dropped to a level that will require the water to be sanitized.**

Other water sources may also be able to be processed into good, drinkable water.

4.6. Best Practices for Managing Water During an Emergency

When treating water to make it drinkable *('potable')* there are some basic rules that you must keep in mind:

- **Always consider the source** - Before treating any water for drinking purposes give careful consideration to its source.

    - Does that water flow past any agricultural areas?

    - Is the water from a source near a road or industrial area that may result in chemical contamination?

    - Is the water from a stagnant or otherwise suspect water supply?

    - Could the water have flowed over any decaying organic material?

  − Has the water been treated chemically (from a swimming pool, etc)?

If the answer to any of these questions is 'yes' then give preferential consideration to other water sources.

- **Pre-filter water whenever possible** - If you pre-filter your water through plain cloth (maybe a clean t-shirt) before processing it through your main filter you can greatly extend the life expectancy of your filter elements.

- **Keep water containers labeled and separated** - Use separate, well-labeled containers for containing processed and un-processed water. Do not consider using a container labeled for un-processed water to contain processed water unless that container has first been thoroughly cleaned and sanitized (with bleach), and re-labeled for its new purpose. **NOTE:** You may even need to organize your containers into 3 groups:

  − **Un-processed water** - water from the original source.

  − **Filtered water** - water that has been filtered but not yet purified.

  − **Purified water** - water that has been filtered, purified and is now fit for human consumption.

- **Nature can be as deadly as man** - Just because water comes from a pristine natural source does not mean it is not loaded with harmful or potentially deadly microbes.

- **A little very low cost preparation can save you a vast amount of cost and work** - Would you rather expend time and energy lugging untold quantities of wood each day to use for boiling water over a fire, or to add a couple of drops of bleach to that water to purify it?

4.7. Ceramic Water Filters

Many water filters feature ceramic elements that have small pore sizes that are capable of effectively filtering bacteria and other microbes. These filters are often impregnated with silver, which has the additional benefit of killing unwanted microorganisms. (**NOTE:** Many ceramic filters have no effect on possible chemical contaminants and/or dissolved heavy metals and salts[23].)

Perhaps the most important benefit of ceramic filters is the resistance they offer to the flow of water. This resistance can help regulate the rate of flow through an activated charcoal filter stage, which is important in enhancing its chemical-scrubbing characteristics. Also, any redundancy in the filtering of biological contaminants is never a bad thing.

> **NOTE:** *Any water treatment system employing ceramic water filters should not rely solely on the ceramic filter element to control biological contaminants. The reason for this is because ceramic filters may develop invisible cracks that can provide a pathway for microbes.*

4.8. Reverse Osmosis Water Filters

Reverse osmosis is a water filtration technology that can remove heavy metals such as arsenic, cadmium, lead and mercury. The technology is based on subjecting water to pressure against a membrane containing molecule-sized pores.[27] Such filters generally also incorporate other filtering technologies discussed here to provide a complete water treatment solution.

While reverse osmosis filters do an excellent job of producing high quality drinking water this advantage comes at a price. Reverse osmosis filters tend to recover only 10 to 15 percent of the water entering the system[27] and require an energy source that may very well be offline during a disaster. Many of the filtering advantages offered by reverse osmosis filters may be realized by simply using rain water.

4.9. Dealing with Chemical Contaminants

The number and variety of chemicals in the modern world is such that the only way to be certain that one's water is chemical-free is to make your own by burning hydrogen and oxygen. This is such a costly (and dangerous) process, however, that it is not practical (particularly in a disaster situation).

While there may not be any perfect guarantee of chemical-free water, there are measures that you can adopt that will reduce the risks substantially. One of the easiest measures is the proper collection of rain water (see section 4.5.1).

Fortunately, water filters that employ activated charcoal filter out many of the common chemical contaminants (such as insecticides). If you believe your water source may be contaminated by agricultural, mining or industrial runoff it is important that your water filtering system employ an activated charcoal stage to help scrub out harmful chemicals.

In order to remove inorganic contaminants or metals such as antimony, arsenic, asbestos, barium, beryllium, cadmium, chromium, copper, fluoride, mercury, nickel, nitrates/nitrites, selenium, sulfate and thallium from water it is generally necessary to distill the water or filter it through a reverse osmosis filter.[1] As rain water is basically distilled, this once again highlights the status of rain water as a good source for drinking water.

4.10. Dealing with Biological Contaminants

4.10.1. Using Bleach to Disinfect Water

Regular household bleach is a great, low-cost chemical that can be used to purify water for drinking. Before using bleach for this purpose be certain that it is labeled as providing between 4% and 6% 'available chlorine'. Also, be certain that it does not contain any other active ingredients such as fragrances or fabric softeners.

To purify water with bleach simply add 8 drops of bleach to a gallon of filtered water and allow it to stand open to the atmosphere for 30 minutes.[8] After 30 minutes the water should have a faint odor of bleach, if not, successively add 2 more drops of bleach and wait for 30 minutes until you can detect that faint bleach odor (but adding no more than a grand total of 16 drops). At this point the water is purified and ready to drink.

CAUTION: *Household bleach begins to degrade after 6 months, and after that eventually becomes worthless. As a result you should not plan on using your stored bleach to sanitize water for longer than 1 year.*

The Nice Solution - Using Calcium Hypochlorite to Make Bleach!

Fortunately you can easily make your own bleach from calcium hypochlorite, and then use that bleach to purify water. If stored properly calcium hypochlorite should retain its potency indefinitely. A single pound of calcium hypochlorite can purify enough water to supply a typical family for several years.

4.10.2. Calcium Hypochlorite for Water Disinfection

Having a supply of *granular calcium hypochlorite (GCHCL)* is easily one of the most cost-effective and important measures that a prepper can take. GCHCL is used to make bleach,

Type of Exposure	Measure
Inhalation	Remove the subject to fresh air and provide artificial respiration if the victim is not breathing. Give oxygen if the subject is experiencing breathing difficulty. Seek professional medical attention for the victim immediately.
Ingestion	**DO NOT INDUCE VOMITING.** If the victim is conscious have them consume large quantities of water. Seek immediate medical attention.
Skin Contact	Remove contaminated clothing and begin flushing affected skin with water for at least 15 minutes. Seek immediate medical attention. Be sure to wash contaminated clothing before reuse.
Eye Contact	Immediately begin to flush the victim's eyes with water for at least 15 minutes, being sure to lift the lower and upper eyelids while flushing. Seek immediate medical attention.

Table 4.1.: First aid procedures for injuries due to calcium hypochlorite exposure.[26]

and bleach can then be used to purify water as well as to sanitize cooking areas, locations where medical procedures are performed, or clothing (which can be critical during an outbreak of diseases such as cholera).

Several pounds of GCHCL can be sufficient to meet the sanitation needs of a small community for a period of years. Because GCHCL is extremely low cost there is simply no reason for a serious prepper not to have a supply of this vital prep.

Handling and Storage

When working with GCHCL you should wear gloves and protective eyewear. If GCHCL comes into contact with any part of your body then that area should be rinsed thoroughly with water.

When using GCHCL to make bleach, the procedure should be performed in a well-ventilated area.

GCHCL should be stored in a sealed plastic or glass container and stored physically apart from any organic substances such as oils, foods, etc.

Table 4.1 provides a list of the first aid measures that should be taken in he event of harmful exposure to GCHCL.

Use for Purifying Water

Using GCHCL to purify water is a 2-step process. The first step is to create a batch of bleach, and the second step is to use the bleach to purify the water (after making bleach it should be labeled and stored for future use).

To create a batch of bleach thoroughly stir a one half of a heaping teaspoon of GCHCL into 1 gallon of water. This will produce 1 gallon of bleach that can be used for any purpose for which you would normally use bleach, including purifying water.[8] (**NOTE:** *Of course you can decrease these quantities of water and GCHCL proportionally to make a smaller batch. Since bleach starts to degrade after 6 months you may want to consider this.*)

Refer to section 4.10.1 for a description of the procedure for using bleach to purify water.

Obtaining Granular Calcium Hypochlorite

Calcium hypochlorite is sold in both granular and pellet form. For purposes of sanitizing relatively small quantities of water you should obtain the granular form (the pelletized form is often used by cities to sanitize municipal water supplies).

GCHCL is most often sold in small quantities as 'pool shock', as one of its principal uses is to sanitize swimming pools. When buying pool shock for purposes of sanitizing water for human consumption you should confirm that it is at least 63% granular calcium hypochlorite and that granular calcium hypochlorite is the **only active ingredient** (some varieties of pool shock may have other active ingredients that could be harmful, and some varieties of pool shock are not based on GCHCL at all, so it is important to confirm this by reading the label).[25]

One source of pool shock that the author has found is at http://www.poolgeek.com/.[24] The name of the product sold there is *GLB Super Charge*, which is sold in 1 pound bags.

4.10.3. Boiling Water for Disinfection

Spores are a dormant state of some bacteria that is part of the bacteria's natural reproductive cycle. They may be thought of as the "seeds of bacteria". As such they are smaller than actual bacteria. Many of these spores are able to survive the temperature of boiling water.

Boiling water is a good and commonly-accepted means of purifying water, however it is not perfect. Some viruses may survive the boiling process, as well as bacteria spores. However, boiling is generally trusted because:

- Viruses are generally not present in most water supplies.

- The pore size of a good water filter will remove many bacterial spores.

- The human body's own defense mechanisms can deal with almost any microbe that survives boiling.

Most harmful microorganisms are killed at temperatures just below that of boiling, so after the water has begun boiling vigorously you know that it has been purified.

The pore size of a good water filter is small enough to prevent the passage of bacterial spores. This highlights the fact that filtration **and** purification are both important to having good drinking water.

There are some notable disadvantages to boiling water for purification. These include:

- **Limited resources** - Sources of wood may, over time, become depleted.

- **Fuel consumption** - Substantial fuel is required to boil water as part of any long-term water sanitation strategy.

- **Time consumption** - Gathering wood for boiling water can be time consuming.

- **Personal risk** - Gathering wood for boiling water, and having to range ever farther to obtain that wood, can increase the risk of conflict with others.

- **Bringing unwanted attention** - Any fire used to boil water will inevitably generate smoke that will be observable for some distance.

Considering the above disadvantages it is strongly recommended that the prepper plan on some means other than boiling to purify drinking water.

4.10.4. Distilling Water

Distillation is the process of heating water to convert it to vapor, then collecting and condensing the vapor back into water. As a result of this process all biological contaminants and many chemical contaminants are eliminated. Additionally, heavy metals and any particulate contamination are eliminated. The only chemical contaminants that are not eliminated by the distillation process are those that have a lower boiling point than water (most notably, chlorine).

4. Emergency Drinking Water

At first blush distillation would seem to be the ideal means to purify water, however it has some significant drawbacks:

- It is very wasteful, producing only a small percentage of output water compared to the amount of water being distilled (this is due to the inefficiencies of capturing water vapor).

- It does not remove chlorine and other *volatile organic chemicals (VOCs)* that have a boiling point less than that of water.

- It makes inefficient use of fuel.

- Depending on your resources and equipment, it may be a slow process that does not produce sufficient water to meet your basic needs.

Considering these factors it is recommended that the prepper not plan on the use of distillation as their primary means for purifying drinking water.

4.10.5. Using Iodine to Disinfect Water

While iodine tablets and/or crystals are used by campers to purify drinking water, it is a poor choice as a water purification method for anyone in a disaster scenario extending beyond a few days. The reason for this is because once the iodine container is opened, its contents must be used within a few days (iodine is generally sold in small glass bottles, rather than having tablets individually wrapped). Additionally, iodine is not a cost-effective means of purifying water compared to the alternatives.

Iodine **is** an effective water purifier if used properly, and can in fact be more effective than bleach (especially against *Giardia cysts*, which can be a **real** problem in an outdoor setting). If you find yourself in a situation in which iodine is the only available solution to purify water then please follow these guidelines:

- Do not use iodine to treat water to be consumed by anyone who has an iodine allergy. (Some people who are allergic to shell fish are also allergic to iodine!)

- The water being purified should be no cooler than 68°F.

- Always read and follow the usage instructions on the iodine bottle.

- Don't drink the purified water until 30 minutes after the iodine tablet or crystal has dissolved.

- If purifying water in a bottle be sure to, after adding the iodine, swish the water around such that the entire interior of the container is made wet.

- Any aftertaste in the purified water can be compensated for by adding vitamin C, fruit flavoring, or by simply pouring the purified water between containers a few times.

4.10.6. Using Sunlight to Disinfect Water (The 'SODIS' Method)

As an alternative to using chemicals to purify water, microbes in water may also be rendered harmless through low-cost use of solar power. To purify water using this technique it should be poured into a transparent, plastic bottle (such as a typical clear, uncolored 2-liter soda bottle with the labels removed) and laid on its side exposed to the sun for 5 hours. The solar energy entering the bottle will kill virtually all harmful microbes. This technique for water purification is referred to as *solar water disinfection (or 'SODIS')*.

The bottle(s) used for SODIS water purification should have a diameter of no more than 4 inches, meaning a 2-liter plastic soda bottle should be considered the maximum size to use. This limitation is due to the inability of the effective wavelengths of light to penetrate water to a depth greater than 4 inches.[21]

The SODIS technique depends on oxygen being dissolved in the water being purified. If the water is obtained from a non-flowing source then it is advisable to manually aerate the water before beginning SODIS. This can be done by vigorously splashing and stirring the water for several seconds before pouring it into the bottle, or by filling the bottle half full, sealing it, and shaking it vigorously for a few seconds, before proceeding to finish filling the bottle.[21]

There are some disadvantages to relying on the SODIS technique to purify water:

- If the weather is overcast then the bottles must be exposed to the sun for a longer period, and all microbes may not be killed.

- Due to the 5+ hours required for the process, several bottles may be needed to provide an adequate quantity of drinking water for even a small group.

CAUTION: *SODIS should be considered one tool in the toolbox of anyone interested in purifying water in a disaster scenario, however it should not be the primary or preferred method.*

4.10.7. Using UV Light to Disinfect Water

Some commercial and home water treatment systems employ *ultraviolet light (UV light)* for water purification. UV light of the proper wavelength and intensity has the ability to kill bacteria and viruses by damaging their DNA.

The advantages to UV systems is that they do not remove important minerals from the water and avoid the addition of chemicals for water purification.

While UV light may be an effective part of a home or commercial water purification strategy it is not particularly applicable for water treatment in disaster scenarios because:

- It requires electrical power.

- Cryptosporidia cysts are fairly resistant to the effects of UV light radiation, and these cysts are a major concern in a disaster scenario.

- The status of the filter can be difficult to monitor (if the UV light source stops working, it might go undetected).

- The water being processed by the UV light must already be clear to allow for the transmission of the UV light.

4.11. Commercial Water Filters

Anyone preparing for a grid-down scenario should be focused on obtaining a quality, gravity-fed water filter.4.2.5 Some gravity-fed filters allow you to increase the rate at which they produce drinkable water by simply installing additional filter elements.

The most widely known and acclaimed brand of filter gravity-fed water filters is the Berkey filter.[3] These *Berkey-brand filters* have a long and successful history of providing drinking water throughout the world.

Another, slightly lower cost gravity-fed water filter is offered by *CeraGrav*[4], and is manufactured by the same company that manufactures the Berkey brand filters. The CeraGrav filter is less costly than the Berkey, and also has a strong reputation.

In addition to the Berkey and CeraGrav brand water filters the *Katadyn* and *Gravidyn* brand water filters also have excellent water filtering characteristics and good reputations.

All 4 brands of water gravity-fed water filters mentioned above are full water purifiers, with a filter pore size of less than 0.5 microns (in the case of the Katadyn filters, less then .2 microns!). Additionally, all 3 filters employ activated carbon to filter out many hazardous chemicals that are found in many environments. If the filtered water is from a trusted source, the water produced from these filters should require no additional processing.

NOTE: *Katadyn also produces several portable (camping) water filters with excellent filtering characteristics.[28] These filters are the gold standard for light, highly-portable water filters.*

4.12. Building a Homemade Water Filter

There are a few reasons to consider fabricating your own water filter:

- *To save costs* - It is much less costly to make your own filter than to purchase a good commercial gravity-fed water filter.

- *Availability* - You will be able to utilize materials at hand to renew your filter virtually indefinitely, while a commercial filter is only useful as long as your supply of purchased filter elements holds out.

- *It's a better fit for your specific situation and plan* - The filter you construct may be more rugged and portable than a purchased water filter.

- *Future barter potential* - In the future you might have the opportunity to create new filters to trade for other things.

There are many ways to construct homemade water filters, with some of them being rather quick and simple. For example, a water filter can be constructed from a plastic soda bottle with a little polyester batting material and some activated charcoal. Such filters are impressively simple, however they are not a good fit for most survival situations because they may very well not provide adequate filtering.

A good compromise between ruggedness and cost is to make your filter from commonly available PVC piping. This will result in a good, rugged filter than you can transport easily. The following parts list and instructions will guide you in building a good, rugged water filter.

CAUTION: *The following instructions are for constructing a water filter, and not a complete purifier. this means that any water produced by this filter must still be subject to an additional purification step.*

---

4. Emergency Drinking Water

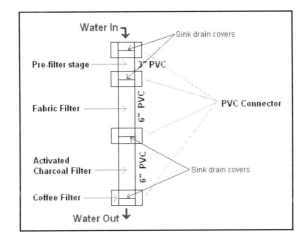

Figure 4.3.: Diagram of a homemade PVC pipe water filter.

Parts needed:

- **From the Hardware Store**

    – Two 6" lengths of 3/4" diameter PVC piping

    – One 3" length of 3/4" diameter PVC piping

    – Four straight 3/4" PVC connection joints

    – Four 3/4" diameter sink drain covers

- **From the Aquarium Section of the Pet Store**

    – Multiple 6-inch-long, oblong aquarium filter bags

    – Containers of activated charcoal (at least 16 ounces)

- **From the Fabric Store**

    – One large bag of polyester batting material

- **From Other Sources**

    – Standard circular paper coffee filters

Notes:

- The sink drain covers serve to separate the various filter segments.

- The pre-filter section contains the same material as the fabric filter (the batting material) but is intended to be replaced more frequently (as it will become fouled more quickly).

- The activated charcoal is contained inside the aquarium filter bag.

- The purpose of the coffee filter paper is actually not to provide filtering, but rather to slow the passage of water through the filter to provide a better opportunity for the activated charcoal to absorb chemical contaminants.

See Figure 4.3 for a depiction a homemade PVC pipe water filter.

4.13. Water Infrastructure and Storage

If you are preparing for a disaster that spans only a few days then water management becomes as simple as storing containers of water, or adding a liner into a bathtub and filling the bathtub with water. If you are preparing for a longer term disaster, read on...

Of course the amount of water you need to store will vary with your specific circumstances. (If you have a highly trusted well that can be operated manually then you may not need to store any water at all.) If you do not have ready access to a good trusted source of water, however, then you may want to give serious consideration to storing rain water in plastic *rain barrels* or some other large food grade containers that you are certain have not ever been used for any purpose other than storing food or water. See chapter 5 for instructions on identifying food quality plastic containers.

If you need to store rain water then the two primary considerations should be the amount of water you need to store and how the rain water will be collected.

The great majority of preppers who collect rain water simply capture the water that flows off the roof of their home and into the gutter. If you choose this approach then it is a good idea to schedule to periodically clean the gutters of your home so that potential contaminants do not accumulate excessively ("Is it just me, or does this water taste like dead squirrel?").

In a disaster situation the average person requires an absolute minimum of 1 gallon of water per day to remain hydrated and for bare essential sanitation purposes (5 gallons is a much more realistic number, and 13 gallons per person is optimal).[6] If your only source of drinking water is to come from rain then the following formula can give you an idea of the quantity of water you need to collect per month:

$$\text{GALLONS} = P \times \text{PGALS} \times 30$$

where...

- P = is the number of people in your group
- $PGALS$ = is the number of gallons per day you wish to allow per person (ranging from a bare minimum of 1 gallon up to 13 gallons).
- 30 = is the average number of days in a month.

To calculate the average number of gallons of water you can collect per month:

$$\text{GALS\_PER\_MONTH} = (\text{SQFT} \times 144 \times I) / 231$$

where...

- $SQFT$ = the number of square feet of your collection area
- 144 = the number of square inches in a square foot
- I = the averages number of inches of rainfall you receive per month
- 231 = the number of cubic inches in a gallon

If the number of gallons you collect per month is less than the number of gallons you need per month then you must increase the size of your water collection surface.

Finally, a formula for calculating the number of gallons of water you need to have the capacity to store is:

$$\text{GALS\_STORED} = (\text{GALS\_PER\_MONTH}/30) * \text{MAX\_DRY\_DAYS}$$

where...

- $GALS\_PER\_MONTH$ is calculated above
- MAX_DRY_DAYS - the maximum number of days you would expect between significant rainfall.

NOTE: *During an extended disaster if you experience a drought you should immediately work to increase your rain collection area. Having some large, reasonably thick plastic sheets stored may be important for this.*

---

5. Emergency Food

"I'll never be hungry again.
No, nor any of my folk.
If I have to lie, steal, cheat or kill.
As God is my witness,
I'll never be hungry again."

by Scarlett O'Hara from *Gone With the Wind*
by Margaret Mitchell

Recently there have been numerous examples of store shelves going bare even before the onset of a major disaster. And, inevitably, fights have broken out as food supplies began to dwindle. In order to meet the basic human need for food there are numerous examples of looting and theft in the wake of disaster. All of these situations are rife with danger to anyone who is desperate for food.

Having a good, well-planned store of emergency food supplies is essential. Not only does a lack of food pose a threat to survival but it also poses the distinct possibility that the refugee will completely lose control of their own fate (those who offer the food may only provide it in exchange for control).

Of course emergency food must remain edible in the event of a prolonged loss of electricity, so the type of food stored and the way in which it is stored are a major consideration. This chapter will discuss the various types of long-shelf-life foods that are available, the advantages and disadvantages of each, and will describe a reasonable, cost-effective emergency food strategy.

Identifying Food Grade Plastic Buckets and Other Containers

When storing food and water in plastic-type containers it is important that you make use of containers that have been rated for this purpose. Non-rated containers may contain carcinogenic chemicals that could leech into your food and water.

Food Type	Shelf Life	Usage
Dry Packed	25-30 years	*e.g. beans and rice* - The low cost and high shelf life of this food makes it the form of food that most preppers should store in bulk quantity. Dry-packed beans and rice provide a much needed source of proteins and carbohydrates.
MREs	3 years	MREs are an ideal source of nutritious meals when you want to 'eat while moving' (on foot or driving). This is because they provide good calories and nutrition, and can even be heated without requiring a source of flame or smoke.
Freeze Dried	25 years	Freeze-dried foods are very light and have a long shelf life. They need only be rehydrated with hot water to quickly provide a good, nutritious meal. These foods also provide a good source of variety. Because these are costly they should primarily be considered a food source for individuals who are traveling medium-to-long distances on foot.
Dehydrated	3-18 months	Dehydrated foods have little benefit to offer the prepper before a disaster. After a disaster this may be considered as a method to prolong the shelf life of some harvested foods.
Canned	2 years	Every prepper should be putting away canned foods before the disaster, and rotating out and consuming them as they approach their expiration dates. Canned foods provide much-needed variety, and can also serve as ingredients that make dry-packed beans and rice much more appetizing.

Table 5.1.: Types of Emergency Food Stores

If your container is labeled *'HDPE'* or you see the number *'2'* inside the universal logo for recycling, and if you know that the container has not been used to contain non-food items previously, then you can trust it for storage of emergency food. If the container is made from *polycarbonate*, *polyester* or *polyethylene*, and it has not been used to contain non-food items, then it can be considered safe.

5.1. Beans and Rice - a Solid Foundation!

Beans and rice have long enjoyed the reputation of being a classic staple for those in a survival mode. There are some very good reasons for this:

- Beans and rice, together, provide a good spectrum of amino acids (the building blocks for protein) and other nutrients that are essential to life.

- Beans and rice are very cost effective.

- If packed properly, beans and rice can store at room temperature and remain edible for as long as thirty years *(see section 5.2 for a description of the procedure for vacuum packing dry foods in mylar)*.

A large inventory of beans and rice packed for long-term storage should be considered the foundation of your emergency food strategy. A survey of several beans and rice recipes indicates that it is common for a beans-and-rice meal to consist of equal quantities of beans and rice (although the volume of dried beans will increase as they are soaked in water for several hours prior to cooking). One gallon of beans and one gallon of rice is sufficient to provide approximately 53 meals. Hence two 5-gallon buckets filled with beans and rice should be expected to provide approximately 53 x 5 = 265 meals. If two meals per day are beans and rice then those two buckets should serve 2 people for about 19 weeks.

If you know how many people you are planning to feed, and your planned time frame for feeding them, then you'll easily be able to calculate the number of buckets of beans and rice required. *These calculations do not take into account the need for other foods for breakfasts and snacks; nor do they take into account the need to incorporate ingredients other than beans and rice into a recipe to create meals that are palatable. You should not plan on subsisting on a diet that consists exclusively of beans and rice.*

NOTE: *When packing beans for long-term storage be sure to pack dried beans. Pinto beans are particularly nutritious. Be sure to identify and test beans and rice recipes to find those that you prefer, and to store those recipes in hard copy form alongside your food stores.*

You should compliment the beans and rice you store with spices required by your recipes along with a stockpile of multivitamins to fill in any nutritional gaps not filled by beans and rice.

5.2. Mylar-packed Dry Foods

Mylar is the metallic fabric that has come into commonplace use. The characteristics of mylar that make it valuable for food storage are its flexibility, its toughness and its ability to hold a vacuum almost indefinitely (if sealed properly).

Beans and rice, along with numerous other dry foods, can be vacuum packed in mylar and stored away in food grade plastic buckets for truly long-term storage (as long as 30 years). The relatively low cost, high nutritional value and long shelf life of beans and rice make them a perfect candidate as a long-term emergency staple. While you may be rotating through your other emergency food provisions, your beans and rice stores will be sitting there waiting patiently for the day they are truly needed.

To dry pack any food in mylar bags you'll need the following:

- A food saver with a vacuum hose attachment. Ideally it will also come with vacuum-sealable jars to save your highly-perishable oxygen absorbers between usages.

- 3- or 5- gallon food grade buckets to store your packed food. The purpose of these buckets is to provide a protective hard outer shell around your mylar-encased foods.

- If your buckets have lids that require hammering down to seal them, then you'll need a rubber mallet to use as the hammer.

- One or more packages of 250cc oxygen absorbers.

- Mylar bags to contain the food that is to be packed. These bags must be at least 4.5 mils thick (the minimum thickness for them to be considered "food quality"). You should be able to use any mylar bag with a thickness between 4.5 and 7 mils. 7 mils thickness is recommended if the food bag is not to be stored in any protective container such as a food-grade plastic bucket, or if the contents being stored has the possibility of puncturing less thick mylar (e.g. dried spaghetti noodles).[32] (**NOTE:** One good source of mylar bags is *usaemergencysupply.com*).

- *(Optional)* Food grade diatomaceous earth powder.

- One large measuring cup.

- One standard clothes iron (to be used to seal the mylar).

- A one-inch-thick board that is about as long as the mylar bags are wide (you'll be using this as a backing for the mylar bags to provide a solid, flat surface to iron against).

- One or more large (40-50lb) bags of rice.

- One or more large (40-50lb) bags of dried beans.

While the food saver has the ability to both vacuum pack and seal food containers it is not really practical to take full advantage of these capabilities when packing food in mylar. This is because the mylar material does not have the high-friction properties of regular food storage bags, and also because many food savers are not wide enough to seal the size of bags you'll be using. Also, these bags are going to be packed sufficiently full that it will not be feasible to lay them on their sides for sealing (as most food savers require).

So, your food saver is more often than not going to be used only for its vacuum feature.

NOTE: Gander Mountain *offers a wide variety of high-quality food savers.*

The procedure for packing food in a mylar bag is:

- Heat the clothes iron to maximum heat.

- Open a mylar bag inside a bucket and place it on the table or floor in front of you.

- Using a large measuring cup, pour the food to be stored into the bag until there is only enough space remaining in the bag to allow the top to be folded over the edge of the one-inch-thick board for sealing.

- **Optionally**, for non-powdery foods being stored, stir in a couple of tablespoons of diatomaceous earth powder. This provides an additional protection against insects.

- Throw two 250cc oxygen absorbers into the bag (if you don't vacuum out the air then you'll need between 1500cc and 2000cc of oxygen absorbers for a bag that would line a 5-gallon bucket[31]).

- Folding the top of the bag over the edge of the one-inch-thick board, run the iron along the board once or twice such that almost one-half of the bag is sealed.

- Run the iron along the other side of the bag, leaving an unsealed opening maybe one inch wide in the top of the bag.

- Place the vacuum hose from the food saver in the unsealed hole in the center of the bag and activate the vacuum to remove virtually all the air from the mylar bag.

- With one fluid motion remove the vacuum hose, fold the top of the mylar bag over the board once again and, using the iron, finish sealing the bag.

- Leave the bucket containing the bag open and set it aside to inspect after 24 hours has passed. At that time the oxygen absorbers should have absorbed any remaining oxygen in the bag, and the enclosed food should almost feel like a brick. If beans are stored in the bag then you should see little bumps in the mylar that are conforming to the enclosed beans. (**NOTE:** *you may wish to pack two or more smaller bags in a single bucket - for example one bag containing rice and another containing dried beans.*)

- For those buckets that pass their post-24-hour inspection, hammer down the gasketed lids and put them in a location where they can be stored at a temperature of $75°$(F) or cooler. In the case of *gamma lids* you will screw the lids into place rather than hammering them into place.

> **'THE CHICKEN CHASE':** *Chickens (and their eggs) represent an almost ideal source of dietary protein. The size of chickens means that the need to preserve their meat is virtually non-existent. While vegetable sources of protein are passable, in a long term grid-down situation you should seriously consider obtaining and raising chickens.*

5.3. Store Bought Canned Foods

Canned foods bought at the store have a total shelf life that is generally between 18 and 24 months (of course it should be noted that this is the shelf life after it is produced and NOT after the date it is purchased). **Before purchasing canned foods always check the expiration date.**

Canned foods play an important part in disaster scenarios because they provide some sense of normalcy and variety to meals. While beans, rice and vitamins may technically be able to sustain human life for the long term, the blandness and monotony could be intolerable for most people. Adding a little canned pork, for example, and maybe some stored spices, to beans and rice would result in a much more palatable food for very little additional price.

Because canned foods expire you should rotate through them based on expiration dates such that those closest to expiration are consumed first. An easy way to do this is to stack the different types of canned foods together in the pantry ordered by date purchased. Add newly-purchased canned foods to the back of the stack, and to pull food that you will be consuming from the front. It's even more convenient if your pantry is accessible from both front and back, in which case you can add new canned foods from the back while pulling older ones from the front.

Canned foods are the heaviest of the emergency food stores, and so they are not as portable. However, even when bugging out it is a good idea to give serious consideration to raiding the pantry for canned foods to take along. **And don't forget the can opener!**

5.4. MRE's

The acronym *MRE* was originally coined by the US military to identify the high-energy, individual meal packages that were formally named *'Meals, Ready to Eat'*. Since originally being developed by the US military MREs have been adopted for a wide range of additional uses ranging from search and rescue operations to disaster response.

NOTE: *Some vendors have been known to sell old MREs. Be sure to check the production date on any MREs you purchase and don't accept any that are more than a few months old.*

The typical MRE consists of one or more individually wrapped food items packaged in a pouch made of layers of plastic and aluminum foil. MRE's may also come packaged with chemical heater pouches that can be used to heat the meal. To heat the meal one simply adds a little water into the heater pad (which initiates the chemical reaction that generates the heat) and place the heater pouch, along with the food to be heated, back into the main package wrapper for about 10 minutes.

The quality of the food provided by MREs is very much like that of regular canned food. In fact, the process used to produce the MRE food packets is really just a variation of the regular food canning process. The MREs packaging does reduce the amount of time the food is heated before packaging, which means that MREs may be perceived as being a little more palatable than canned food.

For the prepper there are a few considerations that indicate the proper role for MREs:

- Calorie-for-calorie, meal-for-meal, MREs are more costly than other forms of long-shelf-life food.

- MREs have a typical shelf life of three years.

- MREs are excellent for eating while on the move (whether by foot or by vehicle). Not only are they fast and easy to prepare but many do not require any external devices for heating (they come equipped with their own built-in chemical heating pouch). Since they do not require fire for heating there is no potential for the presence of smoke to disclose one's location.

As a result, the typical role for MREs is to provide food for those in-transit, especially during an initial bug-out at the onset of disaster, or possibly when hiking overland. One way to determine the quantity of MREs to have on hand is to simply multiply the number of meals one expects to consume in transit by the number of people who will be in the group. It might then be a good idea to multiply this number by some factor to account for other unexpected needs that may emerge. If you end up with what proves to be an excess inventory of MREs then, in a disaster scenario, you should be able to use the excess inventory for barter.

As with canned foods, one should plan to regularly consume MREs as they approach their expiration dates.

5.5. Freeze-Dried Foods

Freeze-dried foods are vacuum-sealed meals from which all moisture has been extracted by a process known as *freeze drying*. This process involves freezing the food in a pressure-controlled environment such that virtually all water is extracted. In this state the food can be stored at room temperature for typically as long as 25 years. Because freeze drying of food does not involve the exposure of the food to additional heat, freeze-dried foods retain virtually all of their original nutritional benefits.

> **NOTE:** *The process of freeze drying food requires costly, highly-specialized equipment. As a result the average person does not have the option of freeze drying food at home.*

Like MREs, freeze-dried foods can play a specific role in disaster scenarios. That role is to provide a food source that is light and very easy to transport (for example, when traveling by foot). This is why the traditional market for freeze-dried foods has historically consisted of hikers and campers.

In a disaster scenario it is possible that you may find yourself relegated to transportation by foot, and in such circumstances it would be very beneficial to carry light-weight freeze-dried meals.

Preparing Freeze Dried Meals

The process of preparing a hot freeze-dried meal is quite simple. First one begins by boiling water. Once the water is boiling simply open the mylar pouch containing the freeze-dried food, pour in the quantity of hot water specified on the label, stir slightly and wait for a couple of minutes (as long as directed by the instructions on the label). The meal is then ready to eat.

Obtaining Freeze Dried Meals

Because the equipment to produce freeze-dried meals is quite costly it is almost always purchased in commercial packages. Two of the bigger names in freeze-dried foods are *Mountain House* and *Alpine Aire*. Through a simple search of the Internet you should be able to locate numerous vendors who offer these brands (particularly the Mountain House brand, which has widespread distribution). Both of these brands enjoy excellent reputations for both the taste and quality of their foods.

Freeze-dried foods generally come packaged in one-meal plastic pouches or in multi-serving #10 cans.

NOTE: *While plastic pouches of freeze-dried foods typically have a shelf life of 7 years, the #10 cans typically have a shelf life of 25-30 years.[50]*

5.6. Dehydrated Foods

Since moisture is required for the growth of bacteria and mold, dehydrated foods have a much longer shelf life than the same foods in a non-dehydrated state. Dehydrated foods are prepared and processed in a food dehydrator or through direct exposure to sunlight, which removes a great percentage of the its moisture content. Before food can be dehydrated it must first be prepared, which involves *blanching* it through immersion in boiling salt water. In the case of fruits and vegetables it is best to select foods just before their peak flavor.

NOTE: *Dehydrated foods should not be confused with freeze-dried foods, as freeze-dried foods have a much longer shelf life and are processed in costly commercial equipment that must regulate temperature, humidity and air pressure.*

Dehydrated foods are not quite as nutritious as fresh foods (for example, the processing destroys some vitamins and, because they are reduced in volume, they contain more calories per unit volume). However, properly dehydrated foods still provide plenty of benefit (in this regard any loss of nutrition is comparable to loss of food value resulting from the wet canning process). To maintain nutritional value, dehydrated foods should ideally be stored in a cool, dark and dry location.[36]

The actual shelf life of dehydrated food depends on the food's composition:[35]

- Dehydrated fruits and vegetables can be stored safely for a full year.

- Dehydrated noodles can be stored up to 1.5 years.

- Dehydrated meats, due to their higher fat content, can be stored up to 3 months. After the first month it is recommended that they be stored refrigerated.

Solar dehydration involves cutting the food to be dried into narrow slices or strips and laying the strips on *drying racks* that are exposed to direct sunlight (the individual slices or strips of food being processed should not be in physical contact with one another). The sun itself provides the energy to draw the moisture from the food. The bottoms of the drying racks on should be made of cheesecloth or other similar light fabric (the use of metal trays can contaminate the food).

To speed the dehydration process, a window pane can be mounted over the food to concentrate the solar energy (in fact, an entire window frame, laid horizontally with the window glass intact, makes an excellent homemade dehydrating box). If insects become a problem during the drying process the food can be shielded with a layer of light fabric similar to that used for the bottom of the tray (this protective layer of fabric should also not be in physical contact with the food being dehydrated).[45]

NOTE: *While solar curing has been used to make jerky from meat for centuries, many health and governmental agencies recommend against this approach).*

In the event of a disaster in which it is anticipated that electricity will be unavailable, it might be useful to dehydrate foods that are currently refrigerated, so as to extend the availability of those foods. In a survival scenario dehydration might be used to store fruits, vegetables and meats that have been produced during the recovery period. This may be particularly useful as a food source for those who travel for extended periods.

5.7. Cured Meats

Curing is the process of saving or preserving meat.[42] Meat curing involves either treating it chemically or smoking it (see section 5.8).

The process extracts water from the meat to create an environment that inhibits the growth of harmful bacteria. This is achieved by packing the raw meat in salt or in nitrate compounds (such as salt peter). It is also not uncommon for sugar to be used in a packing recipe. Sugar has the effect of countering any excessive salty taste in addition to promoting the growth of beneficial bacteria.[43]

Foods can be *dry cured* by trimming as much fat as possible and then packing the meat in salt, sugar, nitrates and seasonings. They can also be *wet cured* through immersion in liquids that draw moisture from the meat. Two typical recipes for dry-curing packing mixtures are:

- One part pink salt, 4.5 parts sugar and 9 parts kosher salt
- One part pink salt, 5.5 parts dextrose and 6 parts kosher salt

The protein content of meat, and most of the other nutritional value, is not significantly diminished by the curing process.

> **NOTE:** *All cured meats (whether cured with chemicals or through dehydration) should be considered to still be raw, and when you are ready to prepare them the first step should be to wash the cured meat thoroughly with fresh water and then to cook it normally.*

Cured meats, other than seafood and poultry, have a shelf-life of about one year. Poultry and seafood should be considered to have a shelf life of 6 months. It is a good practice to consume cured meats within 4 months.

5.8. Smoked Meats

Smoked foods are foods that have been exposed to heat and smoke for a prolonged period in order to increase its shelf life. The heat from the process cooks the meat while simultaneously killing bacteria, while the resin and oils from the wood provide a bacteria-resistant coating for the food. Typically meats are smoked, however sometimes vegetables are as well (most commonly as a means of imparting flavor). The exact shelf life of smoked meats varies with the type of meat, however properly smoked foods can have a shelf life of as long as one year. Smoked fish and poultry have a higher rate of degradation than other meats and should be carefully inspected before an signs of spoilage before being eaten.[37] As a result, it is advisable to store smoked fish and chicken no longer than six months.

Smoked meats are typically smoked as thin strips of meat to provide the assurance that the meat cooks thoroughly during the process.

The type of wood used in smoking foods is also an important factor. Commercial lumber should never be used to smoke food because it has almost certainly been chemically treated.[37] In America the woods commonly used for smoking food include mesquite, hickory, pecan, alder, maple, oak and the wood of fruit trees including apple, cherry and plum.[38]

Vacuum-sealing smoked meats is a great way to ensure the longest possible shelf life while simultaneously doing the best job of preserving the food.

For all practical purposes smoking food should not be considered for long term food preservation, but more as a means of extending the service life of food during "times of plenty".

As such, smoked foods are really significant to the prepper during stage three of the disaster, when the recovery process is under way. During stage three those who survive will be raising and harvesting food once again, and smoking could be useful in the absence of refrigeration, or when members of the community begin to travel for extended periods.

A good use for dehydrated meats is to incorporate them into stews and soups, where they can rehydrate to provide a more normal meal.

Nutrition and Health Concerns

Most commonly it is meats and fish that are smoked. These foods retain much of their nutritional benefits (their protein content) through the smoking process.

It has been shown that smoking fish is often not sufficient to kill germs and parasites[41], so smoking fish should be done carefully and smoked fish should still be cooked before being eaten.[40]

It should be noted that smoking foods has been shown to impart known carcinogenic compounds to the meat.[39] Given the prevalence of smoked foods within society during normal times, in a disaster situation these risks would almost certainly be minor considerations (when the alternative is hunger and death!).

5.9. Home Canning

Canning is the process of sterilizing and storing food in such a way that it will remain edible for an extended period (often as long as two years). The method used to can the food depends on the type of food being canned:

- *Dry foods* should be vacuum-sealed and stored in a dark cool environment.

- *High acid foods (with a pH of less than 4.6)* or foods with high salt or sugar content can be heated in boiling water to kill harmful bacteria and then sealed against future contamination. These include many fruits (e.g. citrus fruits) and pickled vegetables.[47]

- *Low acid foods* such as meats and most vegetables must be heated in a pressure cooker to assure that all harmful bacteria are killed (the pressure cooker allows the food to be heated to temperatures greater than the normal boiling point of water) and then sealed against future contamination.[49]

5.9.1. Dry Canning

Dry canning simply involves putting away dry foods such as beans, rice, noodles, etc in a vacuum-sealed environment that inhibits the growth of harmful bacteria. Since harmful bacteria require both oxygen and moisture to grow, dry packed foods can have a very long shelf life (sometimes as long as thirty years).

Canned foods (whether dry canned or wet canned) retain a great percentage of their original nutritional value.

5.9.2. Wet Canning for High-Acid Foods

For purposes of food canning, high-acid foods are those that have a pH value of less than 4.6. Harmful bacteria cannot live and grow at this acidity level, hence high-acid foods require a less rigorous procedure for canning. Such foods can be canned in a *hot water bath* that does not require the use of a pressure cooker.

High acid foods consist primarily of fruits, although properly pickled vegetables can also be wet canned using the hot water bath method. Tomatoes, figs and certain other foods with a borderline pH value, can also be canned using the hot water bath method if citric acid or lemon juice is added to increase the acidity.[47]

NOTE: *Don't be misled by the name 'canning' into believing that canning only involves storing food in cans. Most home canning is done using* Mason *or* Ball *brand glass jars that have been specifically designed for food canning. In fact the packing of dried foods such as beans and white rice into mylar is a form of dry canning.*

While the procedure for wet canning of high-acid foods is less rigorous than that for low-acid foods, it is still important to exercise due care to assure that the food is stored in as sterile a condition as possible.[46] These procedures include:

- Don't allow anyone who is sick to be in the area where the canning is taking place.

- Before starting be sure that everyone involved in the process washes their hands thoroughly with soap and water.

- Remove all jewelry from the hands and/or arms before starting canning.

- Make use of magnetic canning wands to handle and move lids for cans.

> **CAUTION:** *High-acid canned foods such as fruits, jams, jellies and picked vegetables should be consumed within one year of being canned.[48]*

5.9.3. Wet Canning for Low-Acid Foods

Low-acid foods such as meats and non-pickled vegetables provide an environment in which harmful bacteria may grow (even in the absence of oxygen). As a result, it is necessary to can such foods at temperatures that are guaranteed to kill those bacteria - temperatures which happen to be higher than the boiling point of water. To accomplish this the foods must be boiled in a pressure cooker (the higher pressures in the pressure cooker increase the boiling temperature of water). Of course the same cleanliness and hygiene procedures described above for hot water bath canning should also be observed.

When wet-packing canned foods, whether with the hot water bath method or using a pressure cooker, after the jar is sealed and cools a vacuum will be created within the sterile environment inside the jar. This vacuum causes the jar's lid to curve inward slightly. It is this curvature that provides you with the indication that your jar does not have a vacuum leak and is, therefore, preserving the food as intended.

> **CAUTION:** *Low-acid canned foods such as meats and fish should ideally be consumed within two years of being canned, although such foods have been known to be edible (with reduced nutritional benefits) as long as five years after being canned. After being opened, however, these foods should be kept refrigerated and should be consumed within three to five days.[48]*

Milk can be canned and stored for between nine and fifteen months, depending on its fat content (higher-fat milks actually store longer than lower-fat milks).

Canned Foods and the Risk of Botulism

The biggest concern for food canners is that the bacteria responsible for botulism *(Clostridium botulinum)* might find its way into the canned food. This creates the perfect environment for the bacteria to produce the extremely dangerous *botulism toxin.* Anyone consuming this tasteless, odorless toxin faces the very real possibility of paralysis and/or death.

Fortunately with just a little due care the threat posed by botulism can be avoided. The bacteria that produces the botulism toxin also produces a gas. This results in the loss of the vacuum within the canning jar. If the botulism toxin is present then the lid of the can will be curved slightly outward rather than inward (which indicates the vacuum has been lost). When removing the lid from the can one should notice the lack of a vacuum.

So, it is not just important to be observant while canning the food but also when later opening it.

5.10. Other Important Foods and Suppliments

In addition to the the various primary food sources described in this chapter it is important not to forget the 'extras' that will be necessary for practical survival. These important extras should certainly include:

- Multi-vitamins

- Sugar

- Flour

- Spices

- Honey

- Peanut Butter

- Crackers

- Powdered Protein

- Dry-packed breakfast cereal

- Powdered fat-free or low-fat milk

In addition to the above 'must haves', you should also give serious consideration to other basic provisions such as:

- Pancake mix and syrup

- Powdered drink mixes

- Whole wheat (which stores much longer than milled wheat)

- Candy bars and other treats

5. Emergency Food

As with canned foods, you should plan on rotating through these extra food items over time so that they never have a chance to approach their expiration dates. The availability of these extra provisions will be good for morale in addition to helping maintain overall health.

Please refer to Chapter 13 *('Survival Farming - Achieving Self-Sufficiency')* for information on raising or growing your own food as part of a strategy for long-term survival.

6. Disaster Communications

STRAIGHT THINKING: *A good emergency radio receiver is a necessity.*

If you plan on bugging out in the event of a disaster equip any vehicles you plan on using with CB radios (these will be vital!). For short distance, low-cost communications (within one-half mile reliably) obtain FRS hand-held radio devices. For slightly longer distance communications (within 1-2 miles) obtain GMRS hand-held units (these require an $85 fee for use by you and your immediate family). FRS and GMRS radios are low cost with GMRS units also covering the FRS channels and communicating freely with them. You should consider obtaining not only multiple units but additional battery chargers as well for quick recharging of multiple units.

Obtain a HAM radio unit if you are planning for long distance 2-way radio communications.

Binoculars can also be helpful to increase the range of visual communications. Multiple binoculars are recommended for bidirectional communications.

Signage posted along the perimeter of the areas under your control is a form of communication that works for you 24x7, and which can help you avoid unnecessary conflict.

Good communications can be as important to surviving disaster as having adequate food and water. In day-to-day living communications can save both time and fuel (why walk or drive down the road to make a purchase if you have the means to determine beforehand that there is nothing there available to purchase?). Knowing weather forecasts can help you make the best decisions about how to invest your time on any particularly day. And, of course, communications is essential to both long-term strategic as well as short-term tactical self-defense situations.

> **NOTE:** *Seals and envelopes have been used for centuries to provide the assurance that messages are not seen by third parties while in transit. In a post-disaster scenario these low-tech approaches to guaranteeing message confidentiality may once again become important (especially if the Internet becomes unavailable). While these measures are not foolproof they may very well still provide a high level of confidence that a message was not compromised in transit.*

6.1. Use of Semaphores

Semaphores are physical objects (often hand-held) used for visual communications. A semaphore might be as simple as 'running up the white flag' to communicate surrender or as complex as the use of hand-held flags or light wands in various positions to transmit complete messages. Semaphore systems have been defined that specify individual arm and hand positions that correspond to the letters of the alphabet.[151]

In a post-disaster scenario semaphore communications might be used for communications between a central headquarters and one or more observation posts, or between roadblocks and observation posts or shooters providing covering fire for the roadblock. In larger communities when radio communications is unavailable or undesirable semaphores might be used to quickly communicate a wide range of information across the community.

Semaphores should be considered not only for their use in defensive situations, but as means of saving time and energy. For example, if you can visually see the status of a roadblock from a distance then you do have saved the time and energy of visiting the roadblock to obtain that information. Binoculars could be very helpful in facilitating semaphore communications.

In addition to hand-held objects for semaphore communications, devices such as kites might be useful for communications across greater distances.

6.2. Use of Signage

The best battles are the ones that you avoid altogether. While signs are a decidedly low-tech means of communication, they can also be one of the most important. Well-conceived, well-placed signs work 24x7 to dissuade would-be intruders from infringing on your property. The very presence of a good sign communicates that you are prepared and organized, which is exactly what many potential intruders will be anxious to avoid.

While standard *'No Trespassing'* signs may be adequate for normal times, you may wish to consider placing signs that convey stronger and more potent messages in a post-disaster scenario. Because many potential adversaries may not be literate, it may also be beneficial if such signs communicate their meaning as much through imagery (e.g. a picture of a person in the cross-hairs of a rifle) as well as through words.

6.3. Disinformation and Obfuscation

Disinformation can be a powerful weapon. Putting false information into the hands of a potential adversary can be as useful (if not more useful) than concealing valid information. For example, if you can convince the adversary that you are 'attacking on the left' when you intend to 'attack on the right', then they may very well be at a disadvantage when you do attack. Other uses of disinformation might be less tactical in nature (for example, providing misleading information about resource availability, or information that causes an adversary to relocate to somewhere less threatening).

One way of spreading disinformation is to qualify a message with some code word or through the use of some other means to indicate its veracity. For example, if a community adopts the standard that all messages containing the letter *'k'* in the first four words of a message indicates that the entire message is invalid, then valid and invalid messages can be sent freely between the participants with the knowledge that any third party reading the message will receive incorrect or inconsistent information. A similar (but probably less effective) approach might be to have all messages delivered by a particular courier be invalid.

Obfuscation is the process of concealing the meaning of a message through *information hiding*. Much of the meaning of messages can be concealed through the use of message obfuscation techniques. One good example of message obfuscation is the use of *'ten-codes'* by law enforcement and other public service agencies. These codes provide an easily-understood shorthand method of communications between the speaker and the listener while also doing a reasonable job of concealing the meaning from the casual listener. In reality, obfuscation is a special, low-security form of encryption in which the keys are the sheets that associate the ten-codes to their respective meanings.

A small community of disaster survivors should consider adopting their own set of standard code words to improve communications. This is a good way to facilitate communications while helping to keep communications more secure.

6.4. Radio Communications

History shows that even modest disasters can severely disrupt normal voice and Internet communications. Starting in the first moment of any major disaster good radio communications will become extremely important.

Through radio communications you will stay aware of safe times and places to travel, schedules for any assistance that may arrive, and weather forecasts that will allow you to plan your days for maximum efficiency. Additionally, 2-way radio communications will allow you to coordinate security measures within your local community and to save fuel by avoid nonproductive travel (if you know in advance that there is no food at the local grocery store, or that a bridge is out 10 miles down the road, then you can save yourself time and fuel).

> **CAUTION:** *Any radio device that simply refers to itself with the generic term* 'walkie talkie' *is not suitable for serious use in a disaster scenario.*

6.4.1. Modes of Radio Communications

While there are a few theoretical methods of using radio waves for communication, presently the only modes employed for radio communication are *AM (amplitude modulation)* and *FM (frequency modulation)*. (A special variation of AM known as *SSB (single sideband)* communication is also used by some of the higher-end CB radio devices). AM (and SSB) radio transmission modes are employed by CB radios, while virtually all other forms of radio communication make use of FM signaling. AM radio communications is highly susceptible to noise while FM radio communications is virtually noise free.

6.4.2. VOX Switching

Most 2-way radios only allow communications in one direction at a time, and require the operator to activate some type of switch to transmit (this is referred to as *'half duplex'* communications). In order to provide more natural communications some microphones are able to detect the speaker's voice and automatically switch to transmit mode without the need to physically activate a switch. This capability is known as *voice activated switching* (or *'VOX'*).

In addition to allowing for more natural communications over half duplex radio devices, VOX also allows the operator to communicate handsfree. As a result, VOX switching can be considered to be a significant *'force multiplier'* when used by those who engaged in defensive operations.

6.4.3. Radio Frequency Bands

Radio communications takes place over a wide range of radio frequencies. This range of frequencies has been organized into 'bands' that are assigned to various purposes. Different frequencies also have different characteristics with regard to how the radio waves travel through the atmosphere, which means that it is logical to make use of the different bands for different purposes. The following are radio frequency bands that are commonly used:

- *High Frequency (HF)* - used for shortwave radio, citizens band radio, amateur radio, over-the-horizon aviation communications, radar and marine communications.

- *Very High Frequency (VHF)* - used for FM radio, television, ground-to-air and air-to-air communications, mobile maritime communications, amateur radio and weather radio.

- *Ultra High Frequency (UHF)* - used for television, microwave ovens, microwave communications, radio astronomy, Bluetooth, ZigBee, GPS, FRS radio, GMRS radio and amateur radio (ZigBee is radio communications between 'smart' devices in small enclosed areas, such as the components of home alarm systems).

- *Super High Frequency (SHF)* - used for radio astronomy, wireless LANS, radar systems, and satellite and microwave communications.

- *Extremely High Frequency (EHF)* - used for radio astronomy, amateur radio and directed energy weapons.

6.4.4. FRS - Family Radio Service

FRS radio devices are hand-held 2-way radios with a typical range of between 0.3 and 1 miles.[153] These devices provide 14 channels and have a nice feature for reducing unwanted crosstalk for others using FRS radios (users can provide special 'privacy codes' that allow

6. Disaster Communications

> **NOTE:** *While you may tune a radio to a limitless number of frequencies within a radio band, in practice there must be some standardization on frequencies used so that conversations on nearby frequencies don't 'bleed' over one another. As a result tables of standard frequencies are published.*
>
> *Additionally, simple communications devices such as hand-held FRS and GMRS radios, as well as CB radios, are configured to operate only on specific sets of frequencies. These individual frequencies are sometimes referred to as 'channels'.*

their radio to largely filter out other communications on the same frequency that is not using the same code). The typical cost for a pair of FRS radios is between $30 and $60. When evaluating units for purchase it is a good idea to give stronger consideration to those that come with rechargeable batteries and recharging stations (of course this suggests that you should also have a generator available to provide power to those recharging stations).

Two handheld radios will obviously not be sufficient if you need to enable messaging between multiple locations (e.g. others in your neighborhood who might be part of a neighborhood watch program). Accordingly, it is worthwhile to consider obtaining multiple FRS units.

6.4.5. GMRS - General Mobile Radio Service

GMRS radio devices cover all the channels of FRS plus add an additional 8 channels, and have a longer range of between 1 and 2 miles (and even longer in the case of non-handheld radios with longer and higher antennas).[154] To legally operate GMRS radios outside the FRS channels you are required to purchase an $85 license (no testing required). This license entitles you and your immediate family to make use of GMRS radios for 2-way communications.

It might be worthwhile to consider purchasing all GMRS handheld radios rather than FRS radios for the increased range (the cost of GMRS radios is about the same), especially if you feel there is a need to communicate outside the normal 0.5 mile range of FRS radios.

> **NOTE:** *Types of radios that provide longer communication ranges are often considered preferable to those with shorter ranges, however this is not necessarily the case. A radio with a shorter range generally transmits a weaker signal, which presents fewer opportunities for eavesdropping.*

6.4.6. CB - Citizens Band Radio

CB radios use AM transmission, which is susceptible to noise from the environment. Because these radios do not require the purchase of a license the the 40 CB channels can become quite crowded with voice traffic. Mobile and handheld CB radios typically have an operating range of between 3 and 6 miles[155], however this range may be extended to 20 or more miles for non-mobile units having better-quality and higher-elevated antennas.

Due to the larger antenna requirements CB radios do not lend themselves to being used as handheld devices, however it is very common for them to be mounted inside vehicles.

NOTE: *In the world of CB radios channel 9 is intended for use only for emergency communications or discussion of road conditions. Channel 19 is the channel reserved for 'casual communications'.*

Because CB radios are low cost, widely used and typically have a range of several miles they are ideally-suited for use in any vehicle that may be used for *bugging out*. These radios could easily enable you to avoid traffic snarls and other problems on the road. In this scenario the fact that the radios receive heavy traffic is actually an advantage (more people reporting road conditions to you in advance). **A CB radio is a must-have for any individual or group that is considering the option of relocating in the aftermath of a disaster.** A good, mobile CB radio can be purchased for well under $100. For additional range and increased privacy it might be worthwhile to obtain a higher-end unit that includes the range-boosting *SSB* (single sideband) feature. Another important feature is the ability to scan multiple channels so that you may not miss receiving important information simply because it is being broadcast on a channel other than the one you have currently set.

6.4.7. MURS - Multi-use Radio Service

MURS radios were formerly licensed for business only but have recently been made available for general use within the US without the need for a license. MURS radios have a range similar to that of CB radios, however because they utilize FM modulation they have much less noise.

MURS radios are limited to 5 channels, and can transmit no more than two watts, however can have a longer range than FRS and GMRS. MURS radios should be considered for many of the same uses as CB radios, however due to their history of business use the five channels should be expected to be far less crowded.

For post-disaster usage CB radio should be preferred over MURS simply because the much greater popularity of CB radio provides access to more information.

6.4.8. Amateur Radio - Ham Radio

Because amateur radio (aka 'HAM radio') devices can transmit in a wider range of frequencies and with higher-powered signals, they allow the user to communicate across very large distances (even around the world in some circumstances). HAM radios should be viewed as a means of obtaining regional or national news, longer term weather information and other strategic information.

Every disaster group should have access to HAM radio communications, however it is not necessarily critical for every individual to communicate at this level. HAM operators often have little difficulty communicating with FRS, GMRS and CB users to relay and share information over longer distances.

All HAM radio usage requires that the user obtain a license. In the US there are three levels of HAM licensing available:

- *Technician License* - requires that the applicant pass a 35-question exam and entitles the holder to make use of all frequencies above 30 megahertz. These frequencies have a range that provides good communications across the continental US.

- *General License* - requires that the applicant pass a 35-question exam and entitles the holder to access all Amateur Radio frequencies, which allows for global communications.

- *Amateur Extra License* - requires that the applicant pass a 50-question exam and entitles the holder to make full use of all communications modes within the Amateur Radio frequencies.

There are no government fees associated with obtaining an amateur radio license, however the organization that administers your test may require a fee. Many organizations administer the test at little or no cost.

Two interesting makes of hand-held HAM radios are *Yaesu* and *Wouxun*. The Yaesu units cost around $450, and have a reputation for great quality and ruggedness. The Wouxun radios cost around $140 and have a reputation for being full-featured and low cost. The Wouxun KG-UV3D radio can be 'unlocked' by running a special program from your personal computer (while it is connected to your radio through a USB cable) such that it can additionally send and receive over FRS and GMRS channels. Both makes of radios provide support for *Bluetooth* headsets (although Wouxun support is through an adapter and Yaesu support is direct).

NOTE: *If you make use of a 2-way radio - particularly in a non-disaster situation - you should make yourself aware of and adhere to the laws, rules of behavior and etiquette that pertain to that medium (particularly when making use of a radio that requires a license). Some of the types of rules that you may encounter will include the possible need to refer to yourself by a 'call sign', the maximum time allowed for any single conversation and the minimum amount of time that must elapse before you initiate a new conversation. Also, for some communications gear (e.g. GMRS) in some countries (e.g. the United States) it is illegal to transmit messages with 'hidden meanings'. This means that the use of obfuscation or disinformation is not in strict conformance with the law, and should only be considered as part of a communications strategy under extraordinary circumstances.*

6.4.9. Marine Band Radio

Marine band radios are 88-channel FM radios that operate in the VHF frequency band. These radios may transmit at power levels up to 25 watts, and may have a range of over 5 miles for short antennas and up to 70 miles for elevated antennas[156]

NOTE: *Handheld marine radios will transmit at lower power levels and may have a range of only 1-3 miles.*

Some survivalists advocate the use of marine band radios on land in the aftermath of a major disaster simply because the channels will be much less crowded and will offer a greater degree of privacy. Their reasoning is that under such circumstances the advantages of greater communications privacy outweigh the risks associated with violating the law. There are some radios that combine both marine band communications with other bands such as GMRS. When transmitting from such radios from land great care should be taken not to transmit over the marine channels.

CAUTION: *Marine band radios are intended solely for use by marine vessels, and operators of marine band radios on commercial boats (not recreational boats) must be licensed to legally operate these units. If you transmit over the marine radio channels while not on the water you are transmitting illegally and run the risk of incurring stiff penalties.*

It should also be noted that the marine band radio frequencies may have greater difficulty transmitting over normal terrain, as they are best suited to usage in marine environments with clear lines of sight.

6.4.10. Spread Spectrum Communications for Enhanced Privacy

Virtually all commercially-sold 2-way radios make use of a single frequency for communications, meaning that anything said can be heard by anyone listening on that frequency. Some radio systems may transmit and receive on separate, associated frequencies in order to allow users to speak and listen simultaneously.

Commercial radios featuring *spread spectrum* technology (also known as *'frequency hopping'*) are only now starting to become available. These radios actually sync up to one another and then begin dynamically-hopping frequencies while transmitting and receiving. The result is that your conversations are much more private than with normal radios. As of this writing one of the very few commercial 2-way radios with this feature is the *XRS TSX300 secure hand-held radio* by TriSquare[152] (with a pair, complete with recharging station, being advertised as being available at major retailers for around $75). In a normal urban environment the reliable usable range of these radios is right at one-half mile. These radios also provide the ability to text message between units, which can be good for silent communications. Any number of these radios can be synchronized together to form a local privacy-enhanced network.

Keep in mind that while these radios may hop across multiple frequencies, it is easy to imagine full conversations still being picked up by radio scanners that scan all those frequencies. So, even with this technology privacy is greatly enhanced but is not guaranteed. Obtaining a pair of these radios may still be a good fit for command-and-control communications between locations that are no more than a half-mile apart (a great example might be communications between an observation post and a central headquarters).

6.4.11. Bluetooth Microphones as 'Force Multipliers'

Many portable radios offer support for *Bluetooth* headsets. The use of such a headset may be viewed as a desirable *force multiplier* in a tactical defense situation, as it leaves the hands free for other things. When selecting portable radios that may be used for self-defense it may be good to consider the unit's support for Bluetooth as well as to purchase Bluetooth headsets.

6.4.12. PSK31 Communications

PSK31 is a communications protocol that enables low-cost, real-time text chat between stations at a rate of about 31 baud (about the speed of a fast typist). The advantage of PSK31 is that you can communicate over longer distances and with less interference from others. In order to make use of PSK31 you must have a radio that is capable of SSB communications and which transmits between 5 and 50 watts of power (e.g. a higher-end CB radio). Additionally the radio should have 'line in' and 'line out' jacks which are attached to the 'audio out' and 'audio in' jacks of your computer's sound card. You may then run special software on your computer to communicate with others through a simple text interface.

NOTE: *For PSK31 communications, a dedicated hardware interface between your radio and your computer is recommended for better performance and electrical isolation between your radio and computer. The SignaLink USB device[356] is an excellent product for this purpose.*

6.4.13. WINMOR Communications

Like PSK31, *WINMOR* is a communications protocol that requires a very simple interface between a standard personal computer and an amateur radio transmitter. While PSK31 allows real-time typing between stations, WINMOR provides email-over-radio. The benefits of email communications in disaster scenarios are significant, as the messaging parties are not required to be online simultaneously.

Like PSK31, it is recommended that an electrically-isolating interface between the radio and computer be used, with the SignaLink USB device[356] being a good fit for this need.

6.5. Wired Communications

Voice Communications over wire provides greatly enhanced security compared to radio communications. Such communications is always between stationary locations, such as a central headquarters and observation posts. Given the nature of communications with an observation post, the enhanced security of wired communications makes it a particularly good fit.

Most military-grade wired voice communications devices take the form of *field telephones*, which can either be battery-powered or voice-powered. As the name implies, voice-powered field telephones require no external power source as the speaker's voice provides the energy needed to send the signal down the line. Battery-powered field telephones, however, offer the advantage of greater usable range.

A good example of a voice-powered, military-grade field telephone is Vietnam-era TA-1 device, which has a range of 1 to 3 miles. The more modern TA-312 field telephones have the option to use either battery or voice power, and have a maximum range of 20 to 30 miles (when battery power is used). Both the TA-1 and TA-312 field telephones are designed to use military WD-1 wire between communication points. All of this gear can often be found for sale online at reasonable prices.

Since observation posts are generally very rudimentary structures these rugged, military-grade field telephones are an excellent fit to provide communications with a central head-quarters (or with other observation posts).

6.6. Electronic Cryptography

> **NOTE:** *The science of encryption is a field of mathematics about which entire books can be (and have been) written. The purpose of this section is not to make the reader an expert on encryption but to provide a high level overview to enable the reader to make practical real-world decisions in securing sensitive communications.*

The use of *encryption* to conceal the content of messages has a history that extends to ancient times. Original forms of encryption took the form of simple text character substitutions or other simple manipulations. In those times these simple measures were probably largely effective. Even today such simple techniques can be helpful. For example, if you simply did some text substitutions for a message that you put out on a web page those substitutions would probably cause the various Internet search engines not to allow that content to be search-able (e.g. if my substitution resulted in the text 'cache' being converted to 'xuxyz', then no Internet search on the word 'cache' is going to return a link to my web page).

So, even simple encryption can be useful.

Beyond simple encryption, however, there is often the need to encrypt messages such that one has a *very* high degree of confidence that the information will not become known to unintended recipients. To meet this need two different types of encryption have developed over the years, *public key encryption* and *private key encryption*.

Encryption Keys

In the field of cryptography a *key* is simply a bit of information that is used to encrypt and/or decrypt a message. A key containing more information generally results in an encryption that is more difficult to break (so, for example, a message encrypted with a key of 'xat' is less secure than a message encrypted with a key of 'this is my special key'). Most encryption algorithms make use of a key of a specific length (expressed in number of bits). Encryption algorithms that use longer keys are generally considered to be more secure.

> **NOTE:** *In general electronic encryption keys are simply specially-formatted files stored on a computer. In many cases they can be viewed in a simple text editor.*

An encryption key may not necessarily take the form of readable text. In the world of radio communications a key may take the form of a list of frequencies across which the message will be transmitted, a list of random numbers, or even a voice waveform that is overlaid over the speaker's voice during transmission.

Private Key Encryption

Private key encryption is a form of encryption in which the same key is used to both encrypt and decrypt a message. Until relatively recently private key encryption was the only approach used for encryption. This form of encryption has a major drawback in that you must have a way to securely deliver the key to both sides that are exchanging messages.

Throughout World War II and the Cold War one of the major tasks carried out by spies was to act as couriers for private encryption keys. One can imagine that often those highly-secure, metallic briefcases that were handcuffed to the agents contained nothing more substantial than a scrap of paper with an encryption key.

Public Key Encryption

With public key encryption keys are generated as *key pairs* (a pubic key and a private key) that have a mathematical relationship. Any message encrypted with the public key can only be decrypted with the private key. This approach has the notable advantage that you may broadcast your public key to the world, and anyone in the world can use that key to send you messages that only you may decrypt (imagine all the secret agents that got put out of business with the advent of public key encryption technologies!).

> **NOTE:** *The computer algorithms used for public key encryption do have the disadvantage that they are computationally slower than the simpler private key algorithms. As a result many forms of real time encryption over the Internet (e.g. encrypted web sites) actually use a combination of public and private key encryption. Private key encryption is used to exchange a randomly-generated public key (known as the 'session key'), which is then used to secure the bulk of the communications.*
>
> *Public key encryption is sometimes referred to as 'symmetric encryption', while private key encryption is sometimes referred to as 'asymmetric encryption'. The encryption algorithms themselves are sometimes referred to as 'ciphers'.*

In addition to being useful for encrypting documents, the public/private keys pairs of public key encryption are also very useful for electronic document signing. In this case an individual's *signing key* can be used to encrypt a brief message that indicates a signature, along with a checksum number that is a unique *fingerprint* of the document being signed. Others can then make use of that signer's public key to decrypt the signature accompanying the document and confirm its authenticity. This is very significant when you consider that changing even a single character of the original document will cause the decrypted fingerprint check to fail, which means that it is virtually impossible to successfully tamper with a digitally-signed document.

> **CAUTION:** *It should go without saying that you should protect your private encryption key(s) carefully. It is not uncommon for computer programs to actually encrypt private keys with a regular public key, so that even if your key file is lost it will probably not be usable by others.*

Digital Certificates

Many forms of secure communications require not simply a key for secure communications but rather a *digital certificate* that contains other critical information in addition to a public key. These certificates are simply text files that, in addition to the grantee's public key, contain the name of the grantee, the identity of the organization that issued the certificate (and that organization's public key), an expiration date after which the certificate should be considered invalid, and an optional list of uses for the certificate. The certificate itself is also digitally signed so that it becomes invalid if altered in any way.

Electronic services that require digital certificates may also check the certificate with their granting *certificate authority* to confirm that the certificate has not been revoked.

While the use of simple encryption keys allows the contents of a message to be kept confidential, the use of digital certificates provides the additional advantage of providing the assurance that the user is authorized to see the information. It is helpful to think of a digital certificate as being similar to a driver's license, in that it identifies you, it indicates the permissions you have and it can be checked against a central database to confirm it has not been revoked.

Centralized vs. Decentralized Trust

Digital certificates, as described here, require a centralized *certificate authority* to verify the identity of the individuals or organizations for which certificates are being issued and to create new certificates once those identities have been verified. These certificates can then be validated against that central authority when they are being used for secure communications (which means the certificate authority has the ability to *revoke* certificates it has previously issued). However, if that authority becomes unavailable for any reason the system breaks down.

An alternative to digital certificates has been implemented by email clients that feature PGP (or, in some cases GPG) encryption. This encryption system allows one individual to vouch for other individuals by *signing* their public keys and providing them to others (if Betsy has Alice's key, and you wish to communicate with Alice, Betsy can sign the key that she has used and trusts, and then provide that signed key for you). This decentralized *web of trust* provides a more fault-tolerant means of user authentication, and is employed almost exclusively by email programs for encrypting and decrypting email messages.

E-Mail Encryption

All disasters will not necessarily take down Internet services. Even after the earthquake in Haiti it is certain that some Internet communications to that nation either remained intact or were restored quickly. For the survivalist/prepper the use of encryption technologies to protect the content of email from prying eyes is simply a matter of due diligence.

The most common add-ons for email encryption are *PGP* ('Pretty Good Privacy'), *GPG* ('GnuPG') and *S/MIME*. PGP is the original email add-on, and is now a commercial product. GPG is an open source equivalent to PGP and S/MIME is a certificate-based open standard that is built into many email programs. While PGP and GPG make use of the *web of trust* approach in which users sign one anothers' keys, S/MIME is based on digital certificates and requires the presence of a third party certificate authority as described earlier in this chapter.

111

Any of these technologies should be considered to provide good protection of email messages, although the de-centralized nature of the PGP and GPG add-ons should probably have stronger appeal within the prepper community.

7. Emergency Fuel and Power

*"Go forward until the last round is fired
and the last drop of gas is expended ...
then go forward on foot!"*

General George Patton Jr

Issues related to fuel and energy storage and conservation are critical to anyone trying to survive an extended disaster. Fuel provides heat, light and comfort; all of which are critical to life. While it may have been sufficient for primitive man to gather wood to burn as a source of fuel, in today's world this is not necessarily a good plan. For example, wood can not be used to power modern vehicles, and the use of open fires can be highly inefficient and undesirable in a survival scenario. Time spent gathering wood and the energy spent transporting it might be better used for other purposes.

The prepper should plan not only to have sources of fuel, but also to conserve it. As an alternative to running an air conditioner on a hot day one might swab one's body with water or alcohol as a means of cooling down just enough to get by. Or, rather than expending energy to air condition an entire home throughout the day, one might run a small air conditioner in a single room for 1 or 2 hours per day as a way of providing just the amount of relief that is needed.

This chapter describes the various fuels that are in common use and how they might best be stored and applied in the wake of disaster. Also covered is the use of solar power and emergency electrical generators.

Fuel Storage

When storing **ANY** fuel be certain that it is stored in a container that is rated for that fuel. Also, if possible, fill the container completely to minimize loss due to vaporization. Metal containers are preferred as they are not permeable to vapors or the outside atmosphere. If possible, fuel tanks should be painted with a reflective paint and located in a shaded area to minimize heating due to sunlight exposure.

Fuel	Advantages	Disadvantages
Gasoline	Has many uses.	Short shelf life without being treated. Highly volatile and dangerous to store.
Diesel	Very stable and safe to store. Can be used for many important applications (generators, etc). Can be stored up to six months without being treated	Tends to "attract" water from the atmosphere, which can result in the growth of sludge-forming bacteria.
Kerosene	Very stable and safe to store. Can be used in place of diesel if necessary. Has many applications for heat and light. Requires no special treatment for long term storage. It can be stored in plastic containers. Kerosene-powered appliances are available.	Not very useful for some important applications (e.g. powering vehicles for the long term).
Propane	Stores indefinitely with no treatment needed. Useful for many important applications (e.g. heating, lighting cooking).	Must store under pressure. Difficult to detect leaks in storage. Can become explosive when released into the atmosphere.
Natural Gas	No advantages to the prepper.	Limited usefulness (used almost solely by utility companies).
Wood	Renewable fuel source. Prevalent in many locations.	Limited usefulness. Labor intensive to gather.
Coal	Burns long and steady. Good for heat and cooking.	Limited usefulness.
Solar	Renewable source of energy. Unobtrusive.	Costly. Limited usefulness (electrical devices only). May not provide adequate energy.

Table 7.1.: Pros & Cons of Common Fuels[59]

All above ground fuel storage tanks should be kept off the ground to reduce the accumulation of water in the fuel (which can lead to growth of algae).

CAUTION: *All liquid fuels removed from fuel tanks should not be extracted from the very bottom of the tank, and should be filtered before use.*

7.1. Types of Fuel

7.1.1. Gasoline

Being used to power the great majority of vehicles in the world, *gasoline* is certainly the most commonly used fuel in the modern world. *However, gasoline is not a suitable fuel for many disaster applications - for example, most cook stoves cannot accept gasoline as a source of fuel.*

Modern gasoline, containing ethanol, has an effective shelf-life of 90 to 100 days[55], which will vary depending on the fuel blend (the blends vary by region and season of the year). For longer storage, additives must be added to the gasoline to preserve and/or rejuvenate its chemical properties. These additives can extend the shelf life of gasoline for months and possibly years.[58] The most popular products used for this purpose are:

- PRI-G^{TM}
- STA-BIL^{TM}
- Techron^{TM}

These fuel additives may be purchased from numerous retail sources. Simply add the prescribed quantity of any of these products to the gasoline you are storing and the shelf life will be extended to between 1 and 5 years. Ideally you should re-treat with the additive once each year for maximum fuel preservation.

As you can really have no idea how long gasoline has been stored in tanks prior to your purchasing it, you should not rely on newly-purchased gasoline having its full shelf-life. When storing gasoline you should immediately add a stabalizer to increase its shelf life.

If possible store gasoline in a red container, as this is the industry-standard color for gasoline storage containers. Also, try to keep gasoline containers completely filled with the lids tightly closed for maximum storage life. The NATO metal 5-gallon (20 liter) Jerry Cans are an excellent choice for good storage and transport of gasoline as they provide excellent protection and their square shape allows them to stack well.

7.1.2. Diesel

Diesel is a fuel that is used by some passenger vehicles and by heavy agricultural and commercial equipment. It is a heavier fuel that does not evaporate the way that gasoline does, however diesel does still degrade over time. This degradation is due to the growth of microbes within the tank during storage[56], and can be controlled by preventing water from condensing in the fuel and through the addition of antimicrobials into the stored fuel.

> Diesel is not a highly volatile fuel. If you were to strike a match and throw it into a pool of diesel the match would be extinguished. As such, it is much safer to store than gasoline and propane. While diesel is not volatile, when it does ignite it burns long and hot and produces a dark, oily smoke.

The shelf life of untreated diesel is well over 12 months if stored at or below 68°F, or between 6 and 12 months if stored at 86°F or higher.[57] Diesel that has been treated for long term storage can have a shelf life ranging between 5 and 10 years.[58]

As with gasoline, the shelf life of diesel can be extended with additives. The most popular products used for this purpose are:

- PRI-D^{TM}
- STA-BIL^{TM}

A good diesel storage system should, at a minimum, have provisions for draining off accumulated water from the bottom of the tank, as periodically draining off the water will greatly extend its shelf life. Ideally the system should have a filter that allows the drained fuel to be separated from the water and circulated back into the tank.

Diesel is primarily useful as fuel to power vehicles and heavy equipment that are equipped with diesel engines. Its interest to the prepper depends largely on the situation. Obviously any prepper with a diesel-powered vehicle would be interested in having a supply of diesel fuel. Also many larger power generators are diesel-powered (diesel-powered generators tend to have a longer life expectancy than gasoline-powered generators[354]).

7.1.3. Kerosene

Kerosene is a heavy fuel much like diesel, and in fact shares many properties with diesel, including its non-volatility and easy storage (as with diesel, a lit match tossed into a pool of kerosene will probably be extinguished). Unlike diesel, kerosene can be stored for a long period without any need for treatment with additives.

> **NOTE:** *The fuel used by most jet aircraft is actually a highly-refined and filtered kerosene.*

One interesting and little-known application for kerosene, and an application that every prepper should be aware of, is the ability to power non-electric refrigerators.[62] Such a refrigerator could be invaluable in storing insulin supplies for diabetics during times when normal refrigeration is not available.

Kerosene is so stable and easily stored that it is almost the perfect fuel for the prepper. The only disadvantage (and this is a major disadvantage) is that virtually no non-military vehicles are designed to utilize kerosene for fuel. As a result of this limited usefulness diesel, rather than kerosene, is almost certainly better to stockpile in preparation for disaster.

NOTE: *By general convention gasoline is stored in red containers, kerosene is stored in blue containers and diesel is stored in yellow containers. It's a good idea to to adhere to this convention as much as possible or, failing that, to at least mark your own fuel storage containers accordingly.[54]*

7.1.4. Propane

Propane gas serves as a power source for a wide range of devices ranging from cook stoves to lamps, heaters and generators. As such it is important for the prepper to have some knowledge of this important fuel. Propane is generally transported and stored under pressure and in liquid form, hence it is also often referred to as *liquid propane* or *LP gas*. The gas canisters that connect to virtually all gas grills contain propane. Much outdoor survival equipment is powered by propane as well. There are also electrical generators that use propane for fuel, and adapter kits are available which can convert many gasoline-powered electrical generators to use propane.

Storage of Propane

One positive aspect is that propane can be stored indefinitely without any significant degradation. However, there are some other important considerations when storing propane:

- *Potential undetected loss due to leakage* - because propane becomes a gas at regular atmospheric pressure, a leak in a propane tank might be undetected until all the fuel has been lost through the leak.

- *Dangers associated with leakage* - when propane does leak it tends to combine with air in such proportions as to pose a significant risk of sudden and violent explosion when exposed to a spark or open flame.

- *Locating the storage tank outdoors* - due to the tendency of propane to combine into an explosive mixture with air it should not be stored in any enclosed environment that might allow this mixture to accumulate.

NOTE: *If you suspect that your propane tank may be leaking you might submerge it under water to detect the source of any bubbles. Alternately, you could coat the tank in a mixture of water and dish washing soap to see where bubbles appear.*

7.1.5. Natural Gas

While filling a critical niche in the domestic energy market during normal times, *natural gas (a.k.a. 'methane')* is of very limited interest to the prepper. This is primarily due to infrastructure and application issues. With regard to infrastructure, virtually the only means of delivering natural gas to the end user is through the utility system, which can be expected to be disrupted during a disaster. With regard to application, there are very few options, other than through the normal utility infrastructure, for making use of natural gas if it were available.

Compressed Natural Gas ("CNG") is simply highly-compressed natural gas that is used in many places to power vehicles. The principle advantage of CNG is that it generates fewer CO_2 emissions than other fuel sources per mile driven. As a result CNG is often used to power municipal bus systems and other government-owned fleets. In some countries CNG has found its way to more mainstream use by the general public.

Because CNG fuel is not as prevalent as other common vehicular fuels, and because the production and distribution of CNG is more dependent on a fully-functional economy than other fuel sources (electricity may be necessary to run the compressors to fill CNG fuel tanks, for example) it is anticipated that CNG will be of limited usefulness as a fuel source during a major, long term disaster.

As a result, natural gas will probably play little or no role in a grid-down scenario, and the restoration of natural gas is a good indicator that recovery from the disaster itself is underway.

7.1.6. Wood

Wood is one of the few sources of fuel that is available in most inhabited regions. Unlike other fuels, wood is easy to store and its fuel value does not degrade with the passage of time.

CAUTION: *Burning wood not only produces smoke, but also* carbon dioxide, *which can be fatal in an enclosed environment. As a result, wood should only be burned in a well-ventilated area.*

Wood can be used to produce both light and heat, as well as for cooking. Wood stoves can also be effective in living spaces. Because wood is not useful as a fuel for motors it can only be considered to be part of the prepper's overall energy plan.

NOTE: *Burning wood generates smoke, which can draw unwanted attention. As a result the burning of wood should always be considered from a security perspective.*

In addition to the conventional uses of wood as a fuel, it should also be noted that gaseous hydrocarbon fuels, capable of powering conventional engines in some cases, can be produced from wood through a process known as *gasification*. Wood *gasifiers* are simple devices that can be readily constructed from commonly-available materials and components. Practical considerations, such as the near impossibility of storing the generated gasses due to safety and condensation issues, the physical size of the gasifier, and the fuel needs of the gasifier itself, make the gasifier of limited usefulness[353], however some of those uses (such as generating electricity or providing power for manufacturing processes) could be of significant strategic value during the disaster recovery period.

7.1.7. Coal

Like wood, *Coal* is a potential fuel source that stores easily and, if stored in a dry place, preserves its fuel value indefinitely. Unlike wood, coal cannot be readily obtained from the environment. Any coal that the prepper plans on using as fuel in the event of disaster must be acquired and stored in advance of the disaster.

Some good things to know about coal:

- Coal burns longer and hotter than wood, which also means less need to add fuel to a fire during the night.

- While wood can be burned in a coal stove, coal cannot be burned in a wood stove. This is because the coal stove is designed to handle the greater temperatures produced by coal fire, and also because coal stoves require bottom grates for the removal of ash and soot.

- Coal is historically about 40% cheaper than wood in terms of cost per BTU of energy produced.[61]

Coal is mostly useful for producing heat, including both for heating living spaces as well as cooking. As a result of this limited usefulness coal, like wood, should be considered only a part of the prepper's overall energy plan. Also like wood, the burning of coal generates smoke which may draw unwanted attention. Utilizing any smoke-producing fuel should always be considered from a security perspective.

7.1.8. Solar Power

Imagine spending tens of thousands of dollars to purchase so many solar panels that they cover the roof of your home as well as your yard. Imagine all these panels being connected to 30 car batteries through a costly electrical interfacing device. Then imagine these batteries being wired into another hugely expensive power inverter to convert the 12VDC battery power into AC power you can use in your home.

This is the scenario you might expect if you wanted to completely power your home with *solar power*. Not very practical!

This does not mean that solar power is of no interest to the prepper. Sometimes just a tiny amount of electricity can make a huge difference in quality of life. For example, having the electricity to run an electric drill might be all that is needed to fabricate a pavilion that provides shelter from the sun on a hot day. Or, a solar panel might power a radio transceiver that provides vital communications, or a laptop computer that is used to more efficiently manage an entire community.

Of course, these modest electrical needs could be fulfilled by a conventional generator, however unlike your generator the energy supply from solar power is essentially limitless.

A good case could be made for installing a solar energy generator if its use is well-defined in the site's energy plan.

7.2. Electrical Generators

Electrical generators convert the mechanical power of a fuel-powered motor into useful electrical power. Most households that own generators own gasoline-powered devices that are rated at anywhere from 850 to 5000 *surge watts* of power.

A typical full-size refrigerator uses about 425 watts of electrical power (with a surge of up to 600 watts on power up). A window-mounted room air conditioner requires between 600 and 1400 watts, while a typical central home air conditioning unit may consume 3500 watts or more. Based on your own situation and needs this gives you an idea of the size of generator that is a reasonable fit for your emergency plan.

CAUTION: *The 'surge watts rating' of an electrical generator is the amount of power that can be provided for very limited intervals, such as additional power consumed by devices in the first seconds they are powered up. Many generator vendors provide only this number when it is the 'continuous power rating' that is of greater interest. When you purchase a generator be certain to note its continuous power rating, as this determines how many devices of what type you may power simultaneously.*

Fuel for Generators

Given the self-life and storage considerations associated with gasoline, a gasoline-powered generator is not really a recommended preparation for a longer term disaster. Diesel fuel stores better and more securely than gasoline. Even liquid propane is a better choice than gasoline to provide fuel for a generator (liquid propane has an indefinite shelf life and, while a propane tank could conceivably be ruptured and explode, it is much less likely to do so than a tank filled with gasoline).

NOTE: *There is a reason why virtually all large businesses, hospitals, government agencies and the military have backup generators that are powered by diesel rather than gasoline. Diesel fuel stores better and longer than gasoline, and because diesel engines produce higher torque at lower operating speeds, the life expectancy of a diesel generator should be considerably higher than that of a comparable gas-powered generator.*

Some of the larger appliances in your home require a 240 volt power source, rather than the more common 120 volts. In selecting an emergency generator you should make certain that it supplies both 120 volt and 240 volt output power.

7. Emergency Fuel and Power

If you would like to have your generator power devices in your home without running large extension cords through the house then you should have a qualified electrician install a *transfer switch*. Transfer switches make it very easy to switch your home's primary electrical power between the utility grid and your own generator.

Generator Safety Tips

To avoid accidents and other hazards when making use of an emergency generator you should observe the following guidelines:

- *Do not attempt to wire your generator into your home electrical system yourself* - If you do not have a transfer switch installed in your home by a licensed and qualified electrician then any devices you wish to power from your generator should be connected directly to it via extension cord.

- *Use only heavy duty extension cords to connect your generators to any devices* - light extension cords can become very hot and result in fires.

- *Locate the generator outdoors when being used* - generator exhaust can be very harmful to humans in an enclosed environment.

- *Be careful not to overload your generator.*

- *Don't run electrical cords across any water puddles* - a person handling a current-carrying extension cord while standing in any depth of pooled water may easily get electrocuted.

8. Hunting, Trapping, Fishing and Foraging

"Every moving thing that liveth shall be meat for you; even as the green herb have I given you all things."

Genesis 9:3

STRAIGHT THINKING: *The skills of hunting, fishing, trapping and foraging are important because they bring together so many of the critical and more basic survival skills. To engage in these activities is to hone those skills which may very well be needed for entirely different purposes. Very few people, however, are in a position to be able to benefit predominantly from a hunter-gatherer existence (basically only those who depend on those same skills to survive today).*

Unless you are already an expert on living off the land, don't plan to rely exclusively on these skills for food during a disaster. Otherwise you may be in for a rude awakening!

Many preppers imagine themselves returning to a lifestyle of living from nature in the aftermath of a major disaster. Towards these ends they equip themselves with costly hunting and fishing equipment and all the attendent accessories. After reading this chapter the prepper may have a broader and more realistic view regarding the prospects of living from nature, and will hopefully come to view natural sources of food as being just one more piece of a much larger puzzle.

Several sources quote that the amount of land required to sustain a single person in 'hunter-gatherer' mode ranges between about 2 and 10 square miles.[512]. Assuming, for the sake of simplifying the math, that the average number is 5 square miles, if you divide the number of square miles in the continental US (3,119,885) by 5 you will see that the continental US can sustain about 623,000 hunter-gatherers:

$$3,119,885/5 = 623,977$$

Since the population of the continental US is about 313 million[63] then one must ask .. *"What happens to the 312.5 million inhabitants of the Continental US, and will I be included in that unlucky 99.5% of the population?"* There is simply not enough land to allow even 1% of the US population to live off the land.

This strongly suggests that if the US were to devolve into hunter-gatherer mode, you will probably not have to be too concerned with it, because **you probably won't be around!** This does not mean that a prepper should not be prepared to live from nature, only that they should not plan on living exclusively as a hunter, and also that they should balance the resources allocated for hunting against those needed to meet other important needs (e.g. the ability to grow food).

NOTE: *The good news is that civilization has a* **LONG** *way to fall before reaching hunter-gatherer mode, so we are all not necessarily doomed. However, our modern systems have become so interdependent that even a temporary disruption of modern transportation or electrical systems could result in widespread suffering and loss of life.*

8.1. The Very Real Dangers of Subsisting on Nature in the Aftermath

Acquiring food from the wild is one of the more dangerous aspects of post-disaster survival, and serious consideration should be given before engaging in these activities. Of course there is always an increased chance of injury and infection, and beyond that there is the danger of staking out territory.

If you or your group lays claim to a broad area for hunting and foraging then it is very possible that others may also eventually lay claims to the same or overlapping areas. Such situations carry a very real potential for violent conflict. This may be the reason that, historically, hunter-gatherer populations have been spread thinly.

> **CAUTION:** *All the techniques for hunting, trapping, fishing and foraging discussed in this chapter may not conform to prevailing law in all locations. Laws may control where you can hunt, what you can hunt, the time of year authorized for hunting, the time of day you can hunt, the types of guns and other devices that can be used, the size, number or gender of game and fish you are allowed to take, the type of ammunition that can be used, and sometimes even documentation that must be performed while hunting.*
>
> *Be sure to be aware of and follow any applicable laws and ordinances.*

8.2. Hunting

An important first consideration when planning to hunt is to determine the game you'll be hunting. Large game can provide more food with a single kill, however you are then presented with the need to preserve the meat that is not immediately eaten. Smaller game allows you to kill only the food to meet your immediate needs. (Of course you must also consider the number of people you will be feeding.)

It's not sufficient to just have the hunting gear, you must also have the knives, saws and other equipment needed to butcher the carcass and process the meat. For smaller game this may require a small, sharp knife, clean water and some containers for the meat. Larger game may require heavier equipment, including a way to hang the carcass for butchering. One consideration that is common to butchering all game is the need to keep the meat from being contaminated by the contents of the animal's organs (for example, to keep the animal's feces and urine from coming into contact with the meat). A poor job of butchering can waste an entire carcass.

> **NOTE:** *Hunting is one of the few skills in the modern world that is probably more effectively passed on by word of mouth rather than by books and other media. The best hunters will tend to be those with the most experience. Rather than planning on becoming an 'instant hunter' in the event of a disaster, the prepper with little or no hunting experience may be better served by accompanying an experienced hunter than trying to teach themselves.*

In addition to the gear required to kill and process game, the hunter should have clothing that will allows them to cope with the rigors of the hunt. This includes traveling over rough terrain and walking through thickets, woodlands and sometimes water.

8.2.1. Hunting Methods

There are several techniques for stalking game. The methods used depend primarily on the type of game being hunted. In some cases extreme silence is necessary while in others it is necessary to make noises to attract the game. Some methods require total mobility, while others require the hunter to remain stationary.

Stalking Game

Some wild game, such as quail and pheasant, does not really present a target unless the hunter actively searches it out, locates it and flushes it into the open. Once flushed such game will take flight or run in an attempt to escape. It is after the game is flushed that the hunter will take the shot. This type of hunting requires the hunter to have a good understanding of the game they are hunting, as well as of the terrain and the availability and location of food and water sources.

Stalking game often involves trekking through woods, across fields and prairies and through thickets and swamps. The hunter must be prepared for the demands of such a hunt, which may include carrying food, water (or a portable water filter), a first aid kit and perhaps even a tent for sheltering overnight. For long distance hunting, or hunting in extremely dense terrain, a map and compass may also be needed. Depending on the game being hunted stalking game may also involve using hunting dogs.

NOTE: *Whenever you kill an animal while hunting it is imperative that you try your best to make the animal's death as quick and painless as possible. Not only is this the humane thing to do but often, if an animal does not die quickly, the metabolic and hormonal changes that take place within the animal can have a very adverse affect on the quality of its meat.*

You should also never kill an animal if you do not plan on consuming or pre- serving all of its meat. Wasting food (and life) is simply not consistent with the survival mindset, and is not an acceptable thing to do.

When hunting by foot for extended distances be sure to anticipate weather conditions, the distance that you will be covering and the type of terrain involved.

Blinds and Tree Stands

Many types of game are best hunted from a fixed location. The location may simply be a hill top or open area, or a concealed location such as a *hunting blind*, a *tree stand*, or a spot that offers some degree natural concealment.

Hunting blinds are typically small 'tree houses' built on stilts which have been camouflaged with tree branches and other local natural cover. Hunters wait inside the blind for the game to come within range.

Tree stands are platforms that allow hunter to remain concealed among the upper reaches of a tree. In this case the tree's branches and foliage provide concealment. Hunters using tree stands must remain silent and motionless while waiting for game to come within range.

Baiting and Using Attractants

'*Baiting*' an area is an effective way to draw many forms of game to a '*kill zone*'. The bait used may consist of:

- An aromatic food that is favored by the game being sought.

- A block of salt.

- A attractant that mimics the urine of a competing male or of a female that is in season.

When non-aromatic attractants such as salt are used for bait, an area is often baited days in advance of a hunt in order to give the game an opportunity to locate it. In the case of baiting food for wild hogs, aromatic foods may be buried a few feet underground in order to cause the hogs to remain at the location for a longer period (hogs have a sense of smell that allows them to detect food even when it is buried a few feet underground).

CAUTION: *It should be noted that the practice of baiting for game animals is strictly controlled by law in many areas, and the hunter should take particular care to understand how this law applies in the jurisdiction where they are hunting.*

Also note that the laws regulating baiting in your area may be relaxed if you are hunting nuisance animals such as feral hogs.

Use of Camouflage

Concealment becomes important for hunters who seek game that has a well-developed sense of vision (such as deer and wild turkey). Camouflaged hunter's clothing allows the hunter to better blend into the environment.

Some game, such as deer and rabbit, have sharp eyesight but cannot differentiate well between colors. This allows many camouflage patterns to incorporate bright colors that are distinct to humans such that the hunter stands out from the environment to other hunters while remaining concealed to the game being hunted. Often camouflage that incorporates such highly visible colors uses a bright orange, and is referred to as *'blaze camo'*, or *'orange blaze'*.

The most important aspect of camouflage is not that the hunter's flesh be concealed, but rather that their human-shaped silhouette be concealed. To do this hunters will often attach branches and twigs to their clothing, or wear a *'Ghillie suit'*, which is a body cover originally developed by military snipers for extreme concealment. The Ghillie suit is a body cover that incorporates layers of hanging camouflage strips that are attached to a netting and hang freely. These suits provide highly effective concealment by breaking up virtually any visual indicator of the human form (often at the cost of mobility, as the strips hanging from the suit have a tendency to become tangled with branches and other objects in an outdoor setting).

Camouflage patterns are available for a wide range of environments, including deserts, woodlands and snow-covered areas.

Calling Game

Many game animals can be attracted with sounds that mimic the sounds of members of its own species. These sounds may emulate the sound of a female that is in season, the sound of a male that has invaded territory, or the sound of two males fighting for dominance (such as the rattling of deer antlers). Similarly, many animals can be induced to betray their location with the sounds that mimic their natural predators.

The devices that hunters use to make these sounds are referred to as *'game calls'* (or simply *'calls'*). Calls are available that mimic many animals including ducks, geese, turkey, deer, elk and hawks (a hawk call would be an example of mimicking a predator). Some calls have diaphragms through which the hunter blows while others consist of objects that are rubbed together (or are otherwise used together to generate the sound mechanically).

Often using a call effectively requires practice and tutoring from experienced hunters.

Use of Decoys

A decoy is a physical replica of the animal being hunted that is deployed so as to attract other (real) animals of that species. The best-known decoys are those used for duck hunting. In this case the duck decoys are often deployed floating on water within shooting rage of a duck blind.

As real ducks spot the decoys they will fly close or actually land in the water among the decoys, where they will be within the kill zone.

Decoys are also used when hunting for larger game such as deer, elk and turkey.

Hunting with Dogs

Dogs are sometimes used by hunters to locate and flush prey, as well as to retrieve the prey after it has been killed. Bird dogs are commonly used to locate quail, and retrievers often occupy duck blinds with hunters and are used to quickly retrieve ducks that have been taken. The many breeds of hounds are often used to track and corner game such as rabbits, foxes, raccoons and hogs across large tracts of land.

The hunting instincts of these dogs makes it much easier for them to be trained to perform these tasks, however some training is still required. For example the bird dog must be trained to recognize certain specific voice commands to seek, flush and retrieve quail.

8.2.2. Weapons Used for Hunting

Hunting with Guns

Game is often classified as being *big game* or *small game*. These distinctions are most often made for purposes of licensing (for example, in some jurisdictions a single hunting license may cover all small game animals, while individual licenses may be required for different animals that are classified as 'big game'). This distinction between sizes of prey is also useful in determining the type of guns or other weapons to use for hunting.

There are several common calibers of ammunition that are adequate for killing large game. The 30.06 *(pronounced "thirty ought six")* and .308 Winchester are popular rounds for hunting large game. Either of these rounds should be able to bring down any prey up to and including bear. Another caliber commonly used for larger game is the .243 Winchester round, which has a smaller bullet but a much higher velocity (which translates into longer range).

> **NOTE:** *For the prepper the .308 Winchester and the .243 Winchester cartridges have particular appeal. The .308 is the cartridge most commonly used by modern snipers, which makes it a good dual-purpose weapon for both hunting and long-range home defense. The .243 Winchester cartridge might be a better fit for long range defense in those situations where range is more important than knock-down power.*
>
> *The Remington R-25 is a good example of a semi-automatic rifle in this category. This particular rifle is available in both .308 and .243 calibers.*

For small game the *.22 caliber long rifle hollow point round* is often a good choice. This round has more power than the *.22 caliber short round*, and is often used for hunting small game such as squirrels and rabbits. For some game a larger caliber round may be desirable for killing at greater distance. In other instances, when lower cost of ammunition and reduced noise are important, a good pellet gun might be a better fit.

Shotguns are also commonly used to hunt small game. Because they disperse lead pellets in a pattern that covers a wider area than a single rifle bullet, the shotgun tends to be much more effective against targets that are in motion (which includes most small game and birds). Please refer to Appendix D for more details on the variety of shotguns that are available and the ammunition they can use.

> **CAUTION:** *Due care should be taken when eating the meat of any animal killed with a shotgun, as it is not uncommon to find the individual shot pellets in the meat while eating. Biting down on these pellets can be quite painful and damage teeth.*

Shotguns are available in different *gauges*. The gauge of a shotgun indicates the diameter of the barrel. The formula used to calculate gauge measurements is such that a smaller gauge number actually indicates a **LARGER** barrel (so, a 12 gauge shotgun is more powerful than a 20 gauge shotgun, for example). Table 8.1 describes the best uses for common shotgun gauges.

> **NOTE:** *A 12 gauge shotgun is another good example of a multi-use weapon. Not only is it well suited to hunting a wide range of game, it is also recognized by many experts as being an excellent weapon for indoor defense.*

Size	Description
10 Gauge	This is a rare gauge, and is a shotgun that is too powerful for most small game.
12 Gauge	This is a very common shotgun gauge that packs plenty of killing power for virtually any game smaller than an elephant.
16 Gauge	This is a (rare today) mid-sized shotgun that is well-suited for hunting most birds.
20 Gauge	This is a very common gauge used to hunt small game by those who have difficulties with the weight and recoil of the larger sized shotguns.
.410	This is the smallest modern shotgun, and the size is actually a caliber measurement rather than a gauge. This lower-powered shotgun is a good starter gun for young hunters or those who are too weak or infirm to handle a 20 gauge shotgun.

Table 8.1.: Common shotgun gauges and their typical uses, ordered by size.

Bow Hunting

For specific types of game many modern hunters use a bow rather than a gun. Some hunting seasons for some game animals are divided into a separate *bow hunting season* and *gun hunting season*. Bows are commonly used for hunting medium- to large- sized game, although in the hands of an expert they can also be used effectively to take smaller and faster game such as squirrels and rabbits.

Using a bow requires a greater degree of skill than a gun and the range of a bow is far less than that of a gun. As a result the probability of making a kill with a bow is greatly reduced. However the bow does offer the significant advantage that it kills silently. In a survival scenario the advantages of maintaining silence may outweigh the advantages of hunting with a gun. Another advantage of hunting with a bow is that, in general, the cost of a bow is less than that of a gun.

Traditional bows and arrows are made of wood, however modern bows and arrows are made of better and more durable composite materials. It is recommended that the survivalist obtain bows and arrows based on these more modern technologies, as this will only increase the chances for of a successful hunt.

Special bows are also available that have been designed for *bow fishing*. Such bows incorporate spools to hold a line that is attached to the arrow. The line is then used to retrieve any fish that are successfully targeted.

Hunting bows are available in the classic bow design, or as *compound bows*. Compound bows have a built in system of cams and pulleys that allow the bow to exert less force on the hunter's arm once they are fully drawn. This gives the hunter the ability to make a more steady shot in most cases, as well as the opportunity to wait longer for the best possible shot to present itself. Any hunter in a survival situation should certainly give preferential consideration to a compound bow for these reasons (of course the compound bows tend to be more costly).

Hunting with Spears

It is almost universally inadvisable to use *spears* for purposes of hunting game. There are, however, possible exceptions. After having successfully taken a wild hog with a gun on one hunting trip in the southern United States, President Theodore ("Teddy") Roosevelt was quoted as saying that, in retrospect, the hunt would have been more fair had he used a spear.[501]

As with using a bow, the spear has the advantage of being a stealthy weapon that, unlike a gun, does not have the potential of drawing unwanted attention to the hunter. And of course spears do offer the advantage that there is no concern for depleting ammunition.

Perhaps one of the biggest advantages of the spear is the speed and ease with which it can be constructed with little more than a hatchet, ax or heavy survival knife.

Spears might also be effective in hunting *alligators*, and other medium-to-large game that has a tendency to aggressively charge the hunter (wild hogs are also known to be very aggressive). With a little practice, spears can be very effective in catching fish in clear, shallow streams. Even in these cases, for reasons of safety, the spear should only be considered as a hunting tool of last resort.

8.2.3. Other Hunting Gear

In addition to weapons, ammunition, game calls and other equipment normally associated with hunting, and depending on the environment and circumstances of the hunt, other important equipment should also be considered. Examples of such equipment are:

- *Boots and Clothing* - normal street clothing may not be suitable to the rigors of hunting in a rugged environment. Footwear and clothing should be compatible with the terrain and weather that is anticipated for the hunt.

- *Knives* - Hunting knives can be essential equipment not only in field dressing game, but also as a general tool in numerous outdoors situations.

- *Rope* - Rope can be useful for hanging food to protect it from foraging wildlife, hanging carcasses of larger game for butchering, dragging firewood, hanging clothes to dry and a variety of other purposes.

- *Water Container and Filter* - Anyone hunting for more than an hour or two should carry a supply of drinking water and, in the case of a protracted hunting trip, a portable water filter.

- *Field Dressing Equipment* - If hunting for large game then the hunter needs to be equipped to field dress the game. Equipment needed for this might include:

  - sharp knives

  - soap (for sanitizing knives used to cut a carcass)

  - a 'kill tag' with string attached (required by law in some jurisdictions)

  - string and/or twine (for tying off organs as they are being removed)

  - paper towels

  - water for washing down a carcass, hands and equipment

  - clean cloth

  - buckets (for washing down a carcass)

  - rope and pulley (for hanging a carcass)

  - cloths for cleaning hands

  - a large orange-blaze cloth to hang above the carcass

  - a large self-sealing plastic bag (to receive any internal organs you may wish to keep)

  - a flashlight (for inspecting inside a carcass)

  - a pair of heavy rubber gloves to protect the hands from coming into direct contact with a carcass

- *Shelter and Blinds* - A tent may be necessary for overnight hunting, or some structure may be necessary to serve as a game blind.

- *Salt Block(s)* - If your plan for hunting involves *baiting* an area with salt then a salt block will be needed.

- *Food* - Protracted hunting trips may require that the hunter bring along his/her own food supply to sustain them through the hunt. This might be a good use for freeze-dried food, dehydrated food, or MREs.

- *Communications Gear* - It would be advisable, if possible, to have anyone hunting carry gear that would allow them to communicate among themselves or back to headquarters (in case of injury, the need for additional support, etc.).

- *Toiletries* - Any possible sanitary and personal hygiene needs should be anticipated and provided for.

- *Fire Starter* - Some means of starting a fire may be important for signaling an emergency, staying warm, preparing food or keeping wildlife away from a campsite.

- *First Aid Equipment* - All hunters ranging more than 10 minutes from the community should carry some sort of basic first aid kit to deal with any injuries. This should in particular include antibiotic ointment to treat common cuts and abrasions.

- *Navigation Equipment* - Maps, a compass, a writing implement and possibly a straight edge should be considered for any hunting trips that venture far enough away from the community that the hunter might become disoriented and lost.

- *Lighting / Flashlight* - If the hunter is to be out at nighttime, or camping overnight, then some sort of quick and easy lighting will be needed.

8.2.4. Hunting Rabbits and Hares

Rabbits and hares are abundant throughout the continental United States and can also be found on virtually every continent, although they tend to occupy ranges that are mutually-exclusive. Although rabbits and hares share common roots in the evolutionary tree they also have substantial differences. While rabbits live in underground *'warrens'*, hares have above-ground nests known as *'forms'*. Hares grow about 50% larger than rabbits and rely as much on their speed as on concealment to elude predators. While rabbits will run in short high-speed bursts to elude predators, hares are capable of running at sustained high speeds.[442] Both feed on grasses, weeds and other vegetation.[438] Male rabbits and hares are referred to as *bucks* while female rabbits and hares are referred to as *does*. Newborn rabbits are called *kittens* and newborn hares are called *leverets*.

Rabbits are commonly found throughout the US east of Texas, and down into Mexico, Central America and into the northern part of South America. Hares are found in the western US and north into Canada and throughout the entire state of Alaska. Hares are also found in Northern Europe, the Middle East, Asia and in the southern cone of South America.[440][442]

Rabbit and hare meat is extremely lean and rich in protein and B vitamins, and is eaten widely throughout the world.[440] In many countries rabbits are raised for their meat in large-scale commercial facilities. Both rabbit and hare meat are prepared in the same ways, and can be used as a replacement for chicken in virtually any recipe.[439]

Rabbit habitats range from woods, grasslands and wetlands to meadows, forests and even deserts. They live communally in *'herds'* in their warrens. Hare habitats consist of more open areas such as meadows, grasslands and deserts.

Rabbits and hares often graze on grasses in the later afternoons for about a half-hour, followed by another half-hour of slower, more selective grazing.[438] Rabbits may also graze during other parts of the day. Hares are primarily nocturnal animals, and spend about a third of their lives foraging (generally feeding on more woody vegetation than rabbits). During daytime they hide partially-concealed in their above-ground *forms*.[442]

NOTE: *Rabbits* **love** *clover. If you find an area that has clover then you are highly likely to find rabbits. Clover most often grows in loose, sandy, well-drained soil. Rabbits can also be found near fence rows, or anywhere near blackberries, raspberries and (late in the season) near honeysuckle vines. During the Winter rabbits often must resort to eating the bark from small tree saplings.[446]*

Rabbits and hares may be hunted at a distance or they may be flushed from their places of concealment and shot while on the run. A small caliber rifle (such as a .22 caliber rifle) equipped with a scope is well suited for hunting rabbits at a distance. When hunting in this way the hunter takes up a strategic location that is within shooting distance of a good rabbit grazing habitat and waits for the rabbits to present themselves.

In addition to finding rabbits grazing in open fields, rabbits often seek shelter in brush piles, cane breaks, honeysuckle vines, briar patches and woody forest cover. Rabbits are very good at concealing themselves, and some old-time hunters say that it is better to look for the rabbit's eyes rather than their entire body, as the eyes tend to stand out more from the surrounding environment.[444] Because the wooded environments where rabbits are found can be quite dense, when multiple hunters are working together it is highly advisable to wear standard *'blaze orange'* hunting garments to help prevent a shooting accident.

Hounds (such as beagles) are often used to locate, track and sometimes flush rabbits and hares. Shotguns are most often used to shoot rabbits and hares on the run after having been flushed. Hunting dogs are particularly recommended during the cooler or colder hunting seasons as the dogs are much more energetic. Because rabbit fur is a relatively poor insulator, rabbits tend to be more active at temperatures above 50°F. Rabbit hunting is worst when temperatures are at freezing and below, and particularly when conditions are windy or snowy.[447]

When stalking rabbits on foot without dogs it is a good practice for the hunter to pause for several seconds at random intervals, which has been known to have the effect of causing a hiding rabbit to grow nervous and bolt into view. It is also a good idea for the hunter to glance back over their shoulder occasionally, as rabbits are known to wait for a hunter to pass by before starting to run.[444] When stalking near places where rabbits may be concealed, the hunter should look for rabbit tracks leading into the location with no tracks leading out.[443]

It is not uncommon for rabbits to run in a large loop when attempting to escape capture such that they end up back where they started. These loops tend to be shorter in colder weather.[446] A rabbit will sometimes almost let the hunter step on them before flushing.[445]

In addition to being hunted it is also common in many parts of the world for rabbits and hares to be trapped (particularly hares, as they are nocturnal). Often nets or snares are used. When nets are used they are generally set up at the opening of the rabbit's den and ferrets or other animals (sometimes snakes) are sent into the den to flush the rabbit into the waiting net.[443] Snares can also be set at the opening of the rabbit's den, or along trails that the rabbit uses while feeding or seeking water (see section 8.3.1 for details on trapping game with snares). Rabbits may also be captured in baited traps with doors that close when the rabbit enters the trap and disturbs the bait.

> **CAUTION:** *Capturing rabbits and other animals with snares is illegal in many jurisdictions.*

8.2.5. Hunting Quail

The quail is a mid-sized bird that travels mainly on the ground, where it feeds on various seeds and insects. The various species of quail cover much of the southern two-thirds of the US extending from the Pacific to the Atlantic coasts, with the *California Quail* and its related species existing primarily west of Texas[430] and the *Northern Bobwhite* extending from the western edge of Texas eastward *(see Figure 8.1 for a graphic depiction of the range for quail in North America).*[431] Other species of quail can be found throughout the world in habitats ranging from tropical rain forests to deserts.[432].

The meat of the quail is a white meat that does not at all have a "gamey" taste, and which is considered a delicacy by many. Quail eggs are also treasured as a food in many parts of the world, and some quail are raised specifically for their eggs.[433] Quail meat and eggs, if available, would be an excellent addition to the survival diet.

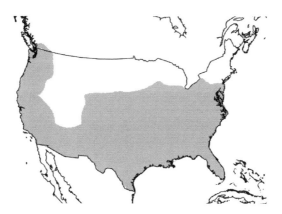

Figure 8.1.: The Range for Quail in the US.

Quail prefer land tracts that offer a combination of open fields and woods.[434] They generally nest in weedy and grassy areas during the night and, in the morning hours, forage through grassy areas for seed and insects. During the mid-day hours quail move into the wooded or other covered areas for shade and shelter, and then move back out in the grasslands during the afternoon hours to continue feeding. The hunter should hunt either along the boundaries between woodlands and grasslands (keeping in mind where the quail should be located based on time of day), and along fence rows and ditches.

The quail is a shy bird that will initially flee any perceived danger by moving quickly across the ground to find cover and concealment. Only as a last resort will the quail take flight, and when doing so it normally flies for only a short distance before settling back to the ground. The quail hunter often must either *'flush'* the quail by kicking at them or, if the bird dog is properly trained, commanding the dog to flush the quail to have them take flight. The hunter then targets the quail with a shotgun.

During the early months of the year quail will travel together in groups known as *'coveys'*, and often a hunter will take multiple birds from a single covey. In later/colder months quail are more commonly found individually, but can still be hunted.[436] There may be up to 15 birds in a covey, and the population density in good habitats can be up to about one bird per acre of ground.[437]

When quail is hunted it is most often hunted with "pointer" and "setter" dogs, which have excellent instincts for locating and signaling the location of quail. Usually hunting parties for quail consist of no more than two hunters, as the quick coordination needed between hunters of these fast-moving birds might otherwise lead to safety issues.

Quail is almost always hunted with shotguns loaded with *bird shot*. The recommended barrel length for a quail gun is 26 inches, which provides an optimal distribution of shotgun pellets for the shooting ranges typically involved.[434] Shotguns used for hunting quail range from 12 gauge on the heavy end to .410 gauge shotguns on the lighter end. If the shotgun has a choke it should be not be set for a tight shot pattern, otherwise the chances of of bringing down a bird are greatly reduced.

Because quail often seek refuge in briar patches and other difficult locations hunters should wear heavy, protective clothing. They should also wear bright orange hunting outfits to reduce the probability that they will inadvertently target one-another when shooting. If two hunters are hunting together then the proper protocol is only point the gun such that it covers half of the arc between yourself and the other hunter. Quail should only be shot when above eye level so that there is little or no chance of shooting the dogs.

When a dog points the hunter should ideally approach the dog directly from behind with the gun pointed upwards and the safety engaged. Only immediately before flushing the birds should the safety be switched to the 'fire' position.[434]

Those who are new to hunting quail are strongly encouraged to begin learning in the company of an experienced quail hunter.

8.2.6. Hunting Pheasant

The pheasant is a mid-sized game bird originally from Russia which, due to its exceptional ability to adapt, has been successfully introduced throughout much of the world. Pheasants range through the northern half of the United States and into the southern half of Canada, and can also be found farther south in Texas and New Mexico *(see Figure 8.2)*.[449] Male pheasants are referred to as *'roosters'* or *'cocks'*, while female pheasants are known as *'hens'*. There are 30 species of pheasant organized into 6 major groups[450], with the *ring-necked pheasant* being the most commonly hunted species.

The pheasant prefers a habitat that consists primarily of crop fields[451] adjacent to woodlands. It feeds on leaves, seed, agricultural crops, fruits, some small animals such as snakes and lizards and occasionally on other birds.[450]

Pheasant meat can be substituted for chicken in most recipes, however pheasant has a darker meat with a more gamey taste. The meat of older pheasants can be tougher, which is why pheasant is often *'hung'* for 3 to 5 days before cooking (so that the meat can become more tender and develop a better flavor). Younger pheasants have a reputation for being very good when roasted. Pheasant hens tend to have more fat and a less gamey taste while older cocks are often cooked in stews and casseroles.

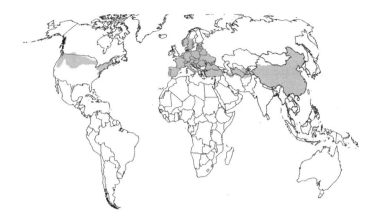

Figure 8.2.: The Range for Pheasant.

Like the quail, the pheasant is largely a ground-dwelling bird that prefers to flee and seek concealment on foot before taking flight. When it does take flight it flies for relatively short distances at speeds up to 60 miles per hour; only flying long enough to find a safe place to land and continue feeding. Unlike the quail the pheasant roosts in the branches of trees at night.[450] The pheasant can tolerate colder weather than the quail, which is why it ranges in the northern part of the United States and Canada while the quail ranges in the southern half of the United States.[434]

The best hunting for pheasant is when it is feeding, which is most often the first 2 hours of daylight and the last hour before sunset, at which time it returns to its roost. Between feedings pheasants will seek shelter in the zone between its feeding area and the wooded area where it roosts.[451] On dry, warm days the pheasant may feed in the field throughout the day and only leave the field to return to its roost at dusk. Occasionally, especially if food sources are plentiful around its roost, a pheasant will stay on its roost through the entire day. During times of extreme cold the pheasant will remain concealed in dense forest cover, often congregating with others of its kind.[452]

Pheasants are commonly hunted by one or more hunters with shotguns; often with Labrador Retrievers or Springer Spaniels along to track, point and possibly flush the birds[450]. Dogs are also very useful in locating birds that have been shot and fallen to the ground, as otherwise it is not uncommon for hunters to shoot a bird only to lose it in dense vegetation.[453] Shotguns commonly used for hunting pheasant range from 12- to 20- gauge, and are typically loaded with birdshot. As dogs are more energetic and alert in cooler and cold weather, they tend to hunt better and longer during the cooler months.[453]

The best fields for hunting pheasant are *'dirty fields'* that have experienced significant large weed growth along with the crop. Crops planted in clean rows tend to be difficult to hunt because dogs become so absorbed in the chase down a straight row that they can forget their training, resulting in birds that take to the air before hunters are positioned to shoot (or possibly resulting in a badly mauled bird).[451] Pheasants may also be found near streams, water-bearing ditches and on the edges of marshlands.[450]

When hunting in clean fields it may be a better strategy to have *'drivers'* (individuals who are along to assist with the hunt) walk across a field and drive the pheasants towards the hunter(s). Ideally the drivers should walk into the wind, should be downhill from the hunters, and should move in a zig-zag pattern through the field to better herd the pheasants (pheasants driven downhill have a tendency to take flight too quickly).[453] When using drivers the hunter must take care to never shoot at or below the level of the horizon so as not to risk any chance of accidentally shooting a driver.

8.2.7. Hunting Squirrel

Squirrels are small, tree-dwelling rodents that have as their habitat vast swathes of North and South America, as well as Europe and Asia. While squirrels are not native to Australia, they have been introduced there and can be found there in limited numbers[458]. There are almost 300 species of squirrels throughout the world.[459][458] They are commonly hunted a source of food as well as for sport and population control. Squirrels reproduce rapidly, so their populations can be large. Most squirrels spend the majority of their lives in trees, eating nuts and tree buds as their primary source of food.[458] Squirrel can be an excellent source of survival food in a grid-down situation, and their small size means that meat preservation is not an issue.

Squirrels can often be found in wooded areas near fields where corn, soybeans, grains are peanuts are grown. In the wild squirrels are particularly attracted to hickory nuts, beechnuts (during the early Fall season) and the acorns of white oaks. Squirrel also will eat the centers of pine cones. Often the empty hulls of the nuts and acorns, or shredded pine cones, can be found at the base of trees where squirrels feed.[457]

While the different species of squirrel have different physical characteristics, the most common varieties of squirrel yield about one-third to one-forth the amount of meat as is found on the average chicken. The meat has a taste that is very much like that of chicken.[454]

Squirrels are commonly hunted and trapped. As described in section 8.3.1, squirrels can be caught with snares as well as in live traps. Bait used in traps can consist of many things, including peanut butter, bird seed and grains. They can be hunted either from a distance by a hunter who has staked out a specific location or on the move while stalking through the woods.

When hunting squirrels from a stationary location they are generally hunted with a small caliber rifle (such as a .22 caliber rifle) or pellet gun, with a scope recommended for increased accuracy when targeting these relatively small animals. When hunting from a fixed position the hunter will wait patiently for the squirrel to present itself and stop moving before shooting. If no squirrels appear within 30 minutes then the stationary squirrel hunter should move to another location.[456]

CAUTION: *When hunting squirrels with a rifle the hunter should always take a shot that provides a solid backstop for the bullet in case the squirrel is missed. Otherwise there is the danger that the bullet may strike an unintended target elsewhere (maybe another hunter!). The use of pellet gun should also be considered due to the reduced noise it makes when firing, so that the hunter is less likely to draw unwanted attention to themselves. Additionally, pellets are far less costly than even .22 caliber ammunition.*

Squirrel hunters that hunt while stalking through the woods typically use a shotgun, which allows them to target the squirrel while it is moving through the trees. While stalking through the woods the hunter should stop periodically to listen for the sounds of squirrels feeding. Some hunters use squirrel calls to excite squirrels in the area to betray their location (and some hunters have reported that the sound made by rubbing two pennies - or other coins - together can also serve to stimulate squirrel activity). In general, squirrels are very sensitive and will flee from hunters with very little provocation.

Whether hunting squirrels from a fixed location or stalking through the woods all squirrel hunters are encouraged to pre-scout hunting locations between hunts or during the off season.

8.2.8. Hunting Wild Turkey

The turkey is a large game bird that is found in every state of the United States except Alaska. It is highly prized for its meat, and would be an excellent food source to augment the human diet in a survival situation. In addition to their range in the United States, one species of turkey can also be found in Mexico's Yucatan Peninsula.[460][466]

The turkey's normal habitat is in mature forest areas; particularly forests with oak, hickory and beech trees. The best turkey hunting can be had in woodlands that border on agricultural fields where grains are grown. Turkeys generally require a habit that consists of at least 40% wooded area.[463] They also must live within 1/4 mile of a permanent water supply.[463] It is not uncommon for turkeys to be spotted along roads in such areas, or even in the back yards of human habitations that border on wooded areas.[466] They feed primarily on fruit, seeds, acorns and insects.[463]

Male turkeys are referred to as *'toms'* or *'gobblers'* and female turkeys are known as *'hens'*. Young turkeys are called *'poults'*, and a group of turkeys together is referred to as a *'flock'*. A flock of turkeys typically contains 20 or more birds. During the Winter, if food is abundant, the flock may require about 50 acres of habitat. During Spring and Summer the flock will require between 640 and 800 acres.[468]

Wild turkeys have a darker, gamier meat than that of turkeys that are grown commercially. During the summer months, when their diet consists more of insects, the meat tends to be at its darkest. Hens and other turkeys feeding more on grain, fruits and seed tend to have a less gamey taste.[467]

Turkey hunters often make use of game calls to either locate a turkey or to draw it into their range of fire. To draw a turkey in the hunter will use a call that mimics the sound of a mating hen. To locate a turkey the hunter will use a call that mimics some predator such as an owl, a hawk or a crow. Such a *predator call* will sometimes elicit a *'shock call'* from a nearby turkey.

These calls take several forms. Some are *'diaphragm calls'* that the hunter must blow through. Others involve scraping or rubbing parts of the call together. The diaphragm calls tend to require the greatest expertise.[461] It is a good idea to practice using these calls in the company of an experienced turkey hunter before taking them on the hunt.

Turkeys roost in trees at night and typically descend to the forest floor at first light to feed and mate during the day. The annual mating season for turkeys extends between mid-March and June.[463] The turkey's mating rituals include the toms displaying themselves prominently. Since turkeys are large birds this means that mating generally takes place in clearings. As they travel from roost to mating area, or to feeding and watering areas, turkeys will prefer the path of least resistance.[464] Wild turkeys are known to be intelligent animals, and will become cautious and flee if things don't seem "quite right" (for example, if a hunter is making excessive use of a call). Turkeys have good vision and an extremely good sense of hearing (they can locate a hen that is calling as far as a mile away).[468][463]

With these characteristics in mind the turkey hunter should try to visit the hunting grounds prior to hunting and locate trees where turkeys go to roost in the evenings. Turkeys tend to gobble as they go to roost, which can greatly help in identifying the locations of their roosts, and when roosting they may shock-gobble in response to a predator call.[465] Most often turkey seasons are during the Spring and Fall, with Spring coinciding with the turkeys' mating season.[461]

If a turkey hunt is taking place during mating season, the hunter should locate cleared areas that turkeys might visit to perform their morning mating rituals. The hunter should also identify natural *'blinds'* - preferably very near large trees - where they can conceal themselves during the hunt to await the approach of turkeys (the purpose of the tree is for the hunter to sit against while waiting. This provides extra concealment and also reduces the chance of getting hit by an errant shot from some other hunter in the area).[462] Ideally, if the hunter is right-handed, the intended killing zone should be off the hunter's left shoulder to provide the widest shooting arc (and of course if the hunter is left-handed, the zone should ideally be off their right shoulder).[464]

While scouting the hunting area the hunter should, keeping in mind the tendency of turkeys to take the *'path of least resistance'*, try to visualize the path a turkey might take from its roost to the mating area or to the nearby water supply.

Turkeys are most commonly hunted with a shotgun, although in some jurisdictions hunting with rifles an and bows is permitted as well. When hunting with a shotgun you should use a shotgun shell that has been specifically designed for turkey hunting. These shells pack a more powerful punch than those used for hunting other, smaller birds. Ideally the shotgun should also have a choke. With a tight pattern (courtesy of the choke) and a high-powered turkey load the maximum killing range should extend to about 40 yards.[469] When shooting at a turkey you should aim for its head (or its neck if it is outstretched).

NOTE: *In many jurisdictions it is illegal to hunt for turkeys with a rifle. Many turkey hunters do not consider it "sporting" to use a rifle, however sportsmanship is a secondary or tertiary consideration in a true survival situation!*

A rifle will provide the turkey hunter with a much greater range. Generally when using a rifle for turkey a smaller caliber cartridge such as the .22 long-rifle is used. When using a rifle to hunt turkey it is advisable to mount a scope for greater precision. As with the shotgun, the hunter should aim for the turkey's head.

Turkey hunts are most productive in calm weather. If hunting on a windy day, or on the day following a windy night, then the hunter's attention should be focused on locations that offer some natural shelter from the wind (such as on the lee-side of a hill). Turkey hunting can also be very productive after a rain. On a hot day after 10am the hunter should focus on areas that provide more shade.[465]

On hunt day the turkey hunter should, by first light, try to stealthily move to a location within 100-200 yards (the closer the better) of a roosting turkey (preferably a tom turkey), and begin making occasional hen calls while listening for replies. The calls should not be too frequent, so as not cause the tom to flee (maybe once in 5 minutes[463]). If the tom answers and flies down to the ground then the hunter should reduce the calls (or possibly stop altogether) and prepare to take the shot. Turkeys are said to respond better to calls that are coming from uphill or from their own level than to calls coming from downhill locations.[465]

If the hunt is during mating season then by 9am the turkeys should begin to meet in clearings for the daily mating ritual. This is when the hunter should be positioned on the edge of a pre-scouted location behind good natural cover. From this position the hunter should patiently wait for the turkey to come to within proper shooting range. Between 9am and 10am the hens begin to lose interest in mating, even though the toms have not. It is from this time through the remainder of the day that toms may be called with good success.[465]

When hunting turkey outside of mating season the turkey's behavior is less predictable, however it can be productive to hunt along the path between the turkey's roost and its water supply. During the winters the flocks of turkey tend to travel more closely together and, if food is sufficient, not range as far afield. Outside of mating season turkey can still be hunted throughout the day (within legal constraints, of course).[462]

8.2.9. Hunting Whitetail and Mule Deer

There are many species of deer distributed across much of the inhabited world. The different species range dramatically in size with the general rule being that the larger deer are to be found in the cooler climates. They occupy habitats ranging from barren plains to deep jungle.

The most common species of deer hunted for sport and food are the whitetail and mule deer of the Americas (the whitetail can be found throughout much of North, Central and South America, while the mule deer is native only to North America, but has also been introduced in Argentina *(see Figure 8.3 for a depiction of the natural range for whitetail and mule deer in North and Central America)* [478]). While the these two species are described in this section, much of the information presented here applies to the hunting of any species of deer (particularly since the whitetail and mule deer occupy a broad range of habitats).

The male deer is referred to as a *'buck'* and the female deer is referred to as a *'doe'*. Young deer are known as *'fawns'* or *'calfs'*.[488]

The meat from deer (known as *venison*) is very palatable to humans, particularly if the meat is processed properly after it is killed.[487] It is an excellent source of protein, is naturally

Figure 8.3.: The Range for Deer in the Americas and Canada.

low in fat, and is rich in vitamins. While a 3-ounce serving of beef provides about 260 calories and 18 grams of fat, the same size serving of venison provides just over 130 calories and 3 grams of fat.[486]

There are some concerns that many wild deer populations are developing a disease known as *Chronic Wasting Disease ('CWD')*, which has symptoms similar to those of *Mad Cow Disease*. There are no records of this disease being transmitted from deer to humans.[486] In the aftermath of a major disaster when the alternative is starvation, most people would find this to be an acceptable risk.[486]

While the whitetail and mule deer have a common genetic ancestry there are significant differences between the two:

- The whitetail deer is found mainly east of the Missouri River in the US, while the mule deer ranges to the west (largely in the Rocky Mountains).[479]

- The mule deer is significantly larger than the whitetail deer, with the mule deer buck ranging between 200 and 460 pounds[478] and the adult whitetail deer buck ranging between 290 and 400 pounds.[479]

- The mule deer has a white tip on its tail, while the whitetail deer has a white tail.

- The mule deer has antlers that bifurcate as they grow, and the whitetail deer's antlers all grow from a single main antler.

- The mule deer is found on sparse and often rocky terrain, while the whitetail deer is found in fields and forests.

Deer have extremely keen senses of smell, hearing and vision. Their sense of smell is so acute that some hunters are known to scrub themselves with baking soda on the day of the hunt and wait until they reach the hunting location to change into their hunting clothes. The deer's vision and hearing are sensitive enough that hunters must remain as motionless and silent as possible as they wait for a deer to come within shooting distance. When movement is absolutely necessary the hunter will move very slowly. The slightest noise, such as a cough or one piece of gear banging into another, is enough to cause a deer to quickly disappear (or not show up at all).

The best success at deer hunting is to be had when they are feeding or seeking a mate. Deer feed on tender leaves, clover, rye, the new shoots of plants, berries and acorns[480], which they often find in the border between fields and woodlands. As most deer tend to feed in the early morning hours and around dusk.[480], these are the best times to hunt them outside of their mating season (also known as *rutting season*). Deer rutting season is generally during the month of November, sometimes extending into December[488]. During this time deer are known to be less cautious and easier to hunt.[480]

Deer can adapt to a wide range of habitats, however they do require a source of drinking water and some sort of concealment in which to sleep. For concealment deer often retreat to wooded areas or swamps.[480] Swamps offer much cover and provide an environment in which it is easier for deer to hear predators and hunters approaching. In general, however, deer prefer a habitat that features wooded areas for sleep and concealment that borders on open spaces for better grazing.

In the wild deer are known to make three distinct sounds for communication:[480]

- *The snort* - a warning of danger to other deer in the area.

- *A bleat* - this is the sound made by fawns or does when in distress.

- *The grunt* - a sound made by bucks to invite does to mate.

Most deer calls replicate the buck's grunt, as this sound will often attract a buck seeking to defend its territory.

In addition to using deer calls, hunters sometimes bring antlers to rattle together to simulate the sound made when bucks are fighting over territory (or they bring devices that mimic this sound). This is also known to attract bucks.[485]

NOTE: *When hunting deer with a bow the hunter should practice with the bow as much as possible in advance. The bow should be set to a reasonable draw weight so that the hunter can hold a drawn arrow as long as necessary to await a good shot. It is not uncommon for a bow string to catch on the folds of loose clothing, so the bow hunter should not wear excessively loose clothing on their upper body.*

Other tips for hunting deer include:

- *Obtain a topographic map of the hunting location in advance* - this map will allow you to better plan your hunt.

- *Scout the hunting location in advance* - look for deer tracks, water supplies, clover patches and patches of other tender green vegetation that border wooded areas, *'scrapes'* (places where deer have been pawing at the ground - especially in wooded areas) and overhanging branches where deer have been rubbing their antlers.[483]

- *Law permitting, bait the hunting area in advance* - If prevailing laws allow, place bait in select hunting locations to attract the deer. Fruits and vegetables such as corn, carrots, apples, cabbage, lettuce, potatoes, beets, acorns, turnips, pumpkins and tomatoes make good bait for deer.

- *Build a deer blind or obtain a good tree stand* - Your chances of bagging a deer will increase exponentially with the quality of your concealment. Drag a rag wetted with a *deer-attractant* around the area surrounding the blind. These attractants either emit the odor of favorite deer foods or, more commonly, emit the scent of deer urine (particularly the urine scent of breeding does).[485]

- *Conceal your scent* - Bathe with a non-scented, non-detergent soap before hunting, and do not eat any pungent foods.[482] Before hunting avoid any activity such as pumping gas that might cause you to emit a scent.

- *Dress strategically* - Deer vision is not sensitive to the bright *'orange blaze'* color worn by many hunters, so you should wear this color to be more visible to other hunters. What ***IS*** important is that you do as much as possible to conceal your human shape from the deer. This concealment could involve hunting from within a blind or attaching foliage to your clothing to break up your shape.[480]

- *Don't give immediate chase to a wounded deer* - If your shot does not immediately kill the deer remain still and watch the deer carefully. Often if you do not give chase the deer will shortly lie down and bleed out. If you give chase, however, you could end up tracking the deer for miles and the release of hormones in the deer's body could be deleterious to the quality of its meat.[482]

- *Be ready to run if attacked* - Deer have been known to occasionally attack hunters, and they are large enough to inflict serious harm. When hunting deer always have an escape plan in mind 'just in case'![482]

- *Make no unnecessary noises, and move very slowly* - If a deer hears you or sees you moving, you will almost certainly never see the deer.[483]

- *Pay more attention upwind* - As a deer that is upwind will not have the opportunity to detect your scent, you should focus more of your attention in that direction.[483]

- *Don't eat internal organs from a deer* - To avoid contracting any disease that may be transmissible from deer to humans do not eat any of the organ meat from a deer.

- *Wear latex or rubber gloves when dressing or butchering a deer*

- *Remove all fat and membranes attached to the meat from a deer*

A Special Note about Hunting Mule Deer

By virtue of its rugged environment with broad, open spaces the hunting of mule deer is a much different experience than hunting whitetail. When hunting mule deer the hunter will not hunt from a stationary position as with whitetail, but rather will stalk the mule deer (often for miles) at a distance while trying to remain concealed by terrain to the greatest extent possible. This means that the mule deer hunter should be in good physical condition and be ready for a long hike back (possibly carrying a very heavy kill).

Guns to Use for Deer Hunting

Deer should be hunted with rifles and higher-powered ammunition that provide a combination of good range and knock-down power. For mule deer the smallest caliber recommended is the .243 cartridge. The .270, Remington .300, .30-06 and .308 cartridges are also quite effective for deer hunting.[484] For the smaller whitetail deer the .227 and .30-30 cartridges should also be effective.

> **NOTE:** *There are many instances of deer being taken with rifle cartridges as small as the .22 Long Rifle, however there is no debating that as the cartridge gets smaller the probability of a good, clean (and humane) kill are reduced.*

In addition to using an appropriate rifle and ammunition, the deer rifle should be equipped with proper scope for precise targeting (see section D.6 for good information on selecting proper scope for hunting larger game).

Field Dressing Deer

In general the procedure described in section 8.2.12 can be followed when field dressing a deer. In addition however, the following two steps should be taken:

- Even before field dressing, cut around the deer's anus, pull it out an inch or two, and tie off the intestines so that no fecal matter will contaminate the deer during transport and/or field dressing.

- Cut around and remove the deer's sex organs as soon as possible to prevent the release of hormones into the carcass.[483]

8.2.10. Hunting Wild Hogs

Wild hog populations today exist on every continent and in the great majority of countries throughout the world. In the United States the population of wild hogs is most dense in the southeast, Hawaii and mid- to northern- California *(see Figure 8.4 for a depiction of the range for wild hogs in the US)*. Due largely to escapes of domestic hogs, there are smaller pockets of wild hog populations spread through much of the rest of the country.

Male hogs are referred to as *'boars'* and female hogs are referred to as *'sows'*. Young wild hogs are referred to as *'piglets'*. Wild hogs can range in size from piglets that weigh just a few pounds to fully-grown boars that can, depending on the species, weigh up to 650 pounds.[471] The average size of a full grown wild hog in the US is about 300 pounds.[474]

Wild hogs are one of the most intelligent game animals.[476]

The characteristics of meat from wild hogs varies with the age, gender and condition of the hog as well as its diet. In general wild hogs will have meat that is noticeably 'gamier' that that of commercial hogs. However, the meat from younger hogs (and often from sows) can be similar to that of commercially-grown hogs, particularly if they have been feeding largely on fruits, nuts or agricultural grains (their preferred foods). However, the meat of large boars can be particularly gamey, and can be virtually inedible if the hog has been feeding on carrion, swill or pine tree roots.

> **NOTE:** *Even the meat from large boars can be made much more palatable through* salt curing *over a period of days. When hog meat is salt cured it is typically soaked in cold brine for 4 or 5 days, with the brine being poured out and replaced after the first day.[470]*

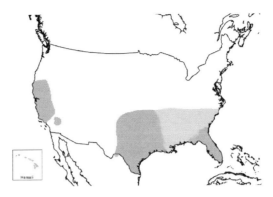

Figure 8.4.: The Range for Wild Hogs in the US
(light gray areas have less dense populations)

Due to the damage they often inflict on crops and private property, as well as their large and quickly-growing populations, wild hogs are considered a nuisance animal in many locations. As a result many of the hunting restrictions that exist for other types of game have been relaxed (or removed altogether) for hog hunting.

Dominant boars generally travel alone except when mating, while sows will often travel with other sows and their piglets. It is common for dominant boars to have a territory as large as 20 square miles, with male boars fighting one another (sometimes to the death) to protect that territory.

While it is not uncommon to see hogs during the daylight hours (particularly in the morning), many wild hogs have become nocturnal in order to avoid hunters.[474] All hogs must live in close proximity to water. These watering holes are used not only for drinking, but also for wallowing and/or just resting in the mud as a means of combating fleas, ticks and other skin parasites. The mud from hog wallows also acts as a sun screen to protect the skin of hogs from excessive exposure to sunlight.

Hogs feed on plants and animals that are near and in the water (in fact, hogs feed on virtually any organic matter, including fruits, vegetables, a wide range of animals, crops and underground roots). Their keen sense of hearing is surpassed only by their extraordinary sense of smell, which can detect food even when buried under several feet of earth.[476] It is not unknown for a herd of wild hogs (also known as a *'drift'* or *'parcel'*) to dig up an entire field of sprouting or freshly-planted crop in a single night! They typically retreat to thickets and/or densely wooded areas when not seeking food or visiting their water source. Young piglets will sometimes emerge from thickets and draw an entire herd into the open.

Wild hogs are hunted in a variety of ways. Most commonly they are hunted from *blinds*, stalked through the woods by foot, or chased down with dogs. Wild hogs (particularly boars) can be extremely dangerous. They can be very aggressive and have two upper and two lower tusks that can be several inches in length and are often razor-sharp.[475][476] In addition to these dangerous tusks they have heavy skulls that have been known to deflect bullets as they charge a hunter, and often have a 1- to 3- inch layer of callus extending from their necks to their lower ribs that has been known to stop some bullets (particularly hollow point bullets that flatten out when striking a target. This callus is often referred to as the hogs 'shield').[472][476] In addition to boars being aggressive, sows that feel their piglets are threatened can also become quite aggressive and dangerous.

CAUTION: *The last/best refuge for a hunter when being charged by an aggressive boar often involves shimmying up the nearest available tree. If you plan to stalk wild hogs on their home territory (as opposed to hunting from an elevated blind) then it is important that you be in good enough physical condition to be able to quickly climb a tree or to hold your legs suspended while clinging to a small tree for a minute or two.*

Many hunters use *bay dogs* and *catch dogs* to corner and capture wild hogs (there are records of such dogs being used extending back to the times of the Roman Empire!). Bay dogs instinctively corner a hog and hold it 'at bay' until the hunter arrives, while catch dogs will actually bite down on the hog's ear and keep it on the ground for the hunter. A hog held in this position may even be dispatched with a knife to the throat if the hunter is brave enough to risk injury from teeth and tusks. Hunters who take hogs live will approach the grounded hog from the rear, grab its hind legs and flip it onto its side before 'hog tying' the legs to prepare it for transport.

Bay dogs tend to be members of the *hound* and *cur* families, while catch dogs are often *boxers*, *pit bulls* or other dogs known to have a strong fighting instinct.[472]

Depending on the hunting style (and the legal restrictions in a particular jurisdiction) wild hogs can be hunted with rifles, shotguns, handguns and bows as well as knifes, spears and even bare-hands (when using dogs). Most often, however, they are hunted with high-powered rifles equipped with scopes for increased accuracy. When shooting wild hogs they should either be shot in the head (most effectively behind the ears) or between the lower front shoulders (where the heart and lungs are located, and well away from the gut).[472] If a wild hog is not cleanly killed then it may run, and the resulting changes to the hogs metabolism may degrade the quality of its meat. Typically handguns, knives and spears are only used to dispatch hogs at close range after they have been cornered or pinned by catch dogs.

Heavy caliber ammunition such as the 30-06, the .308 or the Winchester 300 rounds should be used to quickly and humanely kill wild hogs (other calibers may also be used with heavier or more specialized powder loads or bullets).[472] If using a shotgun then no gun smaller than a 12-gauge should be used, it should be loaded with heavy buckshot, and the hog should not be shot at a range greater than about 30 yards. If a hog taken with a shotgun is not killed with the first shot then it should be quickly dispatched with a follow-up shot to the head at closer range.

If shooting at a hog the hunter should be ready for it (or maybe other hogs nearby) to turn and charge. The hunter should anticipate needing to take an immediate follow-up shot (before heading for the nearest stout tree!).

It is not uncommon for hunters to bait areas with food to attract hogs to a hunting area. Any sort of grain or sweet food (such as donuts) will be attractive to hogs. When baiting a field it's a good idea to bury the bait a foot or two below the ground (typically using a post hole digger).[473] Not only will this cause the hogs to stop and dig for it (as mentioned previously, the wild hog's sense of smell is so sensitive that they can detect food buried several feet underground), it will also preserve the food from other opportunistic feeders such as raccoons. Other tips for hunting wild hogs include:

- If hunting from a blind be sure to camouflage it completely, as wild hogs have a decent sense of sight in addition to their acute senses of hearing and smell.

- If hunting during daylight hours, hunt during the early morning and/or later evening hours.[475]

- Always wear heavy rubber gloves when handling or dressing wild hogs, and avoid contact with the hog's blood or other bodily fluids to prevent getting cut and infected by a diseased animal.

- Before hunting at a location place *trail cams* around the property to identify the best hunting times and places.

NOTE: *While it may not seem humane to hunt younger hogs, the reality is that hogs are an invasive species that destroys the environment for native species. A strong case can be made that* **not** *killing hogs of all ages is inhumane to native species.*

See section 8.2.12 for instructions for field dressing wild hogs and other game.

8.2.11. Hunting Unconventional Game

The person who is struggling to survive will not be particularly concerned that his/her prey always consists of conventional game. There are other good sources of protein that are quite edible. These sources include:

- *Alligators* - Alligator meat has a very conventional taste and texture.[65]

- *Snakes* - Like alligator, the taste and texture of snake can be quite similar to that of other meats.[66]

- *Frogs* - Frogs (frog legs) are served as a gourmet entree in many upscale restaurants.

- *Rats* - Rats are actually not considered a food source in most parts of the world. However rat has been endorsed for human consumption by the government of India.[67] If the alternative is starvation then rat may start to seem reasonable (especially if you are competing with those same rats for the same food sources).

8.2.12. Field Dressing Killed Game

NOTE: *If you have someone else butcher your game it is a good idea to check references from other customers in advance. It is desirable to arrange that the meat you receive from the butcher will not in any way be combined with meat that they receive from others. This is important because other hunters may not kill or handle their meat as carefully and hygienically as you. For example, you have no way of knowing if other meat that might be combined with yours was "gut shot" such that material from the intestines came into contact with the meat. In addition to receiving this assurance from the butcher, you should inquire as to their procedures for cleaning their equipment (e.g. Do they clean regularly? Do they clean their equipment between customers?).*

With all this said you may correctly conclude that the lowest cost butcher is not necessarily the one with whom you should do business. (You may also conclude that you'd rather do your own butchering!)

Field dressing is the first processing of an animal's carcass in preparing it for for human consumption. As the name suggests, this process is sometimes performed 'in the field' where the animal was taken. When this is performed on site it is done to help preserve the quality of the meat and to reduce the weight to transport. Regardless of where the animal is dressed (in the field or at home) the process is, in general, similar for most types of game. It consists of the following steps:

- If working with large game move the carcass under a tree branch (or other structure) from which it may be hung with a rope. The structure needs to be strong enough to support the carcass, and it would be helpful to have a pulley to attach to the structure to facilitate hanging the carcass.

- Make an incision down one hind leg and up the belly.

- Peel back the skin and, taking short strokes with a sharp knife separate the skin from the body as much as possible. Be careful not to cut too deeply into the muscle tissue. Clean the knife occasionally in water as needed. If a good supply of clean water is available then you can also rinse the carcass occasionally.

- Using a sharp knife or a saw (especially for large game), remove the back legs below the bottom joint.

- If you have a pulley, tie it to the branch or other structure from which you will be suspending the carcass.

- Once the skin has largely been cut away from the carcass make holes through the bottom part of the remaining hind legs and run a rope through those holes and over the structure (or through the pulley if you have one) to hoist the carcass into the air.

- Finish trimming the skin from the carcass and remove it.

- Cut a circular hole around the anus such that when the guts are removed the anus will also come with them.

- Make an incision down the the belly of the hanging carcass being careful not to cut so deeply as to cut the internal organs.

- For large game (especially wild hogs) cut the *'brisket bone'* with a saw (this is *'breast bone'*).

- Assist the internal organs in spilling forth from the carcass to the ground, cutting carefully with the knife as needed to separate the organs from the carcass.

- Remove the liver, heart, lungs and kidneys, and inspect the liver for spots (which would indicate that the animal had parasites). If you plan on keeping the liver then trim away the gall bladder from the liver with the knife.

- Using the saw remove the head from the carcass.

- If possible wash the carcass inside and out with clean water, paying particular attention to washing down through the circular hole where the anus was cut.

- The meat is now ready to be transported home or to a butcher to be cut into parts. Depending on the type of game, the condition of the animal, and what the animal had been eating, it may be advisable to cure the meat before freezing or cooking. The curing process, which is often involves immersing the meat in icy brine, will cause the meat to lose much of its *'gamey'* flavor. Curing is particularly important in the case of wild hogs, and almost necessary in the case of large boars. Typically the carcass of a large animal is brine-cured for 3 to 5 days, with the brine being poured out and replaced after the first 24 hours.

8.3. Trapping

Trapping has significant advantages over hunting that should be given serious consideration:

- *Time savings* - It should take far less time to set and check traps than hunting for game in a conventional sense. One need not necessarily be a trained expert to check traps, so there is some potential flexibility in selecting the personnel for that task. (Training personnel to set traps is also certainly much easier than training a new hunter.)

- *Cost savings* - For the cost of a single gun one can purchase many traps.

- *No expendables* - Guns expend valuable ammunition, while traps can be re-baited at low cost (or, in the case of many snares, at no cost!).

- *Draws less attention* - While the sound of gunfire can draw unwanted attention, traps can be set and checked in relative silence (and are often concealed).

Traps can be used to capture animals of any size, however they are most often used to trap animals no larger than deer. There are many approaches to trapping wild game, with the most popular being the use of *cage traps*, *snares* and *deadfalls*:

- *Cage traps* are wire cages with trap doors that can be triggered to close when an animal enters the cage and actuates a trigger (usually by taking some food that was left as bait).

- *Snares* consist of wire nooses on slip knots that will tighten around an animal's neck or legs when they attempt to pass through the noose, or when they actuate some sort of trigger device.

Figure 8.5.: A typical 'twitch-up' snare.

- *Deadfalls* are traps made of natural material that, when triggered, either cause the prey to be killed when a heavy weight falls onto them, or cause the prey to fall into a pit.

Cage traps of all sizes are commonly used to capture wildlife, and are available from a number of commercial sources. They are considered to be humane as they pose very little risk to the captured animal if they are checked on a regular basis. During non-disaster times cage traps are regularly used to capture nuisance animals for relocation.

> **NOTE:** *One of the better sources of cage traps is at Tractor Supply Co., which offers a wide range of traps in all sizes.*

In the wild, most animals make use of *game trails* to travel between their den and locations for food and water (in fact, game trails serve as 'nature's Interstate highway system', with many animals often making use a single trail). The most effective trapping involves setting traps along these trails (or possibly at the opening of an animal's den).[428] Regardless of the type of trap, it is common for the trapper to arrange natural-looking barriers around it so as to 'channel' the game to it.

It is important that the trapper be careful not to leave any human scent on or near a trap, as well as to have the area around a trap appear to be as undisturbed as possible. Human scent can be masked through the use of liquids from the gall or urine bladders of previously trapped animals, by applying smoke to any areas around the trap that may bear human scent, or by handling the trap with hands that have been coated with local mud and dried or rotting local vegetation.

CAUTION: *Just as with other forms of hunting, trapping is regulated by law. Before trapping any game be certain that you are aware of, and to adhere to, the prevailing laws for the location where you intend to be trapping. The use of snares and other types of traps that tend to kill or injure wildlife is outlawed in many jurisdictions, so any such device should only be considered for use in a true life-or-death survival situation.*

8.3.1. Snares

The simplest snares consist of nooses that are tied to stakes in the ground or the trunk of a tree, and which are suspended such that the animal must pass through the noose during its normal travel. The noose tightens around the animal to capture it. More complex snares involve attaching lines to the tops of small flexible trees, or to hanging weights, such that the activation of a simple trigger (often made from natural materials in that area) releases the tree or weight, causing the noose to capture the animal by the legs and pull it into the air. The advantage of these snares is that they not only capture the animal, but also pull it up out of the reach of other predators. Figure 8.5 depicts a *'twitch-up snare'* that uses the flexible body of a freshly-cut sapling to provide tension for the snare, and two simple, notched wooden pegs as the trigger.

Snares are typically placed along game trails. The nooses themselves should be constructed of cord that is easy to conceal and difficult for an animal to break and or bite through. Quite often a thin wire is used for the noose (for example the type of wire that is used to hang pictures). Shoestring and/or un-braided paracord has also been used successfully.[429] The loop of the noose should be about the size of the body of the animal you are trying to capture, and should be positioned so as to either capture the animal by its neck or around its feet.

Squirrel snares consist of branches that are leaned against a tree to which typically several nooses are attached such that squirrels will tend to pass through a noose as they travel up and down the branch. The nooses should be no closer than 18 inches from either end of the branch so that the squirrel will not be able to push against the ground or the tree against which the branch is resting.[429] It is not uncommon to find multiple squirrels trapped on a single branch that has multiple snares affixed to it.

8.3.2. Deadfalls

Deadfalls are traps that, when triggered, cause a heavy log or rock to fall onto the animal and kill it. The triggers used for deadfalls are very similar to those used for snares, with less tension required on the line as it is the weight of the falling object that does the work.

8.4. Fishing

The sports fisherman is often concerned with catching fish of a specific species and size. The survival fisherman, on the other hand, will be much less picky. Some forms of fish have been traditionally shunned due to having many small bones. To the survivalist such fish will be a delicacy. The bottom line is that fishing for survival is a bit different than fishing during better times. This section describes how preppers might plan and equip themselves to fish for survival.

One of the first things the survival fisherman needs to consider is the environment in which they expect to be fishing. Will they be fishing in fresh water or salt water? Will they be fishing from shore or in a boat? Will they be fishing in still water or in a flowing stream? These factors will determine the fishing gear that will be needed.

Most often fish are caught using some form of natural bait or artificial lures. Natural bait attracts fish through smell and taste while lures attract fish through motion and appearance (some lures may have provisions for also appealing to smell and taste as well). The advantage of artificial lures over natural bait is that they may be reused (and in some cases may be more effective). The advantage of natural bait is that it is often better at attracting fish (especially if the artificial lure is not being used by someone with experience) and also requires significantly less work from the fisherman.

For salt water fishing, rods tend to be larger and the reels of line used are most often open reels. For fresh water fishing the rods tend to be smaller and the reels often fully enclose the fishing line. Fresh water fishing rigs tend to require less skill to use, while salt water rigs may require practice to master.

In some cases it is not important that natural bait be alive or freshly killed. For example salt water fisherman often cut up pieces of frozen squid to use as bait. In general, however, live or freshly killed bait provides a big advantage because it is more attractive to a wide range of fish and, unlike frozen bait, it does not have a tendency to fall apart after being cast out into the water and starting to thaw.

8.4.1. Catching Live Bait

Live bait can take many forms including:

- *Worms* - Worms can be used as bait for both fresh and salt water fishing. Often worms can be found under leaves in a cool, shady location (no digging needed). Worms can also be found in rich soil such as in gardens. Typically the worm is pierced with the hook at one end and threaded up the length of the hook so as to conceal the metal of the hook almost entirely.

- *Minnows* - Minnows are very small fresh water fish that make a good bait for fresh water game fish (such as bass). Minnows may often be caught by throwing a fine mesh cast net into freshwater pools. The hook is baited by passing the hook through the back of the minnow one or two times. If the hook is placed properly the minnow will continue to live and swim while on the line, which helps to attract fish.

- *Shiners* - Like minnows, shiners are small fresh water fish (but much larger than minnows) that make a very good bait for fresh water game fish. Shiners can be attracted to a location by putting out oatmeal or horse feed, waiting 20 or 30 minutes, and then using a cast net to catch them as they feed. Alternatively they can be caught individually using a small fishing hook baited with a dough ball. The shiner is placed on the hook in much the same way as a minnow. (NOTE: Shiners are considered the ultimate bait for catching bass.)

- *Crickets, Cockroaches and Palmetto bugs* - Large insects such as crickets, cockroaches and palmetto bugs make excellent bait for fresh water fishing. These insects may be trapped using either moistened sugar or small pieces of over-ripe or rotten banana as bait. Homemade traps can be made from a simple plastic water bottle.[68]

- *Pinfish* - Pinfish are small salt-water fish that can be found near piers and grass beds throughout the southern coastal waters of the US. They are particularly active between early Spring and late Fall and are a good bait for snook, trout, grouper, snapper, redfish, shark, cobia and a variety of other larger fish. Pinfish can be caught with regular fishing equipment using small hooks baited with pieces of squid or shrimp. They may also be caught in cast nets, or trapped in chicken wire traps baited with pieces of fish and resting on the bottom near a grass bed or pier.

- *Shrimp* - Both live and frozen shrimp make an excellent bait for virtually any salt water fish. The best way to catch shrimp is to shine a light near a pier at night, and throw a cast net over the shrimp as they are attracted by the light.

8.4.2. Fishing with Live Bait

Fishing with live bait involves placing the bait on a fishing hook and casting it out, and waiting for a fish to take the bait. Depending on the type of fish you are seeking you may allow the bait to settle to the bottom, or you may use a *'float'* to keep the bait suspended at a particular depth. When fishing on the bottom the fisherman must watch the line to determine when the bait is taken. When fishing with a float the fisherman watches the motion of the float to know when the bait has been taken. *Lead sinkers* are often used to add weight to a line so that it can be cast a greater distance, although excessive weights should be avoided so as to keep the bait as attractive as possible.

NOTE: *Bait fish such as minnows, shiners and pinfish may still be very much alive after being hooked and cast out. With a little experience the fisherman will learn to differentiate between the motion of the bait fish and that of a fish taking the bait.*

8.4.3. Fishing with Artificial Lures

With the exception of plastic worms (see below), when fishing with artificial lures that move below the surface of the water (which covers most artificial lures) the tip of the rod should be held upright and bounced slightly as the lure is reeled in. This will impart a more natural movement to the lure as it travels through the water. If the lure has any sort of grass 'skirt' then varying the speed of retrieval (or even stopping and restarting the retrieval) will help to give a natural motion to that skirt.

Special Considerations when Fishing with Plastic Worms

Plastic worms are used mainly by anglers who are fishing for bass.

In the case of fishing with plastic worms a special plastic worm hook should be used. These hooks tend to be larger, and are constructed to be threaded through the center of the worm (almost like threading a real worm onto a hook).

Special hooks are available for use with plastic worms. These hooks can be easily recognized by their larger size and their particular *'L curve'* just below the eye of the hook where the line is attached (see Figure 8.6). When threading the hook through the worm, the tip of the hook should only emerge slightly from the body of the worm. The reason for this is so that the hook does not snag on vegetation or other objects below the surface.

Some worm hooks feature built-in *'weed guards'* made of thin wire. These also reduce the tendency of the lure to get snagged on submerged objects.

Special weights are also used when fishing with artificial worms. These weights are shaped like little cones, with a hole in the center of the cone through which the fishing line is passed.

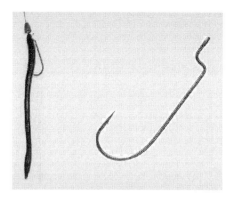

Figure 8.6.: Hook for Use with Plastic Fishing Worms.

This arrangement allows the weight to slide freely with the worm, imparting a more natural movement as it is being retrieved. See figure 8.6 for a depiction of a typical worm that has been hooked and weighted.

When casting the worm it should be allowed to sink to the desired depth before you begin to retrieve it.

As with other artificial lures, the tip of the rod should be held upright and bounced slightly as the worm is retrieved. This also lends a more natural movement to the worm.

Unlike other artificial lures, when a fish strikes at the plastic worm the tip of the rod should be lowered towards the water. In addition to allowing the fish to take the worm this positions the rod to be pulled strongly to 'set the hook' in the fish's mouth. Only the very tip of the hook was exposed through the worm, so you must pull firmly to bring the hook through the plastic worm and embed itself in the fish's lip.

8.4.4. Surface Fishing

A few artificial fishing lures are designed to be plowed across the surface of the water and to attract fish up to take them. For such lures the tip of the rod should be held down towards the water, as it is obviously not desirable for such lures to bounce up and down. Generally the fisherman will try to use a lure like this when the fish don't seem to be interested in anything else (a fisherman's version of the 'Hail Mary Pass').

8.4.5. Bottom Fishing

Some fish spend their time at or near the bottom of a body of water (grouper is a good example). For such fish it is often a good idea to use a natural bait, and to allow it to sink to the bottom. In such cases the fisherman has only to be patient and wait for the line to draw tight when a fish takes the bait. The fisherman then pulls stiffly on the rod to set the hook in the fish.

Some fishermen will put out multiple lines simultaneously in order to increase their chances of catching a fish. In this case they must be observant enough to watch all the lines. Some fishermen have been known to attach tiny bells to the ends of their rods to draw their attention when a fish takes the bait.

8.4.6. Fly Fishing

Proper *fly fishing* is a technical skill that requires much practice. It involves using a special rod to cast a small topwater lure with a series of whipping motions.

Fly fishing can be used when fishing for fresh water fish both in flowing streams as well as in large rivers and lakes. Under certain circumstances fly fishing may be the best or only way to effectively catch fish (such as when the fish are feeding almost exclusively on topwater insects during particular times of year).

Fly fishing requires its own unique rod and tackle. The fly fishing rod is long, slender and flexible to allow the whipping motions used to cast the bait. The baits themselves are small artificial flies that land on top of the water. The fly is generally allowed to rest on the water for a few seconds at most before, with the same whipping motion, the fly fisherman retrieves it and casts it out again.

The reel used for fly fishing is a small, open-faced reel with a lever that retrieves the line when pressed by the fisherman. The fisherman manually feeds the line out from the reel while whipping the fly through the air (often multiple back-and-forth whipping motions are required before the fly can reach its destination). When a fish is caught the fisherman manually retrieves the line while pressing the lever that causes the spring-loaded reel to spool in the slack line.

8.4.7. Fishing with Trotlines

Trotlines are long lines from which baited hooks are suspended to catch fish. A single trotline may contain dozens of baited hooks. The lines are often attached to floats at intervals, which not only keeps the bait suspended at a desired depth but also provides a visual indication that a fish has been caught. Sealed plastic milk jugs are often used as floats for this purpose.

The fisherman generally baits and deploys one or more trotlines from a boat and returns periodically to collect any fish that have been caught and to re-bait the hooks as needed.

The use of trotlines is very compatible with fishing in a disaster scenario because the lines require very little time and energy to check, and the number of lines put out greatly increases the probability of success. The time saved by using trotlines can then be used for other critical activities.

CAUTION: *Before fishing with trotlines be aware of any relevant state or federal fishing laws.*

8.4.8. When and Where to Fish

The fisherman should consider the following guidelines when deciding when and where to fish:

- In general the best times to fish are early morning and mid-evening. Some fish, such as striped bass, feed at night and are best fished at night.

- Spring and early Summer are the best times of year to fish in fresh water lakes and rivers.

- When fishing in salt water the best times to fish are between one hour before and one hour after mean high tide. An incoming tide provides better fishing than an outgoing tide.

- Cloudy (and even rainy) days are best when fishing mid-day.

- A full or new moon is also known to improve fishing. Not only does the full moon result in increased tides (which induces the fish to feed), the additional light has also been shown to stimulate fish activity.

- Fresh and salt water fish tend to be attracted to natural and man-made cover. Fish can be found around piers, buoys, submerged trees, grass and other similar artificial and man-made cover.

CAUTION: *When handling most fish be careful not to brush against fins that protrude along the top or from the side of the fish. These fins can easily puncture skin and contain toxins that can be painful and possibly cause infection.*

The slime that coats the skin of catfish is actually a natural antibiotic.[427] Many fishermen, if they happen to get wounded by the fin of a catfish, will rub the fish against the wound in order to take advantage of these antibacterial properties.

8.4.9. Basic Fishing Equipment (for fresh and salt water)

The basic equipment needed for fishing (*fishing tackle*) is very similar for both fresh and salt water. In general fishing tackle should be of a larger/stronger variety when being used for salt water fishing. As a result, if you expect to fish in both fresh and salt water, it is a good idea to have separate tackle boxes for each. The following is a list of basic equipment needed for fishing in either salt or fresh water:

- *A rod and reel* - quite often the reel is purchased separately from the rod, and heavier rods should be used for salt water.

- *Fishing line* - 8 pound line is a good line for catching small- to medium- sized fish. 20 to 30 pound line is appropriate for larger fish.

- *Sinkers* - a fisherman should have a variety of lead weights to crimp onto fishing lines as needed.

- *Floats* - fishing floats of various sizes enable the fisherman to fish at various depths (the depth can be varied for any float, however differently-sized floats are used to catch specific types and sizes of fish). The ability to adjust the fishing depth can be critical to being successful when fishing without artificial lures.

- *Metal leader line* - A few 12 to 18 inch strands of metal 'leader line' is important when fishing for those fish with sharp teeth capable of cutting regular line (e.g. shark).

- *Fishing swivels* - swivels on the end of a fishing line provide some weight to a line (maybe avoiding the use of lead weights in some cases), and allow the fisherman to quickly switch between various lures, baits and hooks.

- *Fishing hooks* - a variety of fishing hooks of various sizes is important to enable the fisherman to fish for a wider variety of fish.

- *Fishing lures* - fishing lures may be needed to catch specific fish under various circumstances, or to allow the fisherman to fish when natural bait is not available.

- *Regular and needle-nosed pliers* - Needle-nosed pliers are very useful in cutting fishing line and crimping small lead weights onto fishing lines. Regular pliers are useful in removing hooks from the mouths of fish and for adding and removing larger lead fishing weights to and from fishing lines.

- *Stringers* - 'Stringers' are small lengths of narrow rope that typically have a stake attached to one end and a small round hoop attached to the other. The fisherman can loop the stringer through a fish's gills and out of its mouth such that the rope can be staked down to the bank with one or more fish being captive in the water while fishing continues.

NOTE: *One of the best all-around lures for catching fish in both fresh and salt water environments is the 'rooster tail'. The author has personally marveled at the effectiveness of this venerable lure, and seen it used to catch a surprising variety of fish in both fresh and salt water. It is recommended that the survivor/fisherman obtain several rooster tail lures in different sizes and colors. Artificial worms are another artificial lure that would be a good compliment to rooster tails (when one does not produce results, the other very well may).*

8.5. Foraging

Foraging is the process of searching for and exploiting sources of food.[489]. While hunting and fishing technically fit into this definition, for purposes of this section (because hunting and fishing receive their own dedicated treatment in this chapter) this discussion is limited to foraging for fruits, vegetables, insects and worms.

Foraging in an inhabited environment in the wake of a disaster should be considered to be a high-risk activity and should be avoided if at all possible. Simply pulling a fruit from the branch of a tree might be considered by the property owner to be a shooting offense. Such foraging almost inevitably involves trespassing, which once again can result in deadly consequences in a post-disaster situation.

Regardless of your location, **at best foraging should be considered as a means of augmenting your other sources of food**. Studies have indicated that about 1000 acres is required to provide sufficient foraging to sustain a single adult human.[491] This alone would make it impractical for most people in the modern world to depend solely on foraging to meet their total nutritional needs. However, while foraging may not be able to meet a big percentage of your need for bulk macro-nutrients (carbohydrates, proteins and fats), it may be a good source of vitamins and minerals that are also critical to life and health.

CAUTION: *Do not consider a plant to be safe to eat simply because you've seen an animal eating it. There are many plants and berries that are not poisonous to animals, but which are poisonous to humans.[491]*

There are some toxic plants that have a strong physical resemblance to plants that are edible. **NEVER** *consume any wild plant if you have any degree of uncertainty about its safety.*

The woods are home to numerous forms of vegetation that are toxic to humans. While some natural vegetation may be quickly lethal, others can cause severe diarrhea, which in a post-disaster scenario could just as easily prove to be deadly. When planning to forage you should either have excellent references of edible wild plants that include detailed pictures of each, or you should plan on harvesting only those wild foods that you are absolutely certain are safe. The following are some well-known and nutritious foods that are good candidates for foraging:

- *Raspberries* - Raspberries are most commonly found in temperate regions, however they have also been cultivated across the entire United States. They are most plentiful between June and October.

- *Blackberries* - Blackberries grow best in temperate climates. They have a reputation for being one of the easiest fruits to grow, although plant yield may diminish in warmer areas. They typically ripen between June and September and often be harvested twice per year.

- *Blueberries* - Blueberries are typically found only in the northeast due to the humid climate with cool summers, chilly winters and acidic soils. Newer varieties of blueberries now allow for cultivation in a wider range of climates and soils. Blueberries are ripest between June and August.

- *Wild Strawberries* - Wild strawberries grow in most regions but are most commonly found in the eastern half of the United States. Strawberries may be available as early as January and as late as November, although peak season usually lasts between April and June.

- *Wild Muscadine* - Muscadine are native to the southeastern United states but can be found as far west as Texas and Oklahoma and as far north as Delaware and Maryland. Muscadine ripen between September and October.

- *Wild Apples* - The crab apple is the only apple native to North America, however many other types of apples have been introduced and cultivated in the United States. Many varieties of apples require several weeks of near freezing temperatures in order for the tree to bear fruit, and are therefore most commonly found in the north, however some varieties may also be found in Florida and California. Apples are normally harvested from late August to mid November.

- *Wild Peaches* - California is home to the majority of the United States peach production, however peaches are also known to do well in Washington, Pennsylvania, New Jersey and much of the southeast. Peach season begins in the end of June and lasts through the beginning of September.

- *Wild Pears* - Most pears grown in the United States come from Washington, Oregon and California, however pear trees will grow in temperate regions. The fruit requires chilled storage in order to ripen. Pear season ranges from August to May depending on the variety of pear, with pears being most plentiful between October and January.

- *Wild Plums* - Wild plums can be found throughout all of the Midwest, the southern northeast and the northern southeast. They are in season starting in late May until mid October.

- *Wild Oranges* - Oranges grow best in tropical and sub-tropical regions, which make the southern states, Florida and California especially ideal locations for growing oranges. Orange trees may also be found farther north, however the fruit is very sensitive to cold weather and will be considerably less sweet in those climates. Different varieties of Oranges can be found year round, with Navel oranges available from December to April, and Valencia oranges ripening between April and January.

- *Wild Dandelions* - Dandelions grow in every state and province of the United States and Canada. They are best harvested in late Fall to early Spring. It is best to dig the roots out without breaking them to obtain maximum nutritional value from the plant. Dandelions should be harvested just as the bloom bud appears but before the flower blooms.

- *Wild Grapefruit* - Grapefruits grow mostly in Florida, however grapefruit trees also thrive in Texas, California and Arizona and may also occasionally be found in other tropical and subtropical climates. They can be found throughout the year, however the best tasting grapefruit usually ripens between November and June.

- *Wild Acorns* - Acorns are produced by Oak trees, which are found mostly in the eastern half of the United States and the Pacific coast. They are normally harvested in the Autumn months.

- *Wild Chestnuts* - Chestnut trees can be found across the United States and appear to be sufficiently adaptable to both the cold temperature of the northeast and the heat of California or Florida. Wild American Chestnut trees have largely been wiped out due to chestnut blight, however those that do exist can be found in the northeast, and the north-western corner of the American southeast. Chestnuts fall between September and mid-October.

- *Wild Beechnuts* - Beech trees grow in the eastern United States from Maine to the northern parts of Florida. Beechnuts ripen from the prickly burs that grow on the Beech tree in late Fall shortly after the first freeze, however they may also be picked slightly before ripening to avoid having to forage them from the forest floor.

- *Wild Hazelnuts* - Wild American Hazelnut trees are native to the American northeast, midwest, and northern parts of the southeast, however Oregon accounts for almost all of the United States commercial production of hazelnuts. Depending on the variety, they ripen between September and October.

- *Wild Almonds* - The majority of the US almond production comes from the California central valley region, as California is one of the only states with a climate that has sufficiently cool winters and hot enough summers for proper production of almonds. Almonds ripen near the end of summer. **(CAUTION: Most wild almond trees found outside of California produce bitter almonds which are poisonous even in small quantities.)**

- *Wild Cashew* - Cashews grow only in tropical frost-free climates. This restricts cashews in the United States to growing only in southern Florida, Hawaii and Puerto Rico. The nut comes from the cashew apple, which contains caustic oil that can cause blistering of the skin if not handled properly. Cashews are harvested in late Winter and early Spring.

- *Wild Coconut* - Coconuts require constant temperatures over 75°F, 70%+ humidity, high rainfall and lots of direct sunlight. This restricts their range to tropical areas. In the U.S. coconuts are rarely seen outside of south Florida, Hawaii, and other tropical island territories. Coconuts grow and ripen year round.

- *Wild Macadamia* - The Macadamia tree is native to Australia, however Macadamia trees also grow well in Hawaii, Florida and California. Macadamia nuts may be harvested beginning in late October and extending through January.

- *Wild Peanuts* - Peanuts, contrary to their name, are a legume and not an actual nut. They are found in the ground underneath the peanut plant. Peanuts require 120+ frost-free days with moderate rainfall and sandy soil. They are most commonly found in the United States in the southeast and are usually ready for harvest between September and October. Peanuts require several days to dry before being ready to eat.

- *Wild Pine* - Pine nuts come from only a small percentage of pine tree species, and are most typically found in the United States in the wilds of the southwest. The nut comes from the center of the pine cone, and requires a labor-intensive harvesting process that involves cracking the very hard shell around the nut (without crushing the nut itself). Pine nuts are usually ripe in early September through late October.

- *Wild Pistachio* - Pistachio trees are most common in the southwestern U.S. where the climate is arid and hot with mild winters. Pistachio nuts are ready to harvest between August and October.

- *Mint* - Wild Mint is known to grow across the entire United States except a very few southeastern states. Mint requires moist soil and a mix of sunlight and shade. It can be harvested as soon as it begins to flower in the Spring, and one location may be harvested up to two to three times per growing season.

8.5.1. Nuts - One of Nature's True Miracle Foods

Proteins, carbohydrates and fats are the three *macro-nutrients* that are essential to a sustainable human diet. While proteins and carbohydrates can often be stored at room temperature for many months, foods containing fats have a tendency go grow rancid much more quickly. So, it is imperative that the prepper have a plan in place for keeping healthy fats in the diet. Nuts and acorns can be found growing in the wild throughout the world, and they are a great source of vitamins, protein, carbohydrates, dietary fiber and healthy fats.[499] As such they are an ideal fit to augment the prepper's long term food needs. Many of the nuts common to a region are easily recognized by locals, making the locating and harvesting of nuts less challenging (and safer!) than many other naturally occurring foods.

You may find that foraged acorns have a difficult, bitter taste. If so this can be mitigated by extracting and mashing the edible center from the acorn and boiling it for 10 minutes, then discarding the water and boiling it again for 10 minutes in fresh water (this removes much of the naturally-occurring tannic acid that is the source of the bitter taste). If you are unable to boil the water you can place the mashed acorn centers into a clean cloth and submerge them in a flowing stream for 10 to 12 hours. Once the tannic acid has been washed out you can eat the flesh of the acorn raw, toast it, or even dry and pulverize it to make flour for bread.[490]

NOTE: *Regarding dietary fats, it should also be noted that both regular and crunchy peanut butter provide a good source of healthy dietary fats (as well as carbohydrates, protein, vitamins and fiber), and that commercial peanut butter often has a recommended shelf life of up to one year at room temperature (additives to the peanut butter such as salt and/or sodium extend the shelf life beyond that of most foods that contain fats). As a result it is highly recommended that significant quantities of peanut butter be incorporated into the prepper's food store as a means of possibly reducing or avoiding the need to forage.*

8.5.2. Guidelines for Selecting Berries

Edible berries provide a source of natural sugars for energy as well important vitamins and minerals. Like nuts, the benefits derived from berries can often justify the energy required to harvest them. Many berries are poisonous to humans, so care should be taken when gathering berries from the wild for human consumption.

Here are some guidelines to follow when foraging for edible berries:

- The great majority of berries that are colored white or yellow are poisonous to humans.

- Berries that grow in tiny clusters (like raspberries) are generally safe to eat.[492]

- Don't pick berries that are alongside any agricultural areas or other areas that may have been chemically treated.

- Don't trust the little sayings and rhymes that are often cited for identifying safe berries. Many of these sayings are flat wrong and can get you killed. (many contradict one another!)

- Only pick berries that you can recognize as being safe and edible, or which you can identify as being safe with the help of a field guide that includes good, color pictures.

- If for some reason it is absolutely a matter of life-or-death that you eat a berry that you are uncertain of, be careful not to eat its seeds. (It is the seeds of many poisonous berries that actually contain the poison, which is why some wildlife that is incapable of digesting the seeds can consume berries that are poisonous to humans).

- The red berries of the easily-recognized holly plant are poisonous to humans.

*Figure 8.7.: The Cattail Plant is Completely Edible
and is Found in Many Parts of the World.*

8.5.3. Foraging for Dandelions

The often-plentiful dandelion is completely edible from root to flower, and all parts in-between. The flowers have a sweetish taste, and the stems are a good source of vitamins and calcium.[492] The roots of dandelions can be dried and ground up to make a pleasing hot drink.[490] While the dandelion certainly does not offer a fully-balanced diet, it can just as certainly be made part of a balanced diet. As with all foraged plants, be certain that you select dandelions only from sources that have not been chemically treated.

8.5.4. The Highly-Edible Cattail

Figure 8.7 depicts the cattail plant, which is a slender plant that can can be found alongside wetlands in many parts of the world.[500] Many parts of the cattail are edible, including the roots, the lower shoots and the prominent, sausage-shaped *'spikes'*. Archaeological evidence suggests that humans have used the cattail as a source of food for as long as 30,000 years. Cattails have a protein content that is similar to that of rice. The pollen from the cattail's flower can be used as flour or to thicken stews.

Cattails are most often harvested during late Autumn and Early Spring. They reproduce prolifically in any environment where they are established, so over-harvest should not be a major concern. Most often their complete root system is dug up and boiled to prepare it for eating.

Cattails should not be harvested from any wetland that has been polluted by lead or pesticides, as these substances tend to accumulate in the cattail's root system.

8.5.5. Beware Mushrooms!

Many mushrooms found in the wild are extremely toxic and can be lethal if ingested by humans. In some cases poisonous mushrooms bear a close resemblance to mushrooms that are safe to eat. A good rule-of-thumb is to only trust mushrooms from the wild if collected and approved by someone who did this for a living before the disaster. **Otherwise simply do not forage for mushrooms!**

8.5.6. Insects, Earthworms and Grubs as Emergency Food Sources

Insects and worms are eaten in many parts of the world today, and can be an excellent source of protein and other nutrition. It has been scientifically proven that it is more cost effective to grow a pound of protein from insects than it is to grow a pound of beef from a cow. Crickets, grasshoppers and cicadas provide a high quality protein that also has good fat and carbohydrate content, and is rich in vitamins and minerals.[497]. When foraging for and eating insects:[497]

- Remove the legs, wings and other appendages and roast (or boil) them to kill any bacteria or parasites they may contain (roasting also allows to protein to be more readily absorbed by the human body).

- When eating grasshoppers, twist the head and pull it off (which will also remove the internal organs).

- Do not forage for brightly colored or slow-moving insects, or insects with *'fuzzy'* bodies, as they are probably poisonous.

- Do not forage for flies, mosquitoes, ticks or any insects that emit a strong odor.

- Keep in mind that all aquatic insects are edible, and tend to be more palatable to humans than non-aquatic insects.

Earthworms and grubs (the larval form of beetles) are also a good source of protein. Like crickets and grasshoppers earthworms are better roasted over a fire before being eaten. Before roasting an earthworm it should be pulled 2 or 3 times between pinched fingers to cause any dirt and grit within the worm to be expelled. An earthworm or grub can be roasted by simply hanging it from a sharpened stick over a fire. Grubs can be found under stones and rotten logs, as well as in sod.[498]

8.5.7. Other Foraging Tips

Other guidelines when foraging for food include:

- When in doubt, boil it out! - Often boiling foods from the wild can remove toxins and improve taste (the acorn mentioned previously is a good example).

- A bitter taste is often an indicator that an unknown plant is poisonous.

- Not all poisonous plants have a disagreeable taste.[491]

- Some plants that are poisonous to humans are not poisonous to birds and other animals.[491]

- Never collect any food from the wild that you are not certain is safe for human consumption.

- Add one or more illustrated foraging field guides to your survival library so that you have the widest range of foraging options.

- When foraging on property that is not yours always obtain the owner's permission and offer them some compensation, even if it is only some portion of what you collect.

- Always wash all foraged foods with clean water as the first step of preparing them.

- Many varieties of clover are safe for human consumption and provide a source of protein and minerals, however you should confirm the safety of any varieties that you find before collecting. Clover roots provide more calories than the leaves, and are best boiled before being eaten.[492]

- The leaves of violets can be eaten raw or cooked.[490]

- Rose hips are a good Winter source of vitamin C, and tea can be made from rose petals.[490]

- Most varieties of water lilies are edible and available for harvest year-round where they can be found.

- Before foraging learn to identify poison ivy, poison oak and poison sumac so that you can avoid them.[491]

8.6. In Summary

If you are foraging for food sources from nature keep in mind the following:

- Some of the foods available from nature may require you to expend more calories to obtain them than you derive from eating them.

- While some plants are edible and offer nutritional value, your body may have an adverse reaction to those plants if they are new to your system. Be very careful when consuming foods with which you have had no previous experience, and when you do consume a type of plant for the first time consume it very gradually to assess your body's reaction to it.

- **Never** consume any native vegetation that you are not certain is safe for human consumption.

To the extent that you do plan deriving some sustenance from nature here are some key considerations:

- For hunting small game (e.g. squirrels and rabbits), a pellet gun might make more sense than a hunting rifle. A pellet gun produces much less sound, which will potentially draw less unwanted attention. It is also lighter weight and the ammunition for it is far less costly than that for a rifle.

- Traps might be preferable to guns. Rather than spending hours out hunting why not let the game come to you (or, more accurately, to your traps)? That time can then be spent doing other things. In addition to saving you time, traps are silent and several traps can be purchased for the price of a single gun.

- If you are going to hunt larger game, be sure you are trained and equipped to preserve the meat until needed. This includes smoking, curing and/or dehydrating meats (see chapter 5).

As a survival hunter it is as important to conserve game as it is to hunt it. If excess hunting decimates the animal population then you may very well lose a resource that you'll need to survive in the future. You should also take whatever measures are prudent to protect your hunting areas from poachers. These measures might include posting 'No Trespassing' signs around the perimeter of the property (and especially alongside roads and gates that are normal access points to the property).

When hunting on property that is not yours you should always first obtain the permission of the property-owner (otherwise you may have the unfortunate misfortune of learning what measures they have taken to secure their property!). When hunting on property owned by others you might also consider offering to provide them a portion of your kill in exchange for the privilege of hunting on the property.

Proper hunting, even under the most difficult of post-disaster circumstances, is and always should be considered to be a "give-and-take" activity.

9. Hygiene and Sanitation

*"Cleanliness becomes more important when
godliness is unlikely."*

P. J. O'Rourke

We are all under constant attack by potentially-deadly microscopic organisms. Over the centuries our civilization has learned to deal effectively with these threats to the extent that we often take our safety for granted.

In the aftermath of a major disaster, sanitation infrastructure and basic services may very well be disrupted such that these threats re-emerge. A good example is the deadly outbreak of cholera that decimated *Haiti* in the aftermath of the 2010 earthquake. (This took place even with the almost immediate presence of relief agencies and military organizations from around the world!) Before the outbreak had been contained the bodies of thousands of victims were being bulldozed into unmarked pits.

The purpose of this chapter is to provide information to enable the survivor to effectively cope with these threats through basic sanitary practices and other measures.

STRAIGHT THINKING: *Proper management of the disposal of human and animal waste will prevent the great majority of life-threatening diseases that can emerge in the aftermath of a major disaster.*

9.1. Inherently Unsafe/Unsanitary Environments

High-rise apartments and condominiums are going to become irredeemably unsanitary in the event of a loss of power and other utilities. It is important to understand the danger in such environments and to make plans to not be exposed to them when they become uninhabitable.

The problem with stacked living quarters is that, when utilities are disrupted, it becomes virtually impossible for the residents on higher floors to obtain fresh water. Even if some residents do manage to obtain and use water, many of their neighbors will not. The result is that sewage builds up not just in living quarters (bad enough) but in the walls and ceilings surrounding each living space. The entire building becomes a breeding ground for disease and pestilence.

> **NOTE:** *Of course high-rise living spaces will not degenerate instantly, and many such buildings may have backup power systems that keep things running until generator fuel is depleted, however inhabitants should be evacuated from such dwellings as soon as possible.*

It is easy to imagine high-rise dwellings becoming so very contaminated in the aftermath of a major disaster that it eventually becomes necessary to simply demolish them.

9.2. Understanding The Threats - Diseases Caused by Poor Sanitation (and Their Treatment)

9.2.1. Diarrhea

Diarrhea is technically defined as the occurrence of three or more loose or liquid bowel movements per day.[82] The condition is better thought of as a symptom than as a disease, however it is the symptom that can become life-threatening (through dehydration and electrolyte imbalance) if not properly treated. Causes of diarrhea include both bacterial and viral infections, as well as other factors.

Treatment for diarrhea includes both oral rehydration therapy *('ORT')* (see page 226 for instructions on administering ORT) as well as intravenous rehydration (which should only be administered by medical professionals).

In addition to treating the diarrhea itself it is important to diagnose and treat the underlying disease. Depending on the nature of that disease the treatment could range from simple bed rest to a course of orally- and intravenously- administered antibiotics.

9.2.2. Jaundice

> **NOTE:** *Jaundice is not uncommon in babies that are less that one week old, and in this case is not indicative of a life-threatening condition. In the case of babies, jaundice simply indicates that blood cells are breaking down and regenerating at a level higher than the baby's liver is prepared to handle. Babies with this condition are generally treated with fluids, or in extreme cases with phototherapy (exposure to light).[83]*

In adults jaundice is caused by blockage of bile ducts or liver damage, and may result from gallstones, hepatitis, liver cancer, pancreatic cancer or other serious conditions. Even as a symptom, jaundice can have serious and fatal consequences for adults, including *blood poisoning* (*sepsis*), *cirrhosis*, *pancreatitis* and liver and kidney failure - **ALL LIFE-THREATENING!**.

The treatment for jaundice is to treat the underlying condition. Given the nature of the conditions that cause jaundice in adults, immediate attention from a doctor is warranted whenever it is observed.

9.2.3. Cholera

Cholera is an infection in the small intestines that is caused by the *Vibrio cholerae bacteria*; one of the few bacteria that can survive the high-acid environment in the human stomach. Once ingested the bacteria finds its way into the small intestine, where it establishes itself and begins manufacturing the toxins that result in life-threatening dehydration. While the cholera-causing bacteria can be found living freely in nature, cholera is almost always caused by fecal contamination of food and water due to poor sanitation.

The death rate for promptly and properly treated cholera victim is less than 1%, however the mortality rate is over 50% for untreated cases.[72]

The cholera bacteria, once established in the small intestines, causes water to be drawn from the victim's body and excreted as diarrhea. This results in life-threatening dehydration and electrolyte imbalance. The excreted fluids themselves contain the bacteria and spread the disease as they come into human contact.

SYMPTOMS

The primary symptoms of Cholera are extreme, watery *diarrhea* and vomiting. (Often the diarrhea is painless.)[72]

TREATMENT

The primary treatment for cholera is oral rehydration therapy.

Additionally, a one- to three- day course of antibiotics (typically Doxycycline, cotrimoxazole, erythromycin, tetracycline, chloramphenicol, or furazolidone) is administered to reduce the severity of the symptoms.[72]

TRANSMISSION

Cholera is primarily caused by the ingestion of food or water that is contaminated by the diarrhea of an infected person. Once an outbreak occurs it may also be transmitted by coming into contact with materials (e.g. clothing and bedding) that have trace amounts of diarrhea residue from the victim.

PREVENTION

All clothing and other materials (e.g. bedding) that come into contact with a cholera victim should be sterilized by washing in hot water (preferably with chlorine bleach). Any part of a person's body that has come into contact with any material that has been exposed to the body (or bodily fluids) of a cholera victim should be thoroughly cleaned with chlorinated water (or other antimicrobial agents).

All sewage from cholera victims should be treated with chlorine to prevent the disease from entering the water supply. All water consumed in an area experiencing a cholera outbreak should be sterilized by boiling or through the addition of chemicals such as appropriate quantities of chlorine bleach.

Safe and effective vaccines for cholera are available. Generally these vaccines are effective for one to three years.

9.2.4. Typhoid

Typhoid (also known as *typhoid fever*) is a bacterial infection *(Salmonella enterica)* of the intestinal tract (and sometimes the bloodstream) that is spread through ingestion of food or water that has been contaminated with the bodily fluids of infected people. In some cases the disease may spread through human contact with infected people who exhibit no symptoms.

Typhoid cases progress through four distinct phases, each generally lasting about one week:

- *PHASE 1* - A slowly rising fever with headache, malaise and the development of a cough, with possible abdominal pain and episodes of nosebleed.

- *PHASE 2* - The victim is prostrate with a fever up to 104°(F). They may become delirious and experience constipation or diarrhea (with a 'green pea soup' appearance). The spleen and liver may be enlarged and tender, and the lower abdomen may be distended and painful in the lower right quadrant.

- *PHASE 3* - The victim experiences extreme delirium and may grasp at non-existent objects. Intestinal bleeding and sepsis may occur. Fever may actually reduce, although this does not signal any improvement in the victim's condition. These symptoms are life-threatening.

- *PHASE 4* - Coma and death.

CAUTION: *About 5% of people can be* carriers *of typhoid without ever exhibiting symptoms).[74]* **This is significant because it means that typhoid carriers can spread the disease despite quarantine protections.**

With timely antibiotic treatment the fatality rate from typhoid is generally less than 1%. Typhoid is fatal in 10%-50% of untreated cases, depending on environmental factors.

NOTE: *One frequent cause of typhoid outbreaks is flooding that causes the fluids in sewer systems to contaminate food or drinking water sources.* **BEWARE OF FLOODING SITUATIONS!**

SYMPTOMS

The symptoms of typhoid include fever that grows progressively over two to four weeks, profuse sweating, flu-like stomach distress and occasionally a rash that consists of flat, rose-colored splotches.[73] Other symptoms include headache and constipation. Typhoid may also result in enlargement of the liver and/or spleen.[74]

TREATMENT

The victim should be administered with antibiotics (most commonly - in order of preference - Ceftriaxone, Ciprofloxacin, Ampicillin, Chloramphenicol, Trimethoprim-sulfamethoxazole and Amoxicillin) and **receive oral rehydration therapy.**[73]

TRANSMISSION

Typhoid fever results when a bacteria *Salmonella Typhi* (which normally exists only in the intestinal tract of humans) is ingested by a person and subsequently enters the blood stream.[75] It is often spread when untreated sewage comes into contact with food or water or when food handlers or preparers do not adequately wash their hands before handling food. It is not uncommon for typhoid to be spread during floods when untreated sewage contaminates a drinking water supply.

Occasionally individuals may recover from typhoid and yet remain carriers. In such cases they may continue to spread the disease (generally by handling foods without proper hand washing in advance) even though they feel and appear perfectly healthy.[76]

PREVENTION

Typhoid can be avoided by managing food and drinking water supplies in a sanitary fashion and through good hand-washing discipline in the bathroom as well as by those who are involved in food- and water- handling and preparation activities.

In non-industrialized countries it is advisable to avoid typhoid by drinking only bottled water, by avoiding the eating of fresh fruits and by eating only foods that have been thoroughly cooked.

9.2.5. E. coli

E. coli is a bacteria commonly found in the lower intestines of warm-blooded animals as well as on some vegetables. Some strains of this bacteria can cause serious food poisoning in humans.[79]

> **NOTE:** *E. coli poisoning is serious and life-threatening. A doctor and modern diagnostic equipment is necessary to determine the exact source and nature of the disease, as well as to successfully treat it. The most important thing that a non-doctor can do is to EXERCISE PREVENTION. This means adopting very strong hand-washing discipline in the bathroom, handling meat at all times (from butchering to cooking) with due care, not under-cooking meat and peeling and washing fruits and vegetables well during food preparation.[81]*

SYMPTOMS

E. coli can cause a variety of diseases and symptoms:[79]

- *Stomach flu* - fever and extreme abdominal pain.

- *Urinary tract infection* - symptoms include feeling the need to urinate frequently, cloudy urination and pain during urination.

- *Meningitis* - symptoms include headache, fever, confusion, fever, vomiting and extreme sensitivity to light and sound.

- *Hemolytic-uremic syndrome* - mainly affects children - starts with diarrhea and can progress to kidney failure and death. The use of certain antibiotics can actually make this disease worse.

- *Inflammation of the abdominal cavity* - Extreme abdominal pain that is almost always fatal if left untreated. This often requires both antibiotics and surgery.

- *Bloody diarrhea, often with no fever*

- *Sepsis* - (blood poisoning) Symptoms include elevated heart and respiratory rate, abnormal white blood cell count and either elevated or lowered body temperature. This condition requires immediate hospitalization and treatment with intravenous fluids and appropriate antibiotics.

- *Pneumonia* - An inflammation of the lungs that causes cough, chest pain, fever and difficulty breathing. Because this is a bacterial pneumonia it is generally treated with antibiotics (which can vary from one region of the world to another).

TREATMENT

Proper treatment of E. coli poisoning should be determined by a medical doctor. In a disaster situation in which E. coli poisoning is suspected and a doctor or hospital is not available the best one can do is to treat the symptoms and give the best possible care to the sick. If a particular antibiotic treatment seems to worsen the condition then, given the fact that some antibiotics can worsen E. coli poisoning, the treatment should either be modified or terminated entirely.

TRANSMISSION

As the E. coli bacteria normally exists in the lower intestines of warm-blooded organisms (including humans), transmission takes place when fecal material containing the bacteria contaminates a food or drinking water supply. This can result from non-hygienic food handling practices, the inadvertent exposure of food to livestock manure or the irrigation of food from a water supply that has been contaminated with fecal material.[80]

PREVENTION

Proper hand-washing before leaving the bathroom (or other such facilities), coupled with handling, washing and cooking food properly, can greatly reduce the probability of E. coli poisoning.[81] Other important preventive measures include:

- The wearing of gloves by anyone handling foods.

- Cooking foods thoroughly.

- Keeping livestock physically separate from food supplies.

- Adhering to sanitary procedures when butchering livestock for food.

9.2.6. Dysentery

Dysentery is an irritation of the intestines that results in lose diarrhea that displays some blood.[349] Due to the affects of accompanying severe dehydration, dysentery can be life-threatening and should receive immediate attention.

The irritation of the intestinal walls is most often caused by bacterial infection. Other less common sources of such irritation include viral and parasitic infections, as well as exposure to chemical agents.

SYMPTOMS

Symptoms of dysentery include watery diarrhea containing blood, abdominal pain and/or bloating, nausea and flatulence. Severe cases can also lead to elevated heart rate, loss of full consciousness, high fever and dizziness.[350]

TREATMENT

Oral rehydration therapy (ORT) should be administered to anyone displaying a clear indication of dysentery. Depending on the specific cause a round of antibiotic and/or antiparsitic drugs would normally be prescribed by a physician to treat the root cause.

TRANSMISSION

Dysentery is caused by ingesting food and drink, or swimming in water, that has been contaminated with the various bacteria, parasites and/or irritating chemical substances.

PREVENTION

Dysentery may be avoided by adhering to the following practices:

- Handling and preparing food in accordance with best sanitation practices.

- Not consuming foods or liquids from unknown or untrusted sources.

- Not swimming in water that has not be tested for the presence of harmful bacteria or parasitic organisms.

9.2.7. Gastroenteritis

Gastroenteritis, also known as *'stomach flu'*, *'gastric flu'* or simply *'gastro'*, is an inflammation of the stomach and intestines due to viral, bacterial or parasitic infection.[77][78] The common label *'stomach flu'* that has been applied to gastroenteritis is really a misnomer as, unlike influenza, gastroenteritis involves the stomach and digestive tract and is not necessarily always attributable to a viral infection (although most often gastroenteritis is caused by a virus).

SYMPTOMS

Symptoms of gastroenteritis include diarrhea, nausea, vomiting and stomach cramps.

TREATMENT

As with all cases involving diarrhea, oral rehydration therapy (ORT) should be administered in an effort to address the danger of dehydration. A victim may also be administered medications that reduce nausea and vomiting. However, antibiotics and anti-parasitical medicines are generally only administered if the source is identified as being bacterial or parasitic in nature (if the disease lasts more than one or two days then a bacterial infection is probable).

TRANSMISSION

Due to the wide ranges of causes of gastroenteritis, it may be transmitted in a variety of ways. Most often, however, it is transmitted, directly or indirectly, through coming into physical contact with an infected individual or something that has been touched by an infected individual.

PREVENTION

Good hand washing habits, particularly in the bathroom, can do much to prevent the spread of gastroenteritis.

9.2.8. MRSA Infection

Methicillin-resistant Staphylococcus aureus ("MRSA") is a strain of staph bacteria that is resistant to many common antibiotics. MRSA can live for extended periods on many surfaces, and generally results in infections of the skin that manifest themselves as rashes and deep, puss-filled boils. It can also infect wounds or the sites of surgical incisions. MRSA has emerged as an increasingly common threat due to the use of antibiotics.[85]

SYMPTOMS

There are no direct symptoms that are a clear indication of a MRSA infection. Such an infection can only be accurately confirmed through microscopic analysis of a victim's bodily fluids in a medical laboratory. However, if a skin/wound infection does not respond as expected to antibiotic treatments then a physician may presume a MRSA infection and treat accordingly. While there are no symptoms that are clear indicators of a MRSA infection, such infections almost always manifest as skin/wound infections and involve rashes, infected wounds and boils on the skin.[85]

TREATMENT

Treatment for MRSA consists of the administration of special antibiotics to which it has not yet developed a resistance. Many such antibiotics are rare and must be administered intravenously by a qualified medical professional. There is very little literature, either pro or con, regarding the effectiveness of non-prescription antibacterial treatments for MRSA, however in the absence of professional medical care such treatments might be considered (especially given the fact that the infection might actually not be a MRSA infection).

If one of the symptoms accompanying an infection is the occurrence of puss-filled boils on the skin, then care must be taken that the draining of the puss is done properly and hygienically such that other tissue *(theirs OR yours!)* does not become infected by coming into contact with it. Be sure that boils are drained carefully and positioned such that gravity draws the puss downward and away from the body. Once the boil is drained it should be thoroughly cleaned and sanitized (preferably with alcohol or, as a second choice, hydrogen peroxide).

TRANSMISSION

MRSA infections are transmitted when compromised skin comes into physical contact with a surface that contains MRSA bacteria. *'Compromised skin'* includes any wound, cut or skin abrasion.

PREVENTION

The best way to prevent MRSA infections is to sanitize surfaces with which individuals susceptible to skin infections may come into physical contact (see section 9.4.2 about sanitizing surfaces). Alcohol has been shown to be a good sanitizing agent in such cases, with hydrogen peroxide being a somewhat less effective agent.[86] Chlorine bleach, possibly mixed in a diluted solution with white vinegar (see section 9.4.2) can also be an excellent disinfecting agent.[86]

9.2.9. Influenza

Influenza (commonly known as *'the flu'*) is a severe, sudden-onset disease that affects mammals and birds. It is caused by RNA viruses of the family *Orthomyxoviridae*, and is most often transmitted through viruses made airbourne by coughs and sneezes. The flu is responsible for the death of 250,000 to 500,000 people each year, and many times that number during times of pandemic.[143]

The flu most often spreads though populations during identifiable flu *seasons*. Flu season is any time of year when people are less exposed to the sun; for example during the winter time when it is cloudy and people are more indoors, or in the rainy seasons in certain times of year. It has been speculated that the reduced creation of Vitamin D due to reduced sun exposure is the reason for the increases in numbers of flu cases during these times.

SYMPTOMS

Symptoms of the flu include muscle pains, fever, chills, sore throat, headache and weakness (and occasionally nausea and vomiting). A severe case of the flu can lead to the development of life-threatening pneumonia. [143]

TREATMENT

Medications are largely ineffective for treating the root cause of the disease, and victims should rest and consume plenty of liquids during the course of the illness. A healthy individual's own immune system should be sufficient to recover fully from the disease in seven to fourteen days. The victim may be given medicines such as *acetaminophen* to treat the more painful symptoms.

> **CAUTION:** *Children and teenagers suspected of having the flu (particularly those exhibiting fever) should avoid taking aspirin while sick. Otherwise they run the risk of developing* Reye's syndrome, *a potentially lethal disease of the liver.*

TRANSMISSION

The flu virus is commonly spread through the air by the coughs and sneezes of infected individuals. However, it may also be spread when an individual comes into contact with a surface on which the virus has been deposited.

PREVENTION

In the developed world the most common measure taken to prevent the flu is the taking of flu inoculations. However, there are other basic practices that can greatly reduce an individual's probability of succumbing to the flu. These measures consist of:

- *Avoiding coming into close proximity of those who are infected with the flu.*

- *Wearing a medical face mask when in the proximity of those infected with the flu.*

- *Taking Vitamin D regularly during the flu season.*

9.2.10. Key Takeaways on Sanitation and Disease

While this section has shown that there are a number of diseases that can result from poor sanitation, it has also shown that there is great commonality among both the sources and treatments for these diseases. As a result, the following common-sense practices should help greatly to protect you from these serious threats to life and health:

- Keep human and animal sewage well away from food and water supplies.

- Administer ORT for diarrhea to buy time for the patient to recover (see section 10.1.11).

- **Always** seek treatment from a qualified physician whenever possible.

- Wash hands before leaving the restroom, before handling or preparing food and after coming into direct or indirect contact with someone who is ill.

- Avoid uncooked foods from sources that are not completely trusted.

- Sanitize anything that comes into contact with a person having uncontrolled diarrhea.

- Only consume water that is considered to be 'purified'.

- Consider wearing a face mask if near someone suspected of having the flu.

- Get plenty of rest and eat as balanced a diet as possible in order to have a healthy immune system.

9.3. Sanitation Infrastructure

History has demonstrated repeatedly that deadly disease quickly follows in the wake of disaster. This section describes infrastructure the prepper can put into place to meet these vital needs.

In the developed world normal sanitation infrastructure and services are so pervasive that it becomes very easy to overlook or de-emphasize the importance of having backup sanitation measures ready for the day that the normal systems break down. A loss of electricity due to electro-magnetic pulse (EMP) could disable the pumps that keep sewage moving through the system, or disable the electro-mechanical systems that process sewage. A breakdown in the transportation system could disrupt the flow of chemicals needed to treat sewage. Floods could cause sewage waters to merge with drinking water. These are just some of the events that could quickly result in the spread of life-threatening diseases throughout a group or community.

9.3.1. Compost Heaps for Treating Human Waste

It is possible to treat human waste through composting. Not only does composting reduce the volume of the waste by almost a factor of ten, but the resulting waste is suitable for use as a fertilizer.

There are special considerations associated with composting human waste that cause this to be an almost unworkable option in the wake of a major disaster. Unlike compost heaps used to recycle organic refuse, composting systems for human waste require special ventilation and aeration (usually accomplished through mechanical stirring). Both of these require power from some external source - typically electrical power. Hence, in a scenario in which electrical power is disrupted, composting systems for human waste become unusable.

Composting is an example of a 'green' technology that is not particularly applicable to a major disaster scenario.

9.3.2. Latrines

Latrines have been used to dispose of human waste throughout history. A latrine is simply a small structure that facilitates the depositing of human waste into an earthen hole or some other receptacle. When deposited into an earthen hole the waste is often covered with a thin layer of lime and/or dirt. When deposited into a receptacle it must be periodically emptied and the contents transported to some other location for proper disposal.

It is typical that, after an earthen hole latrine is used, a handful of lime power is sprinkled over the waste. This has the effect of altering the pH of the waste such that harmful bacteria are killed, while at the same time greatly reducing emitted odors. Anyone contemplating the use of an earthen latrine in the wake of a disaster should stockpile dried lime powder for this purpose. If storage space permits it might be advisable to store a 50-lb bag of lime for each member of the group.

Latrines may be mobile or stationary. Mobile latrines offer the advantage that the earthen holes that receive the sewage can be smaller, and the sewage can be completely covered over more frequently. Such a mobile latrine may take the form of a simple outhouse that can periodically be moved a few feet.

Latrines should be located downhill from and at least 65 feet away from any dwelling or water source. While latrines should not be near residential structures, for security purposes they should still be easily visible and close enough to defend in the event of a security incident.

9.3.3. Septic Tanks

Simply stated, *septic tanks* are underground tanks that are designed to receive and process human waste into byproducts that can be safely returned to the environment. In a true disaster scenario during which municipal sewage services are disrupted, a residence with a septic tank will be of immeasurable value. Not only does the septic tank provide the safety and convenience of an indoor toilet but, in the absence of a functioning public sewage system, it is also much more hygienic than any alternatives.

Most septics tanks consist of buried tanks to which human waste is routed through one or more pipes. Once in the tank the sewage naturally breaks into three layers - a lower layer of sludge that will be decomposed into its chemical constituents through a bacterial *anaerobic digestive* process, a large central layer of clear fluid and an upper layer of scum that floats on the surface.

Many modern septic tanks contain two such chambers, with holes that allow the central layer of liquid from the first chamber to enter the second to provide a second stage of processing.

A network of piping feeds the separated liquid waste from the septic tank to the *leach field* (also known as the *drain field* or *seepage field*), where it is dispersed into the environment for final filtration by the soil before being returned to the water table. In some cases the processed waste from the septic tank may be routed to a holding pond or to peat moss beds.

Septic tanks are sized to process the waste for a specific number of residents. Problems can arise as the number of individuals making use of the system increases. Solid waste material may accumulate to the point that no more waste can enter the system and sewage backs up. If a septic tank becomes subject to significantly increased use then it it advisable that the tank be checked periodically by a trained professional to determine that sludge is not accumulating excessively.

In addition to tanks and piping, some septic tanks may utilize pumps to move waste materials between stages (particularly when some of the flow is uphill) and aeration units to oxygenate the processed waste before returning it to the environment.

Every few years septic tanks must be pumped to remove accumulated processed solid materials.

9.4. Best Sanitation Practices

9.4.1. Washing Hands with Soap and Water

Thorough hand-washing with soap and water, particularly after expelling solid or liquid waste or before handling food, is critical to preventing some very nasty, life-threatening diseases.

Normal soap does not kill microbes; it simply removes them from the skin and allows them to be rinsed away (which is **hugely** important!). Antibacterial or antimicrobial soap, however, not only removes the microbes, but kills most of them as well. [352]

The rule of thumb should be that anyone providing medical care or involved in any sort of food preparation should prefer to wash their hands with antibacterial/antimicrobial soap, while others should wash thoroughly with regular soap.

All members within a group or household should receive thorough instruction on hand-washing techniques. Anyone washing their hands should be carefully making sure that the cleaning is complete and thorough. Once lathered, hands should be rubbed together rigorously for best cleansing. Additionally, the hands should be washed all the way to the wrists (and maybe a little beyond that). In short, unlike during normal times, the process of hand-washing should not be taken for granted and everyone should receive training that covers proper hand washing techniques.

NOTE: *In a disaster scenario, when washing your hands, try to imagine yourself being a surgeon "scrubbing up" before surgery.* **Thorough hand-washing can save lives!**

There are very good reasons not to use antibacterial/antimicrobial soap in all situations. Over-use of such soaps can give rise to the growth of microbes that are antibiotic-resistant. It is best to conserve such soaps for the situations when it is most critically needed (for example for use by those preparing food or providing medical services).

9.4.2. Sanitizing Surfaces

Many of the tools and substances associated with disaster preparedness (as well as with regular day-to-day life) carry with them an element of risk that is outside most peoples' normal realm of experience. Medications can be abused, the acid in a car battery can destroy human tissue and certainly guns can inflict injury. However, **all of these items and substances can also save lives if used in the proper way.**

The combination of bleach and white vinegar is another example of a substance that can be greatly beneficial **if used properly**, but which can cause great harm if misused.

CAUTION: If you are not prepared to take the information being shared here with deadly seriousness then please skip the remainder of this section and move on to the next. Also be aware that the information provided here is commonly available online.

Mixing any type of vinegar and bleach produces chlorine gas as a by-product. During World War I this gas was known as *'mustard gas'*, and it killed thousands of soldiers. If you mix these two substances together in an inappropriate way (regardless of being indoors or outdoors) somebody is either going to die or spend the next few years wishing they were dead! Mustard gas destroys mucous membranes, including the lining of the lungs, as well as the linings of the nostrils and eyes. **Even if you hold your breath chlorine gas can do you grievous harm.**

Given these serious cautions you may be wondering what possible benefits the combination of bleach and white vinegar may have to offer. The benefit is that, when these substances are **properly diluted in water and combined**, the disinfecting strength of bleach is increased by a factor of 80 to 200![141] The resulting disinfectant has been shown to disinfect non-porous, non-metallic surfaces of both anthrax spores and the dreaded MRSA bacteria. Even the US Environmental Protection Agency has prescribed the use of this mixture for the killing of anthrax spores.[140]

Please note that unless you have the most critical needs for sanitation you should not consider disinfecting with a bleach and white vinegar solution. Examples of exceptions might include cases of suspected anthrax contamination or sanitizing a surface in preparation for *field surgery*.

The steps and considerations for mixing this disinfectant are:

- Wear gloves and protective clothing when making, handling or using this mixture.

- Be sure to use a relatively new bottle of bleach such that the bleach is at or near full strength.

- Create the mixture in a well-ventilated area and, at any point in the process, if you feel any burning of the eyes, lips, tongue, throat or lungs, cease all work and evacuate the area immediately (leaving as many doors and windows open as possible without delaying more than a very few seconds).

- Combine one cup of bleach with one gallon of water.[141]

- Add one cup of white vinegar to the bleach-and-water mixture.[141]

- Pour some or all of this mixture into a spray-mist bottle to spray on surfaces to be sanitized (be sure to mark all containers that come into contact with this mixture as being hazardous).

- Never allow the disinfecting mixture to get any closer to your face than necessary.

- Only disinfect a non-porous, non-metallic surface (bleach compounds can have reactions with metal that can produce toxic substances[142]).

- Clean the surface to be disinfected with regular soap and water.

- To completely disinfect, spray the surface with the disinfecting solution such that it stays wet for 20 minutes (this may require multiple applications).[141]

- When the surface dries it can be considered to be disinfected.

- Dispose of the disinfectant solution within 24 hours.

CAUTION: *Never dispose of any disinfectant solution into a septic system, as this will almost certainly kill the good bacteria within that system that are critical to its internal waste decomposition processes.*

9.5. Use of Face Masks

Face masks masks should be viewed as just one layer of the prepper's fortifications against infectious disease and other airbourne threats. They do not offer complete, guaranteed protection, but rather serve as barriers against some percentage of airbourne particulate threats.

NOTE: *Face masks are mainly designed to protect against viruses and other threats that become airbourne when an infected individual sneezes or coughs. It should also be kept in mind that these same particles may come to rest on surfaces, where they may still be passed to others when they come into physical contact with those surfaces. It is important not to develop a false sense of security from the use of face masks.*

The most common face mask employed for protection in infectious environments is the *N95 mask*, which is produced by numerous manufacturers and available from many sources (a search on *'N95'* on *amazon.com* should quickly locate several vendors). This mask derives it's name from the fact that it has been designed and tested to block the passage of 95% of airbourne particulate threats.

An *N100 mask* is also available which is designed and tested to block greater than 99.9% of all particles.

Normally, N95 and N100 face masks should only be worn once and discarded, as their effectiveness becomes degraded as they are exposed to the moisture of human respiration. Washing and sanitizing these masks only serves to further degrade their effectiveness. In a disaster situation in which resources are highly limited, however, it might be beneficial to store used masks in a box and label them with regard to number of uses (maybe just mark them once after each use). Degraded protection must certainly be better than no protection at all.

NOTE: *Face masks, because they do not form an airtight seal with the face, still provide plenty of opportunity for the transmission of viruses and other infectious agents. The use of face masks is simply a part of what should be a series of reasonable safeguards.*

9.6. Use of Gas Masks

The first step one should take in purchasing gas masks is to define the scenarios for which one anticipates the need. Are you making the purchase in case of some sort of biological warfare, as an isolation device in case of infectious disease, or to be able to function in an environment filled with smoke or tear gas?

While gas masks make a lot of sense for military personnel in case of a biological attack they probably make much less sense for civilian use during such an attack. The reason is because a civilian will almost certainly have contracted the disease before he or she has information that would cause them to put on the mask. Also, considering that the effective lifetime of gas mask filters is 4 to 8 hours, it is not really possible to wear them pro-actively.

One could make the case for having gas masks to deal with smoke or tear gas; but the advantages offered by gas masks in that scenario may be outweighed by the tactical disadvantages.

However the gas mask, if worn properly, does provide an airtight seal with the face and can be very effective at protecting the wearer from the transmission of infectious diseases (particularly *the flu*). So, a reasonable case could be made for the acquisition of a gas mask for dealing with infectious diseases. In such cases one might also consider purchasing a single mask for the care-provider rather than a mask for everyone in the household.

CAUTION: *Excess facial hair may prevent a gas mask from forming an airtight seal, thereby limiting its effectiveness or even rendering it completely useless.*

When acquiring a mask you should exercise extreme care to select one that will truly offer the protection that you expect. Many gas masks and filters being sold are actually 1970's-vintage masks that are no longer reliable. Some old gas masks even have a reputation for themselves being toxic. At the time of this writing if you are paying less than $120 (equivalent to roughly six ounces of 99.9% pure silver) for your gas mask then you almost certainly are buying an outdated model that will probably not offer you the protection you expect. **Older gas masks for former Soviet-bloc nations are particularly inadequate.**

CAUTION: *When buying a gas mask be certain that it comes with printed instructions (written in a language you can read). Before ever trying the mask read the instructions carefully (people have died from not following proper procedures when putting on gas masks).*

Cheap, suspect gas masks can be purchased for as little as $30. Modern, more reliable masks start at around $120. Reliable masks are often manufactured in western nations such as the United States, Israel, or Belgium. Finnish masks also have developed a good reputation.

At the time of this writing reasonable gas mask filters cost around $10 - $12 and have a useful life expectancy of 6 - 8 hours. Filters that cost less than $10 should be suspect.

CAUTION: *All gas mask filters do not fit on all masks. When purchasing a gas mask filter be certain that it is compatible with the intended mask.*

9.7. Medical Quarantine

Quarantine is the isolation of individuals for a defined observation period to ascertain that they are not carrying infectious disease. The use of quarantine as a means of assuring public health is one of he earliest recorded methods for dealing with infectious disease. In a post-disaster scenario in which normal social services and medical care are not available it may be advisable for groups of survivors to adopt quarantine policies in order to help avoid the introduction of disease when others seek to join the group.

Ideally the quarantine facility for any new arrivals to a community should be in its own, dedicated building in order to provide maximum isolation from the general population. The quarantine area may even take the form of a campsite located on the perimeter of the community. If these arrangements are not possible, and if newcomers must be located in the same building as members of the community, then a quarantine space should be identified that does not have any ventilation that is shared with the broader community. Accomplishing this may require the manual blocking of ventilation systems in quarantine areas, and possibly the installation of some new ventilation to the building's exterior.

As some diseases (e.g. infectious mononucleosis and hepatitis A) may not exhibit symptoms for up to six weeks, an ideal quarantine period should be for six weeks. However, where this is not practical a minimum quarantine period of three weeks should be observed. If a three week quarantine period is adopted then it may be advisable to incorporate some additional procedures for the duration of the six week period (such as not sharing eating utensils, avoiding physical contact and remaining physically-segregated to some extent). Also, when quarantine is lifted everyone who was subject to the quarantine should be inspected for rashes, lice, nits, fever, cough, runny nose or any other outward sign of illness.[144]

Eating utensils used by individuals under quarantine should either be kept in the quarantine area until the quarantine is lifted, sterilized by immersion in boiling water for at least five minutes, or washed in a 10% bleach-and-water solution.[144]

If new refugees arrive during a quarantine their own quarantine should be kept completely separate from the ongoing quarantine (or they should be turned away until the quarantine facilities once again become available). Otherwise, if they are directed to a currently ongoing quarantine, it becomes necessary to "restart the quarantine clock" from zero (which is **not** going to be popular with anyone currently quarantined).

Policies associated with quarantine should be defined in advance if possible, so that when they are applied (e.g. someone is turned away for failing a physical examination) there is no suspicion that a refugee was treated unfairly. Additionally, pre-defined quarantine policies provide the opportunity for more thought and energy to be invested in this most critical procedure.

9.8. Handling Bodies of the Deceased

In the aftermath of a major disaster there is the likelihood that those who survive will sometimes need to deal with the *dead bodies* of victims.

In recent times the major earthquake that struck *Haiti* resulted in thousands of deaths from building collapses, and it became necessary for bulldozers to be used to pile the bodies of victims into unmarked *body pits* for disposal. So, there is plenty of precedent for the issue of post-disaster body disposal in the modern world.

While the bodies of victims do pose a nominal health risk they do not necessarily pose a higher risk than a living, breathing human being (after all, dead bodies are not going to be sneezing and coughing to expel viruses into the air!). Most infectious diseases do not exist in a body after it has been dead for 48 hours. HIV exists as a threat in a dead body for as long as 6 days.[145]

Regardless, dead bodies do eventually emit offensive odors and they can be sources of disease, hence they must be properly handled and disposed of. When dealing with the deceased bodies:[145]

- If burying a body, bury it at a depth of at least five feet; otherwise don't be surprised at what the family dog drags in the next day!

- There is no benefit to sprinkling lime or any disinfectant over a body before disposal.

- Try to keep a record of where and how the body was disposed of, and the identity and a description (age, gender, etc.) of the victim if possible.

- To move bodies place them on a plastic or cloth sheet and avoid making physical contact with them to avoid any possibility of disease transmission through touch. Any sheets used to wrap dead bodies should be used exclusively for this purpose.

- Wear boots and gloves when working with dead bodies.

- Do not touch your mouth or face with your hand after handling a body.

- Periodically clean and disinfect any equipment and/or vehicles that have been used in the handling and transportation of dead bodies. A solution of 10% bleach diluted with water should be sufficient to provide such disinfection.

- There is little or no practical benefit for wearing face masks while handling dead bodies.

- In the case of dismembered bodies, treat body parts as individual bodies and do not expend any effort in grouping body parts together.

- Anyone involved in handling and transporting bodies should wash their hands thoroughly with soap and water at the end of the work day.

- Anyone handling or transporting dead bodies should be careful to treat any cuts or wounds received with antibiotic ointments. If antibiotic ointment is not available then then the injury should be thoroughly cleaned with soap and water.

- When burying multiple bodies it is advisable to dig a trench that is at least 5 feet deep and to separate the bodies by a distance of no less than two feet.

- Avoid cremation of bodies in order to conserve fuel. If cremation is used then be prepared to bury those body parts that are not fully incinerated.

- Bodies should not be buried within 1000 feet of a water source or human habitation.

- Bodies should not be buried uphill from a water source.

10. First Aid

The word *'first'* in *'first aid'* implies that there are other levels of care that should be available to those who are ill or injured. If you would not trust an expensive automobile to an amateur mechanic then you also would not want to unnecessarily trust the health of your physical body - the most complex machine in the world - to someone with minimal medical knowledge and experience. However highly-qualified medical personnel cannot always be available at the moment they are needed and following some simple, general guidelines and procedures can preserve life until professional care **does** become available. Following these guidelines and procedures is the essence of providing first aid, and once first aid measures have been followed the caregiver (or the subject) should seek the attention of a medical professional. The purpose of this chapter is to provide information to enable first responders to provide basic first aid for those medical issues that are most likely to be encountered during and in the aftermath of major disaster.

There is a significant overlap in the subject domains of first aid and basic sanitation, particularly in the context of disaster preparedness. As a result this chapter will make liberal references to Chapter 9, *'Hygiene and Sanitation'*.

The first sections of this chapter discuss a variety of general first aid topics, followed by guidelines for addressing a number of common injuries and illnesses which are most likely to be encountered during and after a major disaster.

The term *'patient'* carries with it the implication that a sick or injured individual is receiving care from a medical doctor or other medical professional. Because first aid is often administered by someone who has little or no medical training, this chapter will refer to the individual administering the first aid as the *'caregiver'* and the person receiving the first aid as the *'subject'* or *'victim'*.

STRAIGHT THINKING: *It is not the intent of this chapter to enable the layperson to in any way replace trained professionals in the administration of medical care. When dealing with injury or illness* **ALWAYS** *seek aid from a doctor or other qualified and trained medical professional at the earliest opportunity! First aid should never be confused with professional medical care. While this chapter provides information about antibiotics and other medications, this information is intended solely to enable you to communicate better with your doctor during a disaster. When prescribing a medical treatment your doctor draws from his or her vast experience as well as from knowledge of current disease trends in the community, your own personal health history (as well as that of your family and even your ancestors), and a variety of other sources. Taking medications of any type without the involvement of a medical professional is strongly discouraged and could result in disastrous consequences.*

Please note that of the five additional reference books that are recommended at the end of this book, four are books that cover medical topics. The medical field is **vast***, and a single chapter of this book can can only scratch the surface with regard to the medical information that will be needed in the aftermath of a major, prolonged disaster.*

Never forget that it is far better to avoid illness than to recover from illness. In a disaster scenario you should consider proper hygiene and sanitation, as well as safe working habits, to be as important as food and water. If you observe someone in your group not adhering to proper and safe sanitation or work practices then you should take **whatever measures are necessary** *to modify their behavior.*

10.1. General First Aid Topics

10.1.1. Cleanliness and Sanitation - "An Ounce of Prevention..."

The best first aid is that which you never have to administer. And **the best way to prevent disease is to plan for and adopt good sanitation practices**. Two of the most important sanitation practices are:

- Diligently keeping human and animal fecal material away from food and water supplies.

- Proper hand washing.

Keeping fecal material from contaminating food is not as trivial a challenge as one might think. This involves developing good hygiene practices as well as thoughtfully making use of your property based on its physical layout.

Proper hand washing practices are **absolutely essential** to preventing many diseases that could be life-threatening in a post-disaster scenario. Regular soap actually doesn't kill disease-causing microorganisms, but rather physically removes them from the body. This is accomplished through two chemical processes:

- By causing your skin to become 'slippery' to micro-organisms trying to cling to it.

- By chemically attaching soap's heavy molecules to microorganisms to literally yank them away from the now-slippery skin when rinsed. This is important to note because, unlike the case with antibiotics, biological agents are not going to develop an immunity to this essentially mechanical removal process.

In addition to working like regular soaps to remove microorganisms from the body, *antibacterial soaps* contain additives that kill many harmful microorganisms. However, the use of antibacterial soaps can result in the development of antibiotic-resistant *super bugs*. As a result, it's not a bad idea to limit the use of anti-bacterial soaps to special applications such as scrubbing up before medical procedures and food preparation.

Good sanitation and hygiene is every bit as important to survival as any other aspect of prepping. In the absence of good sanitation deadly diseases can run rampant. Please refer to chapter 9 for a more detailed discussion of this critical topic.

AUTHOR's NOTE: Long before I was a prepper I had always adhered to over-zealous hand washing practices, which basically involved pretending that I was a surgeon scrubbing up for surgery each time I washed my hands.

A few years ago an aspiring inventor entered our offices to demonstrate to us his new invention, which was a device that literally counted the number of microorganisms that inhabited a one-inch square on a person's body. He demonstrated his device on a few of us who were in the office that day by counting an area on the back of each person's hand. As expected, the machine produced a rather large count for everyone's hands except my own. In my case the "germ count" was so small that he started to believe his machine was failing, however a test of the skin of his own hand showed that the machine was operating normally.

This anecdotal story is a great demonstration of the importance and effectiveness of diligent soap-and-water hand washing practices - particularly in the wake of a major disaster.

10.1.2. First Aid Supplies and Equipment

The following items should be included in your *first aid kit* to enable you to provide first aid for many of the situations that may arise:

- Bandaging Supplies

    - Regular and Sterile Bandages

    - Sterile Medical Gauze (you cannot have too much!)

    - Absorbent bandages

    - Medical tape

    - Elastic Bandages (such as "Ace Bandages")

    - Sanitary Napkins (for treatment of wounds)

    - Antiseptic wipes

    - Butterfly bandages

    - Sterile pads

    - Triangular cravat bandages

- Equipment
    - Fever Thermometer (adult and child models)
    - Blood Pressure Cuff
    - Timepiece or Stop Watch (to measure pulse rates)
    - Tweezers
    - Sharp Scissors (for cutting bandages, etc)
    - Lighter (to sanitize implements)
    - Magnifying Glass
    - SAM splints
    - Finger splints
    - Irrigation syringe
    - Water disinfection system
- Topical and Internal Medicines
    - Alcohol
    - Povidone-iodine (brand name *"Betadine"*)
    - Benedryl
    - Benzocaine
    - Clove Oil
    - Antibiotic ointment
    - Alcohol and Hydrogen Peroxide
    - Epinephrine
    - Tincture of benzoin
    - Prescription, broad-spectrum antibiotics
    - Antihistamine to treat allergic reactions
    - Antacid tablets
    - Aspirin
    - Over-the-counter pain medications

- Other Supplies

  - Suture

  - Face Masks

  - Thermal blankets

  - Latex gloves

  - Safety pins

  - First-aid cleansing pads with topical anesthetic

  - Hydrogel-based pads

  - Oval eye pads

  - Cotton swabs

NOTE: *Some medicines should be kept refrigerated (but not frozen) in a dark environment to preserve and extend shelf-life. It is also important to know if a specific medicine simply loses potency over time or becomes toxic.*

10.1.3. Triage and Quarantine

Triage is the process of grouping victims according to their prospects for survivability. The purpose of triage is to provide the assurance that limited medical resources get utilized in such a way as to provide maximum benefit to both the victims and, even more importantly, the broader community.

The concept of triage originated with French battlefield medics during World War I when they were required to prioritize victims for treatment.[371] The French doctors organized the victims into three groups:

- *Group 1* - Those who might survive with treatment.

- *Group 2* - Those who were likely to live if they received no treatment.

- *Group 3* - Those who were likely to die, regardless of any treatment.

Recording Method	Min.	Max.
Oral	95.9	99.5
Armpit	94.5	99.1
Ear	94.6	100.4
Rectal	97.9	100.4

Table 10.1.: Normal Body Temperature Ranges for Various Recording Methods[372]

Those victims in Group #1 would be given the highest priority for transportation and treatment, followed by those in Groups #2 and #3.

In the modern world the concept of triage has evolved dramatically to include triage levels and sub-levels, as well as identifying criteria for reclassifying the sick and injured; and most medical organizations have developed their own standards and procedures around these advanced triage methods. In a disaster scenario, however, it is more practical to return to the 3-level criteria described above. Once the victim moves to a true medical facility they may then be reclassified according to that facility's guidelines.

When you believe that sick person may have an infectious disease it may be necessary to isolate them from those who are not infected. Such isolation is referred to as *quarantine*. Please refer to section 9.7 for a detailed description on recommended quarantine practices and procedures.

10.1.4. Recording a Subject's Vital Signs

When initially assessing the status of a subject it is important to start by observing and recording their vital signs, which include their body temperature, blood pressure and heart rate. Take these measurements occasionally and maintain a record of these observations, including the date and time for each record. This information may be invaluable to others who may later assume responsibility for the subject.

A subject's temperature can be taken either orally, from the arm pit, from the ear or from the rectum, with the best/most accurate measurement being from the rectum. Special costly thermometers are required to take a subject's temperature from the ear. Table 10.1 lists the normal temperature ranges for each method.

When using an oral thermometer first clean the tip of the thermometer with soap and warm water, wipe it with alcohol, and allow it to dry. The armpit method of taking temperature is the least accurate of the four methods. The use of a temperature *strip* on the forehead is considered extremely inaccurate and basically is only sufficient to indicate the presence or absence of fever.

A healthy person's temperature may vary by as much as one degree through the course of a day.

> **NOTE:** *A fever is an indication that the subject is experiencing an infection and is part of the body's defense mechanism. It is highly unlikely that a fever that persists for less than three days will pose a threat to the subject.[372]*

> **CAUTION:** *Never take an oral temperature reading from a child under five years of age or a subject that is incoherent or otherwise mentally incapacitated, as they may bite the thermometer and injure themselves.*

Please refer to section 11.1.10 in the Fitness chapter for instructions on measuring blood pressure and heart rate.

10.1.5. Sprains, Strains and Breaks

Accidents often result in painful damage to bones, muscles and connective tissue within the body. Such damage often takes the form of sprains, strains or broken bones, and of course it is important to understand the type of injury in order to provide the appropriate first aid:

- Sprains - stretches and/or tears to the ligaments that connect the bones.
- Strains - twists or tears of the tendons that connect muscles to bone (or of the muscles themselves).
- Breaks - physical damage to the bone itself (which may take the form of a cracked bone or a bone that is broken through).

Each of these types of injuries can result in extreme pain and greatly inhibited ability to function normally. Of the three types of injuries a broken bone is the most serious. In some cases it is not possible to differentiate between a broken bone and a strain or sprain, however here are some guidelines that may help you to identify a break:

- If you observe bone protruding through the skin.[364]
- If the injured body part appears to be physically out of its normal alignment.[364]

- If the injured area appears deformed in any way.[363]

- If the injury results in any feeling of numbness.[363]

- If it appears that the bone is directly beneath the surface of the skin.[364]

- If the injury is to the lower body and it cannot tolerate any weight at all being placed on it.[365]

- If the pain instantly became intense after the injury.[364]

- If a breaking noise accompanied the injury.[364]

- If the subject absolutely cannot move the body part.[365]

Strains and sprains should be treated with the well-known R.I.C.E. therapy:[327]

Rest - the subject should rest for at least one day.

Ice - ice should be applied to the injury 10-to-15 minutes each hour.

Compression - elastic bandages should be **lightly** wrapped around the injured area.

Elevation - the injured area should be elevated higher than the subject's heart.

Once the R.I.C.E. treatment is initiated the injury should be re-evaluated against the criteria listed above to determine if it might possibly be a broken bone.

Please refer to section 10.2.5 for details on treating the different types of bone fractures.

10.1.6. Infections and Antibiotics

An individual may suffer from bacterial, viral, fungal or parasitic infections. Each of these infections has different treatments and implications.

- *Viral infections* - infections caused by minute biological particles known as viruses. Viruses tend to invade and destroy healthy cells within the body.

- *Bacterial infections* - infections caused by microscopic bacteria. These bacteria grow in open sores and wounds or within the body, and often produce toxins that can be harmful or fatal.

- *Fungal infections* - infections caused by multi-celled fungus organisms. These infections can have effects very similar to those of bacterial infections.

- *Parasitic infections* - infections caused by small parasitic creatures (such as worms) that can result in pain, diarrhea, or destruction of body organs.

NOTE: *Even though viral infections cannot be treated with antibiotics it is not uncommon for viral infections to weaken the body's immune system and give rise to* secondary infections *that are bacterial in nature. As a result doctors sometimes prescribe antibiotics to a subject who is suspected of having a viral infection.[90]*

Beware Meningitis!

Meningitis is an infection of the membranes that enclose the brain and spinal cord. While viral meningitis is generally non-life-threatening, bacterial meningitis poses a very real risk of brain damage or death. If an individual experiences a fever accompanied by a painful or stiff neck (the symptoms of meningitis) then they should seek professional medical treatment immediately.[92]

The antibiotics often used to treat bacterial meningitis include:[91]

- ampicillin
- cefotaxime (commercial brand name *Claforan*)
- ceftriaxone (commercial brand name *Rocephin*)
- gentamicin
- penicillin G
- rifampin
- vancomycin (commercial brand name *Vancocin*) - Often given after other antibiotics have failed.

These antibiotics are most often administered intravenously to treat meningitis.

Bacterial Wound Infections

In a post-disaster scenario it can be expected that there will be a great increase in the incidence of cuts, scrapes and more serious wounds that could lend themselves to infection. In that case the probability of infection is further increased by the fact that basic sanitation will have degraded to some extent. As a result, during a disaster, it is important to remain hyper-vigilant for any sort of skin damage and to properly wash, clean and bandage cuts and abrasions as quickly and carefully as possible.

Infected wounds are indicated by:[89]

- Redness or read streaks near or extending from the wound

- Pain and Tenderness

- Swelling

- Skin that is warm or hot to the touch near the wound site

- The presence of yellow, green or gray/white pus

Infected wounds should be washed with plain water and treated with triple antibiotic ointment at least once per day. If the wound does not obviously appear to be healing within 3 to 4 days then the need for professional medical attention should be considered to be urgent.[89] If the subject exhibits signs of systemic infection (described below) then professional medical attention should be sought immediately.

CAUTION: *Don't use iodine or hydrogen peroxide to treat a wound, as these substances may only further irritate the damaged tissue.[89]*

Exotic, Drug-Resistant Infections

One hears disturbing stories in the news with increasing regularity of terrible, life-threatening bacterial infections that spread quickly and are resistant to many (and sometimes all) antibiotics. The *MRSA ("Methicillin-resistant Staphylococcus aureus")*[85] infection is one example, and more recently similar stories of *CRE ("Carbapenem-resistant Enterobacteriaceae")*[87] infections have started to become common. There are also stories of *"flesh-eating bacteria" ("Streptococcus pyogenes")*[88] that have been carried in the mass media for years. While non-medical-professionals don't have the skills to combat these infections well, knowledge of these infections can help to avoid them altogether or can provide the inspiration to treat potential infections at the very early stages before an infection can become established.

Three extremely important and common measures to combat exotic and deadly bacterial infections are:

- *Good Hygiene* - Many of these infections spread due to poor hand-washing practices.

- *The Human Immune System* - Many of these infections only establish themselves when an individual's immune system is weak.

- *Early and Aggressive Treatment of Potential Infections* - Quick treatment of even the most minor skin wounds through washing and the application of triple-antibiotic ointments can stop a bacterial infection in its tracks.

Many of these deadly infections spread themselves by producing toxins that destroy human tissue. The person providing first aid should take care to avoid coming into direct contact with any infected areas. When draining infected skin boils, care should be taken to quickly remove the drained fluid without it spreading elsewhere on the infected individual (or any caregiver). Once boils have been drained the areas around those boils should be washed with antibiotic soap and covered with gauze to absorb any additional drainage.[85]

Systemic Infections

Systemic infections are infections that have spread to the internal systems within the body. Such infections are very dangerous as they may result in a fatal shut-down of vital organs. The signs of a systemic infection are chills, fever, shaking, fatigue, confusion, achy joints and rapid pulse. Such infections require professional medical treatment that often involves the use of intravenous antibiotics that are specific to the type of infection.

> **NOTE:** *In a disaster situation be certain to wash and treat wounds promptly with antibiotics. Such preventive care can easily prevent a small scratch from evolving into a life-threatening infection. Be particularly watchful for wounds that have been submerged in natural water sources, as such sources provide the worst-case opportunity for microorganisms to enter the wound.*

An important player in the body's battle against infection is the body's own immune system. Consequently, in a post-disaster scenario it is critical to maintain living conditions that are supportive of the immune system. This means that a good, balanced diet and some degree of exercise are vital. Additionally, lately there has been some strong speculation that Vitamins C and D3 play an important role with the body's immune system.[166][167][168] Since the production of Vitamin D3 is promoted by exposure to sunlight it may be prudent for everyone in the community to spend time in the out-of-doors when practical and possible. Vitamin C and D3 supplements are also available, with recommended dosages typically printed on the label. A supply of these important vitamins should be a high priority for any survivalist or prepper.

Emergency Antibiotics

Antibiotics are substances that either kill or inhibit the growth of infectious microorganisms. They take the form of topical liquids and creams applied to the skin, pills, capsules or liquids intended to be administered intravenously.

Because they are ineffective against viruses, antibiotics offer no protection against colds, the flu and other viral infections. Additionally, antibiotics have some toxic effects on the body and, if overused, can result in the development of drug-resistant *super bugs* that can pose a dire health threat to entire communities. As a result of these considerations it is essential that antibiotics only be prescribed judiciously, and when they are prescribed that they be taken exactly as directed. This also means that, ideally, all antibiotic use should be under proper medical supervision.

Some antibiotics are better suited for respiratory problems while others are designed for infections of the gut, bones, throat and mouth. While there are a large number of antibiotics on the market, they are generally organized into a few *'families'* that have similar disease-fighting qualities and other characteristics. See table 10.2 for a description of these families, a list of the names of common antibiotics within these families, and a description of each.

When using antibiotics keep the following rules in mind:[94]

- Antibiotics should only be taken by individuals who are ill.

- Antibiotics should only be taken **ONLY AS PRESCRIBED**.

- Antibiotics are ineffective against all viruses (colds and flu are caused by viruses).

- Some individuals are allergic to some antibiotics. Use of an antibiotic should be discontinued if the person taking it exhibits a rash, itching, hives, swelling, nausea or any other unusual side effect or behavior.

- Antibiotics should always be taken exactly as prescribed by a doctor, or in accordance with directions on the label.

- Antibiotics can increase the effect of anticoagulants. If an individual is taking an anticoagulant then a doctor should be consulted before they begin taking an antibiotic.

- Unless otherwise instructed by a doctor, an individual should not take more than one antibiotic.

- Antibiotics should not be taken with antacids, laxatives or food (antibiotics should be taken no later than one hour before eating or two hours after eating).

Tables 10.4 and 10.5 provide information about antibiotics that would be most in-demand in a disaster scenario.

Most antibiotics have a shelf life of about two years at around 70°F and tend to simply lose potency after the published expiration date. However, some antibiotics (most notably, those in the Tetracycline family - see table 10.2) can become highly toxic some time after they expire. In many cases, if kept in a cool and/or refrigerated (but not frozen) environment and

Family Name	Description	Names of Member Antibiotics
Aminoglycosides	Treat typhus and some forms of pneumonia caused by gram-negative bacteria (bacteria that are not detectable by the "Gram staining protocol"). Aminoglycosides must be injected, and the use of these drugs can result in damage to the ear and kidneys.[96]	Amikacin, Gentamicin, Kanamycin, Neomycin, Netilmicin, Paromomycin, Streptomycin, Tobramycin, Amikin*, Garamycin*, G-Mycin*, Jenamicin*, Kantrex*, Mycifradin*, Myciguent*, Netromycin*, Nebcin*[95]
Penicillins	The first antibiotics. These drugs treat ear, skin, dental, urinary tract and respiratory infections as well as gonorrhea. Penicillin must often be combined with other ingredients for maximum effectiveness against bacteria. Many people are allergic to penicillin.[100]	Amoxicillin, Amoxil*, Polymox*, Trimox*, Wymox*, Ampicillin, Omnipen*, Polycillin*, Polycillin-N*, Principen*, Totacillin*, Bacampicillin, Spectrobid*, Carbenicillin, Geocillin*, Geopen*, Cloxacillin, Cloxapen*, Dicloxacillin, Dynapen*, Dycill*, Pathocil*, Flucloxacillin, Flopen*, Floxapen*, Staphcillin*, Mezlocillin, Mezlin*, Nafcillin, Nafcil*, Nallpen*, Unipen*, Oxacillin, Bactocill*, Prostaphlin*, Penicillin G, Bicillin L-A*, Crysticillin 300 A.S.*, Pentids*, Permapen*, Pfizerpen*, Pfizerpcn ΛS*, Wycillin*, Penicillin V, Beepen-VK*, Betapen-VK*, Ledercillin VK*, V-Cillin K*, Piperacillin, Pipracil*, Pivampicillin, Pivmecillinam, Ticarcillin, Ticar*[95]
Cephalosporins	Used to treat strep throat, pneumonia, tonsillitis, bronchitis, otitis, staph infections, skin infections and gonorrhea. A patient who is allergic to penicillin antibiotics may be allergic to cephalosporins as well.[100]	Cefacetrile (cephacetrile), Celospor*, Celtol*, Cristacef*, Cefadroxil (cefadroxyl), Duricef*, Ultracef*, Cefalonium (cephalonium), , Cefalexin (cephalexin), Keflex*, Keftab*, Cefaloridine (cephaloradine), Cefalotin (cephalothin), Keflin*, Cefaloglycin (cephaloglycin), Kefglycin*, Cefapirin (cephapirin), Cefadyl*, Cefatrizine, Cefazedone, Cefazaflur, Cefradine (cephradine), Velosef*, Cefazolin (cephazolin), Ancef*, Kefzol*, Cefroxadine, Ceftezole*, Cefamandole, Mandol*, Cefaclor, Ceclor*, Ceclor CD*, Distaclor*, Keflor*, Ranicor*, Cefmetazole, Cefotetan, Cefotan*, Cefoxitin, Mefoxin*, Cefprozil (cefproxil), Cefzil*, Cefuroxime, Ceftin*, Kefurox*, Zinacef*, Zinnat*, Cefuzonam*, Cefonicid, Monocid*, Cefcapene, Cefdaloxime, Cefdinir, Omnicef*, Cefdiel*, Cefditoren, Spectracef*, Cefixime, Suprax*, Cefmenoxime, Cefmax*, Cefodizime, Cefotaxime, Claforan*, Cefetamet, Cefpimizole, Ceftazidime, Ceptaz*, Fortum*, Fortaz*, Tazicef*, Tazidime*, Cefpodoxime, Vantin*, Cefteram, Ceftiofur, Excede*, Ceftiolene, Ceftizoxime, Cefizox*, Ceftriaxone, Rocephin*, Ceftibuten, Cedax*, Cefoperazone, Cefobid*, Cefozopran, Cefclidine, Cefepime, Maxipime*, Cefluprenam, Cefoselis, Cefpirome, Cefrom*, Cefquinome*, Cefaclomezine, Cefaloram, Cefaparole, Cefcanel, Cefedrolor, Cefempidone, Cefetrizole, Cefmatilen, Cefmepidium, Cefovecin, Cefivitril, Cefoxazole, Cefsumide, Cefrotil, Cefuracetime, Ceftioxide*[95]

*Brand names

Table 10.2.: Antibiotic Families

Family Name	Description	Names of Member Antibiotics
Sulfonamides	Treat many of the same infections as penicillin. Often used for kidney infections, although these antibiotics have the potential to cause kidney damage. When used the patient should drink good quantities of water to prevent the formation of crystal deposits in the body.[101]	Sulfamethizole, Thiosulfil Forte*, Sulfamethoxazole, Gantanol*, Urobak*, Sulfisoxazole, Gantrisin*, Trimethoprim-Sulfamethoxazole, Bactrim*, Bactrim DS*, Cotrim*, Cotrim DS*, Septra*, Septra DS*, Sulfatrim*, Sulfatrim-DS*[95]
Quinolones (Fluoroquinolones)	Treats respiratory infections such as bronchitis and pneumonia, urinary tract infections, skin infections and sinusitis. Side effects may include stomach pain, upset stomach, nausea, diarrhea and vomiting. Should not be given to pregnant women and children, as these drugs can affect bone growth.[100]	Flumequine, Flubactin*, Nalidixic acid, NegGam*, Wintomylon*, Oxolinic acid, Uroxin*, Piromidic acid, Panacid*, Pipemidic acid, Dolcol*, Rosoxacin, Eradacil*, Ciprofloxacin, Cipro*, Cipro XR*, Ciprobay*, Ciproxin*, Enoxacin, Enroxil*, Penetrex*, Lomefloxacin, Maxaquin*, Nadifloxacin, Acuatim*, Nadoxin*, Nadixa*, Norfloxacin, Lexinor*, Noroxin*, Quinabic*, Janacin*, Ofloxacin, Floxin*, Oxaldin*, Tarivid*, Pefloxacin, Peflacine*, Rufloxacin, Uroflox*, Balofloxacin, Baloxin*, Gatifloxacin, Tequin*, Zymar*, Grepafloxacin, Raxar*, Levofloxacin, Cravit*, Levaquin*, Moxifloxacin, Avelox*, Vigamox*, Pazufloxacin, Pasil*, Pazucross*, Sparfloxacin, Zagam*, Temafloxacin, Omniflox*, Tosufloxacin, Ozex*, Tosacin*, Besifloxacin, Besivance*, Clinafloxacin, Gemifloxacin, Factive*, Sitafloxacin, Gracevit*, Trovafloxacin, Trovan*, Prulifloxacin, Quisnon*[95]
Macrolides	Treats infections of soft tissue including respiratory tract and gastrointestinal infections as well as certain genital infections. Used mainly to treat those who are sensitive to or allergic to the penicillin family antibiotics.[100]	Azithromycin, Zithromax*, Erythromycin, Clarithromycin, Biaxin*, Dirithromycin, Dynabac*, Roxithromycin, Rulid*, Surlid, Telithromycin, Ketek*[95]
Tetracyclines	Treats chlamydial infections, syphilis and malaria. Also effective against mild acne and Lyme disease, Rocky Mountain spotted fever, sexually-transmitted diseases, upper respiratory tract infections, typhus and urinary tract infections.[100]	Demeclocycline, Declomycin*, Doxycycline, Doryx, Vibramycin*, Minocycline, Dynacin, Minocin, Monodox*, Oxytetracycline, Terramycin*, Tetracycline, Achromycin*, Tigecycline, Tygacil*[95]
Carbapenems	This is a broad-spectrum antibiotic that is considered a treatment of last resort for certain drug-resistant bacterial infections (particularly E. coli). Currently only available as an intravenous medication.[97]	Imipenem, Imipenem/cilastatin, Primaxin*, Doripenem, Doribax*, Meropenem, Merrem*, Ertapenem, Invanz*[95]
*Brand names		

Table 10.3.: Antibiotic Families (cont'd)

> **NOTE:** *Due to the buildup of drug resistance and other factors, the effectiveness of certain antibiotics varies from one geographical region to another. As a result, for your locale, there may be a more effective combination of antibiotics than those identified in Tables 10.4 and 10.5.*

protected from exposure to light, the shelf life of antibiotics (with the exception of those in the Tetracycline family) can be extended significantly.

SUGGESTION: If your are without electrical power you maybe able to keep temperature-sensitive medicines (e.g. insulin) cooler by storing them in a source of cool, running water, such as a spring-fed stream.

> **NOTE:** *The antibiotics sold for use with fish aquariums, as well as other veterinary antibiotics, are often chemically identical to those prescribed for humans. Such antibiotics are often available online and at pet stores. They should only be considered for human use under the most exceptional of circumstances. The non-medical-professional may select antibiotics that not only do not help, but which may cause additional harm. If you find yourself in such a dire situation that you do make use of unconventional antibiotics then you should at least keep good records of what you have taken, the quantity taken, and the times they were taken. You should also consult with a medical professional at the earliest opportunity.*

Dosages and Medication Schedules

Obviously if a doctor is available then you can and must turn to them for a proper prescription for any medicine. Determining proper dosages of a particular medication requires medical expertise and case information that is outside the scope of this book. However, if you have a recent prescription for a particular antibiotic for a specific individual then, in a post disaster scenario, you at least have some information with which to work. Even better, the *"Nurse's Drug Guide"* and the *"Nurse's Pocket Drug Guide"* provide a wealth of information related to this topic (the author cannot recommend these references highly enough. Editions of these references from previous years can be purchased at reasonable cost).

Generic Name	Brand Name	Use	Caution
Doxycycline	Vibramycin	Effective in treating malaria and Rocky Mountain Spotted Fever	Long term use (for example by malaria patients) may lead to skin rashes as well as a thinning of the skin and a corresponding photo-sensitivity. Doxycycline is not approved for general use by children, and taking it with food and dairy products can reduce its effectiveness.[134]
Azithromycin	Zithromax, Sumamed, Xithrone	Urinary tract infections, sepsis, abdominal and upper respiratory infecions, gonorrhea and other sexually-transmitted infections, ear infections	Most common side effects are diarrhea, nausea, vomiting and abdominal pain. These effects only cause about 1% of patients to cease taking the medication. [130]
Ampicillan	Principen	Broad spectrum antibiotic used for skin infactions, ear infections, gonorrhea and other sexually-transmitted diseases	Relatively non-toxic and adverse reactons are rare.[131]
Ciprofloxacin	Cipro, Ciproxin, Ciprobay	Urinary tract infections, hospital-acquired pneumonia, anthrax protection, diarrhea infections of the bones and joints	Adverse reactions are rare and usually mild, and include nausea, diarrhea, abnormal liver function, vomiting and rash.[132]
Amoxicillin	Novamox, Amoxil	Used for sinus and upper respiratory infections (ear, nose and throat) and abscesses of the teeth	Adverse reactions are rare and include nausea, vomiting, rashes and diarrhea.[133]

Table 10.4.: Recommended Emergency Antibiotics (1 of 2)

Use of Probiotics to Restore Healthy Bacteria

Antibiotics kill both harmful and beneficial bacteria in the human body. As a result it is important to work to restore the beneficial bacteria after a prescription of antibiotics has been taken. Probiotics are dietary supplements that contain live cultures of beneficial bacteria. It is recommended that an individual taking antibiotics also take probiotics (but to wait a few hours after taking antibiotics before taking the probiotics[93]).

Many yogurts are a good source of probiotics, and *kefir* is known as an **excellent** source of probiotics. Additionally, there are many probiotic supplements available on the market. When purchasing a probiotic supplement be sure to purchase it from a reputable source, as many probiotic supplements have been shown to be selling dead bacterial cultures that provide no benefit.[93]

Generic Name	Brand Name	Use	Caution
Clindamycin	Cleocin	Staph, pneumonia and streptococcal infections. Acne.	Adverse reactions experience by about 1% of patients include diarrhea, nausea, rash, itching, vomiting and abdominal pain. Patients taking higher doses may also experience a metallic taste in their mouth. Often these reactions occur in subjects who lie down for an extended period within 30 minutes of taking this medication.[135]
Metronidazole	Flagyl	Infections caused by anaerobic bacteria and protozoal infections such as the parasitic infection *Giardiasis*.	The most common adverse reactions to this medicine include nausea, diarrhea and a metallic taste in the mouth, with rashes, itching dizziness and headache reported less frequently. It should also be noted that this medication is expected to have some carcinogenic (cancer-causing) properties (this has been demonstrated in animal studies).[136]
Trimethoprim-Sulfamethoxazole	Bactrim, Septra	A broad-spectrum antibiotic used to treat a wide range of bacterial infections, including respiratory, urinary and gastrointestinal tract infections as well as wound and other skin infections.	Use has been associated with some mild allergic reactions as well as liver and kidney failure.[137]

Table 10.5.: Recommended Emergency Antibiotics (2 of 2)

Naturally-occurring Supplements Associated with Antibiotics and Antiviral Properties

In addition to the antibiotic drugs manufactured by the pharmaceutical companies there are some natural substances that are said to possess antibiotic properties. These include:[93]

- *Silver* - Silver and silver compounds (and to a lesser extent other heavy metals such as copper) have long been used for their anti-microbial properties. Today many medical equipment and water filtration equipment manufacturers employ silver coatings and other silver compounds to kill harmful microorganisms. These products rely on the *oligodynamic effect*[127] associated with heavy metals to disrupt cellular activity. In the past some companies have sold a silver suspension called *colloidal silver* for human consumption as an internal antibiotic.

The use of heavy metals to make surfaces disease-resistant is a good and beneficial practice, however because the oligodynamic effect does not discriminate with regard to the types of cells it kills, and because silver has a tendency to accumulate in the body, and because it is speculated that silver may actually suppress or damage the body's own immune system[128], taking any silver compound (or other heavy metal compound) should be considered only as a last resort in a post-disaster scenario. (NOTE: There are anecdotal success stories from satisfied individuals who have ingested colloidal silver regularly for many months without observation of ill effects).

- *Raw Honey* - *Raw Honey* (particularly *Raw Manuka Honey*[511] with an industry rating of UMF 15+ or higher[374]) has been been used for centuries as a natural antibiotic. Honey contains a *defensin-1* protein and other agents that provide substantial antibacterial properties.[510][373]. Entire volumes can (and have) been written that discuss the infection-fighting properties of raw honey. Typically the honey is applied to a pad of gauze which is then applied to the cleaned wound for several seconds or longer. If applied to a shallow scratch or scrape the gauze may be wiped over the injury in a circular motion for a few seconds before being removed. Once removed a regular bandage is applied, the surrounding skin can be washed of any excess honey, and the used, leftover materials discarded.

  There are also numerous claims that honey yields similar antimicrobial benefits when ingested, including fighting stomach infections that are associated with stomach ulcers.[375]

- *Garlic* - The substance allicin, which is produced when fresh garlic is finely chopped or crushed, has antibiotic properties.[377] Crushed, fresh garlic can be eaten with food or incorporated into a poultice and applied over a cut.[378] (An interesting feature of garlic is that it only acts against harmful bacteria, unlike prescribed antibiotics.[377])

  Many natural supplement providers have developed capsules that concentrate and isolate the allicin from garlic.

- *Andrographis* - The leaves and roots of the Andrographis herb (which is indigenous to the countries of Southern Asia) have long been used as a remedy for colds, flus, cancer and some bacterial infections (particularly respiratory infections).[379] Supplements made from the andrographis plant are available as commercial supplements in both capsule and liquid form. The ways in which this herb operates are not yet fully understood, although there is some speculation that it stimulates the human immune system.[380]

  While andrographis is considered to be safe, those using it have been known to experience fatigue, headache, nausea, allergic reactions and diarrhea.[379]

- *Goldenseal* - Goldenseal is a plant that grows in the northeastern United States and southeastern Canada. It was used as a traditional remedy by Native Americans for a wide range of illnesses ranging from respiratory infections to cancer. The roots were typically brewed as a tea and ingested.

There is no good scientific information on the mechanism through which goldenseal may provide any benefits. Due to lack of scientific knowledge on its biological activity goldenseal is not recommended to be taken by children, anyone who is pregnant or anyone taking a prescription medicine. Also, goldenseal should not be considered to be a substitute for more effective commercial medications.[381]

- *Coconut Oil* - Coconut oil is a very good source of lauric acid, which has been shown to have good anti-bacterial and anti-viral properties. It can be ingested or applied as a poultice to fight skin and wound infections.[382]

- *Tea Tree Oil* - Tea Tree oil is an oil that is produced from the leaves of the tea tree. This oil has a long history of being used as a topical antibiotic against bacterial and fungal infections by the aboriginal people of Australia. It is believed that its active component is *terpinen-4-ol*.[383]

- *Echinacea* - Echinacea is a flowering plant found in North America. It was originally an herbal remedy used by Native Americans, and became widely accepted during the early part of the 20th century. It has been used to treat a wide range of conditions ranging from flu to snake bite. Today Echinacia is most frequently used to treat a wide range of internal viral, bacterial and fungal infections as well as skin conditions. It has been used to treat cold and flu, bloodstream infections (septicemia), tonsillitis, gum disease, streptococcus infections, urinary tract infections, vaginal yeast infections, genital herpes, typhoid, syphilis, diphtheria, malaria, rheumatism, chronic fatigue syndrome (CFS), acid indigestion, dizziness, migraines, attention deficit-hyperactivity disorder (ADHD), rattlesnake bites, bee stings, boils, skin wounds, ulcers, abscesses, eczema, psoriasis, UV radiation skin damage, burns, herpes simplex, and hemorrhoids.[384]

Echinacea is available in tablet form in addition to being available with juices and as a tea.[384]

- *Pau D'Arco* - Pau D'Arco is a natural remedy made from the bark of the lapacho tree. It has been used to treat a wide range of infections including the common cold, flu, infectious diarrhea, prostate and bladder infections, ringworm (and other parasitic infections), yeast infections, and sexually transmitted infections such as gonorrhea and syphilis.[385] Additionally, Pau D'Arco has been used to treat cancer, diabetes and lupus.[385][386] Pau D'Arco has not been thoroughly studied and, when taken in excessive quantities, can be harmful.

- *Myrrh* - Myrrh is an antibiotic and antiviral supplement that has been used for centuries. It is used to treat a wide range of viral and bacterial infections such as bronchitis, mouth sores and sore throat. Myrrh can be ingested as well as applied topically to cuts and wounds. It should not be taken internally for more than two weeks, as it may otherwise begin to harm the user's kidneys.[387]

- *Grapefruit Seed Extract* - Grapefruit Seed Extract ('GSE') is a liquid derived from the seed and connective tissue of the grapefruit. It is said to have substantial antibiotic properties that are even effective against drug-resistant bacteria.[388]

- *Olive Leaf Extract* - Olive leaf extract is a liquid that is made from the leaves of olive trees. It has been used for many centuries to treat bacterial and viral infections.[388]

10.1.7. Cautions Regarding some Common Non-prescription Medications

Even non-prescription medications carry with them some risks that should be kept in mind by the first aid provider:

- Aspirin should not be given to anyone less then 20 years of age due to the risk of Reye's syndrome, which is a disease that can lead to coma, brain damage and death.

- Ibuprofen (commercially available as Motrin and Advil) can cause stomach irritation and bleeding. Anyone having a peptic ulcer or who is taking a blood-thinning medication should be cautious when taking Ibuprofen.

- Acetaminophen (commercially available as Tylenol) can, if taken in excess, cause liver damage or failure. Anyone who consumes alcohol regularly or anyone having liver disease should be cautious when using Acetaminophen.

10.1.8. Using an Automated External Defibrillator (AED)

The *Automated External Defibrillator* (AED) is an electronic device that can automatically diagnose serious heart conditions (stopped heartbeats or heart arrhythmia) and apply an electrical stimulation which may restart a normal heart rhythm. The device is sufficiently simple to operate that it may even be used by a layperson who has had proper training.

In general, the steps to use an AED are:[329]

- Turn on the AED and note that it will display instructions.

- Expose the subject's chest and wipe it dry if necessary. If the subject has excessive chest hair you may need to trim it with scissors or a razor that should be included with the AED kit.

- Remove any necklaces or wire-frame bras that the subject may be wearing.

- Attach the electrical pads to the chest, one pad above the person's right nipple and the other just below their left rib cage.

- Plug in the electrical connector if necessary.

- Confirm that no one is in physical contact with the subject.

- If prompted by the instructions, push the button labeled 'analyze'.

- If AED display instructs you to, depress the 'shock' button to administer the electrical stimulation.

- Follow any additional instructions provided by the AED and resume CPR activities as needed.

10.1.9. Executing the Heimlich Maneuver to Clear Blocked Air Passages

The *Heimlich Maneuver* (also known as "abdominal thrusts") is an emergency first aid procedure that is used to clear obstructed breathing passages from individuals who are choking (usually such choking is the result of the subject having eaten something). The procedure to follow is:[327]

- Stand behind the person, place one arm around them and make a fist just above their navel

- Place the other arm around them to grab your fist

- Quickly thrust your fist upwards and inwards as many as 5 times (or until it is apparent that you have cleared the airway).

- Administer up to 5 blows between the shoulder blades with the heel of the hand.

- Cycle repeatedly between abdominal thrusts and back blows as needed.

- If the blockage comes out but the individual is not breathing, administer CPR (see section 10.1.10).

As you are performing the procedure you may see the blockage appear in the individual's mouth. If so then quickly use your finger to clear their mouth (but otherwise do not insert your finger into their mouth).

If performing the Heimlich maneuver on a pregnant or obese person it may be necessary to place the fist just below the breast bone.[328]

It is also possible to perform abdominal thrusts on yourself in the event that you are choking. In that case grab your fist above your naval (or below your breast bone) as described above, bend over a chair or counter, and thrust your fist forcefully upward and inward.[328]

10.1.10. Cardiopulmonary Resuscitation (CPR)

Cardiopulmonary Resuscitation ('CPR') is a first aid procedure administered to individuals who have ceased to breathe on their own. CPR is not intended to restart breathing but rather to 'buy time' by forcing some oxygen and blood flow until the heart can be restarted by some other means (typically through use of a defibrillator, which administers an electric shock to restart the heart). In some cases CPR may establish a weak heart rhythm that can then be more fully restored through standard defibrillation.[331]

Standard CPR consists of two procedures that you alternate between, *rescue breathing* and *chest compressions*, and these specific instructions vary depending on whether the incapacitated person is an adult, a child or an infant. *Hands-Only CPR* consists of performing chest compressions only. Administer hands-only CPR in cases of near-drowning, drug overdose, or cardiac arrest that was not witnessed.[327]

Rescue Breathing for Adults

Rescue breathing for adults consists of the following steps:[334]

- Tilt the subject's head back and lift the chin upwards, then pinch the nose closed.

- Give 2 slow breaths into the mouth. Each time blow into the mouth until the subject's chest gently rises.

- Check the subject's wrist or throat to see if there is a pulse. If you detect a pulse and the subject has begun breathing then you may cease providing CPR.

- Administer 1 slow breath every 5 seconds over a 1 minute time period (which corresponds to administering 12 breaths each minute).

- At the end of each minute re-check the subject to see if the pulse is restored and if they have started to breathe on their own.

- At the end of the first minute call for professional medical assistance if possible, and then resume rescue breathing.

Rescue Breathing for Children

Rescue breathing for children consists of the following steps:[334]

- Tilt the subject's head back and lift the chin upwards, then pinch the nose closed.

- Give 2 slow breaths into the mouth. Each time blow into the mouth until the subject's chest gently rises.

- Check the subject's wrist or throat to see if there is a pulse. If you detect a pulse and the subject has begun breathing then you can cease providing CPR.

- Administer 1 slow breath every 3 seconds over a 1 minute time period (which corresponds to administering 20 breaths each minute).

- At the end of each minute re-check the subject to see if the pulse is restored and if they have started to breathe on their own.

- At the end of the first minute call for professional medical assistance if possible, and then resume rescue breathing.

Rescue Breathing for Infants

Rescue breathing for infants consists of the following steps:[334]

- Tilt the subject's head back slightly and lift the chin upwards.

- Seal your lips tightly around the infant's mouth **and** nose.

- Filling your cheeks with air, give two slow breaths. With each breath wait until the chest rises gently.

- Check the subject's wrist or throat to see if there is a pulse. If you detect a pulse but the subject is still not breathing, then the subject urgently needs professional medical care.

- Fill your cheeks with air and 1 slow breath every 3 seconds over a 1 minute time period (which corresponds to administering 20 breaths each minute).

- Recheck for a pulse and restored breathing at the end of each minute, taking a little time to confirm that medical professionals have been summoned.

Hands-Only CPR

To administer *hands-only CPR* lace the fingers of both hands together and put the heel of one hand on the center of the subject's chest. With arms straight (elbows locked) push down hard on the subject's chest until it pushes inwards about 2 inches. Continue to administer these compressions at a rate of about 100 times per minute (a little faster than once per second) as long as possible or until emergency medical personnel arrive.[327]

Standard CPR for Adults

Standard CPR consists of alternating between performing the chest compressions of hands-only CPR and rescue breathing. Alternate between performing 30 chest compressions and two rescue breaths as long as you can until the subject begins to breathe or until better equipped and trained medical help arrives.[327]

Standard CPR for Children

Standard CPR for children consists of alternating between performing chest compressions and rescue breathing. When performing the chest compressions for children place one hand on top of the other and place the heel of the hand on the chest directly between the nipples. Alternate between performing 30 chest compressions and two rescue breaths as long as you can until the subject begins to breathe or until better equipped and trained medical help arrives.

Each chest compression should compress the chest by about 2 inches, and allow the chest to rise completely before starting a next trust. This should correspond to a rate of about 100 compressions per minute.

Between sets of 30 chest compressions perform rescue breathing by breathing twice into the child's mouth.

If you have altered between chest compressions and rescue breathing for more than two minutes then you should try once again to contact professional medical personnel or look for an automated electronic defibrillator to use on the subject.[327]

Standard CPR for Infants

As with children, standard CPR for infants consists of alternating between performing chest compressions and rescue breathing. If working alone, alternate between performing 30 chest compressions and two rescue breaths as long as you can until the subject begins to breathe or better equipped and trained medical help arrives. If you have assistance then perform sets of 15 chest compressions between sets of two rescue breaths.

For infants the chest should be compressed by about 1.5 inches, and the chest compressions should be performed by placing only two fingers above (but not directly over) the breast bone. Be sure not to exert pressure directly on the ribs.[327]

10.1.11. Recognizing and Treating Dehydration

Dehydration is a dangerous condition in which the subject has experienced an excessive loss of water. This can result from inadequate water intake or from loss of water due to diarrhea, excessive vomiting or a severe burn. The result can be a life-threatening disruption of the body's normal metabolic processes. The symptoms of dehydration include tingling of the limbs, muscle spams, shriveled skin, dim vision, reduced and painful urination and delirium.[369]

While medical professionals may administer intravenous solutions to combat dehydration, for a non-medical-professional providing first aid the best solution is to administer *oral rehydration therapy ('ORT')*. ORT consists of feeding the subject a fluid that, in extreme cases of dehydration, may be as much as 10% of the subject's body weight during the first two to four hours of treatment. If no pre-formulated ORT fluid is available one may be made by mixing 1 liter of boiled (or otherwise sanitized) water, 1 teaspoon of salt, 8 teaspoons of sugar and mashed banana (to provide potassium and improve taste).[73]

10.1.12. Treating Wounds

The basic process of treating wounds is:[339]

- Stop any bleeding (using a tourniquet only if absolutely necessary)
- Clean the wound with clean, clear water or saline solution
- Apply a topical antibiotic if available
- Dress the wound by packing it with clean gauze
- Clean the wound and change the dressings regularly
- Watch for signs of infection
- Seek follow-up care from a trained medical professional

If the subject is not up-to-date with a tetanus immunization and/or a tetanus booster then they should receive the immunization or booster within 48 hours of being injured.[341]

Stopping Bleeding

All but the smallest cuts will require the application of some pressure to (hopefully) stop the bleeding. Pressure should be applied with the most sterile material available (ideally sterile gauze). If no materials are available then the first aid provider can apply pressure directly

> **NOTE:** *If possible and practical it is a good idea to take a few close-up pictures of any serious wound before and during treatment. Later a medical professional may find these pictures helpful in determining the best follow-up treatment.*

with their hand[339] (or have the subject apply the pressure if they are capable of doing so). The pressure should be applied for at least 4 minutes. Retry after 4 minutes if the rate of bleeding is not diminished. If the wound is on an arm or leg then elevating the affected body part may also help to control bleeding.[340]

If the wound is on an extremity and it cannot be made to stop bleeding through the application of pressure, then it may be necessary to apply a tourniquet above the wound to stop the bleeding. This should be considered only as a final option, as the use of a tourniquet may result in dangerous infection (*gangrene*) and ultimately the need to amputate the limb.

> **NOTE:** *Any wound resulting from a human or animal bite is at serious risk of infection, and should receive attention from a medical professional at the earliest possible time.[341]*

Cleaning Wounds

Wounds should be thoroughly washed with either clean water or saline solution. This reduces the risk of infection (tetanus in particular). Ideally the stream of liquid used to clean the wound should be under pressure. This can be accomplished by feeding the water through a tube attached to a plastic bottle while having someone squeeze the bottle. Another common approach is to place the water into a plastic Ziploc bag, cutting a hole in the corner, and squeezing the bag to produce a pressurized stream of water. While cleaning the wound a cotton ball or swab should be used to help remove any unwanted foreign materials.[340]

> **CAUTION:** *Alcohol, soap, iodine and peroxide should* **NOT** *be used to clean a wound, as these substances irritate the healthy cells.[340]*

Applying a Topical Antibiotic to a Wound

Once a wound is cleaned a *topical antibiotic* should be applied to help protect it from external sources of infection. If no such antibiotic is available it is possible to mix a thick paste consisting of a mixture of sugar and Povidone-iodine (*'Sugardine'*) to create a homemade topical antibiotic. If you do this then the Povidone-iodine should only be added in sufficient quantities to change the color of the sugar, but not so much as to cause it to become liquified.[344] If Povidone-iodine is not available then a paste of sugar and clean water can also be used (the affect of the sugar is to destroy bacteria by drawing water through their cell membranes).[342]

> **NOTE:** *Povidone-iodine (better known by its commercial brand name 'Betadine') is an excellent topical antibiotic that kills bacteria, viruses, yeasts, molds and fungi. Due to the nature of its biological activity, microorganisms can never develop a resistance to it.[102] Every prepper's first aid kit should include a good supply of this important antibiotic, along with a good supply of sterile gauze.*

Honey may also be used as a topical antibiotic for wound care. In fact, some studies indicate that honey is more effective than sugar in treating wounds.[343]

If using Sugardine and/or honey the wound dressings should be changed more often than once per day, otherwise the sugar or honey may start to **increase** the probability and severity of infection.[344]

Dressing a Wound

Most small cuts and scrapes can be effectively treated with a single washing, the application of a topical antibiotic and protection with an adhesive bandage. For larger wounds sterile gauze should be used as a dressing. The gauze should be wrapped gently around the wound. Any time you are dressing a wound it should first be re-cleaned (and topical antibiotic re-applied) before the gauze is changed.[340]

Once the wound is dressed, soap and water should be used to clean around the wound.[340]

Cleaning the Wound and Changing the Dressing

Wound dressings should be changed daily, and more often if the dressing becomes dirty or dry, or if a homemade Sugardine antibiotic is being used (the dressing must be changed whenever the granulated sugar becomes liquified). Each time a dressing is replaced the wound should be re-cleaned with water and re-treated with a topical antibiotic.[340]

> **NOTE:** *Because the dressings for wounds must be changed periodically a single wound can require a good quantity of sterile gauze while healing. One way to save gauze might be to pack cotton tampons over the gauze. However, it is a good idea to not have tampons come into direct contact with an injury because they are not sterile and their cotton fibers can irritate the wound and complicate healing.[345]*

Watching for Signs of Infection

While a wound is healing it should be observed for any sign of infection. These signs include swelling, tenderness, the area around the wound being warm to the touch, the presence of pus or red streaks extending from the wound.[340] Any such sign of infection should be be considered a clear indicator that the wound victim has an urgent need for expert medical attention.[341]

> **NOTE:** *Many preppers train themselves to administer stitches to close up wounds. This practice is not recommended for anyone other than a trained medical professional, as the probability of turning a relatively minor wound into a fatal infection is pretty high, and most treatable wounds do not require closure to heal.* **Leave the stitching (and gluing and other forms of closure) of wounds to trained medical professionals!**
>
> *The administering of blood transfusions should also only be attempted by trained medical professionals with proper medical equipment.*

10.2. Treating Common Post-Disaster Illnesses and Trauma

The remainder of this chapter describes procedures for handling the more common first aid needs that can be anticipated during and after a major disaster.

10.2.1. Animal Bites and Rabies

Animal bites carry a high risk of infection (and human bites become infected almost 100% of the time). Consequently, all bites should receive high-priority attention. The procedure for treating a bite is:[327]

- Apply pressure to stop any bleeding

- Wash the wound gently with soap and water

- Apply an topical antibiotic to the injury

- Cover the injury with a sterile bandage

- Seek aid from a medical professional as soon as possible

If the bite was from a domestic animal then you should report the incident as soon as possible to the animal's owner. You should also contact local animal control personnel. The animal itself should be quarantined for observation for 10 days, and if during that time it exhibits erratic and abnormal behavior then it should be assumed to be rabid.

Rabies normally takes 1 to 3 months to develop in an infected person (although gestation periods as short as 4 days and as long as 6 years have been reported[105]). Initial symptoms of rabies include headache, fever and general malaise. As the disease progresses the victim will begin to experience anxiety, insomnia, partial paralysis, hallucinations, agitation, excitability, hypersalivation, hydrophobia and difficulty swallowing. Rabies is generally fatal if allowed to progress to the point that any of these symptoms begin to manifest themselves,[103] so it is essential for any bite victim who suspects they may have been exposed to rabies to receive medical care as early as possible (there are no records of anyone dying who received proper medical treatment within 48 hours of initial exposure to rabies[104]).

In a disaster scenario if it is found that a dog or cat has been exposed to the rabies virus then it should immediately be euthanized.

NOTE: *Dogs, foxes, bats, raccoons, coyotes and wolves are the animals that most commonly transmit rabies to humans through bites.[106] Squirrels, mice, rats, hamsters, gerbils, guinea pigs, chipmunks, rabbits, and hares have very seldom been found to have rabies, and have never been known to cause a case of human rabies in the United States.[107]*

10.2.2. Asthma Attacks

Asthma is a medical condition in which the victim's airways constrict to the point that breathing becomes difficult and simple activities such as walking and talking can become almost impossible. Most asthma sufferers are aware of their condition and will be able to recognize an attack when it occurs.

The procedure for treating an asthma attack is to have the subject sit up, loosen all clothing, and breathe from an asthma inhaler if one is available (the asthma victim may have their own inhaler or one might be obtained from a first aid kit).[327] While relaxation is not generally recognized as a means of treating an asthma attack, the subject should be encouraged to relax and remain as inactive as possible so as not to increase their body's need for oxygen.

Triggers for asthma attacks include allergens (dust, mold, animal dander, pollen, etc.), stress, colds, exercise, sinus infections, very hot and humid air, very cold and dry air, acid reflux (heartburn), strong odors or perfumes and cigarette smoke[108]. If any of these triggers is suspected then the person suffering the asthma attack should be moved to a location where they are no longer exposed.

10.2.3. Blisters

Blisters are liquid-filled bubbles that form on a person's skin due to physical irritation of the skin, exposure to extreme temperatures, insect or spider bites, various diseases and infections or as an adverse reaction to some medications.[129] The blister itself is the body's protective mechanism and, unless the presence of the blister inhibits some necessary physical activity, it should not be disturbed and should simply be covered with an adhesive bandage (in the case of small blisters) or a moisture-absorbent gauze pad (in the case of larger blisters) and allowed to heal naturally.

If a blister must be punctured then the person performing the puncture should prepare by washing their hands thoroughly with soap and warm water and sterilizing the needle by exposure to flame or immersion in boiling water. Prior to being punctured the blister should be swabbed with a topical antibiotic such as Povidone-iodine (Betadine) or antibiotic ointment. It should then be punctured at multiple locations around the edge of the blister, leaving the skin intact, treated once again with a topical antibiotic, and covered with a moisture-absorbing gauze pad and an adhesive bandage.[129]

Several days after being punctured the injury should heal and the dry, dead skin covering the blister can be cut away with sterilized scissors (or other sterilized tool). Care should be taken that only the dry, dead skin is cut away. Once the procedure is completed the area should once again be treated with a topical antibiotic and covered with gauze and an adhesive bandage.[129]

CAUTION: *Diabetics should be particularly careful not to puncture or otherwise damage blisters and seek professional medical treatment for large blisters.[129]*

10.2.4. Blood in Urine

Blood in an individual's urine may present itself as a red, brown, pink or orange color appearing in the urine stream. While most causes of blood in urine are not serious, there are some causes that are. The underlying problem can only be determined by a trained medical professional with sophisticated medical equipment. As a result the subject should seek the assistance of a doctor at the earliest opportunity.[327]

Prior to seeing the doctor note should be made of the color of the urine, the presence of any clots and when during urination the blood is visible. The doctor will also be interested if any pain was involved and, if so, the location of the pain.[327]

10.2.5. Broken Bones

Broken bones are serious injuries that really require the attention of a medical professional. The first step in providing first aid to a subject with a possible broken bone is to determine if the injury is truly a broken bone, or if it might be a sprain or strain. Of course if you can physically see the broken bone then there is no need to consider other injury types. Please refer to page 208 for guidelines to identify broken bones.

If the break subject exhibits symptoms of shock (e.g. fainting or quick, shallow breathing) then have them first lay down with their legs elevated and their head at a slightly lower elevation than the body. The break should be considered a medical emergency if any of the following is observed:[328]

- The subject is unresponsive
- If a foot or hand on a broken leg or arm becomes cold and blue[109]
- The subject is bleeding heavily as a result of the break (including any internal bleeding, which may or may not be observable)
- If a broken bone is protruding through the skin

- If the break results in an observable deformation of the neck, head, hip, pelvis, or upper leg

- If the slightest movement or most gentle pressure to the area results in extreme pain

Any bone break exhibiting any of the above symptoms requires prompt attention from a medical professional.

The general procedure for treating broken bones is:[109]

- If the break has resulted in the deformation of an arm or leg then do **NOT** attempt to straighten it before it receives attention from a medical professional.

- If possible, elevate any broken extremity.

- Immobilize any broken extremity with padding.

- Apply ice (wrapped in a cloth) to the injured area. If possible add water to the ice to allow it to better conform to the body.

- Provide the subject with anti-inflammatory drugs such as ibuprofen or naproxen (subject to the cautions listed on page 221).

- Seek assistance from a trained medical professional.

If the break is to an extremity and it is not causing a deformity then a first follow-up treatment might be to further stabilize it with a splint and to use some sort of weight-and-pulley system to apply traction.[109]

Broken Fingers and Toes

If a finger or toe has a broken bone that has resulted in a break in the skin then the injured area should be wrapped in gauze, a clean diaper or other clean material, any bleeding should be brought under control through elevation of the foot or hand, and application of gentle pressure to the wound (maybe by simply wrapping clean gauze over the wound such that it provides slight pressure).

If a broken finger does not result in a breaking of the skin or deformation of the finger then a splint should be applied to immobilize the finger. The finger may also be taped to an adjacent finger to provide additional support. Swelling and inflammation can then be treated through the application of ice (see above) as well as the taking of anti-inflammatory drugs (see page 221 for cautions).

Broken toes should be treated much like broken fingers with the addition that the foot should be elevated as much as possible for as long as 2 days (to control swelling), and the subject should not apply any weight to the foot until the break has healed (after the broken toe has healed the subject should wear protective footwear for 3-to-4 weeks and avoid putting any pressure on the toe.[327])

Broken Arms

In the case of a broken arm that exhibits redness, swelling or any sort of deformation, or in a case in which the subject refuses to move the arm, no attempt should be made to straighten the arm. Any bleeding should be stopped, the arm should be elevated, and ice should be applied as described above.[327]

If the arm does not exhibit the redness, swelling or deformation described above then a split should be applied to further immobilize the arm.[327]

Broken Ankles

Broken ankles often require x-rays and other modern equipment for a complete diagnosis, although numbness is often a good indication of a broken ankle. The ankle should be elevated, treated with ice as described above and anti-inflammatory and pain-killing drugs should be administered. Small ankle breaks may be treated in much the same manner as sprained ankles, while large breaks may require surgery for proper healing.[330] In all cases the subject should not apply weight to the affected ankle until it is healed.

Broken Legs

Like other breaks, broken legs should be gently straightened and immobilized if no deformation is observed. The immobilization can be with pads and/or pillows and/or the application of a splint (a medical professional with proper equipment may also prescribe that traction be applied to the leg). Ice should then be applied as described above and anti-inflammatory pain-killers provided to the subject.[327]

Other Broken Bones

In case of broken bones that do not involve the extremities any bleeding should be brought under control with the application of gentle pressure (although if a bone is breaking the skin then the area should not be touched until a medical professional arrives). Any jewelry around the affected area should be removed, ice should be applied to the injured area as described above, and anti-inflammatory, pain-killing drugs should be provided to the subject.[327] (See page 221 for cautions.)

10.2.6. Non-Chemical Burns

Burns are classified into three categories based on severity:[327]

- *First degree* - burns that involve only the top layer of skin. These ("superficial burns") appear as reddened skin.

- *Second degree* - burns that involve the top two layers of skin. These *"partial thickness burns"* result in the formation of blisters and are extremely painful (sometimes the pain may be reduced due to nerve damage).

- *Third degree* - burns that penetrate below the second layer of skin. These *"full thickness burns"* involve charred or leathery skin and blisters, and the victim may experience chest pains, rapid breathing, rapid heartbeat or go into shock. Victims of third degree burns require immediate attention from medical professionals.

Each burn category is treated differently. The treatment for first degree burns is:[110]

- Hold the burned area under a stream of cold water for 10 minutes.

- Treat the burned area with a burn cream or other ointment.

- Cover the injury with sterile gauze.

- If needed, provide the subject with an over-the-counter pain relief medication (subject to the cautions listed on page 221).

The treatment for second degree burns is:[110]

- If there are no open blisters, hold the burned area under a stream of cold water for 10 minutes.

- Cover the injury with sterile gauze.

- Do **NOT** apply any burn ointments to the injury without consulting a doctor.

- Seek immediate medical treatment from a trained medical professional.

Victims of third degree burns should be transported immediately to a professional medical facility for care.

10.2.7. Chemical Burns

When faced with a chemical burn first be sure that no one else (including the person providing the first aid) is being exposed to the source of the burn.

The following rules apply to larger chemical burns:[327]

- Anyone administering first aid should protect themselves from the chemical through the use of gloves, apron, etc.
- Do not remove any clothing that is stuck to the burned area unless otherwise indicated by any instructions accompanying the chemical that caused the burn.
- Remove any jewelry or clothing from the victim that may affect or impede treatment.
- Allow a gentle stream of cool water to flow over the affected area for at least 20 minutes.
- Unless otherwise instructed by the instructions for the chemical that caused the burn, do not apply any substances to the burn in an effort to neutralize the chemical (this risks worsening the burn).
- Do not administer any form of antibiotic to the victim.
- For small burns cover the burned area with a sterile gauze or other clean cloth.
- Provide the victim with any over-the-counter pain medicines to help address the accompanying pain (subject to the cautions listed on page 221).
- If the victim has not had a tetanus shot (or tetanus booster shot) within the previous 5 years, consult with a physician about the need for a tetanus shot.

The victim should seek immediate treatment from a medical professional if any of the following is true:[327]

- They show any sign of going into shock (including fainting, pale complexion or rapid breathing).
- The burn penetrated the first layer of skin (often indicated by the presence of blisters).
- The burned area is larger than 3 inches in diameter.
- The burned area included the hands, feet, eye, groin, buttocks or a large joint.
- The person is experiencing severe pain that cannot be controlled with over-the-counter medications.

10.2.8. Chemicals in Eye

The following is a general procedure for treating individuals for chemical exposure to their eyes:[327]

- Instruct the subject not to rub his or her eyes.[328]

- Start by having the subject wash their hands, or any other parts of their body that have come into contact with the chemical.

- Flush the affected eye with water for 20 to 30 minutes. (Flush the eye in a shower if possible for the best possible irrigation.) Allow the water flush to remove any contact lenses if possible. Have the subject open the injured eye as wide as possible while flushing it.

Eye burns from acid and alkali substances should receive immediate attention from a trained medical professional. Alkali and hydrofluoric acid burns tend to be the most severe. Alkali substances include fertilizers, cleaning products such as ammonia, drain cleaners, lye, oven cleaners, plaster and cement.[328]

Acid products include glass cleaners, vinegar and nail polish remover. One of the most common chemical eye burns is from explosions of automobile batteries, which involves exposing the eye to sulfuric acid.[328]

10.2.9. Choking

The Heimlich Maneuver should be performed to assist anyone who is choking. Please refer to page 222 for instructions for performing this procedure.

10.2.10. Cramps

Cramps are sudden and involuntary contractions of muscles that can sometimes cause the muscles to tighten and become very hard. While cramps are usually harmless they can be quite painful, and they can present a danger of drowning if they occur while a person is swimming.

Muscle cramps can be caused by long periods of exercise or physical labor, particularly when performed outside in hot weather. Cramps can also be caused by some medications and some medical conditions.[346]

If a person experiences severely painful or frequent cramps, or cramps that do not have an obvious cause, then they should consult with a physician.

Cramps can normally be treated without a medical professional by taking the following steps: [346]

- Stretch and gently rub the cramped muscle(s).

- For a cramped calf muscle put weight on the leg while bending the knee slightly.

- If unable to stand try pulling the top of the foot on the affected side toward your head with the leg held straight (this is helpful for both calf and hamstring cramps).

- For a cramp of the front thigh grab the foot of the affected leg and try pulling it up behind you towards the buttock.

- Get (and stay) well-hydrated.

It is widely accepted that eating potassium-rich foods such as bananas can prevent and alleviate cramps. Other high-potassium foods include apricots, nectarines, dates, grapes, raisins, beans, cabbage, broccoli, oranges, grapefruit, pork and lamb, potatoes, corn, saltwater fish such as tuna, and tomatoes.[347]

It has been speculated that recurring cramps may be alleviated by having the subject take B Vitamins, however this has not been studied sufficiently to be conclusive.

10.2.11. Diarrhea

Diarrhea is defined as a person experiencing three or more liquid bowel movements in a single day. Diarrhea, when severe enough, can result in life-threatening dehydration. In 2009 it was estimated that over 1 million people aged 5 and over died due to complications arising from diarrhea.[348] In "first world" nations diarrhea is seldom the cause of fatalities however, as was demonstrated in the aftermath of Hurricane Katrina, it is a thin and delicate line that separates the modern world from third world conditions. In a post-disaster scenario diarrhea is a medical condition (and sanitation issue) that should be taken **VERY** seriously.

The challenge to saving lives from diarrhea is to prevent dehydration while either antibiotics or the subject's own immune system overcome the underlying disease. *Oral rehydration therapy ('ORT')* is the widely-accepted treatment for cases of diarrhea that pose the threat of dehydration (in severe cases of dehydration, and in a properly-equipped medical facility, the subject may also be given solutions intravenously).

ORT involves having the subject drink large quantities of *oral rehydration solutions ('ORS')* to replace lost bodily fluids and to restore the balance of electrolytes within the body. These ORS solutions can be made by mixing pre-packaged salt and zinc tablets with water, or by producing homemade ORS. See page 226 for details on oral rehydration therapy and how to produce homemade ORS.

Other practices that can help combat diarrhea include:[327]

- Give children plenty of clear liquids to drink such as water, Ceralyte, Infalyte or Pedialyte (Infalyte is appropriate for treating adults as well as children). If any fruit juices or other common, non-electrolyte-balanced drinks are given they should be diluted with 50% water.

- Avoid providing the subject with milk or any milk-based products, apple juice, alcohol or beverages that contain caffeine until 3 to 5 days after recovery, as they can result in relapse.

- Provide infants with frequent sips of water and/or diluted juice and/or the electrolyte-balanced products mentioned above.

- Do **NOT** augment any drinks provided to infants with salt tablets.

- If the subject is losing more in fluids through diarrhea than they are consuming, then seek professional medical attention for them.

- Make sure the subject gets plenty of rest and avoids strenuous work while they are recovering.

- For recovering infants restart the diet with a mixture of bananas, rice, applesauce and toast if possible.

- For recovering adults low-fiber and semi-solid foods should be re-introduced gradually and spicy, fatty or greasy foods should be avoided until several days after recovery.

A doctor should be certain to see the subject if any of the following are true:[327]

- If there is an apparent need to administer any sort of anti-diarrhea medication (over-the-counter or otherwise).

- If there is a belief that the subject contracted the diarrhea due to travel (particularly due to international travel).

- If the subject is or was taking an antibiotic prior to the diarrhea.

- If there is any observation of mucus or blood in the subject's stool.

- If the subject is losing more fluids through diarrhea than they are consuming.

10.2.12. Dislocated shoulders

Shoulder injuries can be very painful and debilitating. The shoulder consists of a 'ball and socket' joint in which a ball at the end of one bone fits into a socket of another bone, which are then held in place with muscles tendons and ligaments. When the ball is shifted such that it is not resting in its normal position in the socket it is said to be dislocated.

There are 3 forms of shoulder dislocation:[112]

- *Anterior ('forward') dislocation* - 95% of shoulder dislocations are anterior dislocations. These dislocations are typically caused by a blow to an outstretched arm, or a fall onto an outstretched arm. It is often indicated by the subject raising their arm slightly to their side with the hand rotated slightly outward.

- *Posterior ('backward') dislocation* - These dislocations tend to be caused by electrical shocks or seizures, and are indicated by the subject raising their arm slightly to their side with the hand rotated slightly inward.[113]

- *Inferior ('downward') dislocation* - These very rare dislocations are caused by an over-rotation of the arm at the shoulder, and are indicated by the subject having to keep their arm raised and behind their head.

NOTE: *Dislocated shoulders should not be confused with the much more serious condition known as a* separated shoulder. *Separated shoulders are due to a linear force being exerted downward against the top of the shoulder. Major shoulder dislocations require surgery to be corrected.[112]*

The process of physically re-orienting a dislocated shoulder to its proper position in the socket is known as *'reduction'*. 'Closed reductions' are those reductions that do not require surgery (they simply involve external manipulation of the arm). 'Open reductions' are those which require correction via surgery.[112]

Inferior dislocations of the shoulder are complex and can potentially damage tendons, nerves and muscles. As a result they almost always require open reduction to be performed surgically.[112]

Posterior dislocations of the shoulder may be resolved through closed reduction, however in some cases (particularly when the injury has been untreated for more than 6 weeks) such dislocations require surgery. Closed reduction of posterior dislocations involves applying traction to the arm while simultaneously raising the arm straight from the side and rotating it inward until the bone pops into place. This is typically done with the subject rendered unconscious by general anaesthesia.[113]

In discussing shoulder reductions the arm is often described as being (abducted) or (adducted):

- *Abducted* - refers to the arm being rotated at the shoulder such that it is not against the subject's side

- *Adducted* - refers to the arm being held straight against the subject's side

A number of closed reductions have been identified which can be effective in correcting anterior shoulder dislocations. Some techniques are best for cases in which the subject is able to hold their arm in the adducted position, while others are best for those cases in which the arm is held in the abducted position.

It is possible that muscle spasms may prevent any procedure from being effective, in which case it becomes necessary for a doctor to sedate the subject before attempting the reduction.[115] The following sections describe some common shoulder reduction techniques that may possibly be attempted without the administration of a sedative.

Kocher's Method for Shoulder Reduction

Kocher's Method of shoulder reduction is easy to perform and has the highest rate of success of all shoulder reduction methods[114], however it also can be quite painful to the subject and, if performed too quickly or with inappropriate traction applied, can result in significant follow-on complications. This method should be performed for those cases in which the subject prefers to have the reduction performed with the arm in the abducted position.

With this method the subject lies flat on his or her back with their arms against their sides. The affected arm is then bent 90 degrees at the elbow (the person performing the procedure should be holding the subject's wrist with one hand and the elbow with the other). Grasping the hand arm is gently rotated to the outside to an angle of between 70 and 85 degrees until resistance is felt (if the subject is conscious then some effort should be made to keep them distracted during this procedure). The upper arm is then lifted as far as possible and the lower part of the arm is then rotated back towards the body. This should result in the shoulder popping back into its proper position, and the associated pain should diminish.[114]

Milch's Method for Shoulder Reduction

Milche's method is for those who prefer to have the shoulder reduced with the arm being abducted. It involves the subject laying face down on flat surface, with pillows placed under the pectoral muscle of the injured side of the body. The arm is then allowed to hang freely, which in some cases is sufficient to cause the shoulder joint to spontaneously reduce to its normal position.

If the shoulder does not reduce while the arm is hanging then the injured arm is bent 90 degrees at the elbow and the subject's hand rests against the caregiver's forearm at the elbow. The caregiver then grabs the subject's arm at the elbow, with the other hand grasping the upper part of the arm below the tricep and pulling upwards and outwards gently. The injured arm is then rotated slowly away from the subject's head with the intent of causing the shoulder to reduce into its proper position.[114]

Cunningham's Technique for Shoulder Reduction

Cunningham's Technique for the reduction of dislocated shoulders is for those cases in which the subject is able to sit upright with their injured arm held directly to their side (in the *adducted* position). The caregiver has the subject sit upright with their chest out, and bends the subject's arm 90 degrees at the elbow, placing the palm of the subject's hand on the caregiver's shoulder. The caregiver then instructs the subject to shrug the injured shoulder.

The caregiver then begins to massage the middle and upper part of the subject's bicep and behind the injured shoulder. After a few minutes the injured shoulder should spontaneously (and often painlessly) reduce back to its normal position. This entire procedure can take as little as 2 minutes.[115]

The Spaso Technique for Shoulder Reduction

The Spaso technique requires the subject to lay flat on their back. The caregiver raises the arm until it is pointed directly up. With gentle upwards traction applied by the caregiver the arm is rotated away from the body. The result is that the shoulder should spontaneously reduce to its proper position.[114]

The Eskimo Technique for Shoulder Reduction

The Eskimo technique requires the subject to lay sideways on the ground with the uninjured shoulder being on the ground. Two caregivers then raise the injured arm until it is pointed directly upwards and then, holding the arm, pull upwards until the subject is suspended just slightly off the ground. After a few minutes of hanging in this position the shoulder should spontaneously reduce to its proper position.[114]

Post-Reduction Treatment

Once a dislocated shoulder has been successfully reduced the affected arm should be kept in a sling for between 2 to 8 weeks, depending on the severity of the dislocation. Ice should be applied to the shoulder as needed, and anti-inflammatory pain medications may also help.[116] After the arm is removed from the sling an additional 4 to 6 months may be required for a full recovery. During this time the daily exertion of the arm should gradually be increased until it can be used normally.[116]

10.2.13. Dizziness

Dizziness is classified into the following general forms:[118]

- *Vertigo* - A feeling that oneself or one's surroundings are spinning. Vertigo is usually attributed to a change in the balance structures of the inner ear and/or a change in their connection to the brain due to inflammation, a buildup of fluid, a migraine, the presence of a non-cancerous tumor (usually accompanied by hearing loss and/or tinnitus) or other more serious causes such as strokes and brain hemorrage.

- *Disequilibrium* - A feeling of being off balance. Disequilibrium may be caused by problems of the inner ear, sensory disorders such as nerve damage in the legs, problems with joints and muscles, medications or neurological conditions such as Parkinson's disease.

- *Lightheadedness* - A feeling of weakness and fainting. Lightheadedness may be the result in a sudden loss of blood pressure (sometimes experienced when standing up too quickly) or poor blood flow from the heart.

In cases of vertigo the subject's brain often adjusts over a period of a couple of weeks and the vertigo simply ceases. Other cases may be related to inflammation and fluid buildup that may be attributed to infection. (See page 209 for information on treating infections.)

The causes of disequilibrium may be difficult even for medical professionals to deal with, and the subject may need to alter their lifestyle to accommodate the balance problem until professional treatment becomes available. Using a cane to steady themself while walking is one way that the subject may compensate for a feeling of disequilibrium.

Feelings of lightheadedness that do not persist probably offer little cause for concern. However, if the feeling is persistent then the subject should modify their lifestyle until they receive attention from a medical professional.[118]

It should also be noted that dehydration can also be a source of dizziness. If dehydration is suspected then the subject should rest and consume fluids until the dizziness passes. If severe dehydration is suspected then oral rehydration therapy *('ORT')* should be considered (see page 226).

10.2.14. Electrical Shock

When treating an individual for electrical shock it is important to first be assured that the victim is no longer in contact with the source of the shock (otherwise the caregiver may also become a victim!). It is also important early on to ascertain that others have been protected from the source of the shock (that a switch has been turned off, or possibly that the location has been cordoned off).

NOTE: *When dealing with any source of live electricity it is important to keep in mind that it should only be manipulated with a non-conductive tool such as wood or cardboard, and that if high voltages are involved that it is better to cordon off the area until a professional electrician can become involved.*

If the victim is not breathing and does not have a pulse then CPR should be started immediately (see page 223). In order to prevent the victim from going into shock they should be laid down with their legs raised and their head slightly lower than the rest of their body.[328]

If the victim is bleeding then attempt to stop the bleeding by applying pressure to the wound with a sterile or clean cloth (or by applying pressure directly with one's hand if necessary). Check every 4 minutes to see if the bleeding has stopped. (If not then refer to page 226 for instructions for dealing with wounds.)

If the shock has resulted in a burn then refer to page 235 for instructions for treating burns.

10.2.15. Frostbite

Frostbite is the destruction of body tissues due to freezing. The tissue freezing results from the fact that, under extremely cold conditions, the body will constrict the blood vessels of the extremities in order to radiate less heat and better preserve the body's core temperature. The reduced blood flow makes it much easier for the effected body parts to freeze. Due to the destructive way in which water crystallizes within the body's cells when frozen, the effected tissues can be severely damaged. This damage may be sufficiently severe that amputation of the affected body part(s) may become necessary.[117]

Just as with burns, there are different degrees of frostbite:[117]

- *First Degree Frostbite (a.k.a. 'Frostnip')* - Only the surface of the skin is frozen, with yellow, red and white patches visible. The skin may itch and/or be painful but no permanent damage will result.

- *Second Degree Frostbite* - The skin may freeze and harden but the underlying tissues do not freeze. Blisters may form that turn hard and black. No permanent damage results other than possibly the development of temperature sensitivity at the affected areas.

- *Third and Forth Degree Frostbite* - The skin, along with underlying tissue including muscles, blood vessels, tendons and nerves freeze. The skin becomes hard and develops a wax-like texture. Purple, blood-filled blisters form that eventually turn black. The affected part of the body becomes unusable (possibly permanently), and the dead tissue can become gangrenous. It is possible that dead tissue removal and amputations will take place over several months.

In order to minimize the damage done by frostbite some rules can be observed:

- Do not subject the frostbitten body parts to any more movement than is absolutely necessary. In some cases the use of a splint may help to protect the body part from unnecessary motion.

- Do not begin the process of warming the frostbitten body part if it is suspected that it will re-freeze later.

Once the victim reaches shelter the body part can either be allowed to naturally return to room temperature or it may be actively warmed through such means as immersion in warm water.[117] The victim should then receive professional medical care at the first available opportunity.

10.2.16. Heart Attack

The signs of a heart attack include:

- A feeling of uncomfortable pressure, fullness or squeezing pain in the chest

- Prolonged pain in the upper abdomen

- Pain spreading from the chest to the shoulders, neck and/or arms

- Lightheadedness

- Sweating

- Nausea

If it is believed that a person is suffering from a heart attack they should be made as comfortable as possible. If they suffer from a known heart problem for which they have medication, then they should be administered that medication (often heart patients will be prescribed nitroglycerin). If no heart attack medication is available then the subject should be provided with aspirin to chew and swallow (this will thin the blood and reduce the work load imposed on the heart).

If the subject becomes unconscious then CPR should be administered (see page 223).

10.2.17. Heat Cramps

Heat cramps are painful and involuntary muscle spasms that typically occur when an individual is exercising heavily in a hot environment. The individual experiencing a heat cramp should rest briefly and abstain from any strenuous activity for several hours after the cramps subside. During that time they should drink plenty of clear fluids (particularly any fluids that offer balanced electrolytes). It may also be helpful to stretch and gently massage the affected area.[328]

10.2.18. Heat Exhaustion and Heat Stroke

Heat exhaustion is a condition that occurs when a person becomes so hot that they overwhelm their body's own cooling mechanisms. Once this happens the body's temperature begins to rise quickly and any of the following symptoms may manifest themselves:

- Thirst

- Heavy sweating

- Headache

- Fatigue

- Pale, clammy skin

- Rapid heartbeat

- Dizziness or fainting

- Nausea and/or vomiting

- Muscle or abdominal cramps

- Temperature elevations

As heat exhaustion can quickly become a life-threatening *heat stroke* anyone suspected of having heat exhaustion should immediately cease all activity, begin drinking cool (but not cold) liquids, and move themselves to a cool environment. Water should be adequate to deal with heat exhaustion, however it can also be helpful for the subject to drink a sports drink that replenishes electrolytes, or to take any supplements containing calcium, magnesium and/or potassium.[119]

Heat stroke is basically a progression of heat exhaustion in which the body's temperature has been elevated above 105.1°F. The treatment for heat stroke is the same as the treatment for heat exhaustion, however with greatly increased sense of urgency and a greatly increased need for professional medical attention.[120]

> **CAUTION:** *A person who has progressed to heat stroke is at imminent risk of cardiac arrest and death.*

10.2.19. Human Bites

Due to the types of bacteria and viruses that inhabit the human mouth, a human bite actually carries greater risk of dangerous infection than an animal bite. The steps in treating a human bite are:[328]

- Stop the bleeding by applying pressure with a sterile or clean cloth. (If no sterile or clean cloth is available then a hand can be used to apply the pressure.)
- Wash the wound thoroughly with soap and water.
- Apply an antibiotic cream to the injury (preferably a triple-antibiotic cream).
- Cover the bite with a clean bandage.
- If the subject has not had a tetanus shot, or tetanus booster shot, within the past 5 years then seek professional medical attention.

10.2.20. Hypothermia

Hypothermia is a condition in which the body's temperature drops from its normal temperature of 98.6°F to below 95°F. Victims of hypothermia exhibit symptoms of memory loss, loss of consciousness, confusion, slurred speech, numbness of the extremities, shallow breathing and/or shivering.

Proper treatment for hypothermia is to restore body warmth. If the subject is wearing wet clothing then it should first be removed and they should be dried off. They should then be placed under several layers of blankets and/or given dry clothing to wear. Warm the trunk of the subject's body first and wait to warm the hands and feet, as warming the hands and feet first can result in shock.

Do **not** attempt to warm the subject by immersing them in warm water, as warming too quickly can result in heart arrhythmia.[121]

If the subject stops breathing then administer CPR immediately (see page 223 for instructions on performing CPR). If they are conscious then provide them with warm liquids to drink (but not any beverage containing caffeine or alcohol).

In severe cases of hypothermia a medical professional may administer fluids intravenously to the subject, or provide them with warmed oxygen to breathe.[121]

10.2.21. Intestinal Distress

Intestinal distress may take several forms, the most common of which are:[327]

- *Heartburn* - if the subject indicates that they are experiencing heartburn then initial treatment should be for them to be provided with an over-the-counter antacid.

- *Constipation* - the subject should take an over-the-counter stool softener or laxative.

- *Pain* - the subject should take an over-the-counter pain medication (although NSAIDs such as aspirin and Ibuprofen should not be taken as they may cause additional irritation to the abdomen - please refer to page 221 regarding general cautions to considered when taking common pain medications).

Any case fitting any of the following criteria should cause the subject to be referred to the prompt attention of a medical professional:[327]

- Pain that persists for several days

- Blood observed in vomit or a stool

- Difficulty breathing

10.2.22. Nosebleeds

In case of nosebleed have the subject sit up and lean forward slightly while pinching their nose for between 5 and 10 minutes. Leaning forward prevents them from swallowing the blood, and the 5 to 10 minutes of pinching slows the flow of blood and provides the blood a chance to clot. If the individual is taking a blood-thinning medication (such as aspirin) then it may take longer for the blood to clot.[327]

10.2.23. Poisoning

> **NOTE:** *Poisoning victims should receive attention from a medical professional at the earliest possible time. If referring a victim to a medical professional try to gather and provide as much information for them as possible (such as the container with the poison). A non-medical professional should only provide treatment to a poisoning victim as a last resort.*

When confronted with a potential poisoning victim it is first important to try to ascertain that they are not misinterpreting a reaction to a medication or an illness. If the caregiver is unsure that poisoning is involved then they should try to observe physical signs such as the victim having a chemical smell to their breath, redness around the mouth or burns. Symptoms of poisoning include breathing difficulty, some degree of loss of consciousness and vomiting.[328]

The following guidelines apply to cases of potential poisoning:[328]

- If the victim is not breathing then immediately administer CPR. (See page 223 for instructions on providing CPR.)

- If available, check any label that came with the substance for treatment instructions, and follow those instructions.

- If the poison was taken orally then, if the victim is conscious, have them rinse their mouth thoroughly with clean water (spitting the water out, between rinsing).[328]

- Unless otherwise instructed by the label that came with the poison, do not induce vomiting, as this may cause more harm than good.

10.2.24. Pulled Muscles

Pulled muscles are best treated with 'RICE therapy':[327]

> **R**est for at least one day
>
> **I**ce the injury for 10 to 15 minutes each hour
>
> **C**ompress the injury with a bandage (ideally an elastic bandage)
>
> **E**levate the injured area above the level of the heart

The subject may also be provided with an over-the-counter pain medication, subject to the considerations discussed on page 221.

10.2.25. Puncture Wounds

Puncture wounds should be treated very much like other wounds. In general:[328]

- Using sterile gauze, a bandage or a clean cloth apply pressure on the wound to stop the bleeding (if nothing else is available then apply the pressure with either your hand or have the subject apply pressure with their own hand).
- Irrigate the wound with clean water and use sterilized tweezers to remove any small debris from the wound.
- Apply antibiotic ointment to the injury to protect against infection.
- Change the bandage regularly (especially if it becomes wet or dirty).
- Stay vigilant for signs of infection (redness, tenderness, or red streaks extending from the wound)

See section 10.1.12 on page 226 for more detailed instructions for wound care.

10.2.26. Shock

Shock is a condition with symptoms that include partial or complete loss of consciousness, nausea, dilated pupils, slow and shallow breathing, rapid pulse or cool, clammy skin. It is one of the body's reactions to such sources of trauma as heat stroke, allergic reactions, burns, poisoning, blood loss and major infections.[328]

The following guidelines apply to the treatment of shock victims:[328]

- If a pulse and/or breathing cannot be detected administer CPR to the victim immediately and request professional medical attention (see section 10.1.10 for instructions on performing CPR).

- Do **not** provide any oral medications or drinks to the victim initially.

- Lay the victim down flat and still on their back with their feet elevated a foot higher than their head (if the victim is experiencing nausea than have them lay on their side until the nausea passes in order to prevent possible choking if they vomit).

- Loosen any belts or tight clothing the person may be wearing, and make sure they are warm (provide a blanket if necessary).

10.2.27. Skin Cuts and Abrasions

See section 10.1.12 on page 226 ('Treating Wounds') for instructions on providing first aid for skin cuts and abrasions.

10.2.28. Snake Bites

NOTE: *The great majority of snakes in the world are non-venomous, however all bites should be taken seriously as they present the danger of infection.*

The following guidelines apply to the treatment of snake bites:[328]

- Either save the body of the snake or obtain the best possible description of it from witnesses (including the victim). Include not only a description of the physical characteristics of the snake but also where it was located, its behavior and any other details that may help to identify the type of snake.

- Immobilize the area that was bitten and have the victim remain calm so that the spread of any venom into their body will be slowed.

- Remove any tight-fitting clothing and jewelry from the victim in anticipation of swelling.

- Try to position the victim's body such that the bite is at a level that is below their heart.

- Clean the wound and cover it with sterile gauze or a clean cloth.

- Do not apply a tourniquet or ice, and do not allow the victim to drink any caffeine- or alcohol- containing beverages

- Seek professional medical help - particularly if the area begins to swell, change color, or becomes increasingly painful.

- If professional medical care is unavailable, and if an antivenom for the suspected snake type is available, then administer the antivenom in accordance with the accompanying instructions.

NOTE: *Rattlesnakes can actually control the amount of venom they inject based on the circumstances they perceive. About 40% of initial rattlesnake bites (especially from older snakes) do not inject venom.[123]*

10.2.29. Insect Bites and Stings

Insect bites and stings can cause significant pain and result in infection and even life-threatening allergic reactions. The following guidelines should be followed when treating an insect bite:

- If the insect itself is not available then obtain a detailed description of the insect and the circumstances under which the bite or sting took place.

- Remove any stinger that may still be embedded into the victim.

- To control swelling apply ice to the injury and elevate it if possible. Also, remove any tight clothing or any jewelry that is near the injury.

- Provide over-the-counter pain relief medications to the victim (subject to the cautions appearing on page 221), as well as an antihistamine to control itching. If an antihistamine is not available then a paste made of water mixed with baking soda can be applied to the injury to reduce itching.

- If epinephrine is available and if the victim begins to exhibit any signs of an allergic reaction (including hoarseness, tightness of the throat, vomiting, increased heart rate, dizziness, difficulty breathing, or loss of consciousness) then, following the instructions provided, inject the epinephrine into the victim's outer thigh muscle. If no improvement is observed 10 to 20 minutes after the injection, then administer a second injection.

- If the victim stops breathing then administer CPR (see page 223 for instructions for providing CPR). If CPR becomes necessary then it is urgent to also involve a trained medical professional.

10.2.30. Sprained Ankles and Strained Tendons

See section 10.1.5 on page 208 for instructions on providing first aid for sprained ankles and strained tendons.

10.2.31. Sunburns

Sunburns are just a special case of non-chemical burns. Please refer to section 10.2.6 on page 235 for instructions on treating these burns.

10.2.32. Toothache

Cases of toothache really require the attention of a dental professional, however if such care is not available there are some basic steps that can be taken to (hopefully) help:[328][124]

- Rinse the subject's mouth with warm salt water (or with clean water if salt water is not available).

- Use dental floss to remove any particles that may be trapped between the affected teeth.

- If it is available, apply benzocaine or clove oil (clove oil is preferred[125]) to a cotton ball and use it to wipe the affected area of the gums. This should help to reduce the intensity of the pain. (NOTE: The clove oil provides the additional benefit of having antibiotic properties.[125])

- If benzocaine and clove oil are not available you can try applying whisky to the affected gums (there are anecdotal reports of this working that stretch back many decades).

- Provide the subject with an over-the-counter pain medication (subject to the cautions listed on page 221).

- Wrap some ice in a towel and have the subject hold it against their jaw to help numb the pain.

- Have the subject raise their head slightly when laying down.

10.2.33. Gunshot Wounds

When presented with a gunshot wound victim the first response should be to quickly summon a trained medical professional to provide the level of care that is needed for such an injury. Once that task is performed determine if the victim is breathing. If not then administer CPR as described in section 10.1.10 on page 223. If CPR is necessary then, if possible, summon someone to assist in treating the wound itself.

If CPR is not required then then wound should be treated in accordance with the procedures provided in section 10.1.12 on page 226.

> **NOTE:** *In the case bullet wounds to the chest in which the lungs have been penetrated, the covering of the entry and exit wounds with a plastic bag (or other material that blocks the passage of air) can prevent the victim's lungs from collapsing.*

After administering initial treatment for the gunshot wound, if signs of shock are observed, provide additional treatment for shock (refer to section 10.2.26 on page 250 for information on recognizing and treating shock).

10.2.34. Knife Wounds

Some special considerations apply to treating knife wounds:[126]

- Be certain that any potential for violence has subsided before providing treatment.

- If available, the caregiver should wear latex gloves to avoid getting blood on their hands.

- If any wound is in the area around the throat or chest, check for blood in the airways and clear that first.

- If the knife is still in the wound then leave it in place, as removing it may only increase the damage and bleeding.

- If the victim is not breathing then perform CPR before treating the wound (or, if two caregivers are on hand, have one perform CPR while the other treats the wound).

Knife wounds are just a special case of wound treatment, and should be treated in accordance with the guidelines provided in section 10.1.12 on page 226 *('Treating Wounds')*.

After administering initial treatment for the knife wound, if signs of shock are observed then provide additional treatment for shock (refer to section 10.2.26 on page 250 for information on recognizing and treating shock).

11. Fitness and Nutrition

"He who has health, has hope; and he who has hope, has everything."

Thomas Carlyle

STRAIGHT THINKING: *If you are the type of person who has the expectation that you can resume an exercise program with the same or similar intensity months or years after having stopped exercising then you are encouraged to skip this chapter altogether, as there is a high likelihood that you will cause yourself more harm than benefit in resuming an exercise program. This chapter is written for those who have a realistic view of their physical capabilities.*

To paraphrase a well-known movie line ... "A prepper's got to know their limitations!"

The prepper's approach to fitness and nutrition will be very different in the times before and after any major disaster. Before disaster diet and exercise may be pretty conventional. In the aftermath, however, these things can be expected to change dramatically due to time constraints, the demands of day-to-day life, changes in the availability of professional medical care, and changes in eating.

In much of the preparedness literature there is a focus on treating the human body when it is broken, but not as much on physical conditioning to avoid and resist injury. For the serious prepper the body is the ultimate tool. This means that exercise, nutrition and hydration are important at all times. This chapter will address these important topics from a prepping perspective.

11.1. Exercise

11.1.1. Know Thyself!

Any reasonable person driving a well-used car for a long trip would have their mechanic inspect the car closely before the trip. Why would any adult even consider adopting a fitness program without similarly consulting with their doctor? (Even young athletes are often required to subject themselves to physical exams as a prerequisite for participating in sports programs.) In particular, if you are over 35 years of age or have experienced any of the following health issues you should consult with your doctor prior to beginning an exercise program:[506]

- Difficulty in breathing or dizziness during or after physical exertion.

- Heart trouble.

- A family history of heart disease or stroke.

- High blood pressure.

- Problems with tendons, muscles or other connective tissues.

- Arthritis or other bone-related medical conditions.

The results of your medical evaluation will be used by you and your doctor to define a personal fitness plan that makes the best sense for your overall condition. The tests you should consider include:

- *Electrocardiogram ('EKG' or 'ECG')* - This test involves attaching electrodes to the chest to observe and record the overall health and rhythm of the heart, and to possibly detect any heart damage.[502]

- *Oxygen Saturation Test* - This is a simple test that requires a clip to be attached to a fingertip for a few seconds. This test provides a good insight into how efficiently oxygen is being distributed throughout your body.[503]

- *Blood Gas Test* - This is a more involved test than the oxygen saturation test and requires blood to be drawn from an artery (often at the wrist). This test provides more accurate information about how well oxygen is being distributed.[503]

- *General Blood Tests* - Unlike the blood gas test, regular blood tests involve taking a sample of blood from a vein. The doctor will prescribe that various tests be performed on the sample to gain a good insight into your overall physical condition. Typical blood tests include tests for cholesterol and triglyceride levels as well as blood cell counts.

- *Glucose Tolerance Test* - This important test indicates how pre-disposed you are to becoming diabetic. It involves having you fast for several hours, and then eating/drinking a quantity of high-glucose food. Quick blood measurements (similar to the ones that diabetics regularly take with the small lancing devices) are then taken periodically over a couple of hours to build a profile of your body's response to the glucose.

- *Chest X-ray* - This test allows the doctor to visually inspect the size and composition of your lungs, your heart and the major blood cells feeding it.

- *Echocardiogram* - This test allows the doctor to observe an image of your heart in real time as it beats. It is much like the sonograms used by doctors to observe pre-born babies moving in the womb.

- *Vascular Ultrasound* - This test is similar to the echocardiogram, however the sonogram device is used to visually inspect the condition major blood vessels throughout the body.[505]

- *Body Mass Index ('BMI')* - This is calculated as the weight of a person in pounds, divided by the square of their height in inches times 703. BMI is a good general indicator of your fitness level and should figure significantly into the design of your exercise plan.[504]

You will almost certainly not undergo all (or even most) of the tests listed above. Some of these tests are redundant, and others are not necessary unless you are exhibiting certain specific symptoms. However, by being aware that these tests are available you will possess the information you need to carry on a more constructive discussion with your doctor and be more certain that the tests he does conduct will best meet your needs for disaster preparedness. As an example, you may wish to have a blood glucose test performed now so that you can have the opportunity to alter your lifestyle to avoid becoming diabetic during a time you anticipate when medical care (and insulin) is much less available; and without being able to express this need to your doctor he or she may not perform or prescribe the test.

11.1.2. Developing a Realistic Vision for Proper Conditioning

Maybe this traces back to those famous statues of ancient Greece that depict the body shapes of perfect athletes, but we in the Western world tend to have this view of exercise as the pursuit of a perfect body designed to excel in athletic competition. In a survival situation there will certainly be competition, however it will be a competition for scarce resources and a competition against the elements.

To be a prepper is to focus on having provisions, skills and the tools with which to apply those skills. (Even a gun is 'just another tool' in the prepper's toolbox.) **The prepper's most important tool is his or her own body, and preparing that tool to provide maximum utility should be a top priority.** This is why it is a total cop-out for someone to give up on prepping because they "don't have the space for all the gear" - because the most important aspects of prepping - fitness and nutrition - do not necessarily require space (or a budget for that matter!) (and for those who say they "don't have time", the reality is that having a more fit body actually buys you more time!).

Most survivors will not be nearly as well-conditioned as top athletes. Many will, however, need to be capable of erecting fence lines, climbing ladders to repair rooftops, squirming under a car to change the oil, chasing a chicken around a yard and doing whatever is necessary to defend their homes and families. These tasks are going to require bodies that are leaner, stronger and more flexible than those of typical modern-day city dwellers and suburbanites. Please understand that the vision is not to become superhuman, the goal is to become **more capable**. The difference between life and death can sometimes be measured in the ability to simply **endure** for a few more hours - even a slight improvement in fitness can make all the difference!

Suppose a member of a survival group is quite old and physically weak. If that person can increase their strength to the point they can simply hold a pistol and shoot it accurately then they now have the ability to provide security for an entire group while they sleep. **A little fitness can go a long way - and a member's willingness to improve their fitness may be a good indicator as to whether they are a good fit for inclusion in the survival community.**

Most people (even those who have been faithfully going to the gym to exercise for months or years) have at times awakened in the morning to encounter sore muscles from simple tasks performed around the house on the previous day. Often they'll refer to having found *"muscles they didn't know they had"*. Unlike the traditional exercise regime that involves performing certain well-defined routines regularly, the prepper's exercise program should emphasize exercising their entire body - because every muscle will probably be taxed regularly in a post-disaster situation. Since the needs of survival will be different from those of normal life it follows that the exercises to meet those needs may also be different.

With these thoughts in mind, as you read this chapter you should be ready to re-think your concepts of exercise and physical fitness. Your vision should not necessarily be to morph yourself into the aforementioned Greek statue; rather **it should be a more modest and realistic vision of every week being able to physically do a little more than you could the week before.** Because exercise has been shown to boost the immune system you should also envision a body that is better able to resist illness.[366] You should consider exercise and good nutrition to be two equally important sides of the same fitness coin.

As weeks and months pass you should be surprised at the benefits you derive in your day-to-day life (both pre- and post- disaster). And, when disaster does strike, you'll be in much better condition to deal with the new reality.

NOTE: *Regardless of whether you adopt an exercise program pre- or post- disaster it is a good idea to ramp up the intensity of the program gradually. If your exercise program, for example, includes performing 100 sit-ups per day, then on the first day you may only perform 10 or 15 sit-ups, and increase the sit-up count a little each day until you meet your program goals.*

You must give your body time to adapt, otherwise you can do yourself more harm than good.

11.1.3. Pre-Disaster Fitness

Once you have consulted with your doctor and defined your fitness program you should not wait for any impending disaster to begin to follow it. **Now** is the time to begin improving your conditioning. The very fact that you are reading this book is a good indicator that you are concerned with the safety not just of yourself but others as well. To motivate yourself to start your program you need do little more than remind yourself of those you are preparing for.

When defining your regular exercise plan keep in mind that a leaner body with greater endurance is almost certainly going to serve you better than developing excessive muscularity. With this in mind you should consider adopting a plan that places an emphasis on cardiovascular fitness, achieving good body weight and maximizing flexibility.

11.1.4. We're Not in Kansas Anymore! - Post Disaster Fitness

Of course in the aftermath of a major disaster **everything** will change, including diet and fitness programs. If the diet available to you does not provide a sufficient source of protein then exercise will probably do more harm than good. And, even with sufficient protein in the diet, the exercise regime may very well change simply to reduce the risk of injury when professional medical care is no longer as available. For this reason many sports-type activities will probably cease (besides, most of your fellow competitors may no longer be around!).

	Security Role	**Laborer Role**	**Manager Role**	**Kids over 10**
Sit-ups	5 sets of 20	3 sets of 20	2 sets of 20	3 sets of 20
Pushups	5 sets of 20	3 sets of 15	2 sets of 15	2 sets of 10
Leg Squats	5 sets of 10	3 sets of 10	2 sets of 10	2 sets of 10
Run in Place	8 mins	5 mins	5 mins	3 mins
Bench Press	3 sets of 10	2 sets of 10	1 set of 10	(none)

Table 11.1.: Morning Pre-breakfast Exercises (by role).

AUTHOR'S NOTE: *I once visited a customer's office in another city to conduct regularly-scheduled interviews of the employees for a corporate human resources department. While conducting one interview I was surprised to observe that a young man I had interviewed months earlier enter my office in what was virtually a full-body cast. When I asked him the obvious question regarding what horrible fate had befallen him I expected to hear a story that involved an auto accident or a fall from a great height.*

I was shocked when this formerly healthy young man told me that he had "made a bad move in Yoga class"!

The moral to this story is to be very thoughtful when exercising, and particularly so when starting a new exercise program!

This does not mean that exercise should cease as long as it can be worked into the schedule - but only that its form may change. While pre-disaster you may have worked out with heavier weights, post-disaster you may use lighter weights and perform more repetitions to place additional emphasis on cardiovascular health. In the pre-disaster world your fitness program may have placed an emphasis on developing a muscular physique; in the post-disaster world you will probably be better served with a lighter, more nimble body. In the pre-disaster world you may have consumed a protein-rich diet in order to build that muscularity while post-disaster you may very well find yourself rationing protein and consuming only enough to maintain a level of health and fitness.

Another consideration to anticipate is differences of exercise equipment used. Barbells and weights may be impractical to transport during evacuation, while lightweight rubber body-resistance tubes with handles and jump ropes are light enough to carry under almost any circumstance. Rubber tubes and jump ropes may also be much more conducive than weight-lifting to building that *'leaner, meaner'* body.

11.1.5. Chimps, Apes and Orangutans ... OH MY!

In the post-disaster world virtually everyone should play a distinct and vital role in the survival of their group or community.

The classic science fiction movie *'Planet of the Apes'* depicts a world ruled by apes. In this movie there are three types of apes portrayed, each fulfilling a different role in their society. The more intelligent chimps serve as scientists and engineers, the orangutans, being both intelligent and ambitious, serve as the leaders that guide the society, and the tougher and less intelligent gorillas serve in the military and law enforcement. All of these roles are important to the society, and each role has different needs with regard to exercise and nutrition.

Similarly, in a real-world post-disaster human society there will be a variety of roles and a corresponding diversity in needs with regard to diet and exercise. Any exercise and nutrition planning will need to account for this fact. It may not be practical to devise a unique plan for each individual in the group, however it should be practical to develop a few standard plans to provide to individuals based on the roles they will be filling. These plans may then be further tailored for specific individuals. For example, someone performing physically demanding work may have their calorie intake increased, or someone carrying excess body weight might have their caloric intake reduced until they reach a near-normal weight.

While you may develop multiple plans the work involved should not be overwhelming. For example, all plans might state that sit-ups should be performed each morning, with only the number of repetitions varying between roles. In fact, a single plan may meet everyone's needs if it contains tables that specify the differences between the roles. For example, if you define 5 general roles within your group then you may have a table with roles listed across the top, exercises listed down the side, and the number of sets and repetitions to perform per set listed in each cell within the table (see table 11.1).

Another table might list roles across the top and meals down the side, and in each cell list the number of calories and ounces of protein that are allocated for that meal and role (see table 11.2).

These measures may seem draconian, however in a post-disaster situation you may be faced with very limited food resources, and getting the most mileage from those resources may quite literally make the difference between life and death for **every** member of the group. There is probably no better or easier time to make major changes in a individual's behaviors than when there have been major changes in their environment.

	Security Role	**Laborer Role**	**Manager Role**	**Kids over 10**
Breakfast	700/5	700/3	400/2	500/4
Lunch	700/5	550/3	400/3	500/4
Dinner	700/5	500/3	500/2	500/3
Night Snack	300/0	300/0	200/0	200/0

Table 11.2.: Meal Content by Role (cal. / oz. protein)

AUTHOR'S NOTE: *There was a time when my own plan was not to be concerned with fitness until the disaster took place - with the thought being that the "brave new world" would force me to adapt rapidly. Eventually I came to realize that simple loss of electricity (especially in the warmer parts of the country) would cause air conditioning to become a thing of the past, and that many who were not prepared could perish from heat alone before ever having time to adapt. I have now come to realize that* **all preppers should be pursuing health and fitness at all times.**

For me that was 90 pounds ago (which will hopefully be 100 pounds by the time you read this!)

11.1.6. "No Pain, No Gain?"

One expression one hears around the gym is *"No pain, no gain."*. This suggests that in order to become fit one must "exercise until it hurts". Another expression one hears is to *"give one hundred and ten percent"*, which suggests that you must do more than you believe you're physically capable of doing in order to become fit.

Both of these expressions, in addition to a host of other "macho" expressions, may be well suited to a young athlete who has been training for years to compete, however this approach to conditioning is not suitable (and may perhaps be dangerous) to the prepper. Just as you will be gradually accumulating food and equipment to survive, you should also view your physical conditioning as a continuing process. What might start as a simple walk to the end of the road and back will eventually become something remarkably greater as you persist. With any luck when the additional conditioning is needed you'll be ready and free of any exercise-related injuries.

CAUTION: *In a survival situation you should be particularly cautious with your exercise regime. Many exercises involve some risk of injury, and post-disaster you may not have access to medical care.*

11.1.7. Aerobic vs. Anaerobic Exercise

Aerobic exercise is low-intensity, longer-duration exercise that elevates heart and respiration rates, while *anaerobic exercise* is exercise that is more intense and short in duration. Aerobic exercises increase a person's endurance while anaerobic exercises increase strength. Jogging, swimming and rope jumping fall under the category of aerobic exercise, while weight-lifting and short-distance sprinting are good examples of anaerobic exercise.[150]

Obviously disaster scenarios may occasionally require you to have greater physical strength, as well as the stamina to move quickly when necessary. Accordingly, your exercise regime should include both aerobic and anaerobic routines.

11.1.8. Good Exercise Habits

The following general suggestions should fit the exercise needs of most people, however you may need to adapt them based on your own physical conditioning and needs:[506]

- *When exercising, spend the first 5 to 10 minutes of each exercise period performing low intensity exercise such as walking, jogging in place, knee lifts, circling your arms and rotating your torso at the hips.*

- *Train with weights for a minimum of 2 twenty-minute sessions each week.*

- *Perform at least 3 thirty-minute sessions of higher repetition exercises each week that include such activities as calisthenics, push-ups, sit-ups and training with lighter weights.*

- *Schedule at least 3 twenty-minute intervals each week for aerobic exercises such as running, jogging, swimming, cycling, rope-jumping or rowing.*

- *Finish each exercise period with 5 to 10 minutes of low intensity cool-down exercises.*

- *Recognize problems pro-actively* - while exercising if things don't feel 'quite right' for any reason then stop immediately and consider halting your exercise program until you have an opportunity to consult with a physician.

NOTE: *It is not uncommon for a person to experience dizziness after standing up quickly from a sitting position. This is not necessarily an indicator of a medical problem, however anyone experiencing this should consider reducing the intensity of their workout for a while, and consulting with a medical professional at the first opportunity.*

11.1.9. Some Recommended Exercises

The following well-known exercises require little or no equipment and, if combined, can provide your body with a complete workout:

- *Push-ups* - provides good overall exercise for all parts of the arms and shoulders.

- *Abdominal Crunches* - excellent exercise for the abdomen. A safe and easy way for beginners to do this exercise is to perform it from a sitting position on the edge of a bed - the mattress will then provide support to the lower back to help avoid exercise-induced injury that is sometimes associated with abdominal exercises.

- *Pull-ups* - additional arm exercise. By altering the positions of your grips when performing pull-ups you can exercise a wider range of muscle groups.

- *Resistance training* - using resistance devices such as rubber tubes or other resistance equipment can be helpful in strengthening muscles and connective tissues.

- *Jogging, Walking or Swimming* - very good for cardiovascular fitness and developing much-needed stamina.

- *Jump Rope* - excellent for cardiovascular fitness and stamina.

- *Dancing* - very good for stamina and maintaining flexibility.

- *Hula-hoops* - Good for maintaining flexibility and exercising the abdomen.

- *Frisbee throwing* - A good all-around exercise that is great for the cardiovascular system (and **FUN** at the same time!).

- *Yoga, Tai Chi and Qi Song* - these exercises a great for muscle tone and carry very little risk of injury.

Simple repetitive exercises should be done in *sets* consisting of a fixed number of repetitions. You might start with a small set for each exercise and, over time, work your way to performing multiple sets (with more repetitions per set) for each such exercise. Maintaining a diary of your progress is not a bad idea.

CAUTION: *If, while exercising, you ever feel dizzy, light-headed or nauseous then you should* **stop immediately** *and maybe try again the next day. If you feel any strange pain or tingling in your arm, chest or jaw, then you should suspend your exercise program indefinitely until you have had the opportunity to consult with a physician.*

A Special Note About Swimming

Swimming deserves to be highlighted as an almost perfect exercise. **ANYBODY** in virtually any physical condition has the ability to swim, and a swimming pool is ready to let you work as hard as you care to work. Swimmers tend to get very good exposure to sunlight, which is a significant additional health benefit (the vitamin D the human body produces when exposed to sunlight is thought to greatly strengthen the immune system[146]).

Swimming for exercise provides tremendous benefits for improved flexibility, increased muscle tone, and cardiovascular health. Perhaps the most significant benefit offered by swimming is that it provides all these benefits while subjecting the body to virtually zero impact. This means you can condition your body with greatly reduced risk of injury.

Just as you count repetitions of any exercise, while swimming you can track the number of laps that you swim. If you are a beginner you might alter your stroke for each half lap (with one lap being two pool lengths) - for example alternating between swimming the more physically demanding *Australian crawl* with the much easier *backstroke*.

11.1.10. Measuring Your Progress

One of the best indicators of your level of fitness is blood pressure. Blood pressure is expressed in units of *mmHg*, which is the pressure exerted by a one millimeter high column of mercury (chemical symbol 'Hg').

Blood pressure tests actually measure two parameters, *systolic* and *diastolic* blood pressure. These correspond to the two distinct cycles of the heart's pumping action. These pressures are measured in terms of *mmHg* displayed by the testing unit. A healthy adult should have a systolic pressure of between 90mmHg - 119mmHg and a diastolic pressure of between 60mmHg - 79mmHg. For an adult a systolic pressure between 120mmHg and 139mmHg, or a diastolic pressure is between 80mmHg and 89mmHg indicates a state of *'pre-hypertension'*.

NOTE: *A couple of good ideas for upping the intensity of your swimming workout are to count your laps in the pool and to swim with swimmers' gloves (which enable you to work your arms a little harder). If you place a simple child's abacus at the end of the pool and move one bead for each lap completed you do not need to occupy your mind counting laps. Alternatively you may measure your exercise in terms of the time spent swimming rather than the number of laps.*

Coolibar makes a particularly nice pair of web-fingered swimming gloves that, unlike many, don't rob you of the use of your fingers.

CAUTION: *If you experience even slight cramping while swimming you should cease your swimming workout immediately, gently stretch and massage the affected muscle, and exit the pool with a plan of resuming your swim exercise on some other day. When swimming laps, it is a good idea to swim near the side of the pool rather than down the middle, so that you can readily reach the side should you experience a cramp.* **Even experienced swimmers can drown due to sudden cramps, and generally as one ages cramps become more common.**

NOTE: *A good blood pressure cuff should be on every prepper's must-have list!*

A systolic blood pressure between 140mmHg and 159mmHg, or a diastolic pressure between 90mmHg and 99mmHg indicates a state of *stage-one hypertension*. A systolic pressure between 160mmHg and 179mmHg or a diastolic pressure between 100mmHg and 119mmHg indicates a state of *stage-two hypertension*.[357].

A systolic pressure greater than or equal to 180mmHg, or a diastolic pressure greater than or equal to 120mmHg, indicates a state of *hypertensive crisis*. Anyone in this state should seek immediate medical care.[357]

Anyone in a hypertensive or pre-hypertensive state should stop smoking and work to eliminate any use of alcohol or caffeine, as these behaviors have been shown to contribute to increased blood pressure. They should also eliminate excessive calorie intake from their diet and begin to ramp up a reasonable, long-term daily exercise program. The intensity of the exercise program should be increased gradually as tests begin to show blood pressure returning to normal levels.[359]

Normal blood pressure ranges differ for children. Table 11.3 provides the expected normal ranges for children by age group.

Age Range (years)	Normal Systolic Pressure	Normal Diastolic Pressure
3 - 5	104 - 116 (mmHg)	63 - 74 (mmHg)
6 - 9	108 - 121 (mmHg)	71 - 81 (mmHg)
10 - 12	114 - 127 (mmHg)	77 - 83 (mmHg)

Table 11.3.: Normal Blood Pressure Ranges for Children.[358]

Another good measure of fitness level is resting heart rate. For most adults a resting heart rate between 60 and 100 beats per minute is normal[360], with 70 beats per minute being average for men and 75 beats per minute being average for women.[361]. To measure improvements in fitness you should periodically measure and record your resting heart rate, being certain that you are truly in a rested state before taking the measurement.

> **NOTE:** *Normal heart rates for newborns range from 100 to 160 beats per minute. Children between ages 1 and 10 should have a resting heart rate that ranges between 60 and 140. Children between ages 11 and 17 have a normal heart rate ranging between 60 and 100. As with adults, female children tend to have a slightly higher heart rate than male children.[362]*

Of course, exercise itself is intrinsically involved with measuring progress in a variety of ways. Increases in weight lifted and numbers of repetitions performed, as well as distance and time measurements for running and swimming are obvious and natural measures of progress.

One other important progress indicator that is often overlooked is recovery time after intense exercise. As your physical fitness increases you should observe a corresponding decrease in the time required for your body to recover from periods of exertion.

11.2. Nutrition

The human body requires seven nutrients, in varying quantities, to function properly. The nutrients are organized into *macro-nutrients* (nutrients that are needed in large quantity) and *micro-nutrients* (nutrients that are needed in minute quantities).[370]

The macro-nutrients are:

- *Carbohydrates* - *Carbohydrates* provide a source of energy to the body. *Simple carbohydrates* (sugars) are quickly metabolized by the body and result in a spike in the body's insulin levels. *Complex carbohydrates* consist of starches and vegetables that provide a healthier, longer-term source of energy which metabolizes much more slowly.

- *Protein* - *Proteins* are essential to the critical process of rebuilding tissues within the body.

- *Fats* - Like carbohydrates, *fats* provide a source of energy to the body. Fats are essential in the processing of some vitamins.

- *Fiber* - *Fiber* is non-digestible plant matter that helps to regulate the body's water and the movement of food through the digestive system.

- *Water* - The healthy human body is approximately 70% water. Water is essential to a wide range of chemical processes within the body. (See section 11.3 for more information about proper hydration).

The micro-nutrients are:

- *Minerals* - Trace amounts of the minerals potassium, chloride, sodium, calcium, phosphorus, magnesium, zinc, iron, manganese, copper, iodine, selenium and molybdenum are critical to various biochemical processes within the body. The need for these minerals should be met through a balanced diet (in general vegetables are an excellent source of dietary minerals).

- *Vitamins* - Vitamins are water- or fat- soluble substances that are important (and in some cases critical) to maintaining health. See tables 11.5 and 11.6 for more information on the vitamins needed by the human body.

The body obtains energy from carbohydrates proteins and fats. Each gram of carbohydrates and each gram of proteins provides about 4 calories of energy, while each gram of fats provide about 9 calories.[171] Ideally a person should derive about 55% of their calories from complex carbohydrates, about 15% from proteins and about 30% from fats[170].

It should be noted that the number of calories required by an individual varies based on their level of activity, and that in a survival situation the individual's daily caloric needs may be quite different than normal. Diet should be adjusted accordingly. Table 11.4 provides some general guidelines for the number of daily calories typically required by individuals fitting different age and gender profiles. The daily caloric needs of an individual may be more precisely determined for an individual based on observations of undesirable weight gain or loss over time.

	Age in Years	Recommended Daily Calories
Child	2-3	1,000 - 1,400
Male	4-13	2,000
	14-18	1,400 - 2,200
	19-30	2,600 - 2,800
	31-50	2,400 - 2,600
	51+	2,200 - 2,400
Female	4-13	1,400 - 2,000
	14-18	2,000
	19-30	2,000 - 2,200
	31-50	2,000
	51+	1,800

Table 11.4.: Typical Daily Caloric Needs by Age and Gender[169]

11.2.1. Diseases Associated with Vitamin Deficiencies

Three well-known and common diseases associated with vitamin deficiencies are *scurvy*, *rickets* and *beriberi*. Scurvy results from a deficiency of vitamin C, which impairs the body's internal tissue regeneration processes. Initial symptoms of scurvy include lethargy and confusion. As the disease progresses the individual may exhibit bleeding from the gums and other mucous membranes. Ultimately if scurvy is untreated the affected individual will die. Scurvy can be treated by re-introducing vitamin C to the diet. See table 11.6 for a list of dietary sources of vitamin C.[149]

Rickets is a disease that primarily affects children, and which results in softening and deformation of bones. It normally results from a deficiency of vitamin D, and can be corrected with exposure to sunlight on a regular basis and/or by eating foods that have been enriched with vitamin D or vitamin D supplements. In extreme cases surgery may be required to address bone deformities resulting from rickets.[147]

Beriberi is a disease of the nervous system resulting from a deficiency in vitamin B1. Individuals with this disease initially exhibit lethargy and fatigue, and eventually begin to exhibit shortness of breath, irregular heartbeat, confusion and speech impairment.[148] If left untreated beriberi is eventually fatal. Individuals with this disease are treated with thiamine hydrochloride, either in tablet form or as a direct injection. Once this treatment begins

Name	Description
Vitamin A	Sources include meats, milk, a wide variety of green- and non-green vegetables and some fruits. A deficiency may result in night-blindness. It is important to the immune system, vision, skin and bone re-generation.
Vitamin B_1 ('*Thiamine*')	Sources include yeast, pork and cereal grains. A deficiency may result in these disease *beriberi*, which can be fatal. Vitamin B is needed by a wide range of chemical processes with the body.
Vitamin B_2 ('*Riboflavin*')	Sources include milk, cheese and a wide range of vegetables. A deficiency may result in lesions of the mouth. It can be destroyed and/or degraded by exposure to light. Important in biological processes that provide energy to the body.
Vitamin B_3 ('*Niacin*')	Sources include animal organs (liver, heart, kidney), chicken breast, beef, eggs, tomatoes, leafy vegetables, broccoli, carrots, sweet potatoes, nuts, whole grains, beans and mushrooms.[157] A deficiency may result in dementia, diarrhea, dermatitis and severe and negative behavioral changes and mood swings. Important to the normal function of the body's metabolic processes
Vitamin B_5 ('*Pantothenic acid*')	Sources include meats and whole (unprocessed) grains[158]. A deficiency may result in tingling and numbness of the skin, low energy levels (due to impaired metabolism) and irritability. Used by the body for tissue repair and weight regulation.
Vitamin B_6 ('*Pyridoxine*')	Sources include meats, whole grains, nuts and bananas[159]. A deficiency may result in anemia and peripheral neuropathy. Used by certain metabolic processes

Table 11.5.: Vitamins Needed by the Human Body (1 of 2)

recovery tends to be quite rapid, with dramatic improvements becoming apparent within an hour. When thiamine hydrochloride is not available the affected individual should be provided a thiamine-rich diet. In this case recovery will require much longer. Beriberi can be avoided by with normal, balanced diet.

Goiter is a swelling of the thyroid gland that is often caused by a deficiency of iodine in the diet; resulting in a noticeable (and sometimes extreme and debilitating) swelling of the throat. Because many modern foods are enriched with iodine (particularly table salt) goiter has become very uncommon in the developed world. In times when goiter was more prevalent the condition was often attributed to diets that consisted of foods that were grown in iodine-deficient soil.

Treatment for goiter often includes introducing iodine to the diet, the use of thyroid supplements or, in extreme cases, surgical removal of the thyroid gland.[172]

Name	Description
Vitamin B$_7$ ('biotin')	This vitamin is required by some human metabolic processes. It is obtained in small quantities from a wide range of foods[160]. A deficiency may result in dermatitis or enteritis as well as lethargy and hallucinations.
Vitamin B$_9$ ('folic acid')	Used by the body to for cell division and growth. Available from leafy vegetables, beans, peas and animal liver[161]. A deficiency may result in birth defects in newborns as well as diarrhea, general weakness and shortness of breath.
Vitamin B$_{12}$ ('Cobalamin')	Used by the body for DNA synthesis and the production of certain important fatty acids. This vitamin is produced by bacteria within the digestive system[162]. A deficiency may result in severe damage to the nervous system. Symptoms include depression, fatigue and poor memory.
Vitamin C ('Ascorbic acid')	An antioxidant that plays a role in many important biological processes. Available from a wide range of fruits and vegetables, and from he liver of animals.[163] A deficiency may result in scurvy. Some sources also claim that vitamin C is important to the maintenance of a strong immune system.
Vitamin D	Acts as an enabler for the absorption of calcium within the intestines. Vitamin D is synthesized by the body when exposed to sunlight and is also an additive to many common foods.[146] A deficiency may result in rickets and softening of the bone.
Vitamin E	Facilitates proper muscle and connective tissue growth. As an antioxidant it removes free radicals from the tissues. Also facilitates neurological processes. Sources include various vegetable oils, leafy vegetables, avocados and broccoli.[164] A deficiency may, in rare cases, result in anemia in newborns.
Vitamin K	Aids in proper blood clotting and prevention of osteoporosis. Sources include kale, spinach, mustard and turnip greens, broccoli, brussels sprouts, cabbage and other leafy green vegetables.[165] A deficiency may result in excessive bleeding.

Table 11.6.: Vitamins Needed by the Human Body (2 of 2)

11.2.2. Post-Disaster Dietary Strategies

Fortunately a meal of beans and rice provides a reasonably decent balance of proteins, carbohydrates and calories. However, beans and rice alone is far from a balanced diet and, over the medium- to long- term must be supplemented with other foods and nutrients. As already mentioned, it is near optimal for a person to derive 55% of their caloric intake from carbohydrates, 30% from fats and 15% from proteins. A typical meal of beans and rice (consisting of one cup of cooked beans and one cup of cooked rice) provides a total of about 880 calories, 2% of which come from fats, 85% of which come from carbohydrates and 13% of which come from proteins. Clearly what is missing here are fats.

Foods containing fats eventually go rancid. However, you may expect a shelf life of six to nine months for peanut butter, and longer if it is kept refrigerated. Peanut butter also has the advantage of being densely packed and is a good general source of energy. A peanut butter sandwich, made with two slices of wheat bread, provides about 338 calories - 48%

> **NOTE:** *These are just a few examples of many serious health issues that can arise from a diet that does not include a full range of necessary nutrients. The message to the prepper is that you cannot expect to exist indefinitely on stored foods, and that gaining access to a rich and varied diet should be a top priority in a post-disaster scenario.*

from fat, 35% from carbohydrates and 32% from protein.

So, if lunch is a peanut butter sandwich and dinner is beans and rice (one cup of each), a total of 1218 calories is obtained, of which 15% are from fats, 72% are from carbohydrates and 13% are from protein. This is closer to the recommended dietary profile in terms of both number of calories and how they are distributed, however the diet is still deficient in calories from fat, has an excess in percent of calories derived from carbohydrates, and needs additional sources of vitamins and minerals.

Now consider adding a breakfast that consists of two scrambled eggs. These two eggs will contribute about 200 calories of energy. This addition boosts total daily calories from fat to about 22%, total calories from carbohydrates to about 62% and total calories from proteins to about 16% - which begins to approach the ideal calorie distribution. The additional 200 calories also begin to bring this diet up to the number of daily calories needed by most adults.

One reasonable long-term disaster preparation plan would be to store away dried beans and white rice vacuum-sealed in mylar bags and protected in food grade plastic buckets, while also rotating through a substantial supply of peanut butter and bread and/or crackers. The plan should also provide for some access to chickens and eggs. If you do not have the ability to raise chickens of your own then setting aside items to barter for eggs (and possibly chickens) should also be a part of your plan (alcohol, tobacco, weapons, antibiotics, and personal hygiene products are examples of good barter items. If the situation has deteriorated to the point of that you are struggling to find protein sources then precious metals probably are less useful for barter).

In addition to the above, a good supply of multivitamin supplements should be stored (hopefully refrigerated to extend their shelf life) to provide these important nutrients when normal dietary sources are unavailable. And, of course, a good water source and purification equipment should be identified and ready. Sources of fresh vegetables and fruits should also be identified if not already available.

> **NOTE:** *The humble sweet potato has been rated as being, by a very wide margin, the vegetable with the greatest health benefits.[213] Sweet potatoes offer a wealth of vitamins and minerals, as well as fiber (if the potato's skin is eaten). Sweet potatoes are very easy to grow and will grow in a wide range of soils and climates (even sandy soil). The serious prepper should look for any opportunity to grow and store sweet potatoes.*

> **NOTE:** *While beans and rice provide a* **fair** *source of protein they are not perfect. Together they provide a good combination of the amino acids that your body will need to create protein, with some amino acids being present only in modest quantity. It is a good idea to also plan for sources of animal protein - especially for long-term survival. Given the nutritional benefits of eggs (eggs are widely recognized as the best source of dietary protein), having access to chicken eggs should be a cornerstone of your long-term disaster strategy.*

Determining Quantities of Dried Beans and Rice

Dried beans and white rice expand in size by a factor of about 2.5 when cooked. So, if a single meal consists of one cup of cooked rice coupled with one cup of cooked beans, then a 5-gallon bucket of beans and a 5-gallon bucket of rice will store about 200 meals. If you assume two beans and rice meals per day (probably a conservative estimate, as you will have other provisions stored away) then each 5 gallon bucket will provide for three person-months of meals. As an example, if you are preparing to survive largely on beans and rice for six months you should store away 2 5-gallon buckets of beans and 2 5-gallon buckets of rice for each person in your group *(these are just general guidelines as the needs of each group are as unique as the individuals within the group)*.

Ingredients for Typical Beans and Rice Recipes

A meal consisting of pure beans and rice is very non-appetizing. Longer shelf-life ingredients found in many beans-and-rice recipes include bay leaves, bullion cubes, cayenne pepper, celery seed, chili powder, garlic powder, onion powder, coriander, cumin, ground black pepper, ground red pepper, oregano, salt, Tabasco sauce, vinegar, and honey. Shorter shelf-life ingredients include bacon, bell peppers, carrots, celery, cheddar cheese, green peppers, olive oil, red peppers, tomatoes, garlic, onions, and vegetable broth.

11.3. Proper Hydration

Hydration is the presence of sufficient levels of water in the body to meet the body's needs in removing waste, enabling digestion, dissolving minerals and cellular activity. Insufficient hydration results in diminished capacity to do work and less acute mental activity. Severe cases of dehydration may be disabling or may even prove fatal (while a healthy person can live for weeks without food, only a few days without water can result in life-threatening dehydration).[367]

Dehydration is caused by insufficient intake of water (or water-containing substances), or excessive loss of water through sweat, diarrhea, urination or even breathing.

Chronic dehydration has been linked to increased incidence of kidney stones and cancer. Symptoms of dehydration include dry mouth and extreme thirst, dark urine, loss of appetite, fatigue, and lightheadedness [368]

Maintaining Proper Hydration Levels

The body's primary indicator of dehydration is thirst, and people have a natural tendency not to want to drink unless they are thirsty.[367] As a result many people spend a significant portion of their lives in a dehydrated or semi-dehydrated state. Under stressful conditions or under heavy exertion this can have debilitating and/or dangerous consequences.

The average adult male, living a sedentary lifestyle, should consume 2.5 liters of water per day. The average sedentary adult female should consume 2.2.liters per day.[367]

A good way to ensure optimal hydration is to drink about 250 mils of water every 1.5 to 2 hours throughout each day, as well as drinking additional water during and after exercise and as dictated by thirst.

In a post-disaster scenario, and for many active individuals in a non-disaster scenario, it becomes necessary to consume larger quantities of water in order to maintain proper hydration.

NOTE: *It is important that beverages consumed for proper hydration not be caffeinated, as caffeine has a diuretic affect that actually causes the kidneys to draw water out of the body.[367]*

Emergency Re-hydration

In extreme cases of dehydration (such as dehydration due to diarrhea) it may become necessary to initiate emergency re-hydration measures. Oral re-hydration therapy ('ORT') is a treatment that can be administered by anyone to treat dehydration. (See section 10.1.11 for instructions for administering ORT.)

12. Home and Community Defense

*"God made all men,
however Sam Colt made all men equal."*

unknown

STRAIGHT THINKING: *In the aftermath of a major disaster there are going to be two kinds of people - those who took their security seriously and those who are fondly remembered.*

Think of security as existing in 3 layers; indoors security, premises security and community security. Each security layer should incorporate **multiple protections** *and have provisions for avoidance, detection, protection and response.*

One of the better security measures you can adopt is to keep one or more watch dogs or guard dogs. Properly selected dogs act as both detectors and deterrents. And, perhaps most importantly of all, unlike modern-day security systems they don't rely on the availability of electricity to fulfill these vital functions.

The best security strategies incorporate the doctrine of *layered security* which, as the name suggests, consists of multiple security measures that are layered over one another. For example, a home alarm system might be one layer, perimeter security around your property might a second layer and security provisions within the local community a third.

A sound security plan should address the principles of avoidance, detection, protection and response within each layer. For example, home security might consist of no trespassing signs (avoidance), an alarm system that indicates if your home's perimeter has been breached by unauthorized personnel (detection), 'safe zones' with bullet-resistant barriers (protection) and guns for home defense (response). (Avoidance can also include such measures as disinformation, obfuscation and caching.)

Other key concepts that must be addressed by a comprehensive security plan include intelligence (receiving and processing security-related information from surrounding areas) and *defensive posture* (e.g. *rules of engagement* and when to move personnel to defensive stations).

This chapter is oriented towards this three-layer approach to home and community defense.

AUTHOR'S NOTE: *Some readers may be discounting the notion of community defense and may be imagining that it is sufficient to simply defend the property they occupy. Let me suggest a general rule of thumb that, in the wake of major social breakdown, one should ideally hope to secure an area that is sufficiently large that their home is not within "hunting rifle rage" of the perimeter of the secured area. Otherwise an enemy with a commonly-available weapon and the element of surprise could cause* **real** *problems. This is one of the major reasons that I believe that a small town with some industrial base is the best practical environment for surviving the aftermath of a major disaster.*

12.1. Adopting a Security Mindset

The survivor's most powerful weapon in the defense of their home and community is **their mind**. In a defense situation one cannot afford to make mistakes or be in 'learning mode'. The security mindset includes:

- *Questioning anything and everything*

- *Anticipating threats in advance* - by anticipating various types of security incidents before they happen you will be able to react faster and more effectively when they *do* happen!

- *Always looking for vulnerabilities* - never assume that all vulnerabilities have been identified and addressed.

- *Recording and tracking the resolution of identified security vulnerabilities* - it is essential to keep a record of all vulnerabilities that have been identified and track them until they have been fully addressed (in some cases temporary stopgap measures can be instituted).

- *Establishing 'need to know' before sharing sensitive information* - limiting the spreading of sensitive, defense-related information helps provide the assurance that the information will not become known to a potential adversary.

- *"Trust but verify"* - always look for additional confirmation of any important defense-related intelligence information you receive.

- *Managing ongoing security projects* - security should be viewed as a non-stop project that is always underway (even if at a low level of intensity). **There should always be some active project under way to enhance security.**

12.2. The Importance of Drills and Training

Security drills are essential as they enable the group and/or community to identify and correct flaws and weaknesses in security procedures, and also allow individuals to strongly reinforce their knowledge of those procedures. Drills also help to identify any security-related equipment or infrastructure needs, and to test the flow of *command-and-control* within the group when incidents arise. Emphasis should be placed on having drills designed to test **changes in the community's defensive posture**, and the procedures should define the visible and/or audible signals that indicate that a change in defensive posture should take place.

One individual within a group or community should be assigned the role of *Defense Chief ('DC')*. The DC will be responsible for creating (or managing the creation of) defense-related procedures as well as enlisting assistance from others on an as-needed basis to carry out drills.

Before any drill can take place the security standards and procedures must be published and distributed and appropriate training sessions must be conducted. An emphasis should be placed on keeping procedures as few and simple as feasible; otherwise the procedures may very well fall apart under high-stress, real-world community defense scenarios.

The following guidelines should apply to conducting security drills:

- Before each drill performance criteria should be defined for scoring the performance of the group or community. Personnel should also be designated to manage the drill and observe performance.

- Both scheduled and unscheduled drills should be conducted.

- In order to avoid any accidents, when drills are conducted there should be very clear visible indicators that a drill is underway.

- If the drill involves any use of guns, then a special pre-drill sweep should be conducted to remove all ammunition from all guns that might possibly be used as part of the drill.

- After each drill the measured performance should be reviewed, changes to procedures should be identified, and re-training and re-testing should be scheduled.

12.3. Terms and Concepts for Physical Security

This section defines some of the terms that are either used within this chapter or are a general part of the home- and community- defense vocabularies. Many of these terms have been borrowed from military and intelligence organizations. While the use of this terminology by 'normal people' might seem a bit dramatic, the purpose of this chapter is to address dramatic circumstances that many serious thinkers predict will arise in the aftermath of certain major disasters.

12.3.1. Common Terms Associated with Home and Community Defense

- *LP/OP* - acronym for *"Listening Post/Observation Post"*, which is basically a well-equipped and strategically-located lookout station.

- *Military Crest* - refers to a location just below the crest of a hill from which good observations can be made without the observer's human silhouette being visible against the skyline.

- *Intelligence* - security-related information.

- *Counter-intelligence* - the process of working to defeat the intelligence-gathering activities of others.

- *Defensive Posture* - the state of readiness of one or more individuals acting in concert for mutual defense and the protection of others. Defensive posture might describe a combination of stations to be manned, tasks to be performed and procedures to be followed (e.g. "rules of engagement").

- *Defensive Zone* - a location in and around a property that has been pre-designated as a firing location during defensive operations.

- *Disinformation* - false or faulty information that has been planted to mislead potential adversaries.

- *Hard cover* - a location that can offer protection from weapons fire.

- *Soft cover* - a location of concealment that does not necessarily offer protection from weapons fire.

- *Field-of-Fire* - A physical area that can be effectively covered from a defensive location.

- *Dead Zones* - locations around an area (especially an inhabited structure) that are not covered by the field-of-fire of any defined defensive zones.

- *Range Cards* - cards placed at defensive zones that list pre-measured ranges to landmarks around the property **from that specific location**. Range cards are used to approximate the distance to other targets.

- *Avenue of Approach* - a route that an attacker will quite probably take due to terrain features, lack of defenses or ease of travel.

- *Fatal Funnel* - a location selected along an avenue of approach (either indoors or outdoors) that offers the opportunity to perform a surprise attack.

- *Safe Room* - a hardened room at a location that has been designated as a last line of retreat.

- *Area of Operations ('AO')* - the physical geographic area that you occupy and which is under your control.

- *Area of Influence ('AI')* - areas that are outside your AO and which can have a direct affect on the security of your AO.

- *Standard Operating Procedures ('SOP')* - pre-defined procedures that are performed under specific circumstances (such as having an SOP to carry a map when traveling).

- *Operational Security ('OPSEC')* - the practice of not unnecessarily divulging security- and defense- related information.

- *Communications Security ('COMSEC')* - the practice of maintaining secure communications.

- *HQ* - an acronym for 'headquarters'.

12.3.2. Basic Concepts of Physical Security

The four basic concepts of physical security discussed here are avoidance, detection, protection and response. A survival group or community should be constantly re-evaluating its layers of security (home, premises and community) with regard to each of these core concepts (during each security meeting questions should be asked about, for example, how the concept of *'avoidance'* is being applied to in-home security, or how the concept of *'protection'* is being implemented at the community level).

Avoidance

The best way to address a threat is by avoiding it altogether. Measures that you can take to avoid conflict include:

- *Projecting Strength and Confidence* - If you do not seem like an easy target then any person or group looking for easy prey may very look elsewhere. (An extreme case of this might be an Old West-style display of the bodies of the last aggressors that "came a-knockin'"!)

- *Not Making Yourself a Target* - Don't unnecessarily present yourself as having anything that someone else may want or need.

- *Putting up Signage* - Placing serious warning and 'No Trespassing' signs around your AO can dissuade attackers simply because it indicates that you are 'ready and waiting'.

- *Being the 'Gray Man'* - This is really a specific case of not making yourself a target. When you feel at all uncertain of your security situation then simply take yourself out of the spotlight and make a controlled exit.

- *Concealing your Location* - If your location is not visible to passers-by then you are less likely to attract unwanted attention.

- *Trickery and Obfuscation* - Use techniques such as caching supplies, or having one food pantry that has only a few items such that, if an intruder is intent on taking your provisions you can direct them to those meager supplies.

- *Preemptive Strikes* - Sometimes the best defense is a good offense. If you are certain you are in peril then hitting them before they hit you may be a way to avoid a larger conflict.

- *Negotiation* - It may be possible to discuss mutually-beneficial terms with a potential aggressor; especially if you do not appear to them to be an easy target.

- *Adjusting Your Schedule* - If you have some information about the schedule of potential adversaries you may be able to alter your own schedule so as to minimize opportunities for encountering them.

Detection

The ability to detect intruders is a cornerstone of any security plan. In a non-grid-down situation a home alarm can be very useful in this regard, although in today's world of increasingly-common *home invasions* this measure is a little light even in the absence of a major disaster. Technologically-unsophisticated measures, such as stringing wires attached to cans, can play an important role (not only will the noise provide detection, but the wire may also slow their progress or deter the intruder altogether). Another excellent detection system is one or more watch dogs that either have good natural instincts for defending the home or which have been specially trained to do so. Having members of your group on a rotating *'watch schedule'* also helps to meet the needs of detection.

Detection can be greatly improved by augmenting vision. The use of binoculars, telescopes and rife scopes can be very helpful in this regard, and any sort of night-vision gear could be worth its weight in gold for nighttime detection.

If your property is sufficiently large and you have a large enough group, then erecting one or more LP/OPs around the property that have good communications back to a central headquarters is also an excellent idea. In this case the best communications would be over a physical wire that has been run between the LP/OP and HQ such that COMMSEC is virtually guaranteed.

Detection at the community level would be provided by LP/OPs and/or roadblocks (see section 12.9 for a discussion of checkpoints and roadblocks).

Protection

In this chapter *'protection'* refers to having hardened locations from which you can resist or repel an attack. Protective measures should be put into place within the home, on the premises, and within the community. In-home protection might consist of a *safe room* that has been specially hardened and designated for in-home retreat, or it might consist of bullet-resistant barricades that have been installed within the home. Premises protection might consist of:

- A hardened LP/OP.

- Barbed wire and/or razor wire fences.

- Walls (especially walls into which special additional protections have been incorporated such as razor wire, protruding nails, etc.).

- Booby traps, deadfalls and pitfalls.

- Objects or vegetation on the property that might provide hard or soft cover in the event of an attack.

- Pre-identified terrain features such as hills and ditches which might offer shelter from gunfire.

- 'Tanglefoot' (see section 2.3) erected to impede an attacker.

Protection at the community level might consist of the same measures identified above for premises protection in addition to the hardening of designated buildings such that they can provide better shelter from any sort of attack. See section 12.5.3 for a description of materials that are typically used to construct bullet-resistant barriers.

Response

Intrusion detection has little value if you are not ready to respond. The use of guns is one obvious response, however other responses may be more appropriate to specific situations:

- Assuming power is available, audible alarms and/or floodlights may be installed such that they are automatically triggered if an intrusion is detected. These measures may cause an intruder to flee.

- Guard dogs could be released to chase, corner or subdue intruders.

- If a gun is not available then other weapons might be used to confront an intruder (particularly if you are certain that the intruder is **not** carrying a gun).

- The occupants could retreat to a hardened safe-room in hopes that the intruder leaves without penetrating that room.

- The occupants could exit the home and leave it to the intruder (see section 9.4.2 for an idea that might enable you to quickly render the home temporarily uninhabitable).

12.4. Defensive Posture and Threat Level

Typically a group's defensive posture will vary with the perceived *threat level*, possibly in conjunction with other factors and circumstances (such as changes in perceived vulnerability).

> **AUTHOR'S NOTE:** *In the days of the Cold War the defensive posture of the US military was controlled by a DEFCON level ('DEFCON' was an acronym for 'Defense Condition'). During those days, as someone who had some involvement with the 'military industrial complex', I heard it said on more than one occasion that the DEFCON level was upgraded regularly at least once per year, and that was during the Army/Navy football game.*
>
> *In this case the DEFCON level was upgraded due to the increased perceived vulnerability due to so many of the nation's military leaders coming together at a single location.*

For the sake of simplicity (sometimes it really **IS** better to "keep it simple") many survival groups may wish to adopt a well-known 3-level defensive posture that corresponds to the following threat levels:

- *GREEN* - Peacetime, all is well

- *YELLOW* - Be on guard due to an imminent threat

- *RED* - Defensive operations are under way

Regardless, each survival community or *mutual assistance group ('MAG')* should have pre-defined lists of threat levels and defensive postures.

12.5. Selecting and Using Guns for Defense

Due to the widespread proliferation of guns, the use of guns for home and community defense during a period of social breakdown will become a virtual necessity. The following sections provide guidelines for the selection of guns and their use when under fire. Section 12.13 builds on this knowledge and goes into detail about higher level tactics and strategies.

12.5.1. Selecting Guns for Indoor Defense

The most critical issues regarding the use of guns for home defense are:

- *Indoors Maneuverability* - The ability to use the gun effectively in tight quarters (handguns are generally easier to wield in tight quarters).

- *Stopping Power* - How effective will a single shot be at stopping an intruder? Larger calibers such as the .40 and .45 caliber handguns, in addition to 12 gauge shotguns, have a reputation for having serious stopping power (to put stopping power into perspective, many modern law enforcement personnel carry a .40 caliber handgun, while 30 years ago police commonly carried a .38 caliber handgun).

- *Follow-up Speed* - How quickly can one shot be followed by another in the event that multiple shots are required? The relatively low recoil of the 9mm semi-automatic handgun allows for quicker and more accurate follow-up shots, and is the reason that many chose it to be a big part of their home defense strategy.

- *Simplicity and Maintenance* - the issues of ease of use and frequency and level-of-effort for maintenance often play an important role in deciding between the use of a pistol or a revolver when selecting a handgun (revolvers are much lower maintenance and easier to use).

- *Intimidation Factor* - A shotgun tends to have the strongest deterrent affect on anyone who happens to be standing on the wrong end of the barrel. (Shotguns can be quite intimidating without a round being fired. This applies particularly to the pump-action shotgun, which produces a distinctive and easily recognized sound when a shell is being pumped into the firing chamber!) The Remington 870 and Mossberg 500 12-gauge shotguns are often cited by experts on home defense as being excellent and reasonably-priced choices for home defense.

- *Unintended Over-Penetration* - This describes cases in which the shot from a gun passes through a wall and potentially harms someone who was not an intended target. To address this concern many choose to use a shotgun - possibly loaded with lighter 'bird shot' - for in-home defense. To further reduce the chance of over-penetration the shooter may choose to use the the lighter 20-gauge shotgun for in-house defense rather than the heavier 12-gauge shotgun (the 20-gauge shotgun also features substantially less recoil than the 12-gauge shotgun, allowing for a faster follow-up shot if needed).

NOTE: *Some home defenders advocate loading a home defense shotgun with different types of shells such that the first shot is a lighter bird shot (which reduces the risk of over-penetration) and the second is the heavier 00-buckshot. The thought is that the target is either fleeing (and maybe outdoors) when the second shot is fired. This strategy might also anticipate that the second shot would be directed downwards, and therefore the risk of over-penetration is lessened.*

12.5.2. Selecting Guns for Outdoor Defense

When considering guns for outdoor defense it is constructive to think in terms of expected shooting range. There are diverse opinions regarding the effective defensive ranges for various types of firearms. The ranges described here are based on a careful review of numerous expert opinions. For purposes of this book defensive shooting ranges are divided into the following classifications:

- *Close range* - Close range is often considered to be any target within 25 yards. Handguns and shotguns both provide good close-range protection. The advantage of shotguns is that they can also cover the intermediate range, while handguns are easier to carry, faster to deploy and quicker to reload. For those with a limited budget that can only afford a single gun, the shotgun is a strong candidate because it can cover greater range and can be loaded for indoors use as well as outdoors use.

- *Intermediate range* - Intermediate range is often considered to be between 25 and 50 yards from the shooter. For intermediate range the shotgun is a good choice because the wider spread of the pellets increases the probability of hitting a target at those ranges.

- *Long range* - Long range defensive shooting extends from 50 to 600 yards. Assault-style rifles and cartridges are a best fit at these ranges because the shotgun begins to lose its stopping power at 50 yards, while the rifle remains quite effective. The advantage of an assault-style rifle over longer-range 'sniper rifles' is that the assault rifle tends to have a shorter barrel and is, as a result, easier to transport and shoot. Assault-style rifles, which often have regular metal sights rather than having a scope mounted, can withstand much more punishment without sacrificing much accuracy. (The *30-30 caliber rifle*, which is an entry-level hunting rifle that is compact and easy to handle, is also an excellent choice for defense at this range.)

- *Sniper range* - There is no universally-accepted definition of what constitutes *sniper range*, however for defensive purposes it is reasonable to consider that sniper-range starts where long-range stops. The .308 caliber rifle is commonly used within the US military as a sniper rifle (although other calibers are used for the most challenging sniper applications), and many sources claim that 600 yards is the range at which accurate shooting with a .308 starts to require special skills. So, for purpose of this book *sniper range* will be considered any distance beyond 600 yards. Ranges of 800 yards and greater should be considered to require special training that includes the ability to compensate for the *'drop'* of the bullet and the effects of wind.

The type or types of guns that you select for defense will depend on the size of the area and the terrain features at your location. However, it is easy to imagine all four ranges being a concern for most locations. If budget dictates that you acquire your defensive guns gradually then you are advised to start with one or more shotguns and then 'work your way out' to sniper range.

Please refer to Appendix D for information pertaining to the 'care and feeding' of guns.

12.5.3. Guidelines for Gun Defense

The following gun defense guidelines can greatly improve your chances of surviving a gun battle:[507]

- Most situations involving gun combat take place at ranges of 300 yards and closer (with the great majority taking place within a range of 150 yards). When you believe that you are under fire you should methodically scan the surrounding area in an attempt to quickly locate the shooter(s). Start by scanning locations that are closest to you and then, over a period of about 30 seconds, visually work your way out to about 300 yards. If you do not see the shooter try again, successively checking potential places of concealment in range increments of about 50 yards.

- Rifle shots generally produce two sounds, the sound of the bullet as it passes by traveling at super-sonic speed followed by the *'thumping'* sound that the bullet made when leaving the muzzle. The time between these sounds can be measured to help you identify the distance between yourself and the shooter. If possible try to count quickly (5 counts per second) to measure the time between hearing these sounds. This count is will be roughly equal to the distance of the shooter from you in hundreds of yards.

- When using a scoped rifle for defense it is often a good idea to calibrate the scope for a target that is at a range of 250 yards. This allows you to engage targets at ranges of up to 300 yards without the need to take into consideration bullet drop. Any such rifle calibration should be performed as part of regular gun maintenance.

- For longer range shooting, especially with lighter ammunition, wind can play a big factor in accuracy. A light bullet traveling 500 yards in a 20 mile-per-hour crosswind can drift as much as 68 inches, and even a heavier bullet (such as a .308 caliber rifle bullet) can drift 8 inches or more after traveling 500 yards in a stiff cross wind. It is a good idea for you to obtain gun windage charts and study them to have an idea about how to adjust your aim for wind when shooting at distant targets.

- Having cover provided by your own snipers can be a tremendous force multiplier if you come under attack. Snipers should be trained to recognize leaders by their body language, clothing and/or other visual indicators and target them preferentially.

A disruption of an attacker's command structure can often put a quick end to an attack.

- If involved in combat during times of darkness be aware that peripheral vision is more acute in the dark. You are more likely to detect an intruder if you do not gaze directly at the location you are trying to observe. Of course if any night vision equipment is available it should be employed for nighttime defense as well.

- Hard cover that is capable of stopping virtually any bullet should consist of at least 16 inches of sand, 10 inches of concrete or two inches of steel. (As repeated gunfire can degrade such barriers, more shielding is always better.) If using regular packed dirt as a barrier against bullets then 32 to 50 inches of packed earth is required to provide the same degree of protection.

- If possible provide defensive fire from locations other than the central location you are most intent on defending. One rationale for this is that you do not want to attract fire towards the people and provisions you are trying to protect. Another reason is because specifically located and prepared external defensive locations will probably provide better area coverage than defensive locations within a building.

- Incorporate small shooting *'slots'* into external defensive locations such that anyone shooting out has maximum protection. If the wall to the defensive position is thick then the thickness of the walls should be tapered inwards toward the slot to provide the shooter with maximum shooting range (this is a practice that dates back centuries to medieval times when archers fired arrows through similar slotted openings to defend castles from invaders).

12.5.4. Selecting Guns for Long-Range Shooting

Selecting guns for long distance shooting can be thought of much like selecting golf clubs for a particular shot. Each weapon has particular scenarios for which it is the best fit (there is no ideal, one-size-fits-all, gun for long-distance shooting for self defense).

The calibers of weapons most often associated with long-range shooting are the .243, the .308, the 30.06, the .300 and the .50 caliber BMG *("Browning Machine Gun")* (NOTE: There are non-automatic guns that also fire the .50 caliber BMG ammunition). Each of these cartridges has tradeoffs that must be considered.

- The .50 caliber BMG round is, by far, the heaviest and hardest-hitting round, and can stop an attacking vehicle as well as the person driving it. These guns, and their ammunition, are quite costly and are **NOT** the best fit for all long-range shooting needs.

- The .243 caliber rifle cartridge is at the opposite end of the spectrum from the .50 caliber in that the lighter-weight projectile travels much faster (up to 4000 feet-per-second vs. up to about 2900 feet-per-second for the .50 caliber BMG). This translates into longer range (the bullet can travel further before dropping excessively) with less hitting and penetrating power.

- The .308 and 30-06 are very similar rounds, with the .308 having a flatter trajectory and the .30-06 having a bullet that is about 10% more massive. The .308 might be considered the "modern 30.06", with cartridges that are much more common. This is the caliber that is used most commonly by military snipers, as it represents a good tradeoff between range and end-of-trajectory hitting and penetration power.

- The .300 caliber cartridge includes the .300 Winchester Magnum *('WinMag')* and the .300 Weatherby Magnum (with the Weatherby Magnum being the more powerful of the two and the .300 WinMag being the most common). The .300 caliber cartridge fires a faster bullet with a longer range and up to almost twice the end-of-trajectory hitting power of the .308.

AUTHOR'S NOTE: *A couple of additional factors should be noted regarding high-velocity ammunition. Such ammunition tends to wear out the gun's barrel much sooner than other rounds. For example, the barrel for a .243 caliber cartridge may begin to lose accuracy after 1500 rounds have passed through it, while the barrel for a .308 or 30-06 may have 5000 rounds passed through it before accuracy begins to noticeably degrade[401].*

For home defense during disaster scenarios I would suggest that if you're having to use 1500 rounds to defend your property then you might want to consider relocating, as one of these days you're going to end up getting the proverbial "short end of the stick".

*I will also highlight (again, because I think I'm in love with this gun!) Remington's 'R-25' rifle, which is a semi-automatic rifle available for both the .243 and .308 caliber cartridges, as being an attractive multi-use long-distance gun. That .243 with its long range, reduced recoil and semi-automatic firing action seems to be in the 'sweet spot' for both hunting and long-range home defense. (**DISCLAIMER:** The author has no personal vested interest in the Remington company, he just thinks this is a very fine weapon!)*

If you anticipate defending against distant soft targets the .243 has a good chance of letting you "reach out and touch someone" before they "reach out and touch you". If those targets are going to be taking cover along the way then the .300 caliber allows you to possibly penetrate that cover. If you want a long-distance rifle more for hunting than defense then the .308 is a very good choice. And, if you have your dad's old 30.06 rifle and plenty of ammo for it on the shelf then you can at least feel comfortable knowing that "you've got the long-distance needs covered".

Any rifle used for long- and/or sniper- range shooting should be equipped with a scope for maximum accuracy. Section D.6 provides a good general introduction to rifle scopes for both hunting and defense.

12.6. Guard Dogs and Watch Dogs

Dogs that naturally begin barking loudly at the approach of intruders are referred to as *'watch dogs'*. Dogs that will physically attack and restrain intruders are referred to as *'guard dogs'*. While it is not necessary for watch dogs to be physically large and intimidating, they should have a strong enough voice to wake sleeping humans. Guard dogs, on the other hand, must have sufficient size to be able to successfully attack and restrain a person.

Breeds of dog that are commonly used as watch dogs include the Australian Shepherd, the Miniature Schnauzer, the Georgian Shepherd, the Scottish Terrier, the Rottweiler, the Chow Chow, the Akita Inu, the German Shepherd, the Cairn Terrier, the Caucasian Shepherd, the Pit Bull, the Airedale Terrier, and the Doberman Pinscher.[515]

Dog breeds that make good guard dogs include the Belgian Shepherd, the Doberman Pinscher, the Bullmastiff, the German Shepherd, the Giant Schnauzer, the Chow Chow, the American Bulldog, the Black Russian Terrier, the Standard Schnauzer, the Boerboel, the English Mastiff, the Rhodesian Ridgeback, the Tibetan Mastiff, the Bull Terrier, the Pit Bull, the Airedale Terrier, the Boxer, the Spanish Mastiff, and the Rottweiler.[515]

In addition to these pure-breed dogs it is not uncommon for mixed-breed dogs to make excellent watch and guard dogs. While, in the perfect world, dogs would be specifically trained for these roles, many untrained dogs will instinctively fill such roles in a household (the author's own 9-year-old adopted beagle has been doing an excellent job of alerting us to the approach of strangers at our home even before they reach the door!).

If planning to incorporate dogs into your home or community for purposes of security you must be as prepared for their handling and upkeep as you are for that of the human members of your group. Under normal non-disaster conditions you should be careful to provide your dogs with a dog feed that has a high proportion of animal meat (and not *'animal by-products'*!). Any dog food that lists *'meal'* as a primary ingredient should also be avoided, as the meal is a dehydrated grain.[514]

In a disaster scenario it may be more feasible to provide dogs with feed that contains a higher-proportion of grain simply because it will have a longer shelf life. However, if you do so you should also plan on complimenting that feed with other good sources of animal protein.

It is important also to establish a proper *'pecking order'* with any dogs that are part of your household or group (with **yourself** at the **TOP** of that pecking order!). This is generally done by making it clear to the dogs that **you** are the boss. This process does not involve punishment; it consists of being firm and confident in everything that you do with the dog. In also involves training the dog to sit or lie down on command, and not to rise without your command. One easy way to help identify yourself as the boss is to not allow your dog to immediately pass through a doorway when a door is opened; instead close the door to deny the dog's passage and command the dog to sit before entering. Ultimately all of these little signals, added together, will make it abundantly clear that **YOU** are the boss.

When dealing with multiple dogs (more than one dog constitutes a *'pack'*) you should try to identify which of the dogs seems to have the best leadership qualities, and always show some measure of preferential treatment to that dog (especially being certain to feed that dog first). This will establish the pecking order among the dogs, which will cause the pack to function together normally.

12.7. The Need to Gather Intelligence

Intelligence is the acquisition and processing of information that relates to potential current and future security situations. The information gained through intelligence is itself referred to as 'intelligence' (or simply 'intel'). In military literature there is often reference to the importance of the "element of surprise" in determining the outcome of a conflict. The purpose of gathering and processing intel is to deny that advantage to potential adversaries. Sources of intelligence include:[509]

- *Human Intelligence* - information gained from other people who have been actively involved in collecting information or who have simply made important observations in the course of their daily activities. You may obtain this information by simply debriefing travelers as they pass by, through coercion of captured foes (often using a technique that is referred to in the intelligence community as the *'rubber hose method'*), or by actively sending out scouts with clearly-defined instructions and intel-gathering goals.

- *Photographic Intelligence (a.k.a. 'PhotoIntel')* - information gained from photographs (when it comes to threat analysis a picture can be worth far more than one thousand words!).

- *Media Intelligence* - news gained from radio, television, newspapers, The Internet and other sources. You should chose these sources carefully as, even pre-disaster, many of these sources contain *disinformation*.

- *Signals Intelligence* - information gained from monitoring communications (especially radio communications).

- *Measurement Intelligence* - information from measuring devices (such as the way in which seismometers and radiation detectors have been used to detect atomic testing). Another more practical example of measurement intelligence might be obtaining the counts from turnstiles that control access to a sensitive area in order to estimate the number of individuals occupying that area.

The collection and analysis of intel can be as critical before disaster strikes as in the aftermath. Intel gained in the time leading up to disaster may figure into changes made to bugout plans regarding routes taken and criteria for evacuating. For those not bugging out intel may help identify the likely sources of post-disaster threats *('avenues of approach')* so that the site plan (see Appendix B) can be adjusted accordingly.

Good pre- and post- disaster intelligence can literally be a life-saver. If a potential threat observes that you are positioned and in a ready state it is entirely possible that the threat may simply evaporate never to appear again. Or it may enable you the option of testing that old axiom that *"The best defense is a good offense."*

The analysis of intelligence information often involves visualization to identify trends. For example, information related to locations might be pinned to a map so that important additional geographic information becomes apparent. Information might also be pinned to a calendar so that time-based relationships stand out.

A topic closely related to intelligence is *counter-intelligence*, which is the process of denying intel to potential adversaries. In a post disaster scenario counter-intelligence would largely involve spreading disinformation. This disinformation can even be tagged as such in order to not mislead friends. For example, there might be a general understanding that any message containing the letter 'x' in the first sentence should be ignored.

Counter-intelligence could also involve having procedures in place to identify information leaks. Consider the case of a group of individuals in which a spy is suspected. A certain bit of disinformation that would be known to elicit an action by an adversary might be provided to a subset of the group. If that caused a response by an adversary then you would know that the leak came from that subset. A few repeats of this process would eventually identify the spy.

12.8. Other Important Defensive Gear

There is much more involved in defense than simply pointing a gun and pulling a trigger, and effective defensive strategies require additional supplies, tools and equipment. The following additional defensive-related supplies and equipment should be considered:

- Barbed wire or razor wire of sufficient length to cover areas to be protected.

- Spools of thin wire and different thicknesses of fishing line, along with eye bolts and other hardwire that would be helpful in putting together perimeter defenses (it might not be a bad idea to obtain a good number of fishing hooks to go with that fishing line, as this could make any defensive lines run around the perimeter more 'sticky').

- Various sizes and lengths of PVC piping as well as PVC connectors and PVC cement (to possibly be used in quickly assembling other defensive structures).

- Boards and long nails to possibly be laid down along the perimeter to slow down the advance of intruders (great caution should be exercised when deploying such traps, as they are not discriminating with regard to their victims).

- Bows and arrows might serve as backup weapons under certain circumstances.

- Good survival knives may be helpful both as tools and for use in close-range defense (the *'KA-BAR USMC Full-Sized Fighting Knife'* is a good example of a practical survival knife that can be found online for a reasonable price).

- A collection of empty tin cans and/or bells that can be attached to perimeter lines to help alert to the presence of an intruder.

- *Concealable trail cams* can be positioned around the perimeter of an area to collect information continuously.

Basic gear to augment security should also include equipment that can extend an observer's senses and communications range. Such gear includes binoculars, radios and alarm systems.

12.9. Managing Checkpoints and Roadblocks

The proper management of checkpoints and roadblocks is going to be essential to preserving quality of life within a community in a post-disaster scenario. All roads leading into a community should be controlled with roadblocks. These roadblocks should be located at least 1.5 miles from the outermost inhabited location in the community to help protect the members of the community from gunfire originating outside the defensive perimeter. In addition to controlling access to the community by non-community-members, such roadblocks might be used to collect tolls or to enable through travel in a controlled fashion. They may have the appearance of conventional, pre-disaster checkpoints, however additional measures should be taken that reflect the special security needs during times of large-scale disaster.

The following practices will allow roadblocks and checkpoints to be most effective:

- Have good, easily-readable signs at all checkpoints to indicate their purpose and that the checkpoint has armed cover (whether it does or not).

- Have at least two people manning the checkpoint at all times.

- Have at least one concealed observer/shooter providing intelligence and cover to the roadblock crew at all times.

- Have both radio and semaphore-based communications (e.g. flags) between the checkpoint personnel and the concealed observer/shooter.

- Have radio or other electronic communication between all checkpoints and a central headquarters.

- Have individuals ready to reinforce the checkpoints available to be quickly deployed and/or summoned at all times.

12.10. Security Practices While on the Move

When individuals are traveling during a period of disaster they are at their most vulnerable. In order to maximize their security they should follow some basic practices:

- Carry weapons for self-defense.

- Carry extra food, fuel and bathroom tissue if traveling a longer distance to avoid having to make stops as frequently (and to be more selective about where stops are made). NATO-style 5-gallon jerry cans are recommended for transporting extra fuel in this way.

- If traveling by car or truck, have a CB radio installed and be listening on the emergency channel (or, better yet, have a CB that has the ability to scan **all** CB channels).

- If multiple vehicles are traveling together do not travel too closely, and when approaching blind spots, such as the tops of hills or sharp curves, allow one vehicle to go ahead to reconnoiter. Have two-way radios installed in each vehicle and pre-agree to a standard channel for everyone to use for general group communications during travel.

- Each vehicle should have a road map that covers the route to be traveled, and if multiple vehicles are traveling together alternate travel routes should be pre-identified before travel begins.

- Travel during daylight hours if possible, and if it is not expected that circumstances will deteriorate significantly before daybreak.

When traveling off-road the following additional practices should be observed:

- Move in single-file and try to keep 15-20 feet of distance between adult personnel.

- Avoid all unnecessary noise and use pre-arranged hand signs for basic communications.

- When traveling through urban areas consider making use of the areas cleared for utility lines, as these routes are easily traversed and do not receive high traffic.

- Have at least one pair of binoculars so that you can observe potential security-related issues sooner.

12.11. Best Practices for Home and Community Defense

The following practices will allow you to optimize the security of your home:

- Designate an interior room as a *safe room* and plan to provide it with special protections and some sort of quick exit route.

- Identify the *'defensive zones'* in your home from which you can defend against intruders.

- Identify locations for LP/OPs that can be established on the property, and possibly construct those posts to also serve as defensive zones that can provide coverage for the property's critical dead zones.

- Draw a *'security map'* of your home and property that includes a rough floor plan of the rooms in the house (including doors and windows), and any terrain features on the property (trees, shrubs, buildings, etc.) that might be used for hard and soft cover in case of attack.

- On the security map identify those *dead zones* around the house that cannot be covered from any of the defensive zones you have already identified, and develop a plan to put measures in place to provide coverage of those zones (putting up barbed wire and other barricades, setting booby traps, etc.).

- On the security map indicate both indoor and outdoor locations where 'fatal funnels' can be established.

- Try to establish *defense pacts* with neighbors such that each household can provide some coverage of the other's *dead zones*. Define both regular and emergency communications protocol with those neighbors, including defining door-knocks that identify you as a friend. These pacts may also provide for some exchange of weapons, ammunition and other gear in order to enable both households to fulfill their obligations.

The following measures will help to maintain security within the community:

- One community member should be elected as the 'Chief of Police', and be responsible for security within the community itself. Another member should be elected as the 'Defense Chief', and be tasked with all aspects of defending the community from external threats (including the gathering of intelligence information).

- The Chief of Police should:

  - Locate community members to serve as an internal police force and familiarize all members of the community with the authorities they are given.

  - Schedule security patrols such that the community is under their protection 24x7.

  - Designate and harden a building to serve as a security headquarters and secure retreat. In addition to hardening the building against attack, also make provisions for quick exit.

  - Identify a challenge and response phrases that can be used to identify 'friend or foe' within the community.

  - Identify and warehouse vehicles and fuel that are to be used exclusively for security functions for the community.

  - Identify standard public locations for the posting of security-related information, and a location for community security meetings.

  - Document actions to follow when any member of the community ceases to reside within the community.

- The Defense Chief should:

- Develop lists of able-bodied members of the community who are willing and able will help to defend the community if needed.

- Define a regular training program and schedule for all individuals who volunteer for community defense.

- Have manned security roadblocks at all roads leading into the community at all times (see section 12.9).

- Identify a location for the secure storage of defense-related supplies and information (ideally using the same facility as the headquarters).

- Develop an inventory of all weapons and ammunition that members of the community are willing to make available for common defense. Maintain a list of locations and contact information for all such individuals.

- Develop an audible alarm system that can be heard throughout the community, and provide all members of the community with instructions to follow in the event that the alarm is sounded. Schedule periodic drills to test the alarm and the overall community response.

- Develop *rules-of-engagement* for dealing with outsiders and intruders, and make all members of the community aware of those rules.

- Install fencing, alarms, booby traps and other perimeter defenses as needed to protect against intruders. Educate all members of the community with regard to the locations of any concealed traps.

- Position and staff LP/OP structures at strategic points within the community to augment the threat detection capabilities of the checkpoints.

• The Chief of Police and the Defense Chief should work together to define communications channels and protocols to be used for their various security purposes.

For a more detailed description of the formation and running of a disaster community please refer to chapter 14.

12.12. Listening and Observation Posts ("LP/OPs")

'LP/OP' or *'LP-OP'* is a military acronym for *'Listening Post/Observation Post'*, and refers to a simple, concealed structure that is intended for *'keeping watch'*. While an LP/OP might have features that help it to withstand attack, its primary function is the gathering and dissemination of security-related information.

A simple (and typical) LP/OP consists of a trench that is dug to a depth of about 3.5 feet, 4 or more feet wide, and long enough for at least 3 adults to stand abreast. The rectangular trench is often framed with logs or other wooden supports to which a structure is attached such that a makeshift roof and/or camouflage materials can be draped over the top to provide better shelter and concealment. When constructing the LP/OP thought should be given to:

- locating the LP/OP on a hill to provide a wider viewing area and reduced potential for detection.

- if the LP/OP is located on a hill, positioning it at the *'military crest'* such that it and the observers are never framed against the skyline (see definition of the term *'military crest'* in section 12.3.1).

- reinforcing the wooden frame with layers of camouflage-painted sandbags to a thickness of at least 16 inches, and stacked so as not to provide any unobstructed pathways for bullets, to provide a bullet-resistant barrier.

- any needs to house gear such as communications and observation devices or materials such as printed instructions and procedures.

- providing the observers with either hard or soft cover in case there is a need to make an emergency exit (perhaps a wall of camouflage-painted sandbags).

- the addition of a simple raised floor and provision for drainage so that observers are never standing in water.

- proximity to a latrine or other location designated to serve as an *'outdoor toilet'*.

Observers at the LP/OP should, if possible, be equipped with binoculars and listening devices to extend their range of observation, as well as with some means to communicate observations to the HQ. A radio scanner could also be beneficial (particularly to scan the frequencies used by low-power transmitters such as FRS handheld units, as the LP/OP may be able to receive closer/weaker signals that the HQ cannot receive).

12.13. Strategies and Tactics

Simply having weapons and knowing how to use them is only the foundation for employing them as part of defensive or offensive operations. When involved in an armed conflict time- and battle- proven tactics and strategies should be utilized to optimize the group's chances for survival. The following are some well-known strategies and tactics that should be studied and committed to memory by anyone who may be filling a leadership role for group or community defense:

- *Castle Defense* - this strategy involves defending a location from defensive zones at pre-established fortifications.

- *Crossfire* - crossfire involves positioning shooters in two or more positions relative to an adversary such that the adversary finds it difficult (if not impossible) to find effective cover.

- *Flanking* - engaging an adversary frontally with one group while having a second group attack from their side. A flanking maneuver can be countered by a defender by either deploying in a circular formation or by initiating a second frontal defense. If the adversary has sufficient numbers then it should also be considered that a flanking maneuver may itself be accompanied by a secondary flanking maneuver.

  One more effective defense against a flanking maneuver is to anticipate the attempt and have an ambush prepared to meet the flanking forces. Another counter might be to have booby traps or other stealthy protections in place along the avenue of attack (for example, preparing a minefield).

- *Shoot-and-Scoot (a.k.a. 'hit and run')* - this is basically a guerilla warfare strategy that involves carrying out a surprise attack and then quickly moving on before a counter-attack or effected defense can be mounted.

- *Defense in Depth* - deploying defenders in layers with a plan of yielding gradually, but only after inflicting casualties and slowing the adversary's rate of advance while exposing their weaknesses for counter-attack.

- *Hedgehog Defense* - Deploying a series of hardened defensive locations to attract attackers passing through an area. This has the effect of thinning their ranks and making them more vulnerable to counter-attack.

- *Blitz* - An offensive strategy that involves suddenly penetrating and encircling enemy defenses with vastly superior forces.

- *Disruption of Supply Lines* - A strategy of cutting off an attacking force's sources of resupply as a means of 'starving' an opposing force.

- *Ambush* - The tactic of waiting in one or (typically) multiple concealed locations along an adversary's suspected avenue of approach until they move into the designated *kill zone*.

- *Instigation* - This tactic involves employing measures, including disinformation, that result in two potential adversaries attacking one another; thereby eliminating or reducing the threat represented by both.

- *Reverse Slope Defense* - The tactic of laying in wait on the slope of a hill, mountain or ridge facing away from an adversary, such that the terrain provides protection from weapons and observation. When the enemy assaults the position their physical energy has been depleted and they can then be engaged at close range. This tactic is only effective if the adversary does not have 'eyes in the sky'.

- *Guerilla Warfare* - The conduct of a war-of-attrition by small, loosely-organized groups. This form of warfare is asymmetric in that the smaller groups employ weapons and techniques that are very unlike those of the larger group they are attacking. Over time guerilla tactics can damage the resolve of an enemy such that they may later succumb much more easily to a more direct, conventional attack.

- *Infiltration and Subversion* - The process of joining with an adversary or potential adversary so as to disrupt and/or intercept any plans they may have for aggression.

- *Feint Attack* - An attack that is made for the purpose of drawing the adversary's attention and/or forces from the location where the primary attack is planned to take place.

- *Feint Retreat* - A strategic retreat designed to draw the adversary to an ambush or a location where the adversary has a greater disadvantage. Feint retreats can also be used to spread an adversary's forces more thinly, or to exhaust the adversary's resources prior to mounting an attack against them

- *Full Retreat* - The tactic of completely evacuating an area when faced with an adversary who has overwhelming force.

- *Strategic Surrender* - The tactic of yielding and submitting to an adversary with overwhelming force.

Many of the above strategies and tactics may be combined to form more sophisticated strategies. For example, a feint retreat could be used to draw a foe into a Hedge Hog defense, and that retreat might then be turned into a flanking maneuver. Many of these strategies can also be augmented by taking into account such natural factors as terrain, weather and the dark of night.

The management of information flow before and during battle is also a big part of most tactics. Disinformation may be fed to the adversary to affect their allocation of forces, or signaling between groups may be built into the plan such that the timing for phases of the attack is most effective. In the heat of battle this signaling might simply take the form of the blowing of a horn or the waving of a flag.

If, in the future, you feel that you are being threatened by a potential adversary it is recommended that you re-review this chapter prior to developing your plans, as the tactics described here may help you in considering all available options.

13. Survival Farming - Achieving Self-Sufficiency

"Give fools their gold, and knaves their power; let fortune's bubbles rise and fall; who sows a field, or trains a flower, or plants a tree, is more than all."

John Greenleaf Whittier

STRAIGHT THINKING: *Sweet potatoes are the perfect crop. They are low maintenance, low cost, and by far the most nutritious vegetable on the planet.*

Rabbits are the best animal to raise for meat if you have a limited budget and limited space. One male rabbit and two female rabbits can produce offspring with sufficient frequency that you can cook two rabbits per week indefinitely.

Livestock cannot exist without feed. He/she who controls the feed controls the food! In a major disaster non-local sources of feed may become unavailable to local farmers. A simple field of clover could become a good source of income.

Eventually the supplies that one has stored to weather a major disaster will either be consumed or reach their expiration date (which can come more quickly than planned if you are unable to maintain them at a temperature of around 70°F). As a result, if you a preparing for a long-term disaster, then you must plan to be self-sufficient. This means it may be necessary to grow your own vegetables and raise small livestock (chickens, rabbits, goats, etc.).

This chapter is intended to provide a good, strong overview of survival farming so as to allow the reader to determine what (if any) form of survival farming might be a good fit for their particular needs. It will describe the growing of common survival crops as well as the raising of small livestock that can serve as a good source of food and possible commerce.

13.1. Growing Survival Crops

Growing crops is a multi-dimensional topic that cannot be covered completely within the scope of this book. In fact, it can probably not be covered fully within any single book. Of course there is an extremely wide variety of crops to choose from. Additionally there are seasonal, geographical and soil-related considerations that all determine which crops are the best fit for a particular region. And it is precisely for this reason that one of the additional book recommendations appearing at the end of this book is *The Farmer's Handbook.*

While this chapter will provide you a good introduction to survival gardening, *The Farmer's Handbook,* possibly coupled with one or more other books that deal exclusively with gardening, is almost a 'must-have' for anyone planning to grow their own food. Nevertheless, this chapter does provide an important survivalist's perspective on gardening that may not appear in these other references. For example, other books will probably not assume that the crops are being grown in an post-disaster environment when resources that are normally taken for granted are no longer available. Additionally, in discussing the various crops, this book places emphasis on those that are most important as food sources under conditions in which time and resources are limited.

13.1.1. Land Needed

Of course the amount of crops that you can grow in a given area varies greatly depending on many factors (location, ground topology, expected rainfall, soil composition, etc.). On average, however, it is not uncommon for a single acre of decent crop-growing soil to produce sufficient vegetables to meet the dietary needs of 6 to 8 people. Much smaller areas, especially if used for *intensive gardening,* may still provide a yield that is sufficient to make a critical difference. All preppers should be growing some of their own vegetables, if only to be building up their 'green thumb' experience for later use.

13.1.2. Gardening Tools and Supplies

The tools you will need to work in your survival garden will vary depending on the size of the crops and the number of individuals who will be tending it. At the very least you will need a spade, a shovel, a hoe, some string, twine or wire, knives and/or scissors, buckets (including a watering bucket with sprinkler spout) and other containers of various sizes, gloves, a wide-brimmed hat to offer some protection from the sun and water spray bottles and misters. Additionally you will need scissors, knives and other digging implements (such as a digging fork). You should have a weather thermometer so that you know the outside temperature, and a rain gauge so that you can adjust your irrigation schedules to accommodate rainfall.

Other gardening equipment and supplies needed include:

- Hybrid and heirloom crop seeds for multiple planting seasons (including seeds for cover and feed vegetation such as clover and buckwheat).

- Bags of various types of fertilizer, humus and aged livestock manure (different crop types have varying fertilizer needs).

- Commercial fish emulsion fertilizer and *liquid seaweed* (be sure to check on expiration dates).

- Commercial garden insecticides applicable for your location.

- Bags of Epsom salts for soil augmentation (to add magnesium to the soil when needed).

- Large plastic sheets and tarps.

- An assortment of paper and plastic cups in which to grow seedlings.

- Empty egg cartons and other styrofoam boxes (e.g. take-out boxes from restaurants) in which to grow some seedlings.

- A soil thermometer.

- Wooden stakes ranging from 5 to 7 feet in length.

- Lengths of various types of wire fencing (chicken wire, etc).

- Bags of lime for soil augmentation.

- Wooden trellises

- *Flats* on which to sprout seeds.

- Large containers of non-perfumed, non-detergent liquid soap to use as a garden insecticide (liquid *Ivory Soap* is often used for this purpose).

- A garden cart to use for moving young plants in and out of shelter while hardening them off.

- A wheelbarrow for moving large and/or unwieldy loads.

- Hammers, nails, wood and metal screws and screw drivers. Screw-in cup holders and eye-hooks of various sizes.

- Soil and compost thermometers.

- A hoe and a large file (to occasionally sharpen the hoe).

- A soil pH testing kit.

- One or more large bottles of hydrogen peroxide to use as a seed disinfectant for disinfecting pepper seeds before planting.

- Motorized garden tiller.

- Fuel for all motorized gardening devices.

- Plant protectors (e.g. the "Wall O' Water" plant protectors).

- Wire cutters, pliers, vice grip pliers and a full set of US and metric wrenches and sockets.

- Multiple large acid-free envelopes for storing harvested seeds.

- Large markers for making notes on seed envelopes.

- A pitch fork for moving hay and turning compose piles.

- One or more compost bins that are 3 to 5 feet in length, width and height.

- Irrigation water hoses, including drip and/or 'soaker' irrigation hoses if possible.

If your gardens are sufficiently large you may need additional infrastructure and equipment to farm all the available land. This might include tractors with various attachable implements and fuel stores. A larger garden or planted field may also require a garden hose, some piping and/or other related equipment for irrigation.

13.1.3. Obtaining and Storing Seed

In the survivalist community you will see many references to *heirloom seeds*. If you were to research the term you would learn that it really has no clear definition. However, there are some important things that can definitely be said about heirloom seeds:

- They produce seed-bearing vegetables, which allows the survival farmer to harvest seeds for future planting seasons. (Non-heirloom seeds require you to purchase a new supply of seeds for the each growing season.)

- They are more difficult to grow, and often do not produce the yield of non-heirloom seeds.

- They tend to be less resistant to insects and other pests.

- They tend to produce better tasting vegetables.

NOTE: *Many survivalists would recommend that you make use of only heirloom seed when planting your crop so that you can harvest seeds to plant future crops. However, there is a counter argument. The counter argument is that you should start with the more hardy and productive non-heirloom seeds in order to be better assured of success with that first crop, and to be assured of a better yield.*

As is often the case, the answer lies somewhere in the middle. Survival farmers should obtain and plant a mix of heirloom and non-heirloom seeds. In this way they realize the advantages of both. And, in future growing seasons they will have the real-world experience to tackle the challenges of growing purely heirloom crops (when there may be no alternative).

If you store your seeds in a cool, dry location then a good percentage of them can remain viable anywhere from 2 to 5 years. Those seed which are older are almost certainly not going to be as viable as newer seeds, however it does not hurt to plant them and hope for the best. In fact, knowing they will not be as productive, you may plant them a little more densely than normal.

In addition to storing your seeds in a cool, dry place you should also store them in a proper container to realize maximum longevity. There are many references that will suggest storing seed in a vacuum, and even freezing seed. However, seeds are **living things**, and living things cannot exist long in a freezer or a vacuum. Traditionally seeds have been stored in acid-free paper envelopes. Until there is a definitive study conducted you are probably safest storing your seeds in such envelopes and keeping them at as constant a temperature ranging between 40°F and 70°F.

The survivability of different types of seeds can vary significantly. You should research the expected shelf life for any seed you are storing. Be sure to write the storage date on the container or envelope in which the seed is stored.

Of course the amount of seed that you should store will vary depending on the amount of food that you need to grow. If you keep in mind that one acre can feed 8 people then, for any particular crop or set of crops, you should be able to easily calculate the amount of seed that you need. When making the calculation, however, keep in mind that you will be storing seed for at least two planting seasons (in most cases). Also, as mentioned here, be sure to include both heirloom and hybrid seed, making sure to store, track and label them separately.

13.1.4. Gardening Methods

The traditional approach of growing crops in rows spaced about 3 feet apart is a good fit for the survival farmer who has access to ample land. The advantages of this approach are:

- It provides space for the use of machinery and/or farm animals to reduce the amount of human labor required to grow the crop.

- The layout lends itself to mechanical and/or automated irrigation.

- The plants are spaced apart far enough that they only require modest fertilization and watering.

Intensive gardening is an approach to gardening that is a better fit for those who must grow as much as possible in very limited space. Rather than planting crops in rows, the plants are packed as densely as possible on the land available and frames and trellises are used to grow some vegetables (e.g. cucumbers) vertically rather than horizontally. Intensive gardening also involves the growing of vegetables in *raised beds* as a means of further increasing plant density. While intensive gardening allows the survival farmer to grow more crops in less physical space, it has the disadvantages that maintaining the garden is more labor-intensive and it requires significantly more fertilizer and water.

NOTE: Hydroponics *is another form of gardening that involves growing crops* without soil. *With hydroponics the plants are grown such that the roots are exposed to the air, and they are soaked in or sprayed with nutrients. Hydroponics is not a good fit for the survival farmer because the success of this high-tech approach to gardening requires resources and infrastructure that may very well not be available in a grid-down scenario.*

Your choice of planting your garden in rows or practicing intensive gardening will depend on your own unique circumstances. The choice you make will determine the equipment and amount and type of fertilizer and water for which you should plan *(well, ok, there's only one "type" of water!)*.

Vegetable	Nutrition	Needs	Description
Sweet Potatoes	Extremely high	Sandy soil in, 100 frost-free days and good drainage	Sweet potatoes are low maintenance and widely-accepted to be the most nutritious vegetable. In addition to being rich in important dietary minerals, they are high in vitamins A, B6 and C.
Carrots	High	Any type of soil (depending on variety), mature in 50 to 100 days depending on type and growing season	Carrots come in a variety of types, which vary greatly in storage life, taste, shape, and the type of soil in which they can be grown. They are a good source of vitamins A, B1, B2 and C in addition to being an excellent source of alpha and beta carotene.
Kale	High	Grows in rich, slightly acidic soil.	Kale is very high in vitamins an has very strong anti-inflammatory properties.
Spinach	High	Spinach is a cold weather crop that requires nitrogen-rich soil.	Spinach is a good source of many critical vitamins and minerals, including vitamins A, C, E and K.
Purslane	Medium	Grows virtually anywhere, with dry soil being best	Purslane is rich in vitamins and minerals, and is a great alternative to fish as a source of omega-3 fatty oils.
Pumpkin	High	Grows in rich soil and should be fertilized with low-nitrogen fertilizers.	Pumpkins are rich in vitamins A, C and E, and can store for 3 to 6 months.

Table 13.1.: Good Survival Vegetables (1 of 2)

Tables 13.1 and 13.2 provide lists of common vegetables that recommended for cultivation on most survival farms.

13.1.5. Composting, Humus and Mulch

Composting is the process of maintaining a pile of discarded organic materials such that, over time, it decomposes into *humus*, a material that is excellent for augmenting soil used to grow vegetables.[260] Humus is a rich, dark brown substance that increases the nutrient content and water absorption characteristics of soil (because humus is produced by the composting process it is often referred to by the noun *compost*). The composting process involves:

- Identifying a location for your compost bin or pile. (A bin is simply a container that can be used to house and better protect the compost pile.)

Vegetable	Nutrition	Needs	Description
Winter Squash	High	Requires soil rich in organic material.	Winter squash is an excellent source of vitamins A and C as well as the minerals potassium and manganese. It is also high in dietary fiber, iron and beta carotene.[255]
Cabbage	Medium	Soil should contain high organic matter enriched with compost and well-composted manure. Requires fertilizer with balanced nitrogen, potassium and phosphorus.[244]	A good source of vitamins C, K, B1 and B6 as well as minerals calcium, magnesium, phosphorus and potassium.[245]
Onion	Medium	Grows in a wide range of soils. Heavy soils should be augmented with compost or composted manure.[294]	Very good source of Vitamin C, and a good source of Vitamin B6. Also a good source of potassium and manganese.[291]
Corn	Medium	Requires good sunlight and well-drained soil.	A common ingredient for many popular recipes and also serves as good feed for livestock.
Watermelon	Medium	Needs plenty of space, three months of hot weather, and rich, well-drained soil.	While watermelons are not the most nutritious vegetable, and require an abundance of space and attention, they may play an important psychological role as a treat during difficult times.
Cantaloupe	Medium	Needs loose, well-drained soil and 80-100 days of hot weather.	In addition to being an excellent source of vitamins A and C, cantaloupes are a great source of potassium and dietary fiber.

Table 13.2.: Good Survival Vegetables (2 of 2)

- "Feeding" the compost pile with appropriate "green" (high nitrogen) and "brown" (high carbon) organic materials.

- Maintaining the compost pile by occasionally *turning* it with a shovel, compost fork or other implement to provide oxygen to the microorganisms that are responsible for breaking down the organic material.

- Maintaining the moisture level of the pile to facilitate the chemical processes that break down the pile.

- Monitoring the temperature of the pile so that it stays within the bounds that best support the decomposition process.

- Extracting the fully processed humus from the compost pile for soil augmentation and/or mulching use.

NOTE: *Mulching is the process of placing substances and materials on top of the soil for the purpose of regulating soil moisture or temperature, slowing or halting the growth of weeds and dissuading pests. Many substances (some non-organic such as rubber or aluminum foil) may be used as mulch for various purposes. It is not uncommon to use humus as a mulch to reduce weed growth or to allow the soil to better retain moisture (interestingly, aluminum foil has sometimes been used to simply confuse invasive insects).[261]*

Composting is a slow motion "chemical balancing act" in which one must adjust moisture, oxygen content, and the proportion of carbon- and nitrogen- contributing organic substances so as to maximize the speed of decomposition (if not done properly, it can take years for a compost pile to decompose, however if done properly the process can take as little as 3 months). By measuring the temperature of the compost pile, observing moisture content, and monitoring any odors coming from the pile, you are able to adjust oxygen and water levels, as well as the ratio of nitrogen- and carbon- contributing organic substances, so as to decompose discarded organic waste into humus in the shortest time.

"Brown" compost material consists of those organic materials that are high in carbon, including ashes, peanut shells, wood, bark, corn stalks, leaves, shredded newspaper, cardboard, pine needles, sawdust, straw, peat moss and vegetable stalks. "Green" compost material consists of those organic materials that are high in nitrogen, such as algae, manure, clover, food waste, alfalfa, garden waste, grass clippings, hay, coffee grounds, hedge clippings, vegetable scraps, seaweed and weeds. The ratio of browns to greens that is said to result in an optimum rate of decomposition is said to range from 25 to 30 parts of browns for every 1 part of greens.[257]

Planning Your Compost Pile(s)

When planning your compost pile first decide what form it will take. It can be as simple as a place where you keep an open pile of organic material, it can be a homemade bin to help keep the pile better organized (and better concealed), or it may be a commercially-purchased bin that may have special features that make it easier to maintain the pile (for example, commercial compost bins may be free standing and rotate with a hand-crank, rather than requiring you to use a pitchfork or other implement to periodically turn the

NOTE: *The prime benefit to the prepper of having a compost pile is that the humus produced can be used to strategically recondition relatively small garden areas that have the most serious needs. Additionally, the recycling of organic material through the compost pile promotes an important 'waste not, want not' mindset. However, each person in the prepper group generally requires between 1/8 and 1/6 acre of crop growing capacity, and a typical recommendation is to condition soil by working in a layer of humus that is between 1 and 1.5 inches deep. About the maximum size compost bin that is manageable is 5 feet x 5 feet x 5 feet in size (125 cubic feet).*

With a full acre being 43,560 square feet in size, if you wanted to put down one-tenth of a foot (1.2 inches) of compost over 1/6 acre (approximately the land needed to produce for a single person) then you would find that you would need almost 6 compost bins for each person in your group (excluding smaller children, of course). This is almost certainly not realistic or practical for any prepper group. As a result, composting should only be considered a part of a soil-conditioning equation that also includes conventional fertilizing and crop rotation (see section 13.1.17).

If you already have your crop growing area identified then you might also con-sider having humus delivered from a commercial source to condition your soil before disaster strikes (pre-disaster the cost may not be prohibitive). If you do plan on doing this be sure that you have arranged for a means of mechanically spreading the humus and mixing it into the soil, otherwise you'll end up with a small mountain of humus that may never find its way into the soil. Also be aware that, particularly for areas that experience freezing weather during the winter, the best time to augment soil with humus is in the fall before winter sets in (the freezing and thawing cycles tend to better incorporate the humus into the soil). If you have humus disked into your soil with a tractor be sure that the ground is disked repeatedly until the ground is smooth enough to easily walk across.

pile). The recommended size for a compost bin is about 3-5 feet x 3-5 feet x 3-5 feet.[257] This produces a good quantity of compost while not being so large that it is difficult to maintain. Depending on your needs you may wish to have more than one compost pile.

CAUTION: *Be certain not to locate your compost pile near a home, as it may sometimes omit unpleasant odors or may promote the rotting of wood that is nearby. Also, be sure the locate the compost pile such that neighbors are not likely to complain about any odors it may produce, or by it being openly visible from their property.[257] Your compost pile should also be located in a well-ventilated, well-drained area. A area with shade is also good for protecting the pile from over-heating during the summer months.*

Homemade compost bins are generally 3-walled structures, with one side left open to enable you to turn the pile as needed (turning introduces much needed oxygen to the pile). It is not uncommon for homemade bins to be constructed from the types of wooden pallets used by commercial warehouses.[257] All compost piles also require some form of protection from rain. This protection might be as simple as a water-resistant tarp suspended over the pile.

Maintaining a Proper Carbon-to-Nitrogen Ratio

Compost piles are fueled by materials that contribute a proper ratio of carbon and nitrogen. Materials that primarily contribute carbon are often referred to as *'browns'* while materials that primarily contribute nitrogen are referred to as *'greens'* (see page 313 for more information about these compost materials). The optimum ratio of browns to greens is said to range from 25 to 30 parts browns for each part of greens. Managing this ratio will allow you to control unwanted odors produced by the pile as well as to maximize the speed with which the compost decomposes to humus.

Maintaining Your Compost Pile

The primary factors you need to control in your compost pile are heat and moisture, and these factors are controlled by occasionally turning the pile to add oxygen, by adding water to the pile to improve moisture and by adding new organic materials to the pile to maintain an optimum ratio of carbon- to nitrogen- contributing content.

You should use a compost thermometer to measure the temperature of your pile in 3-4 places. The ideal average temperature is between 140°F and 160°F, which is a sufficient temperature to kill any weed seeds in the pile as well as many sources of plant disease.[257] If the average temperature of the pile is less than 104°F or greater than 131°F, or if the pile is emitting any undesirable odors, then you should turn the pile.[258] When turning the pile, if you notice that the material is less moist than a "wrung out sponge"[258], then add water. Also, when turning the pile, attempt to locate the least decomposed material towards the outside of the pile so that it will be exposed to more oxygen. The following measures will provide you with the assurance that your compost pile is operating at maximum efficiency:[257]

- Turn the pile frequently to keep it will oxygenated.

- Add new material to the pile in bulk for better heat generation.

- Locate the pile such that it receives some direct sunlight.

- Shred vegetable matter before adding it to the pile.

- Add compost *activators* (e.g. algae, seaweed, lake weed, aged manure, alfalfa meal, cottonseed meal, blood meal, compost starter or wood ashes) to the pile.

NOTE: *As a compost pile decomposes it may reduce in size by as much as 70%.*

Recognizing When Humus is Fully Decomposed and Ready for Use

Depending on how well you maintain your compost pile the contents may take between 3 and 12 months to fully decompose into humus. Humus that is ready to be applied to soil should be dark brown and have a uniform, grainy texture that crumbles easily, exhibits no clumps or stringiness and does not contain any material that is not fully decomposed. The entire pile will almost certainly not decompose into humus at once, and you should judiciously remove only that humus that is ready, leaving the remainder of the pile to continue its decomposition process.

Vermicomposting

The addition of red worms to a compost pile helps to speed the decomposition process and also results in a humus that is richer in nutrients. Composting with red worms is known is *vermicomposting*. If you plan on vermicomposting then be aware that this process generally requires special, commercially-available composting bins.

Applying Humus

The condition of the soil can be inferred by how well it is growing vegetables, or you may test it more objectively by placing a quantity of the soil into a sealed plastic bag and letting it sit for 1 week. After that time if the contents of the bag develop a sour or ammonia-like scent then the soil could probably benefit from the addition more humus.[259]

While material from the compost pile can be used for mulching at any stage of decomposition, only fully decomposed humus should be used to actually mix into the soil. To mix humus into the soil simply spread a layer of humus over the area being treated (in a quantity consistent with the need) and use a shovel or other gardening tool to dig it into the soil to a depth of 3 to 5 inches.[259] A light composting treatment might consist of mixing in a 1 inch thick layer of humus, while a more intense treatment might consist of mixing in as much as 2 inches.

In the perfect world it would be optimal to routinely treat crop soil with a 1/2 inch layer of humus once every two years in colder climates, and once each year in warmer regions (this time difference is due to the fact that the compost material continues to decompose when the soil is warm).[259]

CAUTION: *Never add meat products to a compost pile, as this will only attract rodents and other unwanted pests, while causing the compost pile to emit undesirable odors.*

13.1.6. Augmenting Soil with Livestock Manure and Other Natural Fertilizers

It is often said that the three basic active ingredients of all fertilizers are nitrogen, phosphorus and potassium. In reality, humus is an important forth ingredient. While nitrogen, phosphorus and potassium directly affect the chemical composition of the soil, humus affects the structure of the soil such that it is better able to absorb and retain nutrients and moisture, and better able to support biological activity that is essential to healthy plant growth. The benefits of humus are covered in detail in section 13.1.5.

CAUTION: *You should only plan on using manure from livestock (cows, horses, goats, sheep, poultry, rabbits, etc.) and not from domesticated or other meat-eating animals or human sources (which have a much higher incidence of disease-causing microorganisms and parasites).[263]*

Animal manure has been used to fertilize soil for thousands of years. Depending on the animal source, manure contains varying quantities of nitrogen, phosphorus, potassium and humus. Cows and horses tend to produce manure that is rich in humus, but provides relatively modest quantities of nitrogen, phosphorus and potassium. Chickens, pigeons, rabbits and goats, on the other hand, produce manure that is richer in these important organic chemicals.

Regardless of the source, all manure should be composted prior to being used to augment soil. This composting process provides the assurance that potential harmful microorganisms are not introduced into the soil. Ideally manure should be composted for 6 months before being applied to soil, however it is possible that manure may be fully decomposed in as little as 2 months. Because manure adds nitrogen to the compost pile, it is important to balance it with the addition of other carbon-contributing composting materials (browns) as well (see section 13.1.5 for a list of carbon-contributing composting materials).

You should cease adding fresh manure to your compost pile 2 months before you anticipate applying it to soil.[262] You will know that manure is fully decomposed when, in relatively dry form, the compost pile is no longer at a temperature greater than that of the surrounding environment.

NOTE: *Manure can be added directly to the soil in the fall after the last crop has been harvested, as the manure will fully decompose in the soil during the winter months.[262]*

To augment soil with manure the fully-composted manure should be spread over the soil to be treated and then mixed in to a depth of 6 to 9 inches. After soil has been augmented with composted manure, at least 1 month should be allowed to pass before planting (so that the sudden increase in organic activity does not harm newly-planted crops).

Using Green Manure

Green manures are crops that are not grown for food, but rather to benefit the soil. Green manure is important to the survival farmer because they are an important means of restoring soil nutrient levels when commercial fertilizers are not available. These green manure crops are ploughed into the ground while they are still green or shortly after flowering.[265] Green manure crops generally fall into one of two classes:

- *legumes such as vetch, cowpeas, annual sweet clover, soybeans, sesbania, and velvet beans'* - these crops are grown for their ability to increase the nitrogen content of the soil.

- *non-leguminous crops such as millet, sorghum, sudangrass and buckwheat* - these crops are grown to suppress the growth of unwanted weeds as well as to improve the structure of the soil.

It would be advisable for the survival farmer to have seeds stored for both leguminous and non-leguminous vegetation as a means of maintaining good soil in the event of a prolonged disaster.

Using Fish for Fertilizer

Fish have been used to fertilize crops for literally thousands of years. Fish fertilizers are among the best fertilizers because, not only do they contribute nitrogen, phosphate and potassium, but they also contribute natural oils that are beneficial to important microorganisms. Additionally, fish-based fertilizers release their nutrients to the crop gradually, resulting in optimal crop growth.

Fish fertilizer comes in three forms:[271]

- *Fish meal* - a powdery fertilizer that retains a fishy smell. Fish meals are made by first heating the raw fish parts and then grinding them into fish meal powder which is then chemically treated. Fish meal is high in nitrogen and phosphorus, making it ideal for good root and leaf development. To the survivalist the disadvantage of fish meal is that creating it requires costly, specialized equipment and chemicals.

- *Fish hydrolysate* - a thick liquid that is made by treating raw fish parts with digestive enzymes that break down the fish parts into a good fertilizer that also contributes beneficial fish oils. To the survivalist the disadvantage of fish hydrolysate fertilizers, as with fish meal fertilizers, is the costly and specialized equipment and chemicals required for production.

- *Fish emulsion* - an organic liquid that is made by composting raw fish parts in a plastic bucket for about 2 weeks. The resulting decomposed fish can then be added to a regular compost pile, with humus from that pile subsequently used to fertilize soil. This form of fish fertilizer is important to the survivalist because it does not require costly and/or specialized equipment or chemicals to produce.

NOTE: *To produce a fish emulsion fertilizer simply place fish parts in a plastic bucket on top of a bed of straw, sawdust or leaves (this bottom layer should fill approximately half of the bucket). If possible, add molasses as a fuel to facilitate the decomposition. The contents of the bucket should then be turned on a daily basis over a 2 week period. After that 2 weeks the contents will have decomposed to a fish emulsion that is ready to be added to a compost pile.[272]*

13.1.7. Augmenting Soil with Commercial Fertilizers

Fertilizers are granular or liquid substances that are applied to soil in order to increase its nutritional content. This is important to the proper growth of many vegetables and other crops. You may create your own fertilizers via composting (see section 13.1.5), or you may purchase commercially-available fertilizers that have been formulated to meet a wide range of needs.

The primary nutrients provided by all fertilizers are nitrogen, phosphate and potassium ('potash'), which are abbreviated as 'N', 'P' and 'K' on standard fertilizer labels.[269] Nitrogen is critical to the development of stalks and leaves, while phosphate and potassium are important to the structure and energy absorption of plants at a cellular level. Different plants have different degrees of needs for each of these nutrients (for example, leafy plants have a larger need for nitrogen). Fertilizers also contain:[266][270]

- *Secondary nutrients* - calcium, sulfur and magnesium (often these are naturally replenished).

- *Micronutrients* - iron, copper, zinc and manganese (easily preserved by recycling vegetable matter).

- *Insecticides* - chemicals to kill harmful insects.

- *Herbicides* - chemicals that kill or inhibit the growth of unwanted weeds.

- *Inert filler materials* - materials packaged with the fertilizer that may help preserve its potency, but which have no effect on plant growth.

All fertilizers are given a three-number rating that indicates the percentage composition by weight of these three critical nutrients. This label takes the form of three numbers separated by dashes. For example, a fertilizer labeled '5-10-20' would contain 5 percent nitrogen, 10 percent phosphate and 20 percent potassium (with the remaining weight being other inactive ingredients). This labelling makes it easy for the farmer or gardener to identify the fertilizer products they can use for their own specific needs.

Not all crops benefit from the application of fertilizer to the soil. For example, peas and beans extract the nitrogen they need directly from the atmosphere. Since soils with a high degree of clay already contain phosphate, no phosphate-enriching fertilizer is needed by clay soils. The phosphate in sandy soil is quickly depleted and must often be replaced through the application of fertilizer.[266] So, it is incumbent on the survival farmer to not only understand the type of soil in which they are growing crops, but also to understand the specific needs of different crops.

NOTE: *Many garden supply centers, country agriculture agents and farm suppliers offer free or low-cost soil testing services to help you better understand your fertilizer needs. In addition to knowing your soil it is equally important to understand the needs of the crops you intend to grow.*

Many lower-cost fertilizers immediately release their nitrogen content into the soil. This immediate release may be more than is needed in the very short term, and may even result in some crop damage if excessive nitrogen is involved. Better fertilizers, known as "controlled release" fertilizers are specifically developed to release nutrients into the soil more gradually. One of the best time-release fertilizers is humus, which you can purchase separately or obtain directly from your own compost pile(s). Compost not only adds fertilizing nutrients to the soil, but also enhances the structure of the soil such that it can better retain nutrients and moisture.[268]

Applying Fertilizer

Fertilizer may be used to augment soil before any crops are planted or after plants are already growing. When adding fertilizer to unplanted soil it should be spread evenly across the soil (typically 1 to 2 pounds per 100 square feet or 200 to 400 pounds per acre). Once spread the soil should immediately be tilled so that the fertilizer is thoroughly mixed in. When fertilizing soil in this way you should allow at least one month to pass before planting.

Fertilizer can also be added to soil alongside individual plants after they have begun to grow. In this case care should be taken to not allow the fertilizer to come into direct contact with the plant, and 1 to 2 tablespoons of fertilizer should be added for each plant.

Applying too much fertilizer can draw moisture from the soil and result in 'burning' the plants.[267] As a result it is better to err on the side of fertilizing too little and then apply more fertilizer as you observe the growth of the plants.[266] Also, in the case of leafy plants that are grown to bear fruit (e.g. tomatoes and pumpkins), excessive nitrogen added to the soil can result in plants that develop very healthy leaves and vines, but develop smaller fruits.

13.1.8. Root Cellars

Several specific vegetables, such as carrots and potatoes, may store well for weeks or months when kept in an environment that is within certain temperature and humidity bounds. In many parts of the world an above- or below- ground room may be used as a place to store produce for longer terms after harvesting. Such storage areas are referred to as *root cellars*. Where the climate makes root cellars feasible their use can enable the survival farmer to enjoy vegetables throughout much of the year.

It should be noted that some vegetables require cool and humid storage, others require cool and dry storage and still others (such as hot peppers) require hot and dry storage (although root cellars are not used for hot and dry storage).

13.1.9. Annual, Biennial and Perennial Plants

Depending on their normal life cycle, plants are categorized as being either *annuals, biennials* or *perennials*. Annuals are plants that have a normal life cycle of one year (and so must be replanted each year). Biennials are plants that have a two-year life cycle, and perennials are plants with a normal life expectancy of greater than two years. Biennials often take different forms and have different characteristics for each of their two years, and if only one of those years produces a crop then the gardener may consider that plant to be an annual.

13.1.10. Thinning Crops

All seeds are not created equal. While one seed for a particular plant may produce a strong and productive plant, another seemingly-identical seed may produce a weaker plant (or completely fail to germinate). This becomes an increasingly important factor when planting seeds that have been on the shelf for longer periods of time. To address this issue it is often important to plant additional seeds and then, as they begin to grow, to selectively remove the weaker plants to provide more space for the strong plants to grow. This process of removing the weaker, redundant plants is referred to as *thinning*.

13.1.11. Dealing with Common Garden Pests

Dealing with Animal Pests

Larger animals pose one of the greatest threats to the survival farmer's crops. These threats include squirrels, mice, voles, moles, raccoons, deer, rabbits, birds and numerous other small- to mid- sized 'varmints'. The most effective protections against these threats are fence barriers. In the case of subterranean threats such as moles these barriers should extend at least 2 feet below the surface of the soil, and in the case of deer the fence should have a height of about 8 feet. In the case of deer it is actually beneficial to have two barriers, one inside the other, if at all possible (with the inside fence being maybe 3 feet in height) as this has been shown to further deter the deer.[286]

Other measures utilized to deal with wild animal pests include:

- *Scarecrows and other visual deterrents* - Scarecrows may help to keep destructive birds away from a crop. Similarly, models of predators such as owls may keep other small pests away from an area.

- *Trapping and snaring* - Animal pests may be trapped and either relocated or, in some cases, killed and used for food.

- *Shooting pests* - The crop owner may simply await the appearance of the unwanted pest and shoot it and possibly use it for food.

- *Poisoning pests* - The crop-owner may put out poison for the pest, although great care should be taken in doing this as it may claim unintended victims or, depending on the poison used, it may render the crops being protected unsafe to consume. Additionally, this approach may very well result in any killed pest also not being eligible for the dinner table.

> **NOTE:** *If you consider killing an animal pest do first make yourself aware of any laws that may prohibit this option (particularly during non-disaster times).*

Dealing with Insect Pests

The first step in dealing with insect pests is to provide the healthiest growing conditions for your plants. Strong plants will not succumb as readily to insects if they are healthy. Make sure that your plants are in an appropriate type of soil with proper exposure to sunlight. Also be certain that they receive adequate watering and use mulching to maintain a proper level of soil moisture.

The two most common ways of dealing with insects you observe on your plants is to physically remove them from the plants and destroy them or, in the case of smaller or more numerous insects, spray the insects with soapy water. An insecticidal soap can be made by mixing 1 to 2 tablespoons of liquid soap in 1 quart of water. To further strengthen the soap you can also add water that has been boiled with ground peppers and other strong spices and strained (although such a mix should be used within 24 hours, as the organic compounds will begin to decompose).[287] The soapy and/or spicy water can then be sprayed on the affected areas of plants. It is possible that soapy water can irritate the plants themselves, so it is important to spray only the affected part of the plant, and observe the effects of a first spraying before applying additional treatments.

Other measures for dealing with insect pests in crops include:

- *Commercial insecticides* - Be sure to read and follow the instructions that accompany any commercial insecticide that you may apply, paying particular attention to the risks of human exposure.

- *Cutworm collars* - Barriers created to encircle the base of a plant to a depth in the soil of 1 inch can form an effective barrier against cutworm infestations. These collars can be made from a wide range of readily-available materials including the cardboard centers of paper towels, tuna cans with the top and bottom cut out, bands or aluminum foil or even rolled-up newspaper (newspaper rolls carry the additional advantage that they eventually decompose and provide nourishment to the plant).[288]

- *Crop rotation* - By varying the crops planted in a particular location from season-to-season the tendency of crop-specific insect populations to increase over time is greatly reduced.

NOTE: *Some insects, worms and larvae are beneficial to vegetable crops because they prey on (or otherwise destroy) harmful insects. Beneficial nematodes are microscopic worms (available for commercial purchase) that emit a bacteria that invades and kills a wide range of destructive soil-borne insects. The lady bug and the praying mantis are beneficial insects that also prey on harmful insects (ladybugs can also be purchased from commercial sources).[290][289]*

13.1.12. Hardening Off Seedlings before Transplanting

Often it is necessary to *'harden off'* seedlings before they are transplanted into your garden. This involves exposes them to the outdoor environment for progressively longer time intervals over a period of between 1 and 2 weeks (but not allowing them to be exposed to excessive rain, wind or sun). This is often most easily accomplished by keeping the seedlings on a gardening cart that can be wheeled in and out of shelter each day. During this hardening process the watering of the plants should be gradually reduced and no fertilizer should be applied. After the hardening process is complete the seedlings are ready for transplant into the garden.[324]

13.1.13. Testing and Adjusting Soil pH Values

The measure of a soil's acidity is referred to as its *pH*. The value of pH can vary between 0 to 14, with a value of 0 indicating the highest degree of acidity and a value of 14 indicating the highest degree of basicity (and a value of 7 being neutral). Most plants experience their best growth in soil pH levels between 6.2 and 6.8[326], although some plants have evolved to flourish in soils with pH levels well outside this range.[325]

Soil pH can be measured in the following ways:

- *The use of litmus paper* - a small sample of the soil is mixed with distilled water and a piece of litmus paper is dipped into the solution. If the litmus paper turns red then a higher acidity is indicated and if it turns blue then a higher basicity is indicated. This approach to measuring soil pH is quick and easy, however the measurement is not very precise.

- *The use of a pH meter* - a metal probe extending from an electronic meter is inserted into soil that has been moistened and the pH of the soil is read from its numeric display.

- *The use of a testing kit* - barium sulfate powder from a small pH testing kit is mixed with a sample of the soil in distilled water, and the water changes color to reflect the acidity or basicity of the soil. Like the litmus paper test, this measure is not very precise.

Once you have determined both the pH of your soil and the pH requirements of the crops you have planned you can augment the soil to bring it within range. Lime, wood ash or oyster shells can be mixed into the soil to increase the pH, while sulfur, iron or aluminum sulfates, acid-reducing fertilizers, urea, decaying plant matter, compost or aged manure can be mixed in to reduce the pH (making the soil more acidic).[325]

13.1.14. The Importance of Knowing Frost Dates

Many crops should not be planted before the last springtime frost. Other crops are sensitive to the last frost of the year. As a result it is important for the survival farmer to know the expected first and last frost dates of every growing year. With these dates in mind the growing season can be planned well in advance. Such planning will inevitably result in better and more productive growing seasons.

13.1.15. Usefulness of a Greenhouse

For the survival farmer the importance of a greenhouse is that it enables them to get a head start on growing plants before the growing season truly starts. For many crops it is essential that they not be planted before the last spring frost, thus a greenhouse allows the gardener to begin growing seedlings earlier in a controlled environment, and to transplant them outside when weather and soil conditions are correct. The result is an extended growing season and increased crop yields.

NOTE: *No book is going to provide you with nearly the knowledge and understanding of gardening issues that are specific to your locale as will conversations with local experienced gardeners. Local experts will be able to identify for you the best varieties of vegetables to plant for your weather and soil types, the best fertilizers and other soil augmentations for the region, and ways to deal with pests that pose the biggest threats in your area.*

Build relationships with the owners of local gardening shops and others with many years of local gardening experience and the chances for your own gardening success will be increased immeasurably!

13.1.16. Storage and Handling of Harvested Seeds

In a time of major disaster a supply of seed for future planting seasons will be worth much more than its weight in gold. As a result it is critical that you store and handle your seed properly. You should always keep in mind that **seeds are living things**, and treat them accordingly.

The first thing to know about seeds is that they are always ready to begin germinating and start the process of growing into full-fledged plants. As a result it is imperative that stored seeds not be exposed to moisture or light. Additionally, because they are living things, seed should not be deprived of exposure to air.

Many experts think nothing of storing seeds in vacuum-sealed packages or jars, however others have serious doubts and report mixed results. Most of the highly experienced gardeners suggest that seed should be stored in acid-free paper envelopes, and kept in cool, dark location with low humidity.

If properly stored the seeds for most garden vegetables should remain viable for between 3 and 5 years.

The result of proper seed handling and storage will be increased yields and stronger, healthier plants when the seeds are finally planted.

13.1.17. Crop Rotation for Healthy Soil and Improved Crop Yields

Crop rotation is the practice of systematically varying the crops that are planted in a given area in such as way as to increase soil nutrition, reduce the effects of erosion, resist plant disease and minimize insect problems. The period of rotation can vary between 1 and 4 years[275], depending on specific needs and type and condition of the soil. There are many systems of crop rotation. All systems tend to organize plants into general classifications and alternate growing them in different locations from one season to the next.

Crop rotation enhances soil nutrient content through the process of alternating the crops planted in an area between those that draw nitrogen from the soil and those that replenish it (legumes).[274] Disease and insect problems are reduced because multiple seasons of planting the same crop have a natural tendency to successively strengthen the presence of harmful microorganisms and insects that target specific categories of crops. By alternating between crops with deep and shallow roots the overall structure of the soil (it's ability to retain moisture and nutrients) is also improved and susceptibility of the soil to erosion is reduced. Crop rotation practices have been credited with increasing crop yields by between 10 and 25 percent.[273]

Generally the best and easiest way to rotate crops is to segment your garden or field into four areas, and to rotate the different classes of crops you plan on growing between these areas from season to season. You might also set aside a fifth area for perennial vegetables that don't benefit from crop rotation *(e.g. rhubarb, asparagus, soft fruits and globe artichokes)*.[275]

Plant Classes

Crops may be considered to be organized into the following four general categories:[276]

- *Leafy and fruiting crops* - for example cabbage, lettuce and tomatoes. These crops are nitrogen-hungry.

- *Root vegetables and herbs* - for example potatoes and carrots. These crops require large quantities of nutrients.

- *Nitrogen-fixing crops* - for example peas, beans and peanuts. These crops add nitrogen to the soil.

- *Cover crops* - vegetation such as clover and buckwheat that enrich and condition the soil while discouraging some pests.

NOTE: *Many soil-borne plant diseases can live in the soil for as long as three or four years, which is why a four-year crop rotation cycle is suggested.*

In addition to rotating growing areas through the crop categories described above, *cover crops* can be planted between growing seasons to further protect the soil, fight pests and reduce soil-borne threats. For example beetle grub problems can be reduced by planting clover and buckwheat as a cover crop. If you have divided your growing area into four zones, each season you would alternate planting the vegetable categories described here in each of the zones. The result will be a reduced need for fertilizing and healthier, more productive crops.[276]

13.1.18. Growing Sweet Potatoes

The sweet potato has been rated by the *Center for Science in the Public Interest (CSPI)* as the most nutritious of all vegetables. In fact, the scientific score they have calculated for the sweet potato is over twice the score for the next most nutritious vegetable (which happens to be the regular baking potato).[213] Sweet potatoes contain high amounts of vitamins A, B6 and C, and the skin is rich in essential minerals including manganese, copper and iron.

In a survival situation the best ways to prepare sweet potatoes for human consumption are by steaming and baking them. These cooking methods preserve maximum nutrition. It is recommended that you consume the skin of the potato as well, which is particularly rich in vitamins and minerals.[217]

Vegetables	Rotation Rules
Garlic and onions	Rotate with legumes and avoid planting these in soil containing non-decomposed organic matter.
Parsnips, coriander, fennel, parsley, dill and carrots	These can be preceded with any other plant classes. Augment with compost before planting, and follow with heavy mulch or legumes.
Brussels sprouts, Broccoli, cabbage, kale, cauliflower, radishes, kohlrabi and turnips	These require a high degree of soil maintenance. Precede with legumes, and follow by cultivating the soil and spreading compost.
Cucumbers, squash, gourds, pumpkins and melons	Precede with wheat or winter rye, and follow with legumes.
Peas, beans, clovers and vetches	These plants add nutrients to the soil and have few pest problems. Rotate freely with other plant classes.
Oats, rye, corn and wheat	Follow with tomato or squash family crops to condition the soil for water retention and to help control weeds.
Potatoes, eggplant, peppers and tomatoes	These plants draw many nutrients from the soil and are susceptible to many fungal threats. They should be preceded with grasses or grain crops and followed with legumes.

Table 13.3.: Crop Rotation Rules for Some Commonly-Grown Crops .[276]

Name	Days to Maturity	Description
Georgia Jets	90-100	Fast growth, high yield, excellent taste
Beauregard	90-100	Fast growth and good shape
Porto Rico	110	Bush type potato, light in color, excellent taste, good for gardens with limited space
Vardaman	110	Bush type potato, very good coloration
Centennials	100	Very common, good size, shape and color
Nancy Hills	110	Sweet, light in color inside and out, one of the best tasting sweet potatoes
White Yams	110	Very white on outside and inside, particularly sweet
O'Henry	90-100	White on inside and out, drier when cooked

Table 13.4.: Types of Sweet Potatoes

In addition to being highly nutritious, given the proper climate and soil, the sweet potato is easy to grow. Sweet potatoes can be grown anywhere that there are 100 consecutive days of no frost, and grow best in sunny locations with loose and sandy soil that has good drainage.

Table 13.4 provides a list of many of the different varieties of sweet potatoes, along with their maturation period and a brief description of each.[214]

Sweet potatoes are grown from *slips* and *cuttings* rather than seeds. A slip is a small, leafy shoot that has grown from an existing potato (or from a piece of a potato). You may purchase ready-to-plant slips from a variety of sources or if you are willing to be patient for them to develop over a 6-week period, you may produce your own from potatoes that you have already grown or purchased.[215] A *cutting* is simply small (maybe 30 cm) length of a potato vine that has been cut and from which all but the smallest leaves at the tip have been removed.

To grow a potato from a cutting simply cover all but the small end leaves with soil and keep the soil wet or damp. The cutting will grow into multiple slips, from which potatoes will grow.

To make a slip, submerge a small potato in water, root side down, until it is about one-third covered with water (often toothpicks are stuck into the potato to keep it suspended at the top of a water-filled jar). Over a period of 4 to 6 weeks the potato will grow slips, which are then separated from the potato and placed separately in water until they begin to form their own small roots. Once the roots are formed the slip may be planted.

Depending on the specific variety of sweet potato that you are planting, it will require anywhere from 90 to 110 days for the potatoes to grow fully and be ready for harvest (you can tell when the potato becomes ready by the thickness of the stem and/or if you see the earth begin to bulge a little above the potato).

NOTE: *In addition to harvesting the potatoes, the leaves and shoots of sweet potatoes have some nutritional value, and may be harvested at any time with no ill effects to the potato itself.[216]*

In the more temperate climates that experience freezing weather, for optimum growth it is advisable to plant sweet potato slips during the springtime, and in open spaces that receive plenty of sunlight. In the subtropical and tropical zones sweet potatoes may be grown year-round, and it is advisable to consider growing them in areas where they have have a little protection from the sun (e.g. under shade trees). In all cases the potatoes should be planted in soil that drains well (if planting in a location with poor drainage it is advisable to plant the potatoes in a raised bed, or in mounds or ridges).[216]

Newly planted cuttings and slips should be watered about twice per week, which should be reduced to maybe once per week after they become established. In fact, after they become established it is a good practice to water them only if the soil seems to be abnormally dry. One month before harvesting you should cease watering them altogether, otherwise they may split prior to being harvested.[219]

NOTE: *If you are in a tropical or semi-tropical location where you can grow sweet potatoes year-round then you should plan on doing so. Otherwise you'll be depriving yourself of an excellent source of nutritious food over much of the year.*

The only pest that threatens the sweet potato is the *sweet potato weevil*, which can completely destroy both the above ground leaves as well as the potato itself. The sweet potato weevil is a small insect, about 1/4 inches in length, that has a blue and orange body.[216] If you do have problems with this pest then you will not be able to grow a permanent potato patch, and you will have to grow your sweet potatoes elsewhere. Whey buying sweet potato slips for planting be certain to only buy slips that have been certified as being free of weevils.

> **CAUTION:** *If you fertilize your sweet potatoes you should use fertilizers that provide high levels of potassium and phosphate and lower levels of nitrogen (such as 8-24-24 or 5-10-10). Otherwise, the potato's foliage will grow nicely, however the potato root itself will be small.*

For best taste and texture, as well longer storage life, sweet potatoes should be cured before being stored in a root cellar (or other dark, cool long term storage facility). To cure sweet potatoes they should be stored for 5 to 10 days at a temperature preferably ranging between 80°F to 85°F and at a relative humidity ranging between 80 and 90 percent. Although the conditions may not be ideal, it is not uncommon for sweet potatoes to be cured by simply being left outside in a shady location and covered with straw and burlap bags. Once cured the sweet potatoes are ready for longer term storage in a root cellar. If kept in a wooden box at a temperature of near 40°F they should store for between 4 and 6 months.[220]

> **CAUTION:** *When sweet potatoes are harvested and stored they should never be wet, as this will only encourage the growth of mold that will ruin the potatoes in storage.*
>
> *Even though fruits and potatoes have very similar storage conditions they should not be stored together, as fruits emit ethylene gas as they ripen, which causes the potatoes to begin to sprout and become inedible.[220]*

Cooked sweet potatoes can be refrigerated for 4 or 5 days.[218] These limited storage times are another reason to plan on growing sweet potatoes year-round if you live in a region that is warm throughout the year.

> **NOTE:** *Irish potatoes should be cured for about 2 weeks at temperatures ranging between 55 and 60°F and at a relative humidity ranging between 85 and 90 percent. They should be stored long term in a root cellar at temperatures ranging between 33 and 38°F and at a relative humidity of about 90 percent.[220]*

13.1.19. Growing Pumpkins for Food

Pumpkins are a very nutritious crop that are easy to grow (and store) in a wide range of climates. They are particularly rich in vitamin A, as well as a good source of vitamins

C and E. In addition to being a good source of vitamins, pumpkins are a good source of dietary fiber and the minerals iron, potassium, copper and manganese (while providing lesser amounts of other important minerals).[228]

NOTE: *There are literally hundreds of varieties of pumpkins that have been developed over generations for various properties. Some are bred for size and shape, others for pest-resistance and others for taste. The survivalist should consider obtaining seed for hybrid pumpkins that have been developed for food and pest-resistance, and also obtaining heirloom pumpkin seeds in order to produce pumpkin seeds for future growing seasons. The hybrid seeds will produce a more hardy pumpkin while you gain the increased gardening skills that may be required to successfully grow heirloom pumpkins.*

Heirloom seeds may produce pumpkins that are not as consistent in size and shape, however these pumpkins will almost certainly provide a better tasting food. And, of course, the fact that they produce seed that can be used to plant the next season's crop is the most compelling advantage of all!

Planting and Growing Pumpkins

If you live in a an area that has a short growing season you can start your pumpkins indoors for the first few weeks, however you should only plan on transplanting pumpkins if it is absolutely necessary, as they can be quite sensitive to this. Pumpkins can be planted when the average air temperature is around 70°F(in many places in the US this will be between late May and late June).

CAUTION: *Be sure to know the type of pumpkin seed you are purchasing, as there are many varieties with entirely different characteristics, and in many cases the seed packages are not adequately labeled.*

Pumpkins should be planted in well-drained soil, with light- to medium- compost added if available. If you experience frequent rain, or if your soil does not have good drainage characteristics, then it is advisable that you plant the seed in a mound of soil to facilitate drainage. Pumpkin seeds should be planted one inch deep. Consult the instructions on the seed packet for the best spacing between seeds. Any fertilizer used for pumpkins should be high in phosphate and potassium, and low in nitrogen.

> **NOTE:** *Pumpkins have many important and delicate roots that grow near the surface. Many pumpkin growers will place wide boards in the rows between their pumpkins in order to distribute their weight when they walk in the rows. This greatly reduces the possibility of root damage.[229]*

Once planted you should check the soil regularly to a depth of about one inch. If the soil is dry then you should give it a good, deep soaking (taking care not to erode the soil around the pumpkin plant itself).

As pumpkins grow you will need to water them only as you observe that the soil is becoming dry. When you do water them, water them in the mornings and avoid getting water on the leaves. This practice will help to minimize possibility of fungus growing on the leaves. If you notice that insects begin to feed on your pumpkin then a good first step is to spray them off with water. This often disrupts them enough for ladybugs to take care of the rest. If you find that you must use some form of insecticide then you should apply it in the early evenings when bees have returned to their hives.

> **NOTE:** *If you grow pumpkins in a garden with other vegetables then you may well notice that the lengthy pumpkin vines will begin to spread throughout the garden and take over. To address this problem you may prune vines that already have 2 or 3 pumpkins or you may choose to trellis your pumpkin vines and construct slings from panty hose that are tied to the trellis to cradle the pumpkin fruits. (If you choose to trellis your pumpkins then you should plant a variety that grows no larger than about the size of a volley ball.) Also, there are some varieties of pumpkins that naturally consume less garden space.[232]*

Do not be surprised if the blossoms of the pumpkins grow and fall to the ground. This is simply part of the pumpkin's normal life cycle. If weeds begin to grow you might first attempt to control the small ones by covering them with fine compost. If this is not sufficient then you may need to dig them up with the hoe (otherwise the weeds will compete with your pumpkins for nutrition and all-important moisture).

Pumpkins take between 85 and 125 days to fully grow and be ready for harvest. There are many indicators when the pumpkins is ready (size, color, the vine is starting to wilt, etc), however the best indicator is the hardening of the outside shell (pumpkins should not be harvested before their outer shell has hardened). If you can penetrate the outer shell with a fingernail, then you know that it is not yet ready to harvest.[229]

NOTE: *Pumpkins will store longer if you stop watering them 7 to 10 days before harvesting them.[229]*

If stored properly pumpkins should keep for between 3 and 6 months (depending on the storage conditions and the variety of pumpkin you have grown). You may also store them at room temperature in your home for 2 to 3 weeks before using them (being careful not to place them on wooden furniture, however, as pumpkin leakage can damage wood). Pumpkins should be stored off any surface that cannot "breath" (e.g. concrete or linoleum). They should not be stacked, and if stored outdoors they should be covered with straw or other insulating material. On particularly cold nights you may also need to cover them with a blanket and/or newspaper to provide additional insulation.

NOTE: *Be particularly watchful for mice when storing pumpkins, as mice love to eat pumpkins, and will even make a home inside a hollowed-out pumpkin! If you already believe you have mice in your storage location then you might set some traps or otherwise deal with that problem in advance of the harvest.*

If a pumpkin begins to soften in storage then you know it is going bad. As long as the flesh of the pumpkin is not moldy, and if the seeds remain firm, then you can still save the seeds for roasting and eating and the flesh is suitable for feeding to livestock (goats and chickens are not at all picky). You can also add the pumpkin to your compost pile, or bury it at least 12 inches deep in your garden to augment the soil for the next planting season. (If you don't bury it at least 12 inches down then it may begin to sprout vines to provide pumpkins for the next growing season!)

NOTE: *Pumpkin seeds are a good source of many important vitamins. A good serving size for an adult individual is 1-2 cups. Pumpkin seeds are often served roasted, with or without salt.*

Harvesting and Storing Pumpkin Seeds

You may save the seeds from any non-hybrid pumpkin for future planting. Simply extract the seeds from the pumpkin, rinse them clean with pure water, and place them over layers of paper towels or newspaper pages to try. Depending on the humidity where you live it may require several weeks for the seeds to dry completely. Once they have dried simply store the seed in acid-free paper envelopes, being sure to mark the envelops with the date when they were stored. The seed can be stored for up to 6 years if necessary.[231]

Preparing Pumpkin for Human Consumption

There are innumerable recipes for cooking pumpkin. Pumpkin can be boiled, steamed or baked. It can be added to muffins, pies or soups. Slices of baked pumpkin can be eaten very similarly to sweet potatoes. Baked pumpkin is often flavored with spices such as cinnamon.

13.1.20. Growing Watermelon

Watermelon is a sweet and refreshing fruit that is most often considered a treat. Beyond that, however, watermelons are low in saturated fat, cholesterol and sodium, a good source of dietary fiber as well as potassium and vitamins A and C. Watermelon is normally cut into pieces and eaten raw. In a survival scenario the role of the watermelon as a treat may be every bit as significant as it's nutritional value, as any sort of treat will provide a welcome break from an otherwise harsh reality.[248]

CAUTION: *Due to their size and high water content, watermelons require relatively large amounts of space and water compared to other crops. Watermelons also require more care and attention than other crops.*

The growing season for watermelons varies depending on climate. Watermelons generally need at least 3 months of weather in which daily temperatures peak between 70°F-90°F (the warmer within this range, the better). Additionally, excessive exposure to moisture can easily result in crop-destroying fungal disease. As a result, in tropical climates watermelons grow best during the fall and winter, while in more temperate climates watermelons grow best during the summer.

If you plan to harvest the seed from your watermelons to use in the next planting season then be sure that the seed you are planting is for an open pollinated, heirloom variety. Otherwise the seed may not germinate or, if it does, will result in melons that will almost certainly not be suitable for human consumption.[249]

Watermelons grow better exposed to direct sunlight and in higher (though not extreme) temperatures. Excessive moisture invites crop-destroying fungal diseases.

Watermelons require rich, well-drained soil. If growing watermelons in a soil that does not drain well, then they should be grown on mounds (or ridges if planting them in a row). The seed should be planted at a depth of about 1 inch, with seeds spaced about 1 foot apart. If using mounds or ridges they should be about 1 foot in height and 3 feet square in area, and contain a good amount of rich compost material. 3 or 4 seeds should be planted together, with all but the strongest seedling later snipped away. Ridges should be spaced about 6 feet apart.

During the first 3 weeks of growth the watermelon plants should receive a good, deep watering once or twice per day. After 3 weeks the watering should be reduced to once every 10 days, and when the vines begin to spread out watering can be reduced to once every 2 weeks. Once the fruit grows to its mature size watering should be ceased altogether to allow the melon to achieve a maximum sweetness and crispness.[250]

NOTE: *Rather than planting watermelons in one area, it may be advisable to distribute solitary plants at various locations in the garden to avoid inviting unwanted pests.*

Fertilizer should **not** be applied to watermelon soil when the seed are planted, however a fertilizer with an even balance between nitrogen, potassium and phosphate can be applied after the vines begin to spread. Later, when the blossoms begin to appear on the vines, fertilizer can be applied a second time.

The visual indicators that a watermelon is ready to harvest include observing that the curly tendril on the stem dries completely or that the part of the watermelon resting on the ground begins to change from green to a yellowish shade. A gardener with a practiced ear can also confirm that the melon is ready harvest by listening for a hollow sound when raping on the melon with his or her knuckles.[249]

An uncut watermelon can typically be stored in a root cellar at 50°F for 2 to 4 weeks. Once a melon is cut it can be wrapped with plastic wrap or enclosed in a plastic container and refrigerated for 3 or 4 days.

The biggest threats to watermelons are the leaf-eating beetles. If these become a problem it is probably a sign that the melon itself is stressed with its environment (e.g. inadequate fertilizer or water, or temperature extremes). The other major threat is mildew, which is a fungal growth that resembles a white powder on the leaves. The best way to address this threat is to avoid getting the leaves wet. If your irrigation system cannot avoid wetting the leaves, then watering in the mornings will provide maximum opportunity for the leaves to dry during the day.[249]

13.1.21. Growing Cantaloupe

Cantaloupe (also known as *muskmelon* and *rockmelon*) is a sweet melon that, in addition to being a good source of dietary fiber, serves as a good source of potassium, Niacin, Folate and vitamins B6, A and C. The naturally-occurring sugars in cantaloupe provide calories for quick energy that may be much needed in a survival scenario.[251] Like watermelon, cantaloupe is a sweet fruit that is almost always eaten raw, and might be as beneficial from a psychological perspective as it is nutritionally.

Cantaloupe should be planted about 3 to 4 weeks before the last frost date. The seed should be planted at a depth of about 1 inch. Because the plants are sensitive to being transplanted it is better to start them directly in the garden than to grow them inside for later transplanting. If your growing season requires you to start the cantaloupe seedlings indoors, then the seed should be planted in peat or paper cups that can be transplanted whole. If planting directly in the garden, the seeds should be planted in a small mound of loose, well-drained soil, with 2 or 3 seeds planted together (as the seedlings grow you'll trim away the weaker seedlings from each group). The seed groups should be planted 3 feet apart from one another (if you're training the vines to grow up a trellis then the plantings can be spaced as close as 12 inches from one another). Prepare the soil by loosening it to a depth of 6 inches. Do not fertilize the soil at the time of planting. The seed should take between 5-10 days to germinate.[252]

NOTE: *If planting cantaloupe seedlings contained in paper cups that were germinated indoors, be sure to cut away the bottom of the paper cup when transplanting so that the growth of the roots is not obstructed. The seedlings should be transplanted 3 weeks after the last frost date.*

Cantaloupe grows best when it receives about an inch of rainfall per week. If you receive less rainfall, then you should plan to water accordingly. The best way to water is with drip irrigation systems or soaker hoses. Regardless of how you water your plants, it is a good practice to avoid getting the fruit, flowers and foliage wet, as that will only increase the opportunity for harmful fungal growth. Because cantaloupe plants have deep roots, it is better to water the plants deeply once per week than to provide smaller, daily waterings. It is not uncommon for the leaves of cantaloupe plants to seem to wilt during the heat of the day, but recover overnight. However, if the leaves appear wilted in the mornings then this indicates the need for more watering. In the final week before harvesting you should cease watering altogether to maximize the sweetness and texture of the harvested fruit.

After your plants reach about 4 inches in height it is advisable to apply a fertilizer that has balanced proportions of nitrogen, potassium and phosphate. When applying the fertilizer keep it away from direct contact with the plant, and distribute it according to the manufacturer's instructions. If using fertilizer granules then apply water to dissolve them into the soil after they have been applied.[253] Later in the growth cycle, after their blossoms appear, the plants can be fertilized a second time, but this time with a fertilizer that has a lower proportion of nitrogen (maybe 5-10-10, or 2-12-12). This will maximize the growth of the fruit.

NOTE: *Because cantaloupe does not store as well as other vegetables it may be a good idea to plant your crop over a period of weeks (climate permitting) such that you have cantaloupes to harvest and enjoy over a longer time frame.*

The main enemies of your cantaloupe crop are:[252]

- Wilt due to inadequate watering.

- Fungal disease, often due to excessive moisture on fruits, vines and leaves (often appearing like a white powder on the leaves).

- Insects such as cucumber beetles (black with yellow stripes) and squash vine borers, both of which eat holes in the vine's leaves. If you observe these insects on your cantaloupe leaves remove and squash them, and treat the leaves with a vegetable-friendly insecticide.

Depending on the variety of cantaloupe that you plant it should reach full maturity within 80-100 days of planting. The outer rind of the melon will take on a texture that resembles a netting with an underlying color. If that color is not green, but rather yellow or cream-colored, then the cantaloupe may be ready for harvesting. Two other indicators will confirm that the melon is ready to harvest:[254]

- The stem of the cantaloupe will smell musky.

- A crack should appear around the stem that allows the fruit to be easily detached from the vine. If this crack does not appear then re-examine the fruit each day until it appears.

Harvested cantaloupe fruit can be immediately cut and served, or it may be refrigerated for serving later. The cut cantaloupe should last refrigerated for 4 to 5 days before it begins to become mushy and less edible. The fruit of cantaloupe can also be removed from the rind and frozen for as long as 6 months before serving.[254] Under ideal storage conditions with temperatures between 36-41°F and 95%-100% humidity whole, uncut cantaloupes can be stored from between 5 and 15 days.

When the cantaloupe vines are no longer productive they can be pulled up and composted.[254]

13.1.22. Growing Onions

Onions are a nutritious, easy-to-grow vegetable that serves as a popular ingredient for soups, breads, salads and casseroles. They are an excellent source of dietary fiber, vitamin B6, folate, potassium, manganese, and vitamin C (onion is a particularly good source of vitamin C). In addition to their nutritional value, onions have excellent anti-inflammatory properties.[291]

Because they are smaller, onions lend themselves to being planted in small spaces within a garden or yard which might otherwise go unused. They come in a variety of cultivars, with some producing large, round bulbs while others produce top-shaped or spindly bulbs. The onion bulbs themselves (the part of the onion that is harvested for food) may be white, yellow or red.

Onion plants are hardy, and can tolerate frost and can be grown in soil ranging from heavy clay to sandy loam. Consider the location in selecting the variety of onions that you will be growing. If you are located in an area that has longer, colder winters then be sure to plant a "long-day" variety that requires 13 to 16 hours of sunlight per day. If planting in warmer locations that have milder winters then plant a "short-day" variety that requires 10 to 12 hours of sunlight.[293]

If possible, identify the areas where you will be planting onions in advance and, if planning on planting in the spring, clear those areas of weeds during the preceding fall. This will greatly reduce the opportunity for *onion thirp* to infest your onion plants during the next growing season. If planting onions in the fall then thoroughly clear any locations where you will be planting of any weeds as far in advance as possible (and keep those locations clear until planting). If planting in the spring then plant 4 to 6 weeks before the last frost.

Ideally you should plant in soil that is slightly acidic (having a pH between 5.5 and 6.5)[292]

Onions can be planted as seed, as transplanted seedlings, or as *sets* (immature bulbs saved from the previous growing season). If sowing onion seed then plant the seeds in rows 1/2 inch deep and about 1/4 inches apart, and intersperse occasional radish seeds (the radishes will help to lure root maggots away from your onions as they begin to grow). The rows should be about 12 inches apart. If transplanting seedlings or planting sets, plant them in a 2-inch deep furrow, keeping them 4 to 6 inches apart. If planting sets be sure the pointed end is facing upwards. After placing the seedlings or sets into the furrow cover them with soil.

> **NOTE:** *Onions require up to 4 mouths to reach maturity when planted from seed, but only about 65 days when planted as seedlings.*

If planting onion seed, be sure that the soil is at least somewhat moist before planting. If the soil is heavy then augment the soil with compost, aged manure or humus before planting.[292] Once the seedlings sprout they should be thinned such that there is about 1 inch between plants. After 4 weeks the onions should be further thinned such that there is about 6 inches between plants (in this case the thinned plants can be harvested as *green onions*).

If you are starting your onions seeds indoors with the intent to transplant them outside, keep them indoors until they are 2 to 3 inches in height and look for an opportunity to expose them to the outside air overnight on a non-freezing night to *harden* the seedlings prior to transplanting.[293] When transplanting the seedlings or planting sets, plant them at least 1 inch apart.

Weeds among the onions should be cut at ground level with a hoe so as not to disturb the shallow root system of the onions. As the onion plants mature mulch can be added around the plants to suppress further weed growth while simultaneously helping to retain moisture in the soil.

The growing onion plants should receive about 1 inch of water each week, with transplanted seedlings requiring more water than onions planted from sets. Excessively dry conditions will cause the onion bulbs to split.[293]

Pests and Disease

Onions plants are subject to a number of factors that can damage them or render them inedible. These factors include:

> **NOTE:** *There are many varieties of onions that come in many shapes, sizes and colors. Some produce very small bulbs that are most suitable for pickling, while others produce large bulbs that are eaten raw or incorporated into a wide range of recipes. Most varieties can be harvested while they are young. These young onions are referred to as 'scallions'. The perennial 'allium fistulosum', which is very resistant to disease and insects, is a bunching variety that is particularly suitable for harvesting as scallions.[294]*

- *Onion maggots* - these are larva that are about 1/3 of an inch in length and burrow into the onion and up into the stem. These may be avoided by not planting onions together in a single location. Also spreading a thin layer of sand on top of the soil around the onion may dissuade the flies from laying the eggs that develop into these larvae.

- *Onion thirp* - these are very tiny insects that cause silvery blotches to appear on the leaves of onion plants. Thirp can be avoided by keeping the planting area well-weeded in the weeks and months before planting (the thirp wait in a dormant state within the weeds). Thirp may also be suppressed by spreading reflective mulch (e.g. aluminum foil) in the garden, which may cause them to become visually disoriented and not recognize the plants as a target for infestation. An early infestation can often be controlled by the spraying of Beauveria bassiana or spinosad, and it is possible that a heavier infestation may be treated with neem.[293]

- *Fungal infection* - these are a series of organisms that can cause roots to shrivel, the growth of black or purplish spores and/or mold to grow on the bulbs, or damage to the stem of the plant. These infections are avoided by rotating where you plant your various crops in the garden, planting onions in a location that drains well, or by preparing the soil before planting with moisture-absorbing humus.[293]

- *Onion fly* - this small insect lays eggs that grow into larvae that can do great damage to young onion bulbs. The fly is attracted by the smell that results from the thinning of an onion crop after the first weeks of growth. Onion flies can be avoided by growing the onions from sets rather than from seed or seedlings, as there is no need to thin the plants when starting onions from sets.

Harvesting and Storage

When the tops of your onions turn yellow you will know that they are ready for harvest. The day before harvesting use the back of your garden rake to push the onion plants over such that the tips are horizontal. This will cause the sap to stop flowing to the stem of the plant and allow it to finish maturing.[293] The next sunny day the onion can be harvested. Simply use your garden fork to lift the bulb from the ground, being careful not to damage the outer skin (the skins around the bulb protect it from microorganisms that will cause it to begin to decay).

Once the bulbs are out they should be cleaned of any soil and set aside to sit in the sun and wind for a few days to dry thoroughly (you'll know they are ready when the tops appear dry and brown).

After you collect your dried onions the tops should be cut off about 3/4 of an inch above the bulb. Any onions that exhibit any signs of decay or damage should be discarded so that they will not contaminate the healthy onions you have harvested while in storage. The harvested onions can then be hung outside for 3 to 4 weeks before being used, or can keep for 4 months to a year if stored in a cool, dry location.

13.1.23. Growing Peppers

Varieties of hot and sweet *peppers* are very popular with gardeners. In addition to being an excellent source of Vitamin C (with red and yellow peppers being particularly good sources of this vitamin), and a good source of Vitamins K and B6, peppers provide much-needed dietary minerals (particularly potassium, copper and manganese) and have strong anti-inflammatory properties and, maybe just as importantly, provide a distinct and pleasing flavor to foods.[304]

Planting and Growing Peppers

Because they require warmer temperatures, pepper plants are often started indoors and transplanted to the garden as seedlings. Pepper seed can be sown about 6 weeks before the garden is ready to receive the plants. The seedlings should only be transplanted to the garden when no more frosts are expected and when the soil has reached an average minimum temperature of 65°F.[305]

If you are purchasing pepper seedlings rather than growing them from seed then be sure to prefer those with dark green leaves, strong stems and no fruit.[306]

Seeds can be pre-soaked before planting for faster germination. Simply drop the seeds into a container of water that contains 1 to 2 teaspoons of standard 3% hydrogen peroxide for every cup of water. The hydrogen peroxide in the solution has the effect of disinfecting the seed before planting. The good seeds will sink to the bottom of the container within 2 to 6 hours. After they sink to the bottom, pour off everything else and collect those seed for planting.[312]

As with other vegetables it is a good idea for the prepper to give strong consideration to raising both hybrid and non-hybrid varieties of pepper plants in order to be assured of a good yield. The purpose of planting the non-hybrid variety, as always, is to obtain seeds from them when harvested that can be used to plant future crops (or even to be used for barter).

If starting seedlings indoors then the seed should be planted in peat pots (3 seeds planted together in each pot)[306] with the seeds being planted just under the soil.[312] Alternately you might plant your pepper seeds in in a seed-starting tray that can be fabricated as easily as punching drainage holes in the top and bottom of a restaurant take-out box. In this case the seeds should be planted about 1/2 inch apart. The seed-starting tray should then be placed in a larger tray of water so that the new seedlings receive water from the 'bottom up'.

Once the seedlings germinate and begin to grow it is important to expose them to light. While light on a window sill may be sufficient, often the new seedlings must stretch and contort themselves in order to receive the best light. As a result it is worthwhile to consider setting up a grow light to provide optimum growing conditions. Even a simple fluorescent light, placed as close as possible to the young seedlings, can result in perfectly healthy seedlings.

If growing seedlings in peat pots, when they are between 2 and 3 inches tall the two least healthy plants in each pot should be thinned out by cutting them flush with the soil. Once the remaining seedlings reach a height of 4 to 6 inches they will be ready for transplanting to the garden.[306]

The seedlings should be hardened off (see section 13.1.12) before being transplanted to the garden. Before transplanting the soil temperature should be about 65°F. The seedlings should be planted at a depth such that the lowest leaves are at ground level, and they should be spaced 16 to 18 inches apart. They should be planted in a well-drained area that receives plenty of sunlight (at least 8 hours of sunlight each day).[305]

For best results it is important to augment the soil before it receives transplanted pepper plant seedlings. The addition of humus or compost conditions the soil to better retain moisture throughout the growing season. Additionally, the soil can be fertilized with 10-10-10 fertilizer 1 to 4 weeks before the seedlings are transplanted.[307]

If available, to deter cutworms, you should consider protecting your transplanted pepper seedlings with cardboard collars, buried about 1 inch in depth. Seedlings should ideally be transplanted on a cloudy day or during early evening to avoid overly traumatizing the plants with *sunscorch*. To keep weeds down and help preserve the moisture content of the soil a thick, light mulch such as straw or grass clippings can be placed around the base of the

> **NOTE:** *Peppers, tomatoes, potatoes and eggplant are all members of the 'nightshade' family. All of these plants draw similar nutrients from the soil and are susceptible to similar diseases. In order to avoid disease and maintain a balance of nutrients in the soil it is a best practice to only grow nightshade plants in a particular location within your garden one out of every four years.[313] Additionally, it is a good practice to, during that three-year off period, look for the opportunity to plant legumes in those same locations, as legumes will replace many of the nutrients in the soil that are drawn out by the nightshade plants.[313] Please refer to section 13.1.17 for more details on rotating crops to maintain soil nutrient levels.*

plants.[306] Any weeds that grow with pepper plants should be pulled by hand to avoid accidentally damaging the plants themselves.

During growth pepper plants should only be fertilized if the leaves on the plant begin to turn a pale green or lighter color. Any fertilizer applied to the soil around pepper plants should **not** be a high-nitrogen fertilizer.

Pests and Disease

Fortunately pepper plants are naturally-repellent to many insects, however one common exception for gardens in warmer areas is the *pepper weevil*, which is a 1/8 inch long brass-colored beetle that has a black or brown snout.[306] Another exception is the larvae of this same beetle, which is white with a beige head and 1/4 inch in length. These pests harm the pepper by chewing holes in the leaves and buds of the plant. Whenever you observe the pepper weevil or its larva you should physically remove them from the plant. These pests are best prevented by not allowing any debris to lay around in the vicinity of your garden.

Other pests that can affect your pepper plants include Colorado potato beetles, aphids, flea beetles, cutworms, and hornworms (please refer to section 13.1.11 for instructions on dealing with a variety of common garden pests).

Proper watering, crop rotation and selection of good, disease-resistant varieties of pepper plants are also critical to protect your plants from pests and disease.

Harvesting and Storing Peppers

Peppers generally change color when they ripen (with different peppers on the same plant sometimes taking on different colors, depending on the variety). When pepper fruits ripen they should be cut away from the plant about 1/4 inch above the top of the pepper (because the plant is fragile it is important to cut the peppers rather than to pull them). You may wish to harvest the fruit of your pepper plants before it has fully ripened in order to encourage faster growth of new fruit (pepper fruits will continue to ripen after being harvested).

Whole peppers have a storage life of only 1 to 2 weeks, with recommended storage conditions of 45°F to 50°F and relative humidity between 85 to 90 percent.[310] Once a pepper is cut open its storage life is greatly reduced and should be consumed within 24 hours if possible.

Options for storing peppers for a longer term include:[311]

- *Freezing* - When fresh or roasted peppers are frozen they should be packed in moisture- and vapor- proof containers. Once frozen peppers are thawed they no longer have their original crispness, however they are still quite suitable for adding flavor (and nutrients) to recipes. *NOTE: Unlike other vegetables there is no need to blanch peppers before freezing them).* Frozen peppers have a storage life of about 9 months.[311]

- *Sun Drying* - Peppers can be sun-dried if the outside daytime temperature is 85°F or warmer. If dew is expected overnight then they must be brought indoors during the night. To sun dry large peppers cut them in half and remove the seeds, stems and internal membranes. To sun dry smaller peppers simply cut a slit in their sides and allow them to dry without removing their internal contents.

- *Air Drying* - In an environment that does not have high humidity peppers may be air-dried by slitting them in the side, running a thread through the stems, and hanging the threaded peppers in a room with good air circulation for a period of 3 to 4 weeks.

- *Dehydrating* - Peppers may be dried in a kitchen dehydrator set at a temperature of 149°F. Large peppers should be split in half with seeds, stems and membranes removed, and sliced or cut into cubes.

- *Pickling* - All peppers can be pickled, which is a good way to preserve the crispness and texture of the peppers. However, because peppers have a low acid content they must be acidified as part of the pickling process. Peppers selected for picking should be firm, fresh and unbruised.

- *Canning* - Roasted peppers can be canned, however because they have low acid content they must be hot canned using a pressure cooker.

Harvesting and Storing Pepper Seeds

Pepper seeds become ready for harvesting at the same time the pepper itself becomes ripe. To harvest the seeds simply cut open the pepper and scrape them out. Drop the seeds into water and those that sink are good. Pour off the water and spread the remaining seeds out on a paper plate and blot them dry with a paper towel. Then let them sit out on a window sill until all the remaining moisture has evaporated. The dried seed can then be stored in an acid-free paper envelope and should be available for re-planting for up to three years (be sure the mark the envelope with the type of pepper seed and the date they were harvested).

NOTE: *Rather than handle individual peppers to extract the seeds you may alternately cut the tops from the peppers, place them in a blender, and blend them at slow speed for several seconds. After blending, pour in water and the good seeds should remain on the bottom of the blender. Pour off everything that is floating and repeat the process (without blending) until all that remains are clean seeds. These seeds can then be set out to dry and stored normally.[309]*

Preparing Peppers for Human Consumption

Peppers are normally incorporated into a wide range of recipes and served with meats and other vegetables. It is also common for them to be sliced and incorporated into salads, or to be stuffed with various foods and roasted. Jalapeño peppers stuffed with cream cheese and wrapped in bacon are particularly tasty when grilled. Peppers may also be incorporated into relishes, pickled or jellied.

13.1.24. Growing Tomatoes

Tomatoes are one of the most universally popular garden crops. They are an excellent source of dietary fiber and are particularly good sources of vitamin A, vitamin C, vitamin K and Potassium. Tomatoes are also a great source of antioxidants, which have been shown to provide a wide range of important health benefits. A tomato has been said to offer the same degree of health benefit as an apple.[296] There are hundreds of varieties of tomatoes with a broad range of characteristics[299], however heirloom variety tomatoes have a reputation for having the best flavor, and can produce seeds that may be used for future plantings. Most varieties of tomato produce a red fruit, however there are some varieties that produce fruit that is yellow, orange, pink, green and white.[296]

In general you should plan on planting 3 to 5 tomato plants per person in your group to accommodate normal usage. If you plan on canning or otherwise preserving your tomatoes then you should increase the number of plants accordingly.[299]

Some varieties of tomatoes are bush-like and grow vines that are only 1 to 3 feet in length. These are referred to as *determinate* varieties. Other varieties grow longer vines and are referred to as *indeterminate* varieties. In the case of determinate varieties the vine stops

347

> **NOTE:** *It is not a bad idea for the prepper to plant a combination of heirloom and non-heirloom tomatoes. The heirloom tomatoes will produce seed that can be used for future planting, while a well-selected non-heirloom tomato will typically be more disease-resistant and provide a better assurance of success. Because tomatoes are one of the more delicate garden plants the planting of hardier varieties becomes more important.*

growing once flowers form at the tips of the vines and the fruit sets over about a 2 week period. This makes determinate varieties a good choice for canning. The vines of indeterminate tomato plants can grow between 6 and 20 feet in length, and produce 3 flower clusters at regular intervals. Indeterminate tomato vines will continue to grow while growing conditions are good, and they continue to produce tomatoes throughout the growing season. The vines of indeterminate tomato plants must be pruned occasionally in order to divert the plant's energy from growing the vine to growing the tomato fruit. Indeterminate tomato plants are often tied to wooden stakes or trellises in order to avoid having the vines consume garden space, as well as to keep the tomato fruit off the ground and away from many destructive pests.[299]

Planting and Growing Tomatoes

If you have identified a specific variety of tomato that you would like to grow then you will probably find that you must grow your plants from seed (the variety of seedlings typically available for purchase is often very limited). Also, tomato plants are very sensitive to soil temperature. These factors result in tomato plants often being grown in three distinct phases:

- **Growing seedlings from seed** - About two months before you anticipate planting out into the garden you should sow your tomato seeds in well-drained *flats*. The seeds should be planted about 1/4 inch in depth and spaced about 1 inch apart. Depending on the temperature the seedlings should germinate in between 1 and 2 weeks. During this phase it is common to place the flats on a window sill so that they can receive proper light. The seedlings should grow in an environment that is between 60 and 85°F. In environments with poor natural lighting or inadequate environmental temperatures it may be necessary to make use of a grow light and/or heating coil.[299] The tomato plants should be well-watered during this phase of growth. (**NOTE: Of course you can avoid this phase altogether if you obtain your plants as seedlings.**)

- **Transplanting seedlings to individual containers** - Once the tomato seedlings have developed their second set of leaves they should be transplanted to individual containers that provide more depth for roots. These containers may be as simple as plastic cups. Whatever container you use should have holes in the bottom to provide for proper drainage. Once transplanted to these containers the frequency of watering should be reduced.

- **Transplanting potted plants to your garden when the soil is ready and the ground has been prepared** - Small tomato plants can be transplanted to your garden as soon as the soil temperatures reach 55 to 60°F. The plants should be hardened off (see page 325) for 1 to 2 weeks before being transplanted. Also, any stakes or other supporting structures for the tomato vines should already be in place. The plants should be separated by a distance of 2 feet if they are to be tied to stakes, or 3 to 4 feet if the tomato vines are going to be allowed to grow along the ground. There should be 3 to 4 feet of space between rows of tomato plants.

You should plan on the time between planting your first seed and harvesting your first tomato to be between 70 and 85 days. In most locations tomatoes can be planted as late as July 1. After June mulch should be applied around tomato plants to help the soil retain water and to inhibit the growth of weeds. An 8 inch layer of straw or used hay makes good mulch for tomato plants, or a 3 inch layer of sawdust can be applied provided that it is augmented with a nitrogen-rich fertilizer (to compensate for the nitrogen deficiency caused when sawdust decays).[297]

If planting tomatoes in clay or sandy soil then the top 6 to 9 inches of the soil should be augmented with organic matter such as compost or peat moss. 3/4 cup of lime and 1/2 cup of 8-8-8 fertilizer should also be worked into the soil around each plant.[298]

NOTE: *Stakes used to guide tomato vines should be between 5 and 7 feet in length, and should be buried between 6 and 8 inches into the ground to provide good support. The tomato vines should be tied to the stake at about 6 inch intervals using soft twine, strips of cloth or panty hose.[299]*

Pests and Disease

Flea beetles, aphids and hornworms are among the insects that are known to plague tomato plants. These and other destructive insects should be removed from tomato plants when they are observed. Tomatoes are also vulnerable to diseases that are endemic to potatoes, cucumbers, dahlias, eggplant and various weeds including ground-cherry, pokeweed, jimson-weed and nightshade. As a result tomatoes should not be planted near these plants, and the area surrounding tomato plants should be cultivated and mulched to reduce the weed population. Another good preventive measure is to allow a two-year interval between plant-ings of tomatoes in a specific location (it is not a bad idea to rotate between tomatoes and potatoes in a particular location). Any tomato plant leaves that are yellowing or otherwise damaged (e.g. brown and decaying) should be promptly removed to prevent the spread of disease to the rest of the plant.[297]

Other measures to assure the production of a good tomato crop include:[297]

- Don't smoke or otherwise handle tobacco before or while handling tomato plants (especially in the plant's first 12 weeks).

- Select varieties of tomatoes that are disease-resistant.

- When fertilizing and otherwise treating the soil in which tomatoes are planted, be sure to read and follow any relevant instructions.

- When watering tomato plants water them early in the day and avoid getting the leaves of the plants wet.[299]

Harvesting and Storing Tomatoes

As soon at tomatoes are ripe on the vine they should be harvested, as leaving them on the vine longer only delays the growth of new fruit. Tomatoes can be stored in a cool, dark location for 2 or 3 days before they start to become over-ripe and subsequently begin to lose their taste and nutritional value. They may be stored several days longer if kept refrigerated. For longer term storage tomatoes may be canned. Properly-canned tomatoes typically have a shelf life of at least 12 months.

> **NOTE:** *Tomatoes have a reputation for often going bad after being canned. This is almost always because the fruits canned were not entirely healthy, which reduced the acidity level (thereby promoting bacterial growth). As a result, tomatoes should be canned carefully and should be inspected prior to canning. These problems can also be avoided by adding lemon juice to the tomatoes when canning to increase acidity or by using a hot canning process.*
>
> *Tomatoes may also be made into tomato ketchup, which has a relatively long shelf life due to it's high acid level as well as the added sugars. Opened ketchup has a shelf life of about 1 month unrefrigerated, and 8 to 12 months when refrigerated.*

Harvesting and Storing Tomato Seeds

You may harvest the seeds produced by heirloom tomatoes for future planting. The process for harvesting the seeds is:[303]

- Wash the tomatoes thoroughly, cut them in half across the middle (not across the stem ends), and gently squeeze the contents of each half tomato into a small glass or plastic cup.

- Allow the glass or cup of tomato seeds and juice to sit for 3 to 5 days until the surface starts to become covered by a white mold (in hotter climates you may need to add some water to the container to keep the seeds floating). After that 3 to 5 days, when the white mold covers much of the surface, use a spoon to remove the mold (being careful that no seeds are removed in the process).

- Fill the container with water and the good seed will sink to the bottom. Pour off the water and the floating seeds, and repeat the process until the remaining seeds are clean. Pour the remaining cleaned seed into a strainer, where they should rinsed and allowed to drain.

- Sprinkle the harvested seeds onto paper plates and allow them to dry for between 1 and 3 days, depending on the humidity in your area (more humid areas should require the full 3 days). During this process do not allow the seed to be exposed to direct sunlight, and stir them once or twice per day so that the seed do not clump together.

- Store the dried tomato seeds in acid-free paper envelopes, being sure to mark each envelop to indicate the variety of tomato and the date stored. These seed should be viable for planting for up to 3 years.

Preparing Tomatoes for Human Consumption

The versatile tomato is most often not consumed alone, but is incorporated into a wide range of recipes. Tomatoes are commonly added to salads and sandwiches, as well as incorporated into soups and casseroles. Tomatoes may also be served stuffed with other foods such as tuna and cottage cheese.

13.1.25. Growing Spinach

Spinach is a cool- to cold- weather crop that is both nutritious and flavorful. It provides an excellent source of vitamins A, C, E and K as well as several of the B-complex vitamins and various essential minerals including calcium, iron, phosphorus, potassium and manganese.[239]

> **CAUTION:** *Spinach is higher in sodium than most vegetables, which should be taken into consideration when incorporating it into any diet.*

Savoyed varieties of spinach have dark green, puckered or crinkled leaves. Savoyed and semi-savoyed varieties of spinach are best for planting in winter, as they become particularly crisp and flavorful when exposed to cold weather.[240] Smooth-leafed spinach produces leaves that are flat and a lighter shade of green. These are more suitable for harvesting the younger, more immature leaves for use in salads.

Spinach can be planted in late winter and in the fall. It is advisable to prepare the soil for the winter crop during the previous autumn, as this will allow you to plant at the earliest possible time (when the ground has just thawed and would otherwise still be unworkable). For winter spinach sow the seed as early as 6 weeks before the last frost. In temperate climates you can continue to plant spinach every 10 days until mid-May in order to be able to spread out your harvest schedule (spinach does not store well once harvested).[241]

When planting in the fall you should plant your spinach 6 to 7 weeks before the date when the first frost is expected. You may also sow spinach seed four weeks before that first fall frost and cover the plants. These plants will then mature in early spring. Any spinach plants that have been overwintered in this way should be fertilized thoroughly with a fish-based fertilizer as they begin to show new growth.[240]

Before planting spinach, the ground should be loosened to a depth of 10 to 12 inches and fertilized with a nitrogen-rich fertilizer (see sidenote). Spinach plants should be planted 1/2 inch deep in rows that are at least 10 inches apart, with the seed planted every 2 inches along the row. As the seedlings begin to appear and grow the rows should be thinned such that the plants are 4 to 6 inches apart.

> **NOTE:** *Because spinach is a leaf crop it benefits most from nitrogen-rich soil, so any fertilizer you use should contain a high proportion of nitrogen. Additionally, fish emulsion and soy meal make good organic fertilizers.[242]*

Six weeks after planting you can begin to pinch off individual leaves from your spinach plants as needed, leaving the central *rosette* intact.[240]

If you have planted non-hybrid spinach then you may wish to save seeds from your crop for planting the following season. Harvest your seeds from a group of plants that are located in close proximity to one another (as the wind will have been much more likely to fertilize the seeds of the female plants with the pollen from the male plants). Wait until the female plants begin to dry before collecting their seed. The collected seed should be stored in an acid-free envelope that is labeled with the seed type and collection date (it's a good idea to include one of your original seed packets inside the envelope as well).

13.1.26. Growing Corn

Corn is a grain crop that is low in saturated fats, cholesterol and sodium, and a good source of vitamin C, thiamin, folate, magnesium, phosphorus and dietary fiber.[279] It has a sweet taste that appeals to many, and can be prepared for eating in a variety of ways. Corn can be roasted, boiled, canned or pickled. Additionally, it is an important ingredient to many recipes, and can be used as feed for livestock. Varieties of corn labeled *'sh2'* in seed catalogs have been created to produce very sweet corn, while those labeled *'su'* have a more traditional flavor and those labeled *'se'* have a flavor that is somewhere between *sh2* and *su*.[280]

In seedling stage corn is sensitive to its environment. As a result you should wait to plant until the soil temperature is at least 60°F (65°F for the super sweet varieties) and no frosts are expected[281]. If a short growing season requires you to begin growing your plants indoors, then grow the seedlings in biodegradable containers so that the process of transferring them to the garden results in minimal shock for the plants. You should plan on planting a minimum of 10 to 15 plants per person. If you wish to have an extended harvest then plant a variety of corn that matures quickly and plant new seed every 2 weeks for up to 6 weeks. An alternative is to simultaneously plant different varieties of corn that have different maturity times.[280] (However, as noted later in this section, care must be taken not to grow different varieties of corn in close proximity to one another.) Newly planted corn should germinate in between 4 and 12 days.

NOTE: *If you are growing corn in a colder climate where the soil is slow to warm, you may cover the ground with a dark material (such as black garbage bags) to speed the warming process.[281]*

For growing corn your garden should be in a location that receives good sunlight and offers some protection from excessive winds. Soil for growing corn should be well-drained. If possible work compost and/or aged manure into the soil the fall before planting season. Ideally you should spread 20 to 30 pounds of compost for every 100 square feet of garden.[280] Because corn is a leafy crop that requires nitrogen, it is beneficial if the corn crop is planted where clover, beans, hairy vetch or other soil-enriching crops have been been planted previously or, alternately, fertilize the soil with a nitrogen-rich fertilizer (always consult the instructions for your specific fertilizer before applying). Corn seed should be planted in 1-inch deep holes that have been punched into the soil, with the individual plants spaced between 9 and 12 inches from one another. After the seedlings have grown to a height of 4 to 5 inches the crop should be thinned such that there is 16 to 23 inches between plants.

> **NOTE:** *Because corn is pollinated by the wind it is better for it to be grown in blocks of short rows rather than in one or two long rows. In this way the corn has the best opportunity to pollinate regardless of the direction in which the wind is blowing. Try to grow at least four rows across, with the rows spaced about 4 feet apart. Proper pollination of the corn crop is important to full development of the kernels.*
>
> *You may also pollinate your corn by hand (particularly important if you are growing your corn in only one or two rows). To do so wait until one morning when there is little or no breeze and shake the pollen from the tassels of your corn into a dry bucket. Then transfer that pollen to a small paper bag and sprinkle it over the silks of your ears of corn. Repeat this process for another day or two and you should realize best results.[280]*
>
> *Cross-pollination of different varieties of corn can result in corn kernels that range from being less tasty to completely inedible. If you are growing multiple varieties of corn then you should avoid cross-pollination by either scheduling the planting such that the varieties will not reach the silk stage within two weeks of one-another, or the different varieties should be separated by a distance of 400 yards or greater.[280]*

When the corn stalks reach a height of 6 inches they can be fertilized. The fertilizer you use should be based on the type of soil and its condition (for example, was the soil previously augmented with aged manure, which contributes nitrogen to the soil?). Consult with your local gardening supplier for their recommendation for your locale. Fertilizer should be applied a second time when the stalks reach about knee height.

For the first month of growth cultivate your corn plants by pulling and/or digging up weeds that grow with your corn. After that first month such cultivation may damage the corn's own root system, so switch to adding mulch to keep weeds suppressed.

Dealing With Pests and Common Problems

If corn leaves begin to wilt or exhibit other symptoms of disease, the affected leaves should be removed. Covering ears of corn with paper bags can reduce damage caused by birds and insects. It is not uncommon for animal pests such as raccoons to attempt their own harvest of your mature corn. Also, an excess of nitrogen in the soil can result in the corn stalks falling over. Other problems can be caused by such factors as inadequate pollination, poorly draining soil and low fertility (often due to low potassium).[282]

Cutworms are the larvae of moths that borrow into moist soil and attack corn stalks at ground level or below. They receive their name because, in borrowing through the corn stalk, they cut it down at or near ground level. The chances of cutworm problems can be reduced by tilling the soil prior to planting (which will kill many of the cutworm larvae). Additionally, the use of fertilizer in the soil, can discourage the cutworm moths from laying eggs there. If cutworm damage is observed it is possible to deal with the problem by simply digging around the plant and finding and killing the larvae manually. Cutworms have also been controlled by encasing the bottoms of corn stalks with buried "collars" made of metal or cardboard.[283]

The *corn earworm* is the larval stage of a moth that lays eggs in both the leaves and the silks of corn. These eggs hatch into larvae that appear in various colors and eat small holes into the leaves and the corn kernels near the tip of the husk. The threat posed by these pests can be minimized by either planting a variety of corn that produces ears that are resistant to the larval penetration, or by planting the corn crop early such that the silk stage of the corn does not coincide with the peak moth population.[284]

The *European corn borer* is the caterpillar stage of a moth that was introduced to the United States from Europe in the early twentieth century. These caterpillars eat their way through the leaves, stalks and ears of the corn, resulting in severely damaged plants and/or the dropping of ears from the plant. Certain wasps and flies that prey on the corn borer caterpillar have been introduced from Europe to the corn-growing regions of the United States as one means of biological control. Other biological controls include ladybird beetles and downy woodpeckers. Other promising methods of controlling this pest are currently under investigation.[285]

The larvae of the *cucumber beetle* (also know as *root worms*), feed on the roots of corn plants, which causes the plants to eventually collapse. At their adult stage they take the form of yellow beetles with black stripes or spots on their backs. In order to kill these pests you must apply Heterorhabditis nematodes *(also known as "beneficial nematodes")* to the soil.

Another common pest in the corn field is the *seed-corn maggot*, which attacks corn kernels that have been planted too deeply. These maggots are about 1/4 inches in length and have pointed heads. If you observe these pests you should wait for warmer weather and re-plant a new corn crop at a shallower depth.

Harvesting and Storage

Depending on the specific variety a corn plant should reach maturity sometime between 63 and 100 days after planting. When ready for harvest the plant silks will become dry and brown with the corn husks themselves being green. The individual corn kernels should be full sized and, when punctured with a fingernail should exhibit a milky liquid (a clear liquid indicates that the corn is not yet fully matured and the absence of liquid indicates that the corn is over-ripe). Maturity can be expected between 17 and 24 days after the first silk strands appear on the ears of corn.[282] Note that each ear on the corn stalk matures independently, however they should all reach maturity within a few days of one another.

Corn does not store well for the long term unless it is frozen. Once harvested it should be kept in cold/moist environment (such as a refrigerator), where it should keep for between 4 and 8 days. Eventually the sugars in the corn will begin to turn to starch, rendering it increasingly inedible.

13.1.27. Growing Carrots

Carrots are a hardy, nutritious plant that is a great addition to the survivalist's meal plan. They come in many types, each with its own distinct properties that are of interest to the prepper (see Table 13.5). Carrots are an excellent source of alpha and beta carotene. Alpha carotene has been said to reduce chronic diseases such as heart disease and cancer, while beta carotene has also been said to inhibit tumor growth. Carrots are also good sources of vitamins A, B1, B2 and C as well as a source of the minerals phosphorus, calcium and iron.[222] in addition to being an excellent source of dietary fiber.

Planting and Growing Season

The wide variety and diverse properties of carrots enable them to be grown in virtually any temperate, tropical or subtropical region. The ideal time of year to plant carrots is when the temperature is peaking between 60 to 70°F, although carrots can be planted in the summer as well (the yield may be significantly reduced for carrots planted during the summer).

Carrots should be planted in loose soil with good drainage. The soil should be loosened to a depth of about one foot prior to planting. If the soil is not rich and sandy then compost and other organic matter should be added (mix in about a 1 inch layer of compost, or a 1/2 inch layer of vermicompost[221]). If manure is added then it should either be composted manure or, if not, it should be added during the fall season, otherwise straight manure fertilizer can result in low yield and malformed carrots.[222]

Carrots grow best in soil that has a pH of 5.8 to 7. If your soil is too acidic then lime can be mixed into the soil to raise the pH. Avoid fertilizing the soil for carrots with high-nitrogen fertilizers. Carrots benefit more from growing in soil that is high in potassium and phosphorous.[221]

Sow carrot seeds about 1/4 inch deep and 2 inches apart. The rows should be at least 10 inches apart. Place a thin layer of compost over the seed. Keep the soil over the seeds moistened until they germinate in 2 to 3 weeks. Once the seedlings are 1 to 2 inches tall the carrots are able to tolerate drier soil.

Once the seedlings are between 2 and 3 inches tall you should thin the rows by removing seedlings such that those that remain are about 1 inch apart. After thinning the rows be sure to dampen the soil for the remaining carrots. This thinning is important to allow the remaining carrots to grow the maximum size (otherwise you'll end up with tangles of small carrots). Once the carrots are about 1/2 inch in diameter they need to be thinned again such that they are about 1.5 inches apart.

As the carrots grow, their soil should receive a good soaking about once per week. If you place mulch around the base of the plants it will allow the soil to better retain moisture between soakings.

Carrots can be harvested at any time after they reach about 70% of their maximum size. When harvesting the carrots it is good to dampen the soil for the benefit of those carrots that you do not harvest, and to possibly use a digging fork (especially in heavier soil) to be sure of not breaking the carrots while extracting them. The green tops of the carrots should be removed, and can be used to feed livestock (especially chickens and rabbits) or can be composted (carrot tops actually are themselves edible, and are rich in vitamins and minerals, however their potassium content tends to give them an unappealing bitter taste).

NOTE: *Different varieties of carrots have different growth characteristics. Be sure to understand the needs and growth characteristics of the specific variety of carrots that you choose to grow based on your locale, eating preferences and other needs.*

It is best to plant carrots before and after the summer season such that the seedlings grow in cooler soil. By planting the carrot seed over time, and by harvesting the grown carrots at different times, you can be harvesting carrots throughout much of the spring, summer and fall seasons.

Your harvested carrots should be stored in a refrigerator or root cellar at the coolest temperature possible at or above 34°F[225]. Most varieties of carrots can be stored refrigerated for up to 8 months.[223] It is not uncommon for carrots to be packed in boxes between layers of straw or damp sand. If carrots are stored in a root cellar they should be stored off the floor.

CAUTION: *Carrots should not be stored near bananas, apples or melon fruits. These fruits emit an ethylene gas that will cause the carrots to become bitter.*

Preparing Carrots

While carrots may be eaten raw, the maximum nutritional benefit from carrots can only be realized if the nutrients are unlocked through either juicing, steaming or cooking. Carrots can also be canned, pickled or dried.

Harvesting Your Own Carrot Seeds

If you wish to harvest your own carrot seeds for future plantings you should first be sure that the carrots you plant are from non-hybrid, heirloom seeds (as any seeds obtained from hybrid carrots will almost certainly not germinate). Because carrots are biennial plants they produce seed every two years, which means that you cannot harvest the carrots you are using for seed (they must grow into their second year to produce the seeds you will be collecting).

In an area that experiences mild winters the seed-producing carrots can simply be left in the ground and covered with mulch through the winter. In the spring the carrot's foliage will re-grow and produce seed. In areas with cold winters carrots can be dug up and stored in dry sand with their tops removed until spring, at which time they may be re-planted to sprout and produce seed.[224]

The seed themselves can be collected from the carrot's top leafage when it starts to turn dry and brown. The seed should be stored in a cool location (or refrigerated at the lowest possible non-freezing temperature) in acid-free paper envelopes. Well-stored seed should be viable for 3 years (or quite possibly longer with reduced yield).

CAUTION: *Any carrots you are growing to produce seed should be kept as far as possible (up to 500 yards) from other types of carrots in order to avoid cross-pollination. Cross-pollinated plants, especially those cross-pollinated with wild carrots, will not produce a good and edible carrots.*

Name	Days to Maturity	Description
Miniature	55-60(spring), 60-70(fall)	Can grow in clay soil, and produce a very sweet carrot.
Chantenay	55-70(spring), 70-110(fall)	Provides a sweeter taste when harvested later in the year.
Nantes	55-70(spring), 60-75(fall)	Grows quickly and suitable for a wide range of soils.
Danvers	70-80(spring), 80-110(fall)	Particularly well-suited for juicing. These carrots store well.
Imperator	55-100(spring), 80-110(fall)	Long carrots that need deep, sandy soil.

Table 13.5.: Types of Carrots[221]

13.1.28. Growing Purslane

Purslane (also known as *pigweed, duckweed, wild portulaca* and *verdolaga*) is a green herb that is as good a source of omega-3 fatty oils as fish (100 grams of fresh purslane leaves provide about 350 mg of linolenic acid), and an excellent source of vitamins A, C and B complex vitamins as well. Purslane is also a good source of numerous essential dietary minerals, and is rich in antioxidants and dietary fiber.[237] Purslane has a crunchy texture and tastes somewhat "lemony".

> **NOTE:** *It should be noted that purslane contains oxalic acid, which is known to cause urinary tract stones in some people. As a result, purslane is not recommend for individuals with a history of oxalac urinary tract stones. Additionally, anyone who does consume purslane should be certain to stay properly hydrated so as to help avoid the potential formation of such stones.*

To many purslane is a weed that grows prolifically, and there is often more effort expended in keeping it away from places where it is not wanted than in growing it as a crop. Purslane can be planted any time within two months of a first frost.

To plant purslane simply scatter the seed over open ground (purslane seed is a tiny, dark seed that is so small that it resembles ground black pepper). Note that purslane grows a little better in dry soil. You can also simply lay purslane cuttings on the ground and water them for a few days (you might consider growing purslane in locations that are not suitable for less hardy plants). Once the plants begin to grow they should require virtually no care at all, other than trimming them back from areas where you do not want them to grow.[238] You can (and should) harvest your purslane regularly.

While purslane will probably re-seed itself you may wish to collect some seeds at the end of the season for planting in the next season.

> **CAUTION:** *If you decide to harvest purslane in the wild you should be certain that it is from a source that has not been chemically treated.*

Purslane can be prepared and served in a variety of ways. The individual leaves can be collected, washed, and simply added to a salad. Additionally, the stems and leaves can be sauteed and stewed and served as a vegetable side-item with fish or fowl, added to soups or served mixed with spinach anywhere.

13.1.29. Growing Kale

Kale is an easy-to-grow plant that is a member of the cabbage family. It is a very good source of vitamins A, C and K (particularly vitamin K) and has very good anti-inflammatory properties.[233] When eaten it is often incorporated into salads or mixed with potatoes or soups. Kale thrives in colder weather, and harvested kale actually develops a better taste after having been exposed to frost.[234]

Kale can be planted in early spring as soon as the temperature of the soil is at least 45°F. Within 8 weeks (or sometimes less) of being planted it is ready for harvest. In warmer climates kale can be planted in summer and fall, as well as in the spring, with kale harvested in the winter often providing the best taste.

The following varieties of kale are commonly grown:[235]

- *Lacinato* - sufficiently tolerant of cold weather that it can be harvested after a snowfall.

- *Vates* - tolerates both hot and cold weather, and excellent taste.

- *Hanover Salad* - grows quickly.

Kale plants can be started indoors and transplanted to an outdoor garden within 4-6 weeks or within 2-4 weeks of the last frost. Kale grows best in a rich, slightly acidic soil (pH = 5.5-6.5) with plenty of organic matter. Kale seed should be planted no more than 1/2 inch in depth and kept moist until the seedlings begin to grow (within 5 to 8 days of planting). Kale plants should be separated by a distance of 12-15 inches (if you are not transplanting from indoors then you may need to move or remove some seedlings to avoid over-crowding). The rows should be 18-24 inches apart.

Kale plants should be regularly watered and surrounded with mulch at their base, which will help them to retain moisture between waterings. Ideally the top of the soil will become dry, but will be moist below the surface.[236] Kale benefits from fertilizers that have a higher nitrogen content.[235] Be sure to follow the directions that accompany the fertilizer that you are using, as some fertilizers may require time to pass between fertilizing and planting.

Kale reaches maturity in 8 weeks or less, so you may have multiple plantings throughout the year.[235] The younger, inner leaves are often harvested for use in salads, while the outer leaves are harvested for cooking as greens. By harvesting only the outermost leaves the plant will continue to grow and produce new leaves.

If you moisten leaves of kale before refrigerating, and leave them exposed to the air, then harvested kale leaves should remain crisp for 1 to 2 weeks.

13.1.30. Growing Cabbage

In addition to being low in cholesterol and saturated fat, *Cabbage* is a good source of vitamin C, vitamin K, vitamin B6, thiamin, folate, iron, calcium, phosphorus, potassium, manganese and magnesium. Additionally it is an excellent source of dietary fiber.[244] As a cool weather crop, cabbage is generally planted in early spring or in the fall. The fall cabbage crop is most popular because it provides a better taste, has fewer problems with pests and can be stored after harvest to be consumed during the fall and winter months. There are a literally hundreds of varieties of cabbage that lend themselves to various uses and planting seasons. The different varieties are organized into major types (see Table 13.6).

Spring cabbage crops grow best in a sandy soil with good drainage, while late-summer crops grow better in a heavier soil that retains moisture better. The soil should have a pH of at least 5.5 (add ground limestone as necessary to raise the pH of the soil). The time between planting and maturity for a cabbage plant is 14 to 16 weeks. You should avoid growing cabbage near pole beans, strawberries, tomatoes, or dill.

You may start your cabbage crop from seed or by transplanting seedlings. If you are planting early-season seedlings in the spring then you should plan on setting them out 4 weeks before the last expected frost date. Cabbage seeds should be sown indoors and planted 1/4 inch deep and 2 inches apart. If you live in a warmer climate (e.g. in the southern US) then you should sow the seeds between mid-January and February. If you live in a cooler climate then you should sow your cabbage seed in March. The indoor environment for planting should have air temperatures between 60 and 70°F. The soil should be kept moist while the seedlings grow. The seedlings can be transplanted outdoors when the outdoor temperature reaches 50°F during the day (at this point the seedlings should have about 3 leaves). They

Type	Description
Green Cabbage	This is the type of cabbage most commonly found at the grocery store. It has pale, tightly wrapped leaves and is often used in soups. Varieties of green cabbage include Charmant, Grenadier and January King.
Red Cabbage	Red cabbage is actually more purple in color, and has a similar taste and texture to the green cabbages. These cabbages are used most often for pickling and making slaw. Varieties of red cabbage include Ruby Ball, Meteor, Red Rodan and Scarlet O'Hara.
Chinese Cabbage (Bok Choy)	The varieties of Chinese cabbage include Pakchoi, Michihli, Pe-Tsai, Tai-sai, and Lei-choi. These cabbages have loosely packed, dark green leaves. The stems and leaves can be cooked. Chinese cabbage has a taste similar to that of celery.
Napa Cabbage	Napa cabbage has a smaller head with light green, crinkled leaves. This cabbage is tasty even when eaten raw, and is most often prepared steamed or stir-fried.
Savory Cabbage	Features yellow-green, crinkled leaves. These cabbages are often steamed or added to stews. Varieties include Promasa, Salarite, Savonarch and Wivoy.

Table 13.6.: Types of Cabbage[246]

should be planted slightly deeper when transplanted than they were indoors, and should be spaced between 6 and 12 inches apart in rows that are 1 to 2 feet apart.[245]

NOTE: *Spacing the cabbage plants further apart produces larger cabbage heads, but smaller heads tend to have a better taste.*

The seeds for a late summer cabbage planting can be sown directly into the garden, or can first be grown indoors into seedlings. In this case the plants should be spaced further apart, and planted in an area where they can receive shade during the afternoon (perhaps alongside taller crops such as corn). For best results:

- Three weeks after planting place a rich compost around the base of the plants.

- Pull weeds by hand rather than using a tool in order to avoid damaging the shallow, delicate root system.

- Apply mulch around the plants to help keep the soil moist.

- Avoid getting the foliage wet in cool weather or during humid weather in order to avoid common diseases.

- If you notice that the leaves begin to become yellow augment the soil with fertilizer that is rich in nitrogen.

If you observe that a cabbage head is about to split then it is advisable to twist the cabbage head a half-turn and pull up the roots slightly to slow the plant's growth (an alternative approach is to sever the plant's roots in a couple of places with a garden spade).[245]

There are a variety of insects, worms and other diseases that can attack your cabbage crop. These should be controlled through the use of insecticidal soaps and/or by hand picking infected leaves. Diseased plants should be removed and destroyed.[245] In the case of persistent disease such as *club root*, it may be necessary to add ground limestone to the soil until it reaches pH of at least 6.8.

When you are ready to harvest your cabbage simply cut the head from the stem, leaving the outer leaves. You may later notice that new, smaller cabbage heads begin to grow where that head was removed. Handle the head carefully to avoid bruising it. Cabbages can be refrigerated, stored in a root cellar or simply hung from their stems in a cool or cold room or building. Also cabbages may be stored in a well-drained earthen trench covered with straw and soil. In this case the cabbages should be placed with the roots downward and the stem extending at a 45 degree angle. Cabbage stored in a root cellar can store for 3 to 4 months.

NOTE: *Late fall / early winter cabbages can be left un-harvested in the garden until there is a heavy freeze.*

13.2. Raising Small Livestock

Most survival farmers will have the need to raise some sort of animals for dietary protein. This section provides details for raising chickens, guinea fowl, rabbits and goats, which are the livestock most relevant to the survival farmer.

General Guidelines on Killing and Butchering Animals for Food

There are some general principles that are common to the killing and butchering of livestock. These principles are:

- Killing the animal in the quickest and most humane fashion.
- Handling of the animal's carcass during butchering.
- Avoiding contamination of the meat from the contents of the digestive system and bladder.

For chickens and other fowl the common way to kill the animal is to break its neck or cut off its head. For chickens a bent nail is often used to hold the head in position while a hand axe or large knife is used to remove the head. In the case of rabbits the killing process involves quickly breaking the neck, while for goats it involves either administering a gunshot between the eyes or cutting across the throat.

Once the animal is killed it is suspended upside down from the legs to allow the blood to drain. For larger animals it is common to slice a hole behind the Achilles tendons of the rear legs through which a rope can be inserted to hang the carcass. Once hung it becomes much easier to cut the carcass, with special care being taken not to puncture the animal's bladder or bowels and risk contaminating the meat. Often the knife used for much of this work is very sharp with the blade being short enough to help avoid puncturing organs.

13.2.1. Raising Chickens for Meat and Eggs

In a worst-case, long term disaster scenario in which the normal supply chain for food is disrupted it may become necessary for you to provide food for yourself. In that case, to meet your protein needs, it is very possible that raising *chickens* might be a good fit to your circumstances. Chickens offer the following advantages:

- They are relatively cheap and easy to raise.

- They are small enough that meat preservation will probably not be an issue.

- The eggs they lay are one of the best sources of protein anywhere.

- They can be raised with very limited space, and even in suburban environments.

- They grow and reproduce quickly.

This section provides you with the information that you need to make an informed decision about raising chickens. If you should decide that it is a good fit for you, then you are **strongly** encouraged to begin raising them well before disaster strikes, as it may no longer be an option for you afterwards.

Adult male and female chickens are referred to as 'cocks' (or 'roosters') and 'hens', respectively. Male and female chickens of less than one year in age are referred to as 'cockrels' and 'pullets', respectively. Baby chickens, regardless of gender, are often simply referred to as 'chicks'.

NOTE: *According to an associate who raised chickens for many years as she was growing up, there are other names by which chickens are known when they escape into the yard and must be rounded up. Apparently these names are quite colorful, but not well suited for sharing here.*

Chickens may be raised for their eggs, for meat, or for both; and different breeds of chickens lend themselves more to one role or the other. The chicken breeds most often raised are:[184]

- *White Leghorns* - usually raised to produce white eggs.

- *Golden Comets and Red Sex Links* - usually raised to produce brown eggs.

- *Cornish Cross* - usually raised for meat.

- *Plymouth Rocks, Susses and Wyandotte* - usually raised for both meat and eggs.

> **NOTE:** *The Cornish Cross chickens have a reputation for producing excellent meat, however they also have a high mortality rate (as high as 30% for novices). The mortality problems can be reduced by raising them in groups of 25 or less.[187]*

Chickens maintain a strict social *pecking order* that dictates which chickens get first access to food, water, roosting locations, etc. If a chicken violates the pecking order then their superior in the pecking order generally pecks at them until they fall back into line. When new chickens are introduced to the flock then the pecking order must be re-established, which can result in an increased stress level (and maybe affect egg production). For this reason new chickens should ideally be introduced gradually to the flock, or chickens should be kept separated by generation.

Shelter and Facility

There are generally three options available for sheltering chickens:

- Provide no shelter at all and just let the chickens *free-range* on the property.
- House the chickens in a chicken coop (a large enclosed box generally made of plywood and chicken wire).
- Provide a hen house for the chickens to return to for roosting at night, with an adjacent fenced *chicken yard* where they can roam, bathe and feed during the day.

The first option of allowing the chickens to free-range 24x7 is very seldom adopted because the chickens (and their eggs) are extremely vulnerable to predators. Also, without a central roosting location it becomes difficult to locate eggs.

The use of a simple chicken coop is fairly common, and provides better protection from predators (especially if the coop is elevated above the ground). However, this is a more stressful environment for the chickens, and results in greatly reduced egg production and increased chicken mortality.

> **NOTE:** *If you must use a chicken coop you should plan on it offering some shade, which can be as simple as draping a cloth over part of the coop.* **All chickens need some shade.**

Hen houses provide reasonable space and roosting and nesting options for the chickens, and also provide maximum protection from predators. It is highly recommended that if you raise chickens that you give serious consideration to erecting a hen house. The hen house should provide two to three square feet of space for each chicken (keeping in mind your future plans for potential growth of the flock).[182] Within the hen house you should provide a series of two-inch wide bars elevated at least ten inches off the floor where the chickens can roost at night. These should allow for at least 10 inches of horizontal space for each chicken.[182]

The hen house should have a door that opens directly to the *chicken run* (or 'chicken yard') where the chickens spend the daytime hours feeding on insects, grass(if available) and grain. The chicken yard should provide at least three to four square feet of space for each chicken.

In addition to roosting, the hen house should feature a 12-inch square *nesting box* for at least every four to five hens.[196]. Each box should be three to four inches deep and contain a good layer of straw and wood shavings. The nesting boxes should be a few inches off the floor and be in darker, more secluded area of the structure. To encourage hens new to egg-laying to make use of the nesting boxes you may place fake eggs and/or golf balls in them temporarily. It is not uncommon for the floor of these boxes to be inclined in such a way that newly-laid eggs will roll away from the nest into a collection area. This reduces or eliminates the chance for the hen to damage and/or eat her own egg (which is known to happen occasionally).

Both chicken coops and hen houses should have a layer of straw and/or wood shavings (often pine) scattered on the floor to provide a good walking surface for the chickens, as well as to absorb chicken urine and manure. This flooring material should be cleaned out and replaced regularly. The chicken coop should also be located adjacent to or inside the chicken yard. Early each morning the coop or hen house should be opened to allow the chickens to roam in the yard.

NOTE: *It is also possible to have the chickens free-range on your property during the day and return to a hen house at night, however this may have disastrous consequences for any grass you have growing and/or any vegetation on the property that you do not want devoured.*

If possible it is also a good idea to have a small room with electricity built into the hen house where you can keep your brooder for new chicks, any egg incubation equipment you may need, as well as other tools. One area of the hen house should also be able to be segregated from the main population to contain new pullets and cockrels that are scheduled to be introduced to the population.

Regardless of how you raise your chickens it is an important part of chicken hygiene for them to be able to take the occasional *dust bath*. This practice removes lice and other parasites from their skin, as well as dead skin cells. Often chickens will create their own dust baths, however if you provide a small container such as a plastic tub that is filled with a combination of dry soil, sand and *diatomaceous earth* powder ("DE powder") then your chickens will realize even greater benefits (the DE powder is excellent for killing small parasites).[198]

Incubating Chicken Eggs

If you have a rooster then you can produce your own fertile eggs, otherwise you can obtain them from another chicken-raiser or from a hatchery. The eggs should be placed into the incubator as soon as possible (if not, they should be stored at 50°F with the large end of the egg pointed upwards[195]) and the incubator should be set and managed according to its own specific instructions. The eggs should hatch at very close to the 21-day mark from when they are placed into the incubator.

> **NOTE:** *For the prepper/survivalist there are some important considerations regarding incubating your own eggs. One consideration is the availability of electricity to provide power to the incubator and the other is that, without an incubator, you may have much more difficulty growing your flock when that growth is most needed. At the very least it is a good idea to have a plan for acquiring, installing and using an incubator quickly as circumstances may warrant. These plans should also take into the account the need for a backup source of electricity should normal sources of electrical power become unavailable.*

Once the chicks have hatched and had a chance to dry and become fluffy they should be placed in a brooder with a heat lamp initially providing a temperature of 90°F (if the chicks are to be kept in the incubator for 1-2 days then the incubator temperature should be lowered to 85°F). Once in the brooder the temperature should be reduced by 5°F each week for six weeks until the new chicks are ready to be introduced into the hen house.

The newly-introduced chicks should be kept in a section of the hen house that is segregated from the general population for a few days before they are released to become part of the flock. Keep a small door to this area open so that it can serve as a retreat for the new chicks if they are picked on too much by the older birds, and keep that area supplied with *grower feed* and clean water.

Obtaining and Raising Baby Chicks

If you decide not to have a rooster to fertilize your own hens' eggs, or to purchase and incubate already-fertilized eggs, then you will have to purchase your new baby chicks from a hatchery. If you do, you may find that there is a need to combine your order with other chicken-raisers to meet the minimum order size required by the hatchery. Also, before making any such purchase, you should understand your options in terms of specifying the gender of the chicks you are ordering.

NOTE: *Some communities have zoning ordinances that allow the raising of chickens but, for noise and other reasons, do not allow you to have roosters.*

Work Routines for Maintaining your Chicken Flock

The following are the regular chores associated with raising chickens:

- When raising new chicks in a brooder their water should be changed twice per day, and their food should be cleaned once per day.

- Each morning the door to the coop or hen house should be opened to allow the chickens to roam in the chicken yard and any new eggs should be collected from nesting areas (nesting chickens should not be released until mid-morning to provide them an additional opportunity to lay eggs).

- Each evening any new eggs that may have been laid during the day should be collected.

- Once every week or two the floor of the hen house or chicken coop should be cleaned.

- Egg-laying chickens should be fed once or twice per day, adjusting the amount of feed given such that they have feed about 80% of the time during the day. Chickens raised for meat should have food available 24 hours per day, and in an environment that has continuous lighting.

Grit and/or small gravel should be made available in the environment for chickens to eat to aid digestion. Also, calcium supplements and/or ground oyster shells should be made available to egg-laying chickens to enable them to produce eggs with harder shells.

The Benefits of Raising Chickens on Pasture

Many chicken raisers choose to raise their chickens in pastures rather than in chicken yards. This provides the chickens with a good supply of grass and bugs to eat (their natural foods), and also allows the chicken manure to serve as a very good fertilizer to the pasture. Additionally, it greatly reduces the cost of feed. It has been shown that both the taste and nutritional value of chicken eggs and meat are dramatically improved when chickens are raised in pasture rather than in fixed pens.

The two practical ways of raising chickens on pasture are by using *chicken tractors* or by rotating the chicken flock through designated paddocks.

Using Chicken Tractors to Raise Chickens on Pasture

Chicken droppings are one of the best natural fertilizers. To capitalize on this many chicken owners have built mobile mini-coops that can be moved across a pasture during the course of the day. These mobile coops have been referred to as *chicken tractors*. A typical chicken tractor would measure from three to ten feet across and from five to twelve feet long (depending on the number of chickens it is intended to house), and should be at least two feet in height.[183] A ten by twelve foot tractor would accommodate about thirty chickens. Multiple tractors are required to accommodate larger numbers of chickens. The chicken tractor should be floor-less, so that the chickens have full access to the pasture.

Rotating Chickens through Paddocks

A practical alternative to the chicken tractor for raising chickens on pasture is to divide the pasture into four or more fenced *paddocks*, and rotate the chickens from one paddock to another every seven to ten days (or when you observe that 30% of the vegetation in the paddock has been consumed).[187] This provides the chickens with ample natural feed in the form of fresh grasses and bugs, while also providing the paddocks time to recover between uses.

Chicken Health Issues

Some of the common health-related issues that you will encounter include:

- Mites

- Molting

- Broody Hens

Mites are tiny insects that can attach themselves in great numbers to a chicken's skin to feed on the chicken's blood. Unchecked this can lead to illness and death. If a chicken will not roost on a nesting box, or if the chicken's eggs exhibit tiny red dots, then mites are indicated. One treatment for mites is to dust all affected nesting boxes with diatomaceous earth powder, and another is to administer the insecticide *permethrin*.[194]

Molting is the annual or semi-annual shedding and replacement of feathers that all chickens experience. During this period of three or more months egg-laying chickens will cease to lay eggs. Molting is simply a natural characteristic of chickens that the chicken farmer must learn to endure.[194]

Hens can sometimes go *broody* and insist on sitting on a clutch of eggs in an effort to hatch them. Under such circumstances the hen may become aggressive when you attempt to collect the eggs. Broodiness may be resolved by moving the hen to another isolated pen for a few days and restricting its access to food and water. Some farmers have also had success by putting ice cubes in the chicken's nest.

Another behavioral problem exhibited by some chickens is the tendency to become cannibalistic (to kill and eat other chickens). Cannibalism is, in fact, one of the main causes of mortality among laying hens. The causes of chicken cannibalism are not yet fully understood, although there is some educated speculation that it may result from a lack of animal protein in the chickens' diets. Some farmers have adopted the practice of 'trimming' the beaks of chickens that exhibit cannibalistic tendencies, however this is regarded by many to be an inhumane, pain-inflicting practice and is not an approach that is widely accepted. Presently the only options for dealing effectively with chicken cannibalism are to either segregate any cannibalistic chickens or to move those chickens to the top of the butcher's list.[200]

Butchering Chickens While Removing Skin

To butcher one or more chickens you will need the following items:

- A sharp knife
- Two bowls, one filled with water
- Some small rope to use for hanging the chicken carcass by the feet
- A level surface such as a table top or a sheet of plywood suspected between two sawhorses
- A sheet of plastic or butcher's paper
- Some sort of low-hanging branch or other object from which to hang the chicken for skinning
- A garden hose
- A thick garbage bag

The procedure for butchering a chicken is as follows:[197]

- Wash your hands thoroughly.
- Tie the chicken's legs together and cut off its head.
- Hang the chicken by its feet from the tree branch or other support.
- Make an incision around the chicken's leg joint just deep enough to cut the skin.

- Cut down the leg and pull the skin down from the leg.

- Pull the chicken skin down the sides while cutting the skin away from the meat with the knife.

- Continue cutting and pulling the skin down around the upper thigh, and down to the breast.

- Cut the wings loose at the first wing joint, then cut and remove the wings.

- Cut the breast from the chicken.

- Cut through each leg such that the main body of the chicken is separated from the non-meaty, scaly legs (the chicken will no longer be hanging from the ropes).

- Push the thigh and drumstick backwards so that the meat comes free from the skin.

- Cut across the upper part of the thigh (about 1 to 2 inches from the anus) to separate it from the carcass.

- Remove any organs that you wish to keep (as well as the neck if you like to keep that).

Butchering Chickens Without Removing Skin

Many people prefer to keep the skin on the chicken for cooking and eating. The process of butchering the chicken to preserve the skin requires the same equipment as the foregoing procedure, and includes the following steps:[199]

- Wash your hands thoroughly.

- Cut off the chicken's head and hang it upside down to allow the blood to drain.

- Heat a large metal container of water (large enough to completely submerge the chicken) to 180°F

- Grabbing the now-bled-out chicken carcass by the feet, dip it into the water and swish it about a couple of times.

- Remove the chicken from the water and you should be able to easily pluck away the feathers (possibly excluding the anus and around the neck, as these will later be cut away).

- If small feathers remain on the carcass you may burn them away by holding the chicken up and passing a flame from a burning, rolled up newspaper across the body (note: due to the smell of burning feathers, this is **definitely** something you should prefer to do outdoors).

- Cut away the feet and legs below the meaty part of the leg.

- Cut away the ends of the chicken's wings (no real meat there!)

- Cut the skin around the base of the neck and discard that skin.

- Peel back the skin at the base of the neck and locate and carefully remove the 'crop' (also known as the 'gizzard').

- Locate the bone between the legs and carefully make a shallow, two inch horizontal cut below that bone (at the bottom of the belly).

- Flip the carcass over and slice across the anus area (also known as the 'vent') to remove that.

- Once again flip the chicken and stretch the 2-inch cut that you made until it is large enough that you can insert your hand fully into the chicken and pull out all of the guts (keeping the livers if you have anyone interested in those). If you are butchering a hen then this process may also extract some eggs that are in various stages of development.

- Make a slice from where you cut away the anus to the front opening such that the entire body cavity of the carcass is now open and empty.

- Wash the inside of the chicken thoroughly with clean water, rubbing your hands around inside the chicken to be sure that no guts remain.

- The chicken is now clean and ready for refrigeration and/or cooking (many recipes may require you to further separate the various parts of the chicken for cooking).

13.2.2. Raising Guinea Fowl for Pest Control

Guineas are fowl that can be raised very much like chickens (in fact, they can be raised side-by-side with chickens). While guineas can be butchered and eaten just like chickens; and while guinea eggs can be collected and eaten just like those of chickens (guinea eggs are about one third smaller than typical chicken eggs), guineas are generally not raised for food. Rather, they are raised to eat unwanted and harmful bugs and weeds (especially ticks!).

Male guineas are called 'cocks' and female guineas are called 'hens'. Very young guineas are referred to as 'keets'.

The guinea owner typically keeps the guineas in a henhouse where they often roost alongside chickens. However, while chickens often, during the day, are limited to scratching around in an enclosed area, guineas typically fly out onto the property to *free-range* during the day, eating harmful insects while doing so.

> **NOTE:** *While chickens have a reputation of wrecking havoc in gardens, guineas can stroll through your garden all day long and cause no damage at all. They will, however, eat every undesirable insect and weed seed they can get their beaks on! (In fact, many guinea owners raise them specifically to help maintain their gardens.)*

Towards the end of the day guineas will simply return to the henhouse to roost with the chickens, only to resume their bug-eating ways the following day!

If you've read anything recently about the life-threatening *lyme disease* carried by ticks then you can appreciate the value that guineas bring to the prepper's world.

Guineas have a strong homing instinct (which is why they reliably return to the henhouse each evening). As a result, older guineas that are introduced to a new environment have a reputation of disappearing (as they attempt to return to their former 'home'). With time and patience older guineas can be re-trained to recognize their new home, however it is recommended that you start with young or day-old keets if at all possible.[181] If you handle your keets personally while they are young and growing then they will quickly come to feel comfortable around you, otherwise as they grow older they will tend to shy away from a human presence.

For the first 6 weeks of their lives (until they are fully feathered) keets need to be kept in a brooder (a brooder is an enclosure, typically with a heat lamp, food and water, in which the young guineas can progress through the critical first stage of growth). For the first week the temperature should be maintained at 95°F and reduced by 5°F each week until the 6 weeks has elapsed and they are fully feathered. While in the brooder the young keets should be fed a medicated turkey starter feed (medicated with Amprolium to prevent diseases that often inflict young keets[181]).

> **CAUTION:** *Guineas have a loud and distinctive call, which they do not hesitate to employ when they are confronted by any number of exceptional situations (including seeing strangers, which is why some guinea owners consider them to be a good alarm system for both human intruders and predators). The males and females each have their own, very distinctive call.*

After the guineas are removed from the brooder they should be relocated to an an area in the guinea/hen house that is separated from the main population by a barrier that allows the new guineas to "see and be seen". They should be kept in this pen for another 6 weeks

Figure 13.1.: Drawing of a Guinea Fowl.

before being introduced to the general population. This process will result in greatly reduced "pecking order" problems when they are introduced, and will also condition the new guineas to consider this to be "home".

Shelter Requirements

The henhouse should be well protected from both the weather and predators. There should be no clear openings between the inside of the henhouse and the outside environment. Additionally, all doors and windows should fit well and close snugly.

The henhouse should have a door that leads to the chicken yard, which should be enclosed by a fence that is high enough to keep ground-based predators away. If the fence is too high for the guineas to fly out into the yard then a *landing board* should be erected in the chicken yard to provide the guineas a staging point from which they can fly out.

Feeding Guineas

Guineas that are part of the general population will fly out onto the property and feed on harmful insects and the seeds of weeds. In the evening, when they return home to roost, there should be a modest amount of feed awaiting them (with the amount of feed increased when there is snow on the ground or during inclimate weather).

Nesting

Guinea hens have a tendency to nest out "on the range" rather than at home, and their nests can be well-concealed. In season the hen may lay one egg each day, and hens may share a single nest. Eventually the hen may "go broody" and roost on the nest at night rather than return to the henhouse. This tendency makes the hen, as well as their eggs, extremely vulnerable to predators. With some close observation you should be able to locate the nest and (very carefully) relocate it to some cozy, secluded, semi-protected corner of the henhouse.

13.2.3. Raising Rabbits for Food

In a survival situation rabbits offer many serious advantages as a source of animal protein:

- They are an excellent source of lean dietary protein.
- They are small enough that there is no real need for meat preservation.
- They are easy to raise, and multiply at a fast rate.
- They require very little space (only the space of their pen).
- They are usually easy to handle and manage, and well-tempered.
- Rabbits do not make any noises that might draw undesired attention.

Male and female rabbits are referred to as 'bucks' and 'does', respectively. When referring to them as parents they are also referred to as the 'sire' and the 'dam'. Newborn rabbits are simply referred to as 'kits'. The process of a rabbit giving birth is called 'kindling'.[201]

NOTE: *Some people live in areas that have such an abundant rabbit population that they imagine themselves living from rabbit meat alone. It should be noted that a person cannot live exclusively from a diet of rabbit meat. While rabbits provide an excellent source of protein, there are other nutrients that are required by humans to live, especially carbohydrates and fats (in fact, the potentially-fatal medical condition resulting from living exclusively on lean meat has been termed 'Rabbit Starvation').*

It is critical for the survivor to supplement their diet from food sources other than rabbit meat.

Shelter and Facility

Rabbits are kept in a wire cage known as a *rabbit hutch*. The mesh of the hutch should be sufficiently small that there is no chance of the rabbit getting its head caught. In general the mesh on the sides and top should be no larger than one inch square, while the mesh on the bottom should be no larger than one-half inch square (to provide better footing). A

Rabbit Size	Cage Size	Feeding	Weight	Breeds
Medium	5 sq. ft.	0.5-1 cup daily	4.5-7 lbs	American Sable,English Angora,French Angora,Satin Angora,Belgian Hare,Standard Chinchilla,English Spot, Florida White,Harlequin,Havana,Lilac,Mini Lop,Rhinelander,Silver,Silver Marten,Tan
Meat	7.5 sq ft.	1.25 cups daily	8-12 lbs	American,Bavarian,Californian, Champagne D'Argent,American Chinchilla,Cinnamon,Creme D'Argent,Hotot, English Lop,French Lop,New Zealand,Palomino,Satin,Silver Fox
Giant	11.12 sq. ft.	1.75 - 2 cups daily	up to 25 lbs	Checkered Giant, Giant Chinchilla, Flemish Giant

Table 13.7.: Feeding and Space Requirements for the Various Sizes of Rabbits[201]

wooden board that has not been chemically-treated should also be placed on the floor of the cage to provide a place where the rabbit can sit without subjecting its paws to the wire mesh (of course this board should be large enough to accommodate the rabbit). The mesh sizes described here should be able to accommodate young as well as adult rabbits.

Depending on the size of the rabbits you intend to raise, the hutch should range from 3 to 4 square feet in size. In addition to the board, the hutch should feature a regular rabbit feeding trough as well as a bottle-supplied water source.[202]

Rabbits are generally classified as being 'medium-sized', 'meat rabbits' or 'giant rabbits'. Table 13.7 describes the space and feeding needs for each class of rabbits.

CAUTION: *Before committing to raising rabbits you should determine if anyone in your household is allergic to them.*

Social Behavior of Rabbits

For mating purposes the male rabbit should always be introduced into the female's cage (otherwise the male rabbit may begin to fight the female in defense of his territory). The male rabbit should also be kept away from any young rabbits.

Young rabbits (especially kits) should be handled seldom (if ever) to avoid the possibility of the doe killing them due to having a foreign scent.

Young rabbits may continue to live in the cage with their mother until 6- to 8- weeks of age, provided that the cage has sufficient space (and also keeping in mind that it has board space for them to stand on so that they are not forced to stand on the wire mesh floor of the cage).

> **NOTE:** *Some people are under the mistaken impressions that rabbits are a form of rodent. Rabbits are mammals and members of the scientific order* Lagomorpha, *while rodents are of the order* Rodentia.

When male rabbits are ready to mate they should exhibit a higher level of energy and restlessness. When female rabbits are in heat they will often begin to rub their heads against their pen. When putting the male rabbit into the female's cage you should be patient and allow the male rabbit at least two opportunities to mate with the female.

Obtaining and Raising Baby Rabbits

You should have little trouble obtaining your first rabbits. They can be acquired from rabbit rescue shelters, from online classified ads, from pet stores or simply from other rabbit owners that make young rabbits available.

Of course, once you have a breeding pair of rabbits you can quickly begin to "grow your own". Does reach sexual maturity after about 6 months of age, while bucks may mature at as early as four weeks of age.[207] The gestation period for pregnant rabbits is just 29 to 33 days.[203]

Housing Rabbits during the Winter

If keeping rabbits outdoors, it is important to provide them with proper accommodations during the colder months. While rabbits do well living in moderately cold temperatures, it is still important for them to be protected from drafts and to have a warm place to sleep. Also, when temperatures plunge to well below freezing it is important to be prepared to provide additional protections. Measures you can take to preserve your rabbits through the winter months include:[211]

- Keep the rabbit hutch in good repair, being sure to pay special attention to any evidence of water leakage.

- Keep the rabbit hutch elevated an inch above any cold surface (using bricks provides a good ventilation space below the hutch). This protects the hutch from dampness and wood rot.

- Enclose the sides of the hutch with clear plastic wrap to provide protection from cold wind and drafts.

- Provide a cozy, somewhat compact bedding area that is well-insulated with newspaper shreds, straw or other insulating bedding materials.

- Provide the rabbits with a spacious area in which to move about and exercise during the day (making sure that it provides ready access to the warmer bedding area).

- To provide increased warmth, consider layering a blanket and other insulating materials over the hutch (leaving open and end of the hutch that is not exposed exposed directly to the wind).

- Under extremely cold conditions, consider moving the hutch to an enclosed building or garage (without exposing the rabbits to car exhaust), or provide additional heat with a greenhouse heater.

- Provide the rabbits with a diet that offers increased calories to enable them to better maintain body temperature.

If, during cold weather, you notice that your rabbits seem to be sleeping excessively then seek immediate medical attention for them (rabbits do not hibernate during the winter!).

Daily Routine for Raising Rabbits

If possible you should have more than one rabbit, and keep the cages in close proximity to one another. This provides the rabbits with some companionship. Additionally, mature and adolescent rabbits should receive human attention at least a couple of times most days.

Feeding and Watering Rabbits

Basically there are four types of food that are commonly fed to rabbits, with each type having its own feeding rules:[206]

- *Rabbit feed pellets* - Nutritionally-balanced food pellets available from most animal feed stores, as well as pet stores, are the food most commonly fed to rabbits. Rabbit pellets can be part of your rabbit's feeding program, however you should look for pellets that are high in fiber and low in protein (especially in the case of adult rabbits). Rabbits may refuse to eat pellets that have become old and stale.

- *High-calorie alfalfa hay* - Alfalfa hay, which is high in calories, should be fed regularly to rabbits in their first 4-6 weeks of growth, and thereafter fed only sparingly to fully matured rabbits (when you suspect that could benefit from an increase in dietary calories).

- *Regular Rabbit hay* - This hay (e.g. timothy, orchard, brome and meadow hay) can and should be made available to rabbits at all times. This is essential to maintaining the rabbit's health. Timothy hay and oat hay are particularly well-liked and healthy for rabbits.

- *Rabbit treats* - Almonds, fruits (e.g. banana and strawberry), green carrot tops and parsley are treats for rabbits that should be fed sparingly to avoid having a severely overweight and unhappy rabbit. Occasional treats, in small quantity (a couple of tablespoons), may be good to maintain the rabbit's overall mental health (rabbits have brains too!). Other treats include romaine lettuce, dandelion greens, cilantro, mint, dill, radiccio, celery leaves, beet greens, bok choy, basil, clover, collard greens, kale, mustard greens and water cress.

In addition to the foods described above, rabbits should have an ample supply of cool, clean water available at all times. Any changes to a rabbit's diet should be made as gradually as possible to avoid causing the rabbit any undue stress which might affect its overall health.

CAUTION: *In addition to these four types of rabbit food, it should also be kept in mind that certain foods can be* **harmful and/or fatal** *to rabbits. These problem foods include non-romaine lettuce, cabbage, potatoes and tomato leaves. These foods can form gas in the rabbit's digestive system that it has no way to eliminate, resulting in serious medical problems.*

While green grass clippings can be fed to rabbits, if they are fed to a caged rabbit they should be free of moisture. Wet grass clippings can also be fatal to caged rabbits.

Sexing Rabbits

The process of determining a rabbit's gender is referred to as 'sexing' the rabbit. This is, of course, important in knowing which rabbits to introduce to one another for breeding purposes.

To sex a rabbit simply hold the rabbit such that it is laying on its back, and look between its legs. You should see two openings, with the one nearest the tail being the anus. Gently press down with your fingers on either side of the other opening (the one not near the tail). If you see the rabbit's testicles or a small penis then you know that the rabbit is male. If you observe a small slit (the rabbit's vagina) then you know the rabbit is female (note that some rabbit vaginas can be slightly raised, and if not observed carefully they can be mistaken for a penis).[208]

Identifying and Caring for Sick Rabbits

Sick rabbits often do not exhibit extremely visible indicators that they are ill (this is likely a survival behavior, as sick rabbits may appear to be easy prey to predators). However, if you notice that a rabbit is not eating normally, or exhibiting some other abnormal behavior (maybe occupying a different location in the pen than normal, or drinking less water), then it is very possible that the rabbit is ill.[210] You might want to offer the rabbit one or two of its favorite treats to further identify if it is ill. If it refuses its favorite treats, then you should check its temperature.

To take a rabbit's temperature cradle the rabbit in your arms such that it is facing upwards with it's body positioned such that it is laying in a slightly-curled 'C' position. Lubricate and gently insert a thermometer no more than one inch into the rabbit's anus to take its temperature.

If the rabbit's temperature is higher than 104°F then you should take steps to cool the rabbit immediately (place ice packs or perhaps bags of frozen vegetables across its body) and take it immediately to the veterinarian. If its temperature is less then 100°F (hypothermia) then you should also take it to the veterinarian immediately.

CAUTION: *When attempting to take the rabbit's temperature, if the rabbit begins to kick or otherwise demonstrate that it is uncomfortable with the procedure, then stop immediately, set the rabbit back on its feet, and stroke it to provide reassurance until you believe the nervousness has passed. Several attempts may be necessary, and you should be patient, gentle and reassuring to the rabbit throughout the process.*

If the rabbit's temperature is between 100°F-104°F then you should listen to the sounds in its belly (hopefully with an inexpensive stethoscope, which is recommended equipment for all rabbit owners). If there is no noise then the rabbit may be suffering from Gastrointestinal Stasis (ileus) and you should arrange to take the rabbit to the doctor as soon as possible.

If you detect a strong gurgling sound in the rabbit's stomach then it may be suffering from an acute gas attack. If this is the case try gently massaging the sides of the rabbit's belly while stroking its hind quarters. You might also try gently lifting its hindquarters into the air. This may release the gas and allow the rabbit to begin to recover. If, during these processes, the rabbit begins to kick or otherwise act in a panicky fashion then you should cease the procedure, place the rabbit on its legs, and stroke it and provide reassurances until it is (hopefully) quieted and ready to try again.

Butchering Rabbits

Rabbits butchered for meat should be butchered at between 6- and 12- weeks of age. Older rabbits tend to yield tougher, less desirable meat. Domestic rabbits produce all white meat, while the meat of game rabbits is not all white.

The first step in butchering a rabbit is to kill the rabbit. The quickest and most humane way to kill a rabbit is to break its neck. One way to quickly break a rabbit's neck is with a *killing board*. This board contains a long notch cut down the length of the board that becomes progressively more narrow. The shape of this notch is similar to the shape of your index and ring fingers separated slightly, and of course the end of the notch must be wide enough to accept the rabbit's neck.

This board is suspended at just over a person's head height such that the rabbit can be hung from it by the neck.

To kill the rabbit simply hang it from the notch, grasp its hind legs, and give the rabbit a quick, somewhat forceful backward jerk. You should hear the rabbit's neck snap, and the rabbit will be killed instantly.

NOTE: *An alternate, low-cost way to humanely kill a rabbit is to shoot it in the back of the head, at the base of the skull, with a pellet gun.*

Once the rabbit is killed the process of butchering is:

- Hang the rabbit from its back legs such that you have easy access for skinning.

- With a sharp knife, cut the skin around the ankles without cutting the Achilles tendon.

- Cut down the inside of both legs such that the cuts meet between the legs.

- Cut across the tail and 'vent area' of the carcass, such that the skin can be pulled down without without involving these parts of the body.

- Using a pair of shears, cut off the front paws.

- Begin pulling the skin from the legs down the carcass, being ready to carefully cut the skin away from the belly as needed (you want to be careful not to accidentally open the belly).

- Pull the skin down until the front legs are half revealed, and cut the membrane there that connects the leg to the pelt.

- Continue pulling the pelt until it comes free from the legs (this last part may require some effort).

- Pull the skin down to the neck and, with larger shears, remove and discard the head, and remove the pelt completely (which can also be discarded, or saved for tanning if you prefer).

- With the shears, remove the back feet such that the carcass is no longer hanging.

- Pull the skin down from the tail and vent area and cut away this entire area.

- Carefully cut across the bottom of the belly so as not to puncture the bladder, and pull out the guts, being sure to get the kidneys (which may be encased in fat) and the heart, longs and diaphragm (located in the upper part of the body).

- Split the ribs of the rabbit to allow for easy cleaning of the body cavity.

- Wash the inside of the body with clean water, and place the cleaned rabbit into a freezer bag for refrigeration.

- Separate the gall bladder from the liver if you wish to save the liver (if the liver exhibits any small white dots or squiggly lines, then it must be discarded).

- If you wish to keep the heart, cut off the top of the heart before washing and saving it.

If the rabbit was 12 or more weeks in age then the meat is generally too tough for frying and should be considered a 'roaster' (the slow cooking associated with roasting serves to tenderize the less tender meat).

A freshly butchered rabbit should either be cooked immediately (before it goes into rigor), or be refrigerated for 3 to 4 days before being cooked or frozen (to give the rabbit carcass time to come out of rigor).[212]

13.2.4. Raising Goats

Their relatively manageable small size, ability to graze on a wide range of vegetation and ability to provide good milk as well as meat make *goats* a viable food source for the survivor. While goats require open spaces of vegetation on which to graze, they are much less difficult to manage and raise than cattle. This section is intended to provide a good, high-level overview of raising goats for food. Should you decide that raising goats is a good fit for your own specific circumstances then you are encouraged to augment the information presented here with additional, more detailed references.

The male goat is known as a 'buck', the female is known as a 'doe' and young goats are referred to as 'kids'. When raising goats you should be prepared to deal with issues of goat mortality. Goats do not have lengthy life spans and are susceptible to a range of diseases.[173]

> **NOTE:** *NOTE: Because goats are larger, in the absence of refrigeration goats raised for meat should only be slaughtered to feed a sufficiently large group. As a result, goats should be considered a meat source for larger groups, and it should be expected that in the aftermath of a major disaster it may take some time for such communities to begin to form.*
>
> *Accordingly, goats should not be raised as the sole source of meat and smaller livestock such as chickens, rabbits and/or fish should also be raised.*

The nutritional value of goat milk is similar to that of milk from cows, with goat milk providing different levels of vitamins and other nutrients than cow milk. A single *nanny goat* is capable of producing about one gallon of milk per day.[175]

Goat meat is actually the most consumed meat on Earth. It is typically much more lean and healthy than beef, and rich in many vitamins and other nutrients. Younger goats tend to produce better, more tender meat than older goats.

Begin building your goat herd by purchasing 5 or 6 goats that are 4 to 6 months in age and weighing at least 60 pounds.[175] At a minimum start with 2 goats, as goats are social. The best types of goats to purchase are those that are most commonly raised in your area, as this gives you better options in selling excess stock as the herd grows.

There are many breeds of goat that vary greatly in size and body shape. As a general rule, the larger goat breeds are more appropriate when raising goats for meat, while the mid-sized goats are better for dairy. Common breeds used for dairy include LaMancha, Nubian, Oberhasli and French Alpine. LaMancha and Nubian, while popular, produce a little less milk per day than the others. Common breeds raised for meat are Boer, Kiko, Saanen, Toggenburg and Nubian, with Boer being the most popular goat to raise for meat.

Feeding Goats

Ideally you will feed your goats regular mixed goat feed in the mornings and hay in the evenings (and, during the winter also feed hay at midday). The goat feed should be a livestock feed that contains 30-50 parts-per-million of the the essential nutrient copper.[179]

(if a goat feed containing copper is not available then consider substituting horse feed). The best hay for goats (unlike for cattle) is hay that is "weedy". Even though weedy hay may be considered to be lower grade of hay you should still be certain that the hay was harvested and stored dry, so that it contains no mold. Between these feedings the goats should be put out to pasture to graze (the word "pasture" is a little misleading here, as wooded areas also offer very nice grazing for goats).

The needs of grazing animals such as goats, sheep and cattle are quantified in units known as DSEs (*dry sheep equivalent*). This standard unit makes it easy to characterize the grazing acreage requirements for combinations of different animals of different genders and size. A grown goat buck is rated at 1.5 DSEs, while a non-milk-producing ('dry') doe is rated at 0.75 DSEs, a breeding doe is rated at 1.5 DSEs and a young goat less than one year old is rated at 0.7 DSEs.[178] **One acre of goat-grazing land should support the grazing of 8 DSE of goats.**

Note that while goats can graze on grasses, they very much prefer leaves, flowering plants (as many goat-owners have learned painfully) and tree bark (another source of some painful lessons). This means that the ideal grazing area for goats should not necessarily be pure pasture. Also, goats prefer to eat the more tender plants, which means that the seed used for the pasture should contain a mix of appropriate seed.

There is no exact formula for mixing seeds to apply to grazing pasture, however a blend of 20% fescue, 15% orchardgrass, 20% bluegrass, 10% red clover, 10% ladino clover, 10% lespedeza and 10% alfalfa has been used successfully.[179]. You can almost certainly vary this blend significantly on an as-needed basis although, as stated above, these changes should be made as gradually as possible. The seed can be spread over the grazing pasture by hand or other means. Also note that, in particular, rye grass can be used as a substitute for fescue.

The grazing area for goats (especially pasture lands where the goats graze close to the ground) should be divided into at least 4 fenced lots ('paddocks'), with each lot able to support the full grazing herd. The herd should then be rotated through the paddocks every 3 weeks. This 3-week period corresponds to the life expectancy of the stomach worms that can cause serious health problems for goats, and greatly reduces the chances of the goats infecting one another by grazing on grass that has been temporarily contaminated.

NOTE: *Keep in mind that each grazing paddock should confirm to the 8 DSE-per-acre guideline mentioned previously. This means that, in reality, your total acreage needs are something similar to 2 DSEs per acre.*

Ideally goat fences should be at least 4 feet in height and have openings no larger than 4x4 inches (to keep the goats from getting their heads stuck in the fence). If the fencing is elevated slightly off the ground then it will prevent rusting. If possible a shorter electric fence extending along the outside of the main fence serves as a nice deterrent to larger predators such as feral dogs, and a shorter electric fence extending across the top or just inside the main fence deters goats from attempting to climb the fence (a common source of fence problems).

> **CAUTION:** *Young kids less than 2-4 weeks in age should not be exposed to electric fences.*

It is important to make any changes to the feeding of goats in a gradual manner so that they may adapt. Otherwise sudden changes could have severe adverse affects on the health of the herd.[179]

Goat Shelters and Fencing

Your goat shed should be have 3 or 4 walls (4 walls if you are in a colder climate, or possibly 3 walls with the open side facing south if you are in a warmer climate). Regardless of the number of walls, you should feel that it provides the goats with protection from being exposed to wind-driven rain and shelter from drafts (goats can be very sensitive to drafts, and a drafty shed can cause a routine illness to become much more serious or fatal).

The goat shed needs to allow 15 square feet per adult goat.[175] Additionally, the shelter should include a separate birthing stall of 15-20 square feet, feed and water troughs and a loft for storing hay. If possible it is also nice to have an attached room with electrical power where you may keep supplies and possibly a refrigerator/freezer to store excess goats' milk in case it may be needed by newborn kids in the future.

Milking Goats

Goats should be milked at a *milking station* that has a platform that leads to a small feed trough. Before milking you should place about one pound of feed in the trough. The station should be constructed in such a way that the goat must place it's head through a stanchion that can be closed so that it fits just close enough to prevent the goat from withdrawing from the feed trough (a stanchion may simply consist of two vertical boards that can be moved together on either side of the goat's head).

Once the goat is secured to the milking station the udder and teats should be cleaned with a sterile cloth and warm water. A milking bucket can then be placed under the goat and the teats gently squeezed (but not pulled) to expel milk into the bucket (the fingers should be squeezed in sequence so as to force the milk down into the bucket rather than back into the udder). After the milk has been collected and the bucket set aside, the teats should be dipped in an iodine solution to inhibit bacterial growth. The doe can then be released and led back to rejoin the herd.

NOTE: *Once a doe has become accustomed to being milked you should have very little trouble getting her to step up to the milking platform.*

Supplies, Equipment and Infrastructure Needed to Raise Goats

Equipment needed for the proper upkeep of goats includes:

- A goat shed

- An office with electrical power and a refrigerator/freezer (for storing goat colostrum).

- A pitchfork for distributing hay.

- Extra fencing

- Hammers, nails, fencing equipment

- Feed and water troughs

- Hay (and a loft for storing hay out of the weather).

- Feeding tubes and one or more feeding syringes

- Feeding bottles

- Pasture seed mix

- Copper-enriched goat (or horse) feed

- Debudding iron

- Iodine solution for treating goat teats after milking

- Space heater or heating lamp

- Meat saw and butchering knife

Recognizing and Caring for Sick Goats

A sick goat can be recognized by any of the following symptoms:

- Diarrhea or feces not appearing pelletized

- Unsteadily walking

- Hot or warm udders

- Ears pointing at odd or abnormal angles

- Abnormal or improper eating or drinking

- Discolored gums

- Irregular heartbeat or abnormal stomach sounds

- Crusty eyes

- Dehydration (pinch the skin in front of the upper shoulder and confirm that is returns to normal shape quickly when released.)

If you believe your goat is sick it is a good idea to call your veterinarian as soon as possible - being sure to ask if there is anything that they recommend that you do before seeing them. Also, try to keep sick goats away from any sources of draft.

Birthing and Raising Kids

The gestation (pregnancy) period for a doe is about 150 days. If the expectant doe is a milk-producer then she should be 'dried' two months before delivery.[177] This can be accomplished by reducing the milking frequency gradually until you stop milking altogether.

On delivery day the doe will begin to moan and/or bleat in a way that is not typical. You should have a well-sheltered birthing stall prepared in advance. The birthing stall should be about 15-20 square feet in size (larger is OK), have a nice bed of clean straw and be draft-free. If the kid is being delivered during cold weather then it may also be advisable to have a heat lamp well anchored to the wall of the birthing stall (this anchoring is important, as there are many examples of goat sheds being destroyed by fire resulting from poorly-anchored heat lamps).

When giving birth, the dark water-sack will first appear from the birth canal, normally followed by either the front or rear hooves. In this normal orientation the mother should not require any assistance in giving birth.

If the newborn kid is mis-oriented then human assistance could be necessary. The person assisting should scrub their hands and forearms with soapy water and rinse completely. Once properly cleaned the assistant should manually re-orient the kid and assist the doe as needed in giving birth. Goats normally give birth to a single kid during their first pregnancy, but may give birth to as many as four.

Once born, if the weather is cold and a heat lamp is available, it should be turned on.

The newborn kid should begin nursing from its mother shortly after birth. In some cases if the kid has difficulty it may be necessary for a human attendant to provide some manual guidance. If for some reason the new kid cannot or will not nurse, or if the mother does not allow the kid to nurse, then it may be necessary for the attendant to resort to bottle feeding. The bottle should have a special 'kid nipple' for nursing the newborn kid.

NOTE: *The nutrient- and antibody- rich milk produced by the mother doe during the first two days after giving birth is referred to as 'colostrum'. It is important that the new kid receive the colostrum in it's first couple of days after birth. If the mother's colostrum is not available then frozen colostrum from other mothers may be thawed and bottle-fed to the new kid.*

If the colostrum is heated between 133° F-139° F for one hour (and allowed to cool) before feeding then potentially arthritis-causing viruses in the colostrum will not cause any problems.

If the newborn kid refuses the bottle then it may be necessary to extend a feeding tube into the kid's mouth, feed it down to the stomach, and force 20cc of colostrum into the kid's stomach (normally this is done with a syringe) for each feeding until the kid begins to take the bottle or transitions to eating regular hay and feed.

Newborn kids should begin eating grain and hay within about 4 days, and within two weeks be feeding normally with the herd. During those two weeks the kid should be fed the best available feed grains, preferably mixed with molasses, and have access to plenty of clean water.

Disbudding is the process of treating the young kid such that it will never grow horns (horns can cause real problems later in life, and serve no useful purpose for goats that are not living in the wild). This disbudding should (preferably) be performed by someone with experience, and involves applying a hot iron (similar to a branding iron) to the locations on the kid's head where the horns would normally develop. While this is not pleasant for the kid, it will avoid many other painful situations in the future.

Killing and Butchering Goats

The best, fastest and most painless way to kill a goat is to shoot it at close range right between the eyes. The goat should drop dead instantly (if not, follow up immediately with another shot to the head). Once the goat drops you should immediately cut its throat (being careful to sever both the jugular veins on either side of the windpipe) so that the goat immediately begins to bleed out. Once this is completed, the procedure is:

- With a sharp knife, slit the skin from the back of the ankle on the back legs to the anus, and then slit the skin from the bottom of the belly up to the neck.

- Using your knife, separate the skin from the meat on the front of the body.

- Make holes behind the ankle tendons of the back legs so that a rope can be run through the holes to hang the carcass. Hang the carcass high enough that you can continue working without straining your back.

- Finish skinning the goat and remove its head (use a meat saw to remove the head quickly and safely).

- Taking care not to cut the intestines, cut open the belly to the breast bone, and then using a meat saw continue cutting up the breast bone to the throat.

- Allow the stomach and intestines to begin to spill forward a little. Without cutting the intestine or rectum, cut the anus away from the goat on the inside.

- Let the stomach, intestine and rectum spill out of the body.

- Remove the heart and liver. Cut the heart, wash out any blood and put both in cold water for later refrigeration.

- Remove the esophagus and trachea from the throat.

- Using the meat saw cut the carcass in half lengthwise, and wash both sides with clean water. The meat is now ready for hanging and curing (refer to section 5.7 for information on curing meat).

14. Forming a Disaster Community

"No man is an island, entire of itself;
every man is a piece of the continent, a part of
the main."

from *No Man Is An Island* by John Donne

STRAIGHT THINKING: *If you're faced with an imminent disaster that threatens to disrupt society, or if the disaster has already taken place, do not be fooled by the fact that you're not hungry or surrounded by desperate people now ...* **you will be soon enough!**. *If you want to maximize your chances to survive then you need to begin to help get your community organized immediately.*

In general, the more geographical territory your community can control, the better!

When disaster strikes, response time is critical. In the near term people will begin to grow restless, hungry and violent. Shortly thereafter death and disease will begin to take their toll, possibly on a massive scale. The best defense against this hellish fate is for survival groups or communities to become as organized as possible as quickly as possible. When faced with such circumstances there is no time for any sort of *'constitutional convention'* to define some utopia. In fact, very few people have the capacity for clear thought under the stress that will accompany a major disaster; but they certainly have the capacity to **ACT**!

This chapter is intended to provide a guideline for that action; providing those affected with the information necessary to quickly and efficiently establish a disaster response community *('DRC')*. The community might consist of groups ranging in size from as few as 20 members to the size of a mid-sized city with a population of up to 50,000 or more. This is accomplished by providing *'action lists'* and a charter that sets forth the basic rules that govern the community and defines the key roles and responsibilities of both elected and appointed leaders. **As a safety precaution the charter for the community is self-expiring after one year unless it is renewed by a vote of at least 75% of the voting-age population.**

14.1. Key Terms Used in this Chapter

For purposes of The Community Charter the following definitions apply:

- *Disaster Response Community ('DRC')* - A group of individuals who are coming together to form a physical community in order to maximize their probability of surviving a major disaster.

- *Citizen* - any individual who lives within the borders of The Community for at least 8 months of the year.

- *Council* - the group of 7 (or possibly fewer) democratically-elected Citizens who define rules and laws within The Community and control the government of The Community in accordance with the Rights defined in The Community Charter.

- *Citizenship Committee* - a 3-person committee appointed by The Council to review and process petitions for citizenship into The Community, prescribing the wages for all employees of The Community and assessing values of real property.

- *Quorum* - any group consisting of a majority of the members of The Council.

- *Share* - The basic unit of currency within the The Community which is the least that anyone 18 years of age or older working within The Community can be compensated for one hour of work.

- *Mil* - a unit of value equal to one thousandth of one Share.

- *Super Majority Vote* - a vote that is carried by The Council with no more than one vote that is not affirmative.

AUTHOR'S NOTE: *This chapter is an adaptation of a standalone white paper I authored in 2010 as a charter for forming a disaster community. Since that time I have received feedback on that document (which I came to realize defined far too 'communistic' a system). This chapter embodies all those "lessons learned".*

14.2. First Things First

There are a few items to attend to before adopting The Community Charter, voting in members, and getting The Community started. Those items are:

- Perform any pending critical tasks before voting in The Council (e.g filling and placing sandbags before a flood, saving victims, etc.).

- Take votes to determine if The Community will support capital and corporal punishment as the maximum and standard punishments, respectively, for certain crimes. Please read or present section 14.22.1 to all voters to be certain that this is given full consideration.

Once the above items are addressed elections can be held, additional leadership positions can be appointed, and work can commence on the tasks that are defined (see section 14.32).

14.3. Preamble to the Charter

Recognizing **freedom** and **security** of individuals and an **opportunity for prosperity** as being basic and inalienable human rights for all People, this charter is being adopted for the formation of The Community known as _____ for purposes of enabling its Citizens to live and work together in the face of adversity to achieve and safeguard these basic rights for all members of The Community.

14.4. Introduction

This is a charter for a Disaster Response Community ('DRC') to be formed under circumstances in which there is a complete breakdown of social order. Because time will be critical under such circumstances, the definition of this charter in advance should enable the DRC to be formed rapidly while being based on a well-considered foundation. In the absence of such a document it could reasonably be expected that an extensive period of debate might adversely affect the safety and security of all Citizens.

> **NOTE:** *It is imperative to understand that this Charter is intended to organize a community during a time of crisis, and as such to define a system of 'benevolent martial law' that is specifically designed to eventually fall back to a democratic form of self-government. The provisions of this charter are designed to assure basic human survival as the top priority.*

In addition to facilitating the startup of DRC's, this Charter is also intended to define a society that preserves the maximum freedom of its Citizens. Without such a document The Community could easily devolve into a more totalitarian structure that does not exist for the benefit of the Citizens.

Originally it was considered that this charter should be very similar (if not identical to) the US Constitution. However, it quickly became apparent that national constitutions are designed for a much larger community than is anticipated for a DRC, and as such was not a good model for the charter of a DRC. However, once a legitimate rule-of-law is re-established any provision of this charter that is in conflict with the prevailing authority of a national constitution will be rendered null and void.

> **NOTE:** *The section of this chapter entitled 'Rights of Citizens' is inspired and modeled after those rights enumerated in the US Constitution.*

While it is the intention of this model charter document to be comprehensive, it is fully expected that it may be tailored to meet the needs of specific DRC's, and that once DRC's are established that this charter will be amended in accordance with the provisions for amendment outlined herein. It is acknowledged that a Community may become sufficiently large that any such charter may be dropped and replaced by a formal, possibly pre-existing Constitution.

Once this charter is reviewed, possibly revised, and deemed ready, the members of The Community should simply begin performing the comprehensive list of tasks in section 14.32 (in fact, even the review and revision process is included in this comprehensive task list).

14.5. Rights of Citizens

All Citizens of The Community have the following fundamental rights, which cannot be infringed by any other rule or law within The Community:

- *Freedom of Political Speech* - all Citizens shall be free to express, by spoken word or writing (in person or in recorded form), and without fear of persecution or harassment by the governing bodies within The Community, any opinion or belief that relates to the administration, Charter, rules and laws of The Community. All such speech that takes place within Council meetings must be in accordance with established rules of order.

- *Freedom of Religion* - all Citizens shall be free to practice any religion approved by The Council.

- *Right to Bear Arms* - all Citizens are free to own and carry any weapon for personal and Community defense, and for any other lawful purpose.

- *Involuntary Quartering* - no Citizen shall be required, against their will, to provide any lodging or other accommodation to any individual.

- *Search and Seizure* - neither any Citizen, nor any property of any Citizen, shall be subject to search and seizure unless it is specifically authorized by a member of The Council or by a judge who has been appointed by The Council.

- *Compensation for Takings* - no Citizen shall be deprived of life, liberty, or property without due process of law; nor shall the private property of any Citizen be taken for public use, without just compensation.

- *Right to Speedy Trial* - all Citizens accused of any unlawful activity will be subject to a speedy trial and will have the right to provide for their own defense.

- *Trial by Jury* - all trials of Citizens will be adjudicated by a member of The Council (or the Council member's designate) and will be decided by a jury consisting of five randomly-selected Citizens. The accused will be judged guilty only on unanimous agreement among the members of the jury.

- *Punishment* - after a jury has returned a verdict, the judge for a trial can specify any punishment for the offense (except in the case of High Crimes), solely based on that judge's own discretion. Once the punishment is pronounced the defendant has the option to appeal the punishment (not the verdict) before the full Council, in which case The Council may vote to amend or sustain the punishment.

  Since the punishment for High Crimes (see section 14.23) is the Maximum Punishment, there is no appeal in the case of a guilty verdict for the commission of a High

Crime. As a last recourse, a unanimous vote of The Council can grant clemency from or reduce any punishment, including the Maximum Punishment. The punishment assigned by a judge to a defendant in a trial may consist of (but is not limited to) loss of any and all rights granted to Citizens under this charter, including the right to possess weapons and to vote (see section 14.23 for more details on crimes and punishments).

Any rights and responsibilities that are not specifically granted to The Community Government by this Charter are reserved for the Citizens.

14.6. Property Ownership

On initiation of this charter anyone holding clear title to any real estate within the jurisdiction of The Community, or anyone holding a mortgage for any such property, will be deemed by The Community to have full ownership of said property and all rights to do as they wish with said property subject to the rules and laws of The Community. Furthermore, anyone paying rent for any commercial or residential real estate to any entity that is outside The Community will similarly be deemed to have full ownership of said property.

Those who rent real estate from members of The Community will convert the amount paid for their rent payment to community Shares, with the converted Share-based rent payment to be determined by The Community Appraiser (all terms of such rental agreements other than this conversion of monetary amounts to Shares will remain fully in force).

Ownership of all tangible property that is not real estate will be retained by the pre-disaster owner.

Ownership of all other residential and non-residential real estate within the borders of The Community will revert to the ownership of The Community to be used and/or disposed of in any way that is judged to be to the general benefit of The Community as determined by a majority vote of The Council.

In addition to the above, if it is deemed to be in the best interest of The Community, The Council may vote to award ownership or temporary custodianship of a property to one more more Citizens.

14.7. Wages and Initial Distribution of Shares

NOTE: *It is widely believed that any sound form of currency should be based on some durable physical asset such as precious metals. However, very few communities are sitting atop mountains of gold or silver.*

One 'commodity' that all communities do have, however, is the physical potential of their population to actually do work. As a result, this charter is defining critical rules that specify minimum wages. The fundamental unit of value in The Community is the 'Share'. The total number of Shares minted will be regulated so as to preserve their value, and Shares will immediately be distributed to all Citizens of The Community to help jump-start the economy.

This is critical for the survival of The Community, because it will allow commercial activity to resume quickly. **Minting and distributing Shares is the highest priority task in the action lists that accompany this Charter.**

Just as with nations today that produce their own paper bills and metallic coins as currency, the disaster community must print or mint the currency representing it's Shares. Suitable stocks of paper for paper currency and/or metal that can be minted into coins should be identified, as well as the printing devices and metal-stamping and engraving equipment to produce coins. It should also be kept in mind that, if the initial currency or coins are somewhat primitive in appearance, new coins and currency can be produced later to exchange for the originals. (Who would not exchange their old Shares and Mils for new ones if they knew the old ones had a date after which they would become worthless?)

The very survival of the community depends on only a certain quantity of currency being in circulation, and any attempt made at counterfeiting should be met with the harshest of punishments.

The following graduated minimum wage structure is defined to provide a healthy incentive for all workers entering The Community's work force to increase the value they deliver to their employer. If they don't 'work their way up the ladder' in their early years then they will naturally be supplanted by younger workers entering the workforce behind them. The following rules govern the minimum wages that must be paid to anyone performing work within The Community or for any Citizen of The Community:

- All able-bodied and able-minded members of The Community who are 18 years of age or older must be paid no less than one Share for each hour worked.

- Any Citizen who is less than 18 but older than 16 must be compensated at a rate of no less then 700 Mils for each hour worked.

- Any Citizen who is less than 16 but older than 14 must be compensated at a rate no less than 500 Mils for each hour worked.

- No member of The Community who is younger than 14 years of age is permitted to work.

- Anyone who is certified by the Public Health Administrator as not being able-bodied or able-minded can receive special permission to work for a minimum wage that is designated for them by that administrator and approved by The Council.

Any person or organization found to be in violation of minimum wage rules may be required to pay fines as high as 10 times the wages they otherwise would have legitimately paid.

To jump-start the economy within The Community, all working-age Citizens will have distributed to them (or their parent(s) if they are younger than 16 years of age) an 'instant bonus' equal to 2080 hours of minimum wages for their age. The Council will have an additional 9 years of minimum wages for all Citizens minted which it will use to make strategic purchases for purposes of maintaining operations and further stimulating the economy. The total number of Shares will never change thereafter except to adjust for fluctuations in the population of The Community. At a time no sooner than 18 months after The Community is started, or after the initial Community funding is depleted such that 3 months of operating expenses are remaining, The Council will institute some forms of taxation to maintain Community government operations.

NOTE: *It is fully expected that these rules will, over time, be amended - particularly with regard to the compensation of business founders.*

14.8. Compensation of Council Members

Council Members are compensated an amount of 320 Shares for each month they serve in office. This rate is calculated to be approximately twice the minimum wage. This constitutes the total compensation and benefits for participation in The Council. Membership in The Council does not preclude Council members from participating in other income-generating activities. Council members must exercise their own judgment in recusing themselves from Council decisions that are in conflict with any such external income-generating activities.

14.9. Compensation of Community Employees and Consultants

The amount and terms of compensation of anyone employed directly by The Community will be negotiated individually between that employee and the Citizenship Committee.

14.10. Re-Authorization of this Charter

One year after the adoption of this Charter it will automatically expire unless voted into permanence by at least a 75% majority vote of voting-age Citizens. This re-authorization will not include any amendments that have been made to the Charter during that year. The re-authorization of all such amendments will require separate individual votes that must pass by a simple majority vote of all voting-age Citizens.

14.11. Citizen Voting and Election of The Council

Only community members who are 18 years of age or older are qualified to cast any votes within The Community. If an individual's age is questioned by more then 3 voting-age members of The Community then the appointed Public Health Administrator will inspect and interview the individual and declare the individual's age.

Candidates for membership on The Council will be nominated and seconded by all citizens at least one month prior to the election (with the exception of the first Council, which will be nominated and elected on the day that The Community is initially formed). During the month following the nominations the candidates for Council will be able to present the case for their election.

Recognizing the fact that tie votes indicate lack of any clear preference by The Community, all tie votes under all circumstances will be decided by fair coin tosses. This practical and fair approach is used simply as a means to save precious time.

14.12. Organization of Government

The government of The Community will be controlled by a seven-member democratically-elected Council (an odd number of Council members is specified here to avoid tie votes on critical issues). If The Community is of such size that 7 Council candidates cannot be found, then the largest odd number of Council members that can be found will be elected. The Council will be elected on the first day of November of each year (see section 14.11 for details). The exact date of these elections is specified here in order to synchronize the voting across multiple communities, which is intended to facilitate merging of communities. If a Council has not been in place for at least six months then the election will be waived and the term of The Council will be extended for an additional 12 months (the intent of this rule is to avoid two elections in quick succession when The Community first comes into existence or after a no-confidence vote). The Council will meet once each month to consider and implement new and revised laws, with all such laws being subject to the rights of Citizens defined herein.

The election of The Council will first consist of the nomination of candidates. Any voting-age Citizen will qualify to be a candidate if they are nominated by any other voting-age Citizen and that nomination is seconded by a third voting-age Citizen. Each person making or seconding such a nomination is given no more than two minutes to speak on behalf of their nominee. After all nominations have been made and all candidates have been selected a general vote will be conducted in such a way that all votes are cast in secret.

Because there are multiple Council positions being decided by this single vote, each voter may cast as many as 3 votes, with each vote being for a different candidate. If there are fewer than seven nominees then the number of Council members elected will be the 'N' nominees receiving the highest number of votes, where 'N' is the highest odd number less than or equal to the number of nominees.

Once candidates are identified through the nomination process each candidate is allowed, prior to the election, to give a speech of up to five minutes in support of their candidacy.

NOTE: *While a person may not nominate themselves, all members of the group are allowed to speak for up to two minutes to make the case for receiving nominations from others. This rule is intended to allow highly-qualified individuals who are not necessarily known to the group to be given due consideration.*

The Council member receiving the largest number of votes will serve as the President of The Council.

The Council President will be responsible for:

- Presiding over all Council meetings (The Council will have scheduled monthly meetings as well as unscheduled meetings on an as-needed basis, with all such meetings being open to all Citizens).

- Setting the agenda for all Council meetings.

In the event that two or more candidates receive the same number of votes the winner will be decided by a fair coin toss (a coin toss is used, rather than a runoff election, in recognition of the fact that time will be critical).

After elections The Council will determine among themselves which of The Council members will be assigned the roles of:

- *Secretary* - responsible for maintaining minutes of all Council meetings and maintaining a roll-call of all citizens.

- *Treasurer* - responsible for maintaining The Community's money supply and the administration of The Community Store.

The following positions will be filled by a vote of the The Council:

- *Defense Chief* - responsible for the defense of The Community from external human threats. This includes responsibility for defining and maintaining a secure perimeter around The Community, constructing community-defense structures within The Community, training of community members for defensive operations and the gathering and analysis of intelligence information.

- *Chief of Police* - responsible for enforcing the laws adopted within The Community and selecting and training all Community members who will be participating in the community police force.

- *Public Health Administrator* - responsible for defining, implementing and enforcing measures within The Community that help to assure the health of all Citizens. Also responsible for appointing personnel to organize, manage and staff all public utility and sanitation departments.

- *Facilities Manager* - responsible for managing and appraising all developed properties owned by The Community.

- *School Superintendent* - responsible for the organizing and administration of public schools within The Community.

- *Director of Agriculture* - responsible for regulating all agricultural activity within The Community.

- *Community Librarian* - responsible for managing all stores of information that are owned by The Community (in The Community Library) as well as maintaining an accurate Census Record of all Citizens.

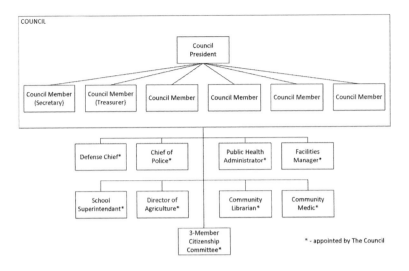

Figure 14.1.: Community Org Chart.

- *Community Medic* - in charge of all medical facilities within The Community. Appointed by the Public Health Administrator subject to approval by The Council. The Community Medic has authority to hire additional personnel for the Community clinic on a probationary basis, subject to final approval by the Public Health Administrator and The Council at the next scheduled regular monthly meeting of The Council.

In a small community it is entirely possible that a single individual may fill multiple roles. FIGURE 14.1 is an org chart that depicts the various elected and appointed positions within The Community. In addition to approving all government employees within The Community, The Council can, at any time and for any reason, terminate the employment of any government employee with a simple majority vote.

14.13. Spontaneous No-Confidence Votes and Re-Elections

A group consisting of at least 65% of all voting-age Citizens can call for a "no-confidence" vote at any time. A no-confidence vote that passes by a 75% majority of the voting-age Citizens will result in the immediate election of a new Council and President.

14.14. The Community Bank

The Community Bank is owned by The Community and consists of location(s) where accounts are tracked and where Share deposits, withdrawals and transfers can be made. Newly minted coins and currency are provided to the Bank to meet these needs, and the Bank is responsible for recording and destroying any worn coins or currency. All fees charged by the Community Bank must be approved by a majority vote of The Council. The Community Bank will be organized and directed by The Community Treasurer and staffed by any personnel appointed by the Treasurer and approved by The Council.

14.15. Licensing of Businesses

No business will operate within The Community without having purchased a license through The Community Bank. Such licenses must be renewed on an annual basis by all businesses. The costs of such licenses, expressed in Shares, will be specified by The Council and may vary based on the maximum number of individuals approved to be employed by the business. The intent of such licensing is not so much to generate revenue as it is a means of tracking and regulating those businesses operating within The Community.

14.16. Education and Child Care

It is required that all members of The Community who are younger than 17 years of age must attend school grades 1-12 (unless they have already completed the curriculum). Citizens or organizations wishing to operate schools must obtain the consent of The Council, which will consider the qualifications and other capabilities of the petitioning entity before granting such authorization.

All children within The Community under the age of thirteen must be subject to the supervision of Citizens 15 years of age or older at all times.

14.17. Public Health

In the interest of public health The Council may require Citizens to temporarily relocate their residence as a means of isolating potentially infectious individuals to prevent the spread of disease. The Council may also require Citizens to obtain specified medical treatments as part of the protocol for returning to the normal routines of their lives. The costs of such treatments shall be born by the Citizen or The Community, as determined by The Council on a per-incident basis.

14.18. Admission of New Citizens to The Community

Families or individuals wishing to join The Community are subject to individual negotiation with the 3-member Citizenship Committee that is appointed by The Council. This committee is authorized to offer terms to any individual or group wishing to join The Community. New Citizens admitted to The Community are subject to a 90-day probationary period after which the Citizenship Committee will either formally induct them into The Community or reject their application (see section 14.28 for a more detailed description of the process for inducting new Citizens). When a citizen is admitted for a probationary period the Community Librarian will add that individual's name and other information to this Census Record, indicating that their status is probationary.

Any individuals who, after their probationary period, are rejected for citizenship will be allowed to make purchases of any goods or services offered by The Community in exchange for any Shares in The Community which they have accumulated during the probationary period. On such rejection the Community Librarian will remove entries for those individuals from the Census Record.

14.19. Departure of Citizens from The Community

Any Citizen in good standing is free to depart and disassociate from The Community at any time. On departure they will lose all rights as Citizens granted within this Charter, but may retain ownership of any Community Shares or other physical property which they own, and may subsequently use their Shares to purchase goods and services from The Community. It is the responsibility of the Community Librarian to remove the entries for each such departing Citizen from the Census Record at the earliest opportune time after (or coincident with) the departure.

14.20. Removing Council Members from Office

Any Council Member convicted of breaking a major law of of The Community will immediately be dropped from The Council, and another Citizen will be appointed by the remaining Council members to replace the dropped member for the duration of that member's term.

An individual Council member may also be so removed from office by a no-confidence vote of 75% of all voting-age Citizens. The procedure for replacing that Council member is the same as if they had been found guilty of willfully and intentionally breaking a law.

14.21. Community Defense and Law Enforcement

The Defense Chief is responsible for the defense of The Community from external human threats. This includes responsibility for defining and maintaining a secure perimeter around The Community, constructing community-defense structures within The Community, training of community members for defensive operations and the gathering and analysis of intelligence information. The guiding principle of The Community defenses is that they should be sufficient to convince any potential aggressor that the cost of overcoming the defenses far outweighs any benefit that will be derived from having done so.

All able-bodied members of The Community 17 or more years of age may be requested by the Defense Chief to volunteer to become part of The Community Defensive Forces and to participate in training, drills and other defense-related activities.

The Chief of Police is responsible for enforcing the laws adopted within The Community and selecting and training all Community members who will be participating in The Community Police Force.

Any compensation for participation in The Community Defensive Forces or The Community Police Force shall be determined by The Council.

14.22. Institution and Publication of Rules and Laws

It is the responsibility of The Council to define and modify all rules and laws that apply to individuals, groups and organizations within The Community. All such laws must be fully consistent with this Charter and passed by The Council with a simple majority vote. Such laws shall be recorded in a Book of Rules and Laws that is maintained by the Community Librarian in The Community Library and made available to all Citizens.

No law or rule put into force within The Community will be specific to any individual or organization. All laws and rules will apply equally to all Citizens and other organizations within The Community.

14.22.1. The Cases for Capital and Corporal Punishment

The Case for Capital Punishment

In a survival Community it is imperative that everyone who consumes The Community's resources also contribute positively to The Community. This is in direct conflict with the notion of incarcerating a criminal around the clock. In fact, not only does that prisoner consume The Community's resources but they also require the time and efforts of members of The Community to provide oversight.

Those individuals who have been found to have committed minor offenses might simply be compelled to perform additional labor each day, however those who have committed the most egregious offenses (and received the harshest punishment) would almost certainly commit future violent acts or attempt to escape, which would further consume The Community's resources.

If the worst offenders were simply banished from The Community then they might very well return in the future to cause additional problems, or otherwise consume resources outside The Community that would be in direct competition with The Community.

So, the case for capital punishment is simply that a Community that is fighting for the survival of those who are innocent cannot afford to risk its survival for the benefit of those who have perpetrated the most serious crimes. Only capital punishment provides the guarantee that they will no longer be a threat to The Community.

The Case for Corporal Punishment

The incarceration of prisoners for even minor offenses consumes the time and resources of any community. This is time and resources that The Community could be using to assure the survival of its Citizens. Additionally, the labor that could be performed by the guilty individual would be lost. If corporal punishment were to be publicly administered, rather than incarceration, then it could act as a strong deterrent to potential future crimes for both the offender as well as any other potential perpetrators who observe the punishment and its effects.

The case can also be made that imprisoning an individual for a major percentage of their life is a far more harsh punishment than the administration of corporal punishment.

14.23. Crime and Punishment

This section provides rules and guidelines for dealing with crimes committed against and within The Community. The punishments prescribed herein reflect the fact that The Community exists during times of dire emergency when the traditional incarceration and maintenance of prisoners is simply impractical. Any community adopting this charter is urged to review and possibly amend these terms based on a majority vote that expresses The Community's own beliefs. Section 14.22.1 of this charter describes the cases in favor of adopting capital and corporal punishment, rather than adopting more traditional punishments such as incarceration. Any changes to this section should be legibly written in ink prior to voting to adopt the charter.

Punishments known as *'Maximum Punishment'*, *'Banishment'* and *'Standard Punishment'* are referenced in various places within this charter. For this community charter these punishments are described as follows:

- *Maximum Punishment* - The maximum punishment to be administered for the most severe crimes committed within and against The Community and its Citizens is capital punishment, with such punishment administered with the most practical and humane means possible.

- *Banishment* - Certain crimes are of such a nature that The Community's best response is to eject the guilty party from The Community.

- *Standard Punishment* - The standard punishment within The Community is *corporal punishment*. Corporal punishment may be carried out against those found guilty of lesser crimes, with the degree of such punishments being proportional to the severity of the crime. Corporal punishment will consist of lashes from a whip administered by a duly authorized member of The Community. The number of lashes administered shall be prescribed by the judge who presided over the trial, and be in accordance with any guidelines that have been set forth by The Council.

NOTE: *At the discretion of The Council the Standard Punishment may be replaced with a monetary fine expressed in community Shares. In such cases the fine must be paid immediately by the guilty party, with the amount of the fine being designated by The Council based on the nature of the case. The amounts of any such fines must be made part of the public record.*

Banishment for Vote Fraud

Anyone found guilty of intentionally corrupting any aspect of the election and voting process will be permanently banished from The Community, with all ownership of community Shares and property transferred to The Community and no remuneration and/or material assistance provided. Such banishment will be immediate following a guilty verdict.

Banishment of Citizens Due to a No-Confidence Vote

Any Citizen who is not a member of The Council may make a report of no-confidence to The Council with regard to any other Citizen. Any Citizen for whom three or more such reports are received (each for different incidents) is subject to a no-confidence vote by The Council. If a super majority of The Council so decides, such individual will be banished from The Community. In this case the banished individual may retain ownership of all Shares and non-fixed property, but all fixed property will revert to the ownership of The Community.

If The Council votes not to banish the individual then the number of no-confidence votes for that individual is set to one, and their status in The Community remains unchanged.

Anyone found by The Council to be abusing the privilege of filing no-confidence votes may, at The Council's discretion, also be subject to a super majority vote for banishment by The Council, with such banishment being subject to the same terms as those described in the preceding paragraphs.

Maximum Punishment for High Crimes

Certain High Crimes are subject to the Maximum Punishment. These crimes are murder, conspiracy, treason, looting, rape, kidnapping and counterfeiting. The severity of this punishment reflects the serious threat that such crimes pose to the survival of the Citizens and The Community. The Community Librarian should remove or update the records for any criminal who is subjected to capital punishment in the Census Record after the punishment has been administered.

Punishments for Bribery

In addition to possible other punishments, any elected or appointed official convicted of accepting bribes in exchange for exercise the influence of their trusted positions, and any Citizen convicted of offering such a bribe, will immediately lose their Citizenship and be banished from The Community. All the property and fixed possessions and community Shares owned by such individuals will be forfeit to The Community.

Penalties for Counterfeiting

Any individual found to be engaged in the counterfeiting of community Shares may be subject to the Maximum Penalty as defined in this Charter. Any external group or community found to be counterfeiting community Shares may, as directed by The Council, be dealt with as though they had launched a physical attack against The Community.

Punishments for Other Crimes

The punishment for other crimes will be the punishment defined in the charter as the *'Standard Punishment'* (see section 14.23). To degree to which the punishment is administered will be determined by the judge presiding over the trial, and in conformance with any applicable guidelines that have been provided by The Council.

14.24. Grievance Resolution

During each monthly Council meeting the opportunity is given for any Citizen to petition The Council with grievances against The Community or against other Citizens. If a majority of The Council agrees with the grievance, then a court will be authorized to formally hear and adjudicate the grievance. Such courts consist of the plaintiff and the accused and their representatives (or, in the case that the grievance is against The Community, the accused is represented by a Council member who is not directly affected by the case). The Council will also appoint a Citizen to serve as judge for the case, with said judge compensated as designated by The Council. In such cases the verdict of the judge is considered final. Judges may also assess fines against any party for filing a redundant or frivolous claim, or for any word or deed which is deemed by the judge to be an assault, threat or slander against the court.

> **NOTE:** *Grievances may include any challenge to the compatibility of any law or rule with this Charter.*

14.25. Re-Integration and Merging of Communities

In the case of a merger with another community based on this or a similar charter, The Council positions for the merged community will be filled through a simple, single coin toss between each pair of counterparts on The Council from each community, with one of each pair flipping the coin and the second calling *'heads or tails'*. Once established, the new council will be free to reassign all appointed positions at its discretion. Those council members displaced by the merger will be entitled to a paid position within the new community (determined by the new council) that compensates them at 150% of the rate of pay they were receiving for participating on The Council, with such employment to extend for a period of two years (this 150% is intended as a *'golden parachute'* to help provide the assurance that transitions of power go smoothly).

In the case that normal rule of law is re-established by legitimate authorities The Community may be disbanded by a super majority vote of The Council members. Immediately after such vote, and before the disbanding is consummated, all items in The Community store will be auctioned to members of The Community.

Any merger between The Community and any other community or government must take into account The community Shares owned by Citizens. One simple resolution to this matter is to allow both currencies to exist for a prescribed period with a conversion rate defined between them. During that assimilation period new Shares in the merged community can be minted and exchanged for the currency being obsoleted.

14.26. Amendment of this Charter

This Charter may be amended only by a super majority vote of The Council, and such vote must first be proposed and seconded by Citizens of The Community as part of a regular monthly meeting. The vote itself may be conducted during the course of that meeting or may be deferred by The Council until the subsequent monthly meeting.

14.27. Oaths

14.27.1. Citizen Oath

Any new Citizen being admitted to The Community must take the following oath:

"I _____ do solemnly and freely pledge my loyalty to the _____ Community and declare my unqualified support for its governing Charter. I pledge to do my best to defend The Community at all times, and to work diligently for the benefit of myself, my family and The Community."

14.27.2. Oath for Officers:

Any Council member or other full- or part- time employee of The Community being inducted into office must take the following oath:

"I _____ do solemnly and freely pledge to uphold the Charter of the _____ Community, to commit myself to the betterment of the condition of all Citizens of The Community, and to discharge the duties and responsibilities of my office to the greatest extent of my abilities throughout the term of my employment."

14.28. Induction of New Citizens

The Citizenship Committee is responsible for interviewing and vetting all prospective new citizens for The Community, as well as for negotiating any terms for acceptance. These terms could include incentive payments in the case of individuals with skills that are much-needed, as well as purchase prices for items that these prospects are bringing into The Community.

The initial vetting process includes an interview of the newcomer(s) by the Committee as well as an initial assessment of their mental and physical worthiness to contribute to The Community. Based on this initial vetting the Committee may elect to reject them immediately or to grant probationary Citizen status to them.

All newcomers will be assigned an escort who will be responsible for spending time with them during their 90-day probationary period as directed by the Committee. The time, schedule and any compensation for the escort will be determined by the Committee on a case-by-base basis. The purposes of the escort are:

- To provide the newcomer(s) with orientation to The Community, and to provide introductions to other Community members.

- To monitor the newcomer for any signs that they may not be positive additions to The Community (including any observations of substance abuse, negative personality traits, lawless behavior, inability to accomplish tasks, health issues, etc.).

- To possibly gain some of the skills and/or knowledge from the newcomer for the general enrichment of The Community.

- To provide reports, as requested by the Citizenship Committee, regarding the worthiness of the newcomer to become a fully vested Citizen.

Once the probationary period has passed the newcomer will be scheduled to appear with their escort before the Citizenship Committee and the Community Librarian. The Committee will receive the recommendation of the escort and consider the case. If the newcomers are granted full citizenship in The Community then, after they have been administered the Oath of Citizenship (see section 14.27) the Community Librarian will update the citizen Census Record accordingly.

14.29. Valuation Guide for the Community Appraiser

The Community Appraiser is the member of the Citizenship Committee who is responsible for appraising the value of all tangible assets (including physical property). With such a wide scope of responsibility the job may seem daunting to anyone faced with this task. This section is intended to provide the Community Appraiser with some guidelines and suggestions that may make the responsibility less challenging.

It is suggested here that the appraised value of an item be calculated as the product of the pre-disaster value of the items multiplied times a *community need factor* that is determined on a case-by-case basis by the Community Appraiser. Considering that the value of a community Share is intended to be a *living minimum wage*, which prior to the disaster might have been approximately $15.00/hour (US), then the pre-disaster value expressed in community Shares might be calculated as the pre-disaster value in US dollars divided by 15 (of course the $15.00/hour living wage may change through inflation by the time this book is needed).

As an example, consider the case of a prospective newcomer wishing to enter the Community and bringing with them a shotgun with a pre-disaster value of $300. The Community Appraiser would use the same type of calculation as was used above to determine an appropriate appraised value. In this case maybe the need factor is 2.5, so the offered price for the shotgun would be ($300/15) Shares times 2.5 = 50 Shares.

This same type of calculation can be applied to anything being appraised (including real estate).

Alternate Approach to Appraising Values

In some cases a different approach might be employed for appraising the value of items. Given a pre-disaster living wage for an adult of $15/hour, the Community Appraiser might estimate the number of 8-hour days such a worker would be willing to work to purchase the item. If the answer is 1.5 days, then the appraised value of the item in question might be calculated as 1.5 * 8.0 hrs/day * 1 Share/hour = 12 Shares.

14.30. The Case for a Strong Defense Establishment

Inevitably there will be debates on the amount of public funds to expend for defense. When this discussion arises it is important that the following point be considered. If The Community is forcibly overrun by some other group then the value of all Shares owned by all Citizens, as well as all their personal property, disappears. With a strong defense establishment such attempts may be repelled or, in other cases, there may be a controlled merger of the two communities (see section 14.25) that preserves property and Share values.

14.31. The Case for Aggressive Expansion and Annexation

The decision to expand The Community should be driven primarily by security and survival concerns. Reasons to expand include:

- To make The Community more defensible (for example, by expanding to include choke points where access to The Community can be better monitored and controlled, or by expanding to move inhabited homes outside of normal gun range).

- To provide additional land for the growing of crops and the raising of livestock.

- To add additional commercial or manufacturing facilities that may either be critical to the survival of The Community or which may help to stimulate The Community's economy.

The cost of expansion is almost certainly going to be least during the time immediately following the disaster, when those affected will be most anxious to join The Community in exchange for increased security. **Hence it is incumbent on The Community to, at the earliest possible time, define its policy with regard to expansion and annexation of territory and act on that policy.**

Such expansion of The Community may often affect others who occupy territory being annexed by The Community. When this is the case every effort should be made by The Community to entice such affected individuals to join The Community. When such annexation is resisted by the affected parties, The Council should decide whether an involuntary annexation is to be pursued or perhaps to the annex property surrounding the affected parties, and to exclude the affected parties from all benefits of Community membership.

Reasonable offers of community Shares should be considered as one possible means of peacefully inducing individuals who resist annexation.

14.32. Master Action Lists

The section defines a list of tasks to be performed to quickly stand up The Community. These startup tasks are organized into 3 distinct phases, with each phase initiated at a public Council meeting. Many of these tasks may require the effort of multiple contributors, who may be selected directly by the Council or who may be selected by The Council's appointees. While the Council normally meets on a monthly basis, these first three meetings will be held on an as-ready basis.

Phase 1 - Define the Leadership, Get Organized and Begin Establishing a New Economy

- Convene all members of The Community, take nominations for Council members, and elect The Council. The Council will be those seven (or highest odd number of available) candidates with the greatest number of votes, with the President of The Council being The Council member with the greatest number of votes. (When voting for Council members all Citizens are allowed to vote for as many as 3 candidates.)

- The Council conducts interviews and votes among themselves to appoint the Defense Chief, the Chief of Police, the Public Health Administrator, the Facilities Manager, the Community Librarian, the Treasurer, the School Superintendent and the Director of Agriculture. The Council should also appoint the members of a 3-member 'Citizenship Committee', and have that committee designate one member to be the Community Appraiser (the one full-time working position within the committee, which involves appraising values for any and all physical assets, tracking ownership of all residential and commercial real estate and determining wages for government employees).

- Identify a location for The Community Store (the location should have accommodations for climate-controlled storage and refrigeration if possible. If not, then work should be started on constructing root cellars for longer-term storage of perishable items. The location should feature a large vacant lot where larger assets (trailers, etc.) might be stored. Establishing cool/cold storage should be treated as an urgent priority.

> **NOTE:** *Even tropical or sub-tropical environments may be able to provide natural cool storage with some ingenuity (for example, the spring-fed waters of Central Florida can be quite cool).*

- Identify a location for The Community Bank and equip the bank with furniture and provisions necessary to perform its function. This should include ledgers of accounts, etc. (Initially all record keeping should be done using pen and paper, and not electronically).

- The Treasurer should be tasked to begin developing a means to mint coins or print paper currency that represent Shares and Mils, as well as developing recommendations for reasonable fees for business licenses (with such fees requiring approval from The Council).

- The School Superintendent should be tasked to begin developing an Education Plan for the community school system, and enlist members of The Community to identify supporting textbooks and curriculums. Emphasis should be placed on basic reading, writing and arithmetic skills as well as history, philosophy, agriculture and home economics. The Superintendent should present regular school system status reports to The Council during its regularly scheduled monthly meetings.

- The Public Heath Administrator should be tasked to begin developing a Water Plan for The Community that identifies both immediate and future sources of water for all Citizens. He/she should also begin to develop a community Sanitation Plan and basic sanitation guidelines to be distributed to all Citizens.

- The Facilities Manager is responsible for the care and maintenance of all properties owned by The Community.

- The Pubic Health Administrator should be tasked to interview candidates for the position of Community Medic.

- The Defense Chief should be tasked to begin developing a Defense Plan for The Community. This plan should include recommendations for Citizen participation in the defense system, plans for regular training, plans for equipping defenders, and recommendations and rationale for facilities and locations to be reserved for defense-related purposes. This plan should also include a plan for expansion of The Community through annexation, community mergers and other means, including detailed rationale for such expansion (see section 14.31).

  The Defense Chief should also purchase all firearms and ammunition from those Citizens willing to sell them for community Shares.

- The Chief of Police should be tasked to begin developing a Community Policing Plan for The Community (local law enforcement and patrolling). This plan should include recommendations for Citizen participation, training and equipment, and recommendations and rationale for facilities and locations (e.g. detainment facilities) to be used for internal security purposes (including detainment of criminals and suspects prior to trial).

- The Community Librarian should be tasked to begin developing a Library Plan for the acquisition, storage and tracking of Community information, including selecting a location to serve as The Community Library.

  The Community Librarian should also develop a master list of all citizens (the Census Record), including names, dates of birth, living address and other contact information. This record should include address information as well as the date the citizen joined The Community (which for the initial list will be the date The Community was created). Depending on anticipated amount of work required to develop the initial Census Record, the Community Librarian may temporarily hire other Citizens to assist with that task.

- The Director of Agriculture should start by immediately assigning one or (preferably) more individuals to the tasks of growing sweet potatoes, raising chickens, raising rabbits and harvesting any nuts that grow locally. Once these assignments are made, the Director should begin developing an Agriculture Plan, which should include:

  - Identifying additional staff that will be needed to support the Director.

  - Describing how the Director is going to work with and support local farmers.

  - Identifying additional Community-owned land and facilities that may be needed.

  - Detailing plans for the Community itself growing, raising and otherwise acquiring (e.g. hunting and fishing) food supplies.

  - Detailing plans for regulating hunting within The Community such that food resources are not over-harvested.

  - Describing any special needs for the raising, harvesting, processing and storing of food grown within The Community.

Phase 2: Institute Community Controls and Review Plans Appointed Officials

- The Defense Chief should be tasked to establish security checkpoints for all roads leading into The Community and to assign firearms and ammunition as necessary. If possible all such checkpoints should be manned by at least two trained personnel and provided cover by a trained and preferably-concealed sniper. These checkpoints should ideally be located at least 1.5 miles from any habitation that is within the DRC.

- The Pubic Health Administrator should be tasked to review the collected Community food stores and develop a Food Rationing Plan for The Community. Additionally, he/she should identify a location to serve as The Community's clinic.

- The Citizenship Committee should be tasked to identify a location (preferably near The Community Store) for processing Citizenship petitions, to establish a schedule for regular meetings, and to appoint the 'Community Appraiser' role to a member of their committee. This appraiser will be responsible for assessing valuations for tangible property, tracking ownership of all residential and commercial real estate and setting wages for all government employees. The Community Appraiser should occupy the Citizenship Committee facility every day during regular work hours (unless working afield in that capacity), as assessments will be in high demand (see section 14.29 for guidelines for the appraisal process).

- The Council should meet with the Public Health Administrator to define revisions for the Water and Sanitation Plans and to vote to approve The Community Medic that has been recommended by the administrator.

- The Council should meet with the Community Librarian to revise and approve the Library Plan.

- The Council should meet with the Treasurer to approve the plan for minting coins and printing currency, as well as to review and approve any business licensing fees and policies recommended by the Treasurer.

- The Council should meet with the Defense Chief to review and approve the Defense Plan.

- The Council should meet with the Chief of Police to review and approve the Community Policing Plan.

- The Council should meet with the Director of Agriculture to review and approve the Agriculture Plan.

- The Council should meet with the School Superintendent to review and approve the Education Plan.

Phase 3: First Regular Council Meeting to Review Progress

- The Council should meet with the Public Health Administrator to define revisions for the Food Rationing Plan.

- The Public Health Administrator should report on progress putting the Sanitation and Water Plans into action.

- The Community Medic should report progress on establishing the community clinic, report progress in defining the standard practices and identify supplies and personnel needed by the clinic.

- The Community Librarian should report on the status of putting the Library Plan into action.

- The Defense Chief should report on the progress of putting the Defense Plan into action and should begin discussing a plan for physically expanding The Community (and possibly merging with other communities) in such as way as to reduce the threat from external sources (this plan should be reviewed by The Council in subsequent meetings, revised and put into action).

- The Chief of Police should report on progress in putting the Community Policing Plan into action.

- The Treasurer should report on the status of the plan for minting coins, printing currency, and supplying the coins and currency to the Community Bank.

- The next regular monthly Council meeting should be scheduled.

15. Next Steps

"Do the difficult things while they are easy
and do the great things while they are small.
A journey of a thousand miles
must begin with a single step."

-Lao Tzu

STRAIGHT THINKING: *The time is now to begin carefully initiating communications with others, developing your disaster plan, and obtaining the food and supplies your plan calls for. If you aren't already, this is also the time to begin working to improve your health and fitness and acquiring new skills that will allow you to generate income in a post-disaster economy.*

Having read this book you should have good knowledge of a broad range of important survival topics and many solutions to the challenges that will be posed by any major disaster. Closing the back cover and placing it on the shelf is not an end however, **but rather a beginning**. When it comes to survival, "thinking" must be accompanied by **taking action**! The tasks ahead include:

- **Working to Become more Fit and Healthy** - adopting a sensible, long-term diet and exercise program can make the difference between life and death.

- **Planning** - developing a General Disaster Plan and Site Plans (see Chapter 3).

- **Personal Networking** - cautiously and gradually attempting to bring friends and family members on-board the prepping bandwagon.

- **Continuing to Gear Up** - obtaining the food and gear identified in your disaster plans.

419

- **Learning** - gaining additional knowledge in strategically selected subject areas.

- **Diversifying your Personal Economy** - starting or becoming part of a business that will be in demand in the aftermath of a major disaster.

- **Community Building** - becoming part of a broader community with others who share common interests and concerns regarding disaster preparedness.

15.1. Working to Become more Fit and Healthy

If physically-demanding times lay ahead, then now is the time to begin to prepare your body to be able to better deal with that reality. Many adults have become so accustomed to luxuries of civilized life such as air conditioning and automobiles that the sudden loss of those luxuries could be disastrous. **Now** is the time to become tougher and more self-sufficient. Even the most modest diet and exercise program performed regularly can greatly improve your chances for survival. **Working on health and fitness is the most important thing that a prepper can do, and it does not require any budget or storage space.**

15.2. Planning

Imagine how impossible it would be to develop a disaster plan when the disaster is already taking place all around you! Conversely, if your disaster plans are ready for action then you can begin acting immediately and channelling your nervous energy in a constructive (and potentially life-saving) direction!

When disaster does strike you must already have your plans prepared. Chapter 3 describes developing both a *General Disaster Plan* and one or more *Site Plans*, and the information needed for each. As with becoming physically prepared, disaster planning is also an activity that can require very little budget or storage space.

15.3. Personal Networking

When it comes to prepping, communicating with others is a sensitive issue that deserves thoughtful consideration. One thing you can be certain of is that, if word of your preparations goes public, there are going to be individuals who simply state that **their** disaster plan will be to come pay you an extended visit. Others will state (half in jest and half in deadly seriousness) that their plan is simply going to be to *"shoot him and take his stuff"*.

Even in the face of these risks there are good reasons that you may need to confide in others with regard to your preparations:

- They are close family members that you are planning to protect.

- They play a key role in your plans.

- They have critical skills, equipment or knowledge that you may need as part of your own plans.

- You are certain that you and they have very similar interests in preparing, and that exchanging information will be in your mutual best interests.

In the US military a person is only provided with access to protected information if they have **both** an adequate security clearance level and a 'need to know' that information. You might adopt a similar approach yourself, replacing the 'security clearance' criteria with a 'trustworthiness' criteria (e.g. 'Is an individual trustworthy and is there a strong case for making them aware of your preparations?'). In this case being 'trustworthy' simply means you are certain that they have the ability to maintain confidentiality with regard to any sensitive information you choose to share with them.

You should also consider the *degree* to which you are willing to share information. For example, you may confide in someone that you are "studying disaster preparedness", while with others you may share details about your preparations.

If those you wish to confide in are not themselves preppers then you should be prepared to be patient and gradual in your communications with them. You might start by expressing some concerns with the news of the day and events unfolding elsewhere in the world (and in *"countries not unlike our own!"*). You might also mention events that have transpired elsewhere in recent history (e.g. the Nazis taking over Germany, or the fact that now-desolate cities around the world were once sought-after vacation spots). You might characterize prepping as *"just another form of insurance - and a cheap one at that!"*.

Limit the amount of information you share with others such that it is proportionate to the degree to which your message resonates with them. If they express only minor concern then you might tell them that you are only putting back a little food *"just in case"* or that you are only doing your *"due diligence"*. You might mention that you are *"... only playing catch-up with the Joneses down the street, who may not be preppers but are much better prepared than me!"*. As time passes, and they have the opportunity to think things through, you may find that those with whom you have these discussions become ready for more details.

15.4. Becoming a "Jack of all Trades ..."

There is an old saying that reads *"Jack of all trades, master of none."*, which is intended to describe the many among us who know "a lot about a lot" but have not attained total mastery in any one area. The prepper should adopt a variation of this philosophy, *"Jack of all trades, master of one"*.

In the aftermath of a major disaster those who survive are going to do so because they became part of survival communities. Those communities are going to be looking for members who bring specific skills to the table. Consequently, the modern prepper should be gaining a good, broad spectrum of knowledge while also pursuing one or more areas of specialized knowledge that will make them indispensable to a survival community.

15.5. Gaining New Knowledge

While this book attempts to cover the full scope of disaster preparedness, the breadth of the subject does not allow it to go into total detail on many topics. For example, while gardening and nutrition is covered, this book does not totally identify the crops that can be grown in various geographic regions. Hence, it is important that you obtain additional sources of information - particularly with regard to your specific location and the role that you imagine yourself filling in a post-disaster world. If you imagine yourself providing security services, then you need additional references that will provide you with greater details on weapons, alarm systems, night vision, structural reenforcement, guard dogs and all other aspects of security. If you imagine yourself providing communications services then you'll need similar additional details on communications systems and protocols.

NOTE: *This book should serve as the foundation of a broader disaster-preparedness library. If you plan on relying on electronic books then be certain that you have a power source that can enable you to gain access to them in a grid-down situation (as an example the company SolarFocus, Inc. - http://www.solarmio.com/en/ - offers a solar-powered carrying case for the Amazon Kindle e-book reader).*

15.6. Diversifying your Personal Economy

In a post-disaster economy there are some goods and services that will experience greater demand. Examples include sewing and leather work, mechanic and auto repair services, security services, plumbing, agricultural feed supplies, and handyman and general repair services. If you can start such a business then you may find yourself able to weather even the longest-term disaster.

Keep in mind that it is not necessary to actually **do** all these things yourself - you could simply have the tools needed by a mechanic who works for you, and maybe plan to pay yourself to work scheduling appointments and ordering and picking up parts. You might even be a 'silent investor' who simply takes in the profit.

15.7. Community Building

Many preppers subscribe to the philosophy that it is better to keep to themselves than to become part of a larger community. In the event of a major disaster these preppers are going to face some harsh realities. A small group that cannot secure a land area that keeps the occupants substantially out of shooting range is going to be a group that lives under constant stress. Similarly, a small group will be challenged to guard its provisions "twenty-four by seven".

For the many preppers who see the advantages to strength in numbers it becomes important to begin the community-building process as early as possible. In some cases these communities will take the form of individuals who do not live clustered together in one neighborhood, but who anticipate finding ways to come together in the aftermath of disaster. In other cases a small town could become a survival community. Probably smaller towns with populations between 5,000 and 10,000 would be well-suited, as towns of this size have a sufficient population to discharge the full range of duties that will be required, while also being small enough that *'everyone knows everyone'*. Communities of such a size will also inevitably have some forms of infrastructure that might be useful in jump-starting a local economy if it becomes necessary.

The prepper's goal in becoming part of a survival community is to transition from a condition of gradually diminishing stored resources to becoming a member of a secure, self-contained and self-sustaining community that is capable of surviving and possibly even thriving.

> **NOTE:** *Imagine a group of decent and caring people who already know one another and share strong bonds, and who have formed a community that may already have some modest infrastructure - possibly including a building with common gathering areas, a kitchen, some land and maybe even a basketball hoop. This is a description of a group of people who, even with modest means, have a strong chance of survival.*
>
> *It is also a description of tens of thousands of churches!*

15.8. Continuing to Gear Up and Build Your Stores

It is necessary that you not only gain knowledge in disaster preparedness, but also that you acquire the supplies and gear designated in your plans. This step can be a difficult one to take because you are now parting with *'green money'* to prepare for a disaster that is not necessarily well-defined and which may not even take place. (And which you **HOPE** will never take place!)

However, food and equipment acquisition is no different than buying fire insurance for your home, and should be considered in much the same way. There are certain potential situations that you are willing to expend money to avoid.

Also, when acquiring your preps, do keep in mind that you may have the option to resell many of them in the future - with some actually appreciating in value. Guns, ammunition and gun accessories are examples of preparedness items that can preserve their value (and probably even grow in value). Indeed, many aspects of prepping could very well be considered as being akin to a savings program.

Other preparedness items may be dual use and may contribute in a positive way to your daily life in addition to providing great value in the event of a long-term disaster. Building a smokehouse for smoking and curing meat is one example, as is filling your cupboard with a substantial supply of canned foods which you can and should consume (and replenish) as part of your normal routine. Another great example of preparedness gear that can enhance your pre-disaster life is a high-quality gravity-fed water filter.

Some equipment you will simply have to write off as insurance against that worst-case scenario. The following are some suggestions for additional items you should consider procuring:

- *Solar Oven* - Can be used to heat food after the supply of cooking fuel is exhausted.

- *Emergency LED Flashlights* - Rugged LED flashlights with a brightness of at least 180 lumens are an excellent general-purpose survival tool. The 180 lumen brightness is sufficient to visually disable an attacker at close range.

- *Portable One-Room Air Conditioner* - During a grid-down situation running an air conditioner in a single room for even just one or two hours per day can provide important relief from heat.

- *Electrical Generator* - A generator can provide a source of power for a small air conditioner or other small appliances on a limited basis during the initial (and probably most dangerous) phase of a major disaster.

- *Leather Boots* - The biggest reason to have rugged footwear is not so much for walking over rough terrain, but more importantly to provide the assurance that your footware won't wear out during the course of a multi-year disaster. (NOTE: While many leather boots made for construction workers feature built-in steel toe guards, this feature may not be desirable for a general-purpose daily-wear boot.) Ebay (http://ebay.com/) is an excellent place to find good deals on overstocked boots and discounted boots with minor cosmetic defects.

- *Stackable Plastic Container Bins* - In the preparedness community there is much talk of *'bug out bags'* that are used to carry emergency provisions when traveling by foot. However, many evacuations will be by vehicle, which presents the opportunity to carry a larger quantity of food and gear. Large, inexpensive, stackable plastic container bins not only can provide additional protections for food stores, but are easily moved and stacked in a vehicle prior to evacuation. Even in non-evacuation scenarios these bins offer some nice benefits for protecting stores and conserving storage space.

- *Survival Knives* - Good survival knives are tools that can be useful in a variety of ways during a disaster. The *'USMC fighting knife'* is a good mid-sized survival knife, and the *'Becker BK7'* is a good example of a large, heavy-duty survival knife (this knife is heavy enough to clear brush). The biggest decision to make when selecting a survival knife is whether to obtain one made of regular or stainless steel. Regular steel knives sharpen better and more easily, while stainless steel knives are not subject to corrosion when exposed to salt water.

- *Paracord* - Paracord (also referred to as *'550 paracord'* or simply *'550 cord'* due to it's rated weight capacity of 550 lbs.) is a thin, multi-strand, multi-purpose nylon rope originally used as parachute cord during World War II. It is known as a good general-purpose line that can be adapted to many useful purposes in a survival situation.

- *Fire Starters* - Fire starters provide an alternate means of quickly starting a fire in the event that matches or lighters are not available.

- *Medium-Gauge Wire* - Used to build defensive barriers.

- *Household and Mechanic's Tools* - Useful to repair equipment as well as for barter.

- *Propane Cook Stove and Fuel Cannisters* - Provides a backup means of cooking in a grid-down scenario.

- *CB Radios with SSB and Channel-Scanning Features* - For learning about local road conditions and possible security hazards.

- *Dehydrated Sponges* - For personal hygiene.

- *Dry Lime* - To treat human waste when it is buried or otherwise disposed of (see section 9.3.2).

- *Granular Calcium Hypochlorite* - To make bleach for water purification and other purposes (see section 4.10.2 - requires special handling and storage).

Other recommended gear includes:

- Emergency Radio

- Radio Scanner

- First Aid Kit

- Antibiotic Ointment

- Regular and Antibacterial Soap

- Guns and Ammunition

- Multi-compartment Backpacks

- Hand-held 2-way Radios

- Road Emergency Kit

15.9. Recommended Prepping Information Sources

- **Books:**

  - *Where There is No Doctor* - The information in this book will enable you to begin to care for those with injuries and illness until they can receive attention from trained medical professionals (as well as to recognize when they need such attention).

– *Ditch Medicine: Advanced Field Procedures For Emergencies* - This book provides specific details on treating the types of traumatic injuries that are found on the battlefield and during major disasters.

– *Where There is No Dentist* - The information contained in this book will allow you to possibly avoid or alleviate some dental problems, and to recognize when a problem may require attention from a dental professional.

– *Nurse's Drug Guide* or *Nurse's Pocket Drug Guide*- **Excellent** references on a broad range of medications, their usages and dosages.

– *The Farmer's Handbook* - This very-old-but-excellent farmer's reference (published in 1912) is available as a free download on the Internet. It is well-written and contains a wealth of still-relevant information pertaining to all aspects of growing crops and raising livestock.

- **Video Resources:**

   – *After Armageddon (http://www.youtube.com/watch?v=R8rYaPfFLgo)* - This is a 90-minute video produced by the History Channel that is believed by the author to best represent the type of disaster scenario and dangers anticipated in this book. All readers are encouraged to watch this and discuss it with others who may be interested. As of this printing it is available online.

   – *ThePatriotNurse's YouTube Channel (http://www.youtube.com/user/ThePatriotNurse)* - The Patriot Nurse's videos on YouTube provide a wealth of information on disaster-related health and medical care.

   – *The Nutnfancy YouTube Channel (http://www.youtube.com/user/nutnfancy)* - Excellent reviews of a wide range of preparedness gear, with an emphasis on guns and knives.

   – *The Southern Prepper YouTube Channel (http://www.youtube.com/user/southernprepper1)* - A YouTube channel with a focus on the human element of prepping.

   – *The Paladin Press YouTube Channel (http://www.youtube.com/user/PaladinPress)* - A YouTube channel that provides good information related to practical self-defense.

- **Web Sites and Blogs:**

  – *American Preppers Network (http://americanpreppersnetwork.com/)* - A US-based national organization of preppers with groups that meet throughout the US and an online community where prepping topics are discussed in depth.

  – *SurvivalBlog.com (http://survivalblog.com/)* - A well-known blog that contains a wealth of articles on every aspect of disaster preparedness.

  – *The Urban Survival Skills Blog (http://get-urban-survival-skills.blogspot.com/)* - A great collection of preparedness-related articles.

  – *The Survival Mom Blog (http://thesurvivalmom.com/)* - A blog that presents preparedness from a woman's perspective.

  – *The SHTF Plan Blog (http://www.shtfplan.com/)* - A preparedness blog that presents today's news from a prepper's perspective

  – *The SurvivalTopics Blog (http://survivaltopics.com/)* - A survival blog with an excellent collection of articles on outdoor survival.

The serious prepper is strongly encouraged to obtain and/or visit these excellent references and resources to compliment the information contained here.

AUTHOR'S NOTE: *My goal in writing this book has been to distill and share hard-won knowledge with the prepper (particularly the novice prepper) such that they can immediately begin building on this knowledge and contributing back to the prepper community. Through this process we all become as prepared as we can be as quickly as possible - prepared to become new people who are ready to live, and eventually perhaps even thrive, in the very different world that confronts us all.*

A. An Example General Disaster Plan ("GDP")

> **NOTE:** *This document is a General Disaster Plan ('GDP') for the (fictitious) Morris family of Tampa, Florida.*

The information contained in this General Disaster Plan applies to everyone at all locations that are or may be occupied by members of the extended Morris family during or in the aftermath of a major disaster.

In addition to this general plan, each site has a more detailed Site Plan. Each individual at each location should have a copy of the this GDP in addition to a copy of all Site Plans. This will better enable everyone to render assistance to other group members if they experience difficulties while traveling between sites.

A *chain of authority* is defined such that, even if the group leader becomes incapacitated or otherwise unavailable, the next acting group leader is pre-defined. Only the group leader is able to declare a disaster and declare the alert level. If a particular site is out of communication with other sites then the individual at that site who is highest on the chain of authority will assume the role of group leader at that site until communications are re-established.

Alert levels are important to both the GDP and the Site Plans because certain tasks are contingent on the alert level. Table A.1 identifies the alert levels and the criteria for declaring each.

Table A.2 provides a comprehensive list of contacts, along with addresses, phone numbers and optional additional notes for each.

Alert Level	Description
Level 0	No alert - all is normal
Level 1	Maintain heightened awareness, perform reasonable preparations
Level 2	Major societal disruption expected for less than 1 week
Level 3	Major societal disruption for 1-2 week
Level 4	Major societal disruption for 2-4 weeks
Level 5	Major societal disruption for 4-8 weeks
Level 6	Major societal disruption for longer than 8 weeks

Table A.1.: Disaster Alert Levels.

A.1. Chain of Authority

The chain of authority for the Morris family, with highest authority appearing on top, is:

- John Morris Sr.
- Betty Morris
- Mark Morris.

For any site covered by the GDP the available individual on this list who is highest in this chain of authority is the group leader. The group leader is responsible for assuring that the disaster plans are followed as well as for declaring disasters and alert levels.

A.2. Supplies and Equipment Needed

In addition to any supplies and equipment specified in the site plan for a particular site, it is important for all sites to have certain basic supplies on hand in advance of any disaster. These supplies include:

- Water Bottles
- 10 MREs per person (or other portable foods)
- Emergency Flashlight
- Propane cook stove with propane cylinders
- First Aid Kit
- Standard Bugout Bag

- N95 Face Masks

- Duct Tape

- Regular Unscented Household Bleach

- Blankets or Sleeping Bags

- Non-electric Can Opener

- Non-electric Clock or other Timepiece

- Old-fashioned Analog Plug-in Phone

- Important Family Business Documents (birth certificates, deeds, car titles, etc).

- Card Decks and/or Board Games

- Candles

- Large Boxes of Wooden Matches

- Propane Tank(s) for Grill (if there is a propane grill at the location)

- Portable Radio

- Assortment of Batteries (for radios, and other critical electronic devices)

- Stockpile of Medications

- Whistles

- Plastic Trash Bags

- Heavy Gloves and Shoes/Boots

- Bathroom Tissue and Various other Needed Toiletries

- Paper Plates and Plastic Forks, Spoons, Knives

- Road Flares

- Emergency Traffic Signalling Reflectors

- Car-battery-powered Tire Inflater

- Spare Tire, Lug Wrench and Car Jack for each Evacuation Vehicle

- General Tool Box

- Road Atlas for the State and Surrounding States

A. An Example General Disaster Plan ("GDP")

Name	Phone	Address	Radio Chan./Freq.
Tallahassee Police	813-555-1001		
Tampa Police	812-555-1012		
Ocala Police	715-555-1722		
George Watts	715-555-1325	1902 Briarcrest, Ocala, FL	CB channel 15
John Morris	813-555-1212	75 Hickory LN, Gainesville, FL	
Betty Morris	613-555-3312	221 Orange Blvd, Tampa, FL	CB channel 15
Mark Morris	623-555-3312	221 Branch Raines Rd., Orlando, FL	CB channel 15

Table A.2.: Emergency Contacts

A.3. Disaster Communications

Good communications are extremely important during and in the aftermath of a major disaster. In addition to providing vital information regarding weather and disaster relief information, radio communications is important for effective community defense as well as for staying aware of the local security situation.

A.3.1. Communications Guidelines

To the greatest extent possible, and unless preempted by overriding considerations, the following rules governing disaster communications should be adhered to by all members of the group:

- Emergency radio channels are always monitored by all groups between 9pm - 10pm ET each evening.

- CB channel 15 is used as the general communications channel by all members of the group.

- Group members should periodically identify themselves with the code words 'Bravo Tango'.

- *'Ten-codes'* (see the next section) should be used when communicating with other group members by radio.

- Unnecessary radio communications should be avoided.

A.3.2. 'Ten Codes' for Disaster Communications

To facilitate communications and provide greater security when communicating using un-encrypted radios, a series of *ten-codes* has been defined that should be used for radio communications during a disaster. These codes have been organized into the following groups of 10:

- *0 thru 9* - Communication status

- *10 thru 19* - Routine activities

- *20 thru 29* - Informational

- *30 thru 39* - Personnel movement

- *40 thru 49* - Internal incidents

- *50 thru 59* - Equipment breakdown

- *60 thru 69* - Medical alerts

- *70 thru 79* - Security alerts

- *80 thru 89* - Incursions

- *90 thru 99* - Tactical maneuvers

With the exception of the first four code words, the following group-specific *'ten-codes'* are consistent with the numeric classifications listed above and have been defined to facilitate and help secure radio communications within the group:

- *Code Black* - Declaration of dire emergency

- *Code Red* - Declaration of a high alert condition

- *Code Yellow* - Declaration a suspicious or abnormal situation

- *Code Green* - Declaration that an emergency condition has been resolved

- *10-2* - Stand by for update

- *10-4* - General acknowledgement

- *10-6* - Experiencing technical difficulties

- *10-7* - Going offline briefly

- *10-8* - Going offline for a prolonged period

- *10-9* - Request escalation to leadership

A. An Example General Disaster Plan ("GDP")

- *10-10* - Restroom break
- *10-11* - Rest break
- *10-12* - Food break
- *10-13* - In meeting
- *10-20* - All is normal
- *10-21* - News item to note
- *10-22* - News item to escalate to leadership
- *10-30* - Deploying to standard patrol
- *10 31* - Coming into headquarters
- *10-41* - Unruly group member
- *10-42* - Unruly group members
- *10-43* - Domestic disturbance
- *10-50* - Weapons malfunction
- *10-51* - Critical systems malfunction
- *10-52* - General mechanical or electrical failure
- *10-53* - Out of fuel condition
- *10-60* - Minor injury
- *10-61* - Blunt force trauma injury
- *10-62* - Heavy bleeding injury
- *10-67* - Other injury
- *10-68* - Life-threatening injury
- *10-71* - Unruly outsider
- *10-72* - Small group of unruly outsiders
- *10-73* - Medium-sized group of unruly outsiders
- *10-74* - Large group of unruly outsiders
- *10-81* - Incursion by single outsider
- *10-82* - Incursion by small group of outsiders

- *10-83* - Incursion by medium-sized group of outsiders

- *10-84* - Incursion by large group of outsiders

- *10-90* - Gathering tactical information

- *10-91* - Request flanking maneuver

- *10-92* - Request crossfire maneuver

- *10-93* - Tactical positioning

- *10-94* - Under fire

- *10-95* - Requesting reinforcements

- *10-96* - On the attack

- *10-97* - Retreating

- *10-99* - Overrun condition, loss of effectiveness

A.4. Travel Information and Guidelines

When traveling during a disaster scenario the following travel-related guidelines should be followed:

- A weapon (or weapons) should be ready for quick use should a life-threatening situation present itself.

- Gas tanks should be kept as full as possible, and vehicles should be refueled as frequently as practical.

- During travel, radio and cell phone communications should be used as much as necessary to provide the assurance that vehicles do not get separated.

- If traveling in multiple vehicles with good communications, allow a 1/2 mile buffer between the lead vehicle and others such that any following vehicles have an opportunity to react to any troubles reported by the lead vehicle.

- Road maps should be kept available for quick access.

- Any changes to travel routes and/or other evacuation plans should be communicated to other group members (including remote group members if possible).

- Consideration should be given to carrying additional fuel.

A. An Example General Disaster Plan ("GDP")

Map Label	Name	Location/Address	Phone	Notes
Rest Areas				
R1	I10 - Exit 75 Rest Stop	I-10	212-555-1212	
R2	I10 - Exit 25 Rest Stop	I-10	212-555-1723	
R3	I75 - Exit 170 Rest Stop	I-75	N/A	
R4	I75 - Exit 40 Rest Stop	I-75	813-555-1010	
Lodging				
L1	Shamrock Motel	226 Davis Road	214-555-1942	
L3	Daized Inn	1720 Howard Lane	215-555-1720	
L3	Armageddon Inn	24 Abrador	217-555-0138	
L4	Hennington's Motel	722 Walkabout Ln.	809-555-2020	
L5	Treasure Cove Lodging	12 Russell Parkway	817-555-7532	
L6	Pine Valley Hotel	Mile 23 - State Rd. 17	819-555-7322	
L7	Traveller's Paradise	223 Trent Road	818-555-3223	
L8	Bohemian Grove Inn	75 State Rd. 51	817-457-1225	
Fuel Stops				
F1	Jack's Truck Stop	I-10, Exit 75	212-555-1710	Monitors CB chan 9
F2	Bently's Service	I-10, Exit 25	214-555-1229	Repair + Fuel
F3	The Truck Stops Here!	I-10, Exit 75	216-555-7663	Food + Fuel
F4	Farmingdale Quickmart	I-75, Exit 150	215-555-8724	Monitors CB chan 9 (food)
F5	Shelly's Fuel and Food	I-75, exit 75	813-555-1830	Eat-in restaurant
F6	BMR Fuel Depot	I-75, Exit 50	813-555-2273	Monitors CB chan 9
F7	Larry's Trading Post	223 State Rd. 17	214-555-1742	
F8	Onestop Quickmart	I75 Norwich Rd.	215-555.1217	Food + Fuel

Figure A.1.: Bugout Map Waypoints.

- Consideration should be given to carrying food (particularly MREs) to eliminate the need for food stops. Stops for food should be combined with stops to meet other needs to minimize risk and reduce travel disruptions. All food should be eaten while on the move.

A.4.1. Travel Maps and Resources

This section contains annotated evacuation maps. Preferred travel routes are highlighted with annotations for important waypoints such as food, fuel and rest stops. Table A.1 provides additional details for the travel resources annotated on these maps.

436

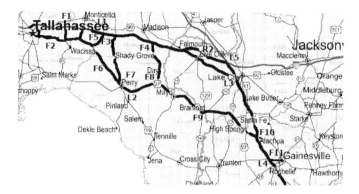

Figure A.2.: Travel Routes from Tallahassee to Gainesville.

Figure A.3.: North Travel Routes between Gainesville, Ocala and Tampa.

A. An Example General Disaster Plan ("GDP")

Figure A.4.: South Travel Routes between Gainesville and Tampa.

B. An Example Site Plan

NOTE: *This appendix provides an example disaster site plan for a family located in Tampa, Florida with a remote college student in Tallahassee and a pre-established bugout destination in Ocala.*

While this may represent a typical disaster plan, a plan for a well-located bugout destination could/should be substantially more detailed. For example, a site with more options for defense and/or growing food would be expected to contain more information on those topics.

This Site Plan defines disaster preparedness measures specific to the Morris family home in Tampa. As it is intended to build on the standards specified in the General Disaster Plan ("GDP"), both plans apply to the Tampa location. For any case in which the Tampa plan is in conflict with the GDP, the Tampa Plan will take precedence.

B.1. Tampa Inventory List

In addition to the supplies and equipment specified in the GDP, the Tampa Site should also have the following supplies and equipment available and ready for use at all times:

- 40 caliber magazine-fed pistol

- 2x tactical home defense 12-gauge shotguns

- 3x large 'No Trespassing' signs with large text

- 500 rounds of 22 caliber long rifle cartridges

- 200 rounds of 40 caliber ammunition

- 200 rounds of 9mm ammunition

B. An Example Site Plan

- 200 12 gauge birdshot shells
- 200 12 gauge 00-buckshot shells
- 20x 5-gal buckets of dried beans
- 20x 5-gal buckets of dried white rice
- 2x 1/2 gal of raw, unfiltered locally-produced honey
- 4x 32oz containers of crunchy peanut butter
- 10x tubes of antibiotic ointment
- 2x large Frisbees
- Emergency weather radio
- CB Radio in Ford Expedition
- CB Radio in Crown Victoria
- 60x 1 oz silver bullion bars
- Full spice rack
- 8x #10 cans of dehydrated pork, chicken and/or beef
- Gravity-fed Water Filter with 8 elements
- 200 sq. feet of heavy plastic tarps
- 2x #10 cans of fruit-flavored drink mix
- 50 bags of freeze-dried meals
- 10 small bells
- 200 ft. rope
- 500 ft. paracord
- 500ft spool of thin-gauge wire
- 4x propane tanks for grill
- 6x FRS hand-held radios
- 20x 6-gal 5+ mil thickness mylar bags
- 20x 3-gal 5+ mil thickness mylar bags

B.2. Tampa Procurement Plan

This procurement plan is intended to be carried out in the event that a disaster of alert level 2 or greater is declared by the group leader (see Appendix A). This plan is organized into three parts:

- *Pre-procurement* - tasks to be performed before beginning any procurement trips.

- *Procurement* - items to procure and where they can be procured.

- *Post-procurement* - tasks to be performed once procurements are completed.

Tampa Pre-Procurement Tasks

If an alert level of 2 or higher has been declared then the following steps should be performed prior to commencing procurements.

- Fuel tanks of all vehicles, as well as any emergency fuel containers, should be filled.

- Attempts should be made to contact Mark in Tallahassee to inform him that a family disaster has been declared as well as the alert level. (Any and all modes of communication, including email and phone text messaging, should be attempted.)

- Defensive weapons should be positioned in all vehicles that will be used for procurements.

- City Hardware should be faxed the pre-prepared hardware list for pick-up, and a follow-up call should be made to confirm the fax was received and that someone will be coming by for a pick-up shortly. (The fax number for City Hardware is 212-555-7721.)

- If possible a neighbor should be contacted to keep watch over the house while the procurement trips are taking place.

Tampa Procurement Plan

This plan defines two shopping trips, with trip #1 being carried out by John Morris and trip #2 being carried out by Betty Morris. Table B.1 lists the locations and items to be procured by John on trip #1 and table B.2 lists the locations and items to be procured by Betty on trip #2.

Tampa Post-Procurement Plan

Once all procurement trips have been completed the following tasks should be performed:

- All procured supplies and equipment should be moved to appropriate storage locations.

B. An Example Site Plan

Location	Alert Levels	Qty and Item
City Hardware	4-6	(faxed order)
Walmart	2-6	10x plastic storage bins
	3-6	10x lg camping propane tanks
	3-6	(Assortment of tools)
	3-6	(Assortment of batteries, all sizes)
	4-6	Rechargeable batteries with charging station
	3-6	2x high-lumen LED flashlights
	3-6	5x box of 12 ga. 00-buckshot shells
	3-6	500 .22 cal long rifle rounds
	4-6	200 40 cal rounds
	4-6	200 9m rounds
Home Depot	4-6	8x sheets 5'x5' plywood
	4-6	(assorted screws and nails)
	4-6	50ft 1" PVC pipe
	4-6	150ft 1/2" PVC pipe

Table B.1.: Procurement Trip #1

- Radio and television stations should be monitored for news updates.

- If electrical power is available, procured antibiotics should be vacuum-sealed in mylar, labeled with the date and contents, and put into the refrigerator for cold storage.

- Plastic "bugout bins" should be loaded with supplies, with each bin used to store supplies of the same category (e.g. toiletries) and stacked beside the carport door in the kitchen.

- Defensive weapons should be loaded and kept within easy access within the house. Every member of the household should be informed of these standard weapons locations.

- The plastic bathtub liner should be installed in the downstairs bathtub, and the bathtub should be filled with water.

- The emergency, gravity-fed water filter should be filled and water collected from it moved to 5-gallon water bottles (stored in the garage) until they are completely filled.

- The swimming pool should be treated with pool shock and covered with the pool tarp.

- There should be a follow-up communication with Mark in Tallahassee to coordinate, plan and possibly decide if he should evacuate based on any news received.

- The full GDP and Site Plan for Tampa should be reviewed and discussed by everyone in the household.

Location	Alert Levels	Qty and Item
SAMS	4-6	5 lb. powdered milk
	4-6	5 lb. flour
	4-6	5 lb. salt
	4-6	5 lb. sugar
	4-6	80 lb. dried pinto (or other) beans
	4-6	80 lb. dried white rice
	4-6	Assorted freeze-dried food packages
	4-6	5x large pkgs bathroom tissue
	4-6	2x large containers of hand soap
	4-6	2x large containers of antibacterial hand soap
	4-6	Plastic plates, cups, spoons, forks & knives
Wins Grocery	3-6	Assorted beef jerky packages
	3-6	Assorted dried beans (not pinto)
	3-6	Assorted packages of candy bars & other treats
Tampa Feed	3-6	2x 50lb bags of dried lime
	4-6	Assorted crop seeds
	4-6	Assorted fertilizers

Table B.2.: Procurement Trip #2

- If possible a schedule should be defined such that someone is awake and monitoring the property and any available news media at all times.

- If the alert level is 3 or higher then the Ford Expedition should be hooked to the trailer and facing outward from the car port, and all plastic bug-out bins and 5-gallon water bottles should be loaded and locked inside the trailer.

- Place the 3 large *'no trespassing'* signs strategically around the property with at least one being easily visible from the street.

B.3. Tampa Defense Plan

The following measures have been defined to defend the family home in Tampa from looters and other malicious intruders:

- *Deterrence* - Large "No Trespassing" signs with large lettering have been purchased and will be posted around the property. These signs indicate (both with words and images) that lethal force can and will be used to protect the property.

- *Intrusion Detection* - A home alarm system has been installed, which has an extra secure mode that utilizes in-house motion detectors for downstairs during the evenings. Additionally, the family dog is a German Shepherd that has an excellent history of recognizing and detecting strangers and barking loudly when they approach.

- *Use of Deception* - Boxes containing litter and other items have been placed near the front door to be scattered if needed to present the image of a property that has already been looted. Additionally, the majority of food in the pantry will be relocated to a more obscure location in the home if lawlessness becomes evident.

- *Intelligence Gathering and Communications* - 2-way handheld radios have been purchased to enable local communications and the sharing of security-related information.

- *Layered Defenses* - In addition to our German Shepherd, guns have been purchased to provide an additional means of defending against potential intruders.

- *Fixed Fortifications and Defenses* - Wire and other hardware has been purchased to be strung as a 'tanglefoot' barrier near vulnerable areas around the home. Additionally, a 3-foot-tall concrete barrier along the east-facing wall of the tool shed offers effective protection against small caliber weapons fire.

- *Response* - As a result of any intrusion attempt Betty and Mark will retreat into the house's designated *safe room* and direct their weapons towards both entrances to the room. John will be armed with the shotgun and defend the hallway that leads to the safe room.

- *Community Defense* - Additional weapons, ammunition and portable FRS radios have been purchased to distribute to neighbors in order to allow more individuals to participate in defense of the neighborhood.

B.4. Tampa Energy Plan

During periods of power outage the emergency generator will be run according to the schedule described in table B.3. Regular refilling of the 3-gallon jerry can will be treated as a high priority during times when fuel is available and personal risk is not excessive. Each day the contents of the refrigerator will be reviewed to determine if would be advantageous to cease devoting energy to it (although it may be important to have the option of refrigerating canned foods that have been opened).

Hours of Operation	Authorized Usage
12am – 5am	Refrigerator only
7am – 9am	Refrigerator only
10am – 1pm	Refrigerator only
2pm – 4pm	Refrigerator only
6pm – 7pm	Refrigerator only
8pm – 10pm	Refrigerator, two 60-watt lamps, one 30-watt fan

Table B.3.: Emergency Generator Usage Schedule.

B.5. Tampa Food Plan

The stored food plan for the Tampa location consists of three parts:

- A fully-stocked food cupboard with an inventory that is used regularly during non-disaster times so that the food is never near its expiration date.

- A supply of dried foods that is sufficient to feed the family two meals per day for a period of 6 months.

- 10 MREs for each family member to be held in reserve for travel.

B.6. Tampa Water Plan

The water plan for the Tampa location includes:

- A 50-gallon water barrel has been installed in the back yard and the gutter system has been adapted to direct rain water into this barrel.

- A commercial, gravity-fed water filter has been purchased for use during disaster. Sufficient spare elements have been purchased to provide the family with 3 gallons of pure water per person for 2 years.

- 5 pounds of calcium hypochlorite have been purchased and stored away to make bleach for water purification.

Time	John	Betty	Mark
12am - 4am	Guard duty		
4am - 8am		Guard duty	
8am - 8:30am		Prepare Breakfast	
8:30am - 9:30am	Breakfast	Breakfast	Breakfast
9:30am - 11:30am	Equip. maint.		Monitor media
11:30am - 12:30pm		Monitor media	
12:30pm - 1pm			Latrine duty
1:30pm - 3pm	Exercise	Exercise	Exercise
5pm - 6pm		Prepare dinner	
6pm - 7pm	dinner	dinner	dinner
7pm - 8pm	Monitor media		dishes/laundry
8pm - 10pm	free time	free time	free time
10pm - 12am			Guard duty

Table B.4.: Daily Activity Schedule for Tampa

B.7. Tampa Sanitation Plan

100 pounds of chlorinated lime powder has been stored locked in the outside tool shed for use in helping to treat human waste. Additionally, a hunter's "camp toilet" has been purchased for use in case running water becomes unavailable in the home. Two one-gallon bottles of regular hand soap and two one-gallon bottles of antibacterial soap have also been stored away to use for hand-washing. Two one-gallon containers of plain, unscented bleach have also been stored to purify water and help sanitize surface areas around the property as needed.

All human waste will be disposed of in a trench that will be dug along the wall that borders the east side of the property. Before dirt is shoveled over any human waste a handful of chlorinated lime powder will be spread over the waste to help control the growth of bacteria.

B.8. Tampa Daily Activity Plan

In order to provide the assurance that critical tasks are not overlooked a daily activity schedule had been developed for the Tampa location. Activities include guard duty, equipment maintenance, monitoring radio and television, food preparation and eating, sanitation and entertainment. Table B.4 depicts the schedule organized by both time of day and responsible individual.

B.9. Tampa Medical and Quarantine Plan

The Tampa home is located near a major medical clinic, which will be the first choice for treatment of any and all medical issues that arise during any disaster.

As a backup, in case the nearby medical clinic is not available or travel to it is not possible, a professional first aid kit, a supply of bandages and antibiotic ointments have been acquired and are stored in the home. Additionally, the family has collected a number of books that describe basic diagnostic, medical and first aid procedures. If the clinic becomes unavailable these references will be consulted to determine how the affected individual may be treated at home.

Safety and hygiene issues will be a regular topic during the family's night meetings in order to prevent medical issues from arising and/or receiving inadequate attention.

After the announcement of disaster any newcomers to the group will be subject to a 3-week primary quarantine period and an additional 3-week secondary quarantine period. During the primary quarantine period the new individuals should be kept fully isolated from the group and, when outdoors, should not approach any group member closer than 20 feet. Additionally, any food, clothing and eating utensils used by the quarantined individual(s) should be kept separate during that period.

During the secondary quarantine period the quarantined individual(s) should avoid any close physical contact with group members and sleep in separate quarters.

B.10. Tampa Commerce Plan

In addition to storing supplies that are expected to be necessary to the family's needs during disaster, other items have been stored in expectation that there may be future opportunities to barter for goods and services. Additionally, extra food has been stored for this purpose as well.

With John's previous years of experience as an automotive mechanic it is also anticipated that the family will be able to offer basic auto mechanic services to others in the community.

B.11. Tampa Evacuation/Bugout Plan

In the event of a disaster of sufficient severity it may become necessary for the Tampa location to be evacuated. This section outlines the criteria and procedures for bugging out.

Tampa Pre-Evacuation Checklist

If the disaster severity is level 3 or higher then evacuation from Tampa should be initiated at the earliest possible time. Before evacuating the following tasks should be performed:

- If Mark is in Tallahassee communicate with him that the Tampa evacuation is under way.
- Contact George Watts in Ocala to inform him of the evacuation and authorize him to begin working on the Ocala task list.
- If possible confirm that all gas tanks on all vehicles used for evacuation are topped off.
- Confirm that each vehicle used has a copy of the evacuation plans with maps.
- Confirm that each vehicle used had at least one weapon to use for defense.
- Confirm that each vehicle has a spare tire and all hardware needed to change a flat tire.
- Retrieve all 'No Trespassing' signs from the property and place them in the trailer for transport.
- Load all MREs into the passenger compartments of the vehicles.
- Load the trailer with all pre-packed storage bins and attach the trailer to the SUV.
- Load canned food from the pantry into plastic bins for each transport.
- Load the trailer with all dried food stores and all plastic bins containing canned food.
- Load the trailer with all stored dog food.
- Load the trailer with all stored garden seeds.
- Load the trailer with all stored PVC piping, tools and miscellaneous construction hardware such as nails and screws.
- Load the emergency water filter and all spare filter elements.
- Test all CB radios in vehicles being used for evacuation.

- Listen to local media, if possible, to identify possible road hazards and travel routes.

- Notify neighbors of departure

On arrival at the Ocala evacuation destination the following tasks should be performed immediately:

- Call George Watts and notify him of arrival.

- If Mark is not with the evacuation group attempt to contact him and notify him of the arrival in Ocala.

- Unload all vehicles and the trailer and store supplies in appropriate and secure locations.

- Park all vehicles behind the house such that they are not visible from the road.

- Conduct a group meeting and review the Site Plan for the Ocala evacuation site.

- Deploy all weapons as described in the defense section of the Ocala Site Plan.

- Activate and implement all security measures defined in the Defense Plan section of the Ocala Site Plan.

- Work within the house and make any preparations for long-term occupancy.

- Identify and begin preparing for any meals for the remainder of the day. Also identify the other regularly scheduled activities specified in the Ocala Site Daily Activity Plan that should be conducted on the first day of the evacuation (e.g. overnight guard duty).

C. Acquiring Precious Metals as a Preparedness Strategy

STRAIGHT THINKING: *Investing in precious metals is a way to preserve the buying power of your money during times of high-inflation and/or to preserve its buying power in the recovery period following a major disaster. During the disaster event itself you may very well find that basic survival supplies such as food and ammunition are of* **far** *greater value than all the gold and silver in the world.*

Before you consider investing in precious metals, first make sure you have acquired the "3 B's" (bullets, beans and band-aids)!

There has been much spirited debate within the prepper community regarding the wisdom of purchasing precious metals as part of an overall preparedness strategy. Those who advocate buying metals point out that purchasing physical assets with real value is a good protection against the loss of the dollar's value due to inflation. Those who disagree make the point that, in a worst-case scenario, bullets will appreciate in value much faster than gold. Other detractors will simply state ... *"You can't eat gold!"*

This appendix will provide some different (and seldom discussed) perspectives on this important topic to help you to define for yourself how the acquisition of precious metals might fit into your overall preparedness strategy. First there are some basic terms to become familiar with:

- *Numismatic Value* - The value of a coin based on its collectibility, rather than on the metals it contains.

- *Junk Silver* - Refers to silver coins that have no collectable (or *'numismatic'*) value but which derive their value purely from the metals they contain. Most junk coins from the US were minted before 1965.

- *Troy Ounce* - A unit of weight, used mainly for measuring precious metals, that is almost exactly 10% heavier than the *avoirdupois ounce* used commonly in North America.

- *Spot Price* - The current market price of a troy ounce of a 99.9% pure precious metal.

- *Premium* - This is the "markup" over spot price that a vendor will charge you when you purchase metals. This amount varies with supply and demand. (If everybody is buying metals today, then expect the premium to be higher.)

- *Bullion* - Refers to metals in various forms that are bought and sold purely for the value of the material they contain. Bullion usually takes the form of bars of various sizes or "coin-like" circular pieces; and typically has intricate engravings to indicate authenticity.

- *Coins* - Refers to engraved metallic disks that are produced by governments for use as currency.

- *Rounds* - Refers to bullion that is produced in a coin-like form (including engraving) but which is not issued as legal currency by any nation.

- *Private Mint* - Institutions that produce bullion as bars or rounds.

- *Assaying* - Refers to the process of analyzing precious metals to determine their purity and authenticity.

C.1. Price vs. Value

Many purveyors of precious metals claim that the metals investor is going to make a ton of money when the price of gold rises. While this may be technically true it can also be a little misleading. Consider the case of a metals investor purchasing a quantity of gold at a price equal to the going price of 1000 gallons of regular gasoline. That quantity of gasoline represents a certain real **value** (the value associated with being able to drive a certain number of miles down the road). Now, suppose many years later the price of gold, as expressed in dollars, has increased dramatically, and that same investor sells it for many more dollars than he/she paid for it. The investor has made "good profits".

However, during that period the price of **everything** has increased due to inflation. In fact, the dollars the investor received when he sold the gold is still only enough to purchase the same 1000 gallons of regular gasoline. **In this very possible case the price of gold has gone up while its real value has not changed!** However, had the investor not purchased gold the value of their paper money would have gone down substantially, and they would be in a much worse overall position.

> **NOTE: FIRST PREPPER RULE OF INVESTING IN METALS:** *It's not about "making profit", it's about "preserving value".*

C.2. Why Metals Rather than Other Commodities or Investments?

To those who successfully invest in bullion gold, silver and other precious metals are "just commodities" like wheat or pork bellies, however they are commodities with characteristics that make them more interesting as an investment. Those characteristics are:

- **Precious metals are fungible** - all ounces of a particular metal and particular purity have exactly the same value (this is one thing that differentiates investing in metals from investing in precious gems, for example).

- **Precious metals retain their value over time** - while wheat and pork bellies spoil with the passage of time; gold, silver and other precious metals can be stored for centuries without appreciable loss of value.

- **Precious metals are relatively easy to transport and conceal** - Because precious metals pack a lot of value into a relatively small space it is much easier to transport and conceal a certain value stored as precious metals than it is to, for example, store or transport an equivalent value expressed in wheat or pork bellies.

> **NOTE: SECOND PREPPER RULE OF INVESTING IN METALS:** *Always buy the physical metal and not any sort of certificate that entitles you to take possession of the metal at some time in the future.*

Investments in precious metals also differ from other investments in important ways:

- Real estate is not portable, and may very well be subject to property taxes. During periods of economic decline real estate will, in general, **decrease** in value. (It should be pointed out that, while precious metals may not be subject to taxes after being purchased, there is precedent in the US for the confiscation of precious metals.[393])

- The value for the stocks of good, stable companies may also increase so as to adjust for inflation. The difference between physical metals and stocks is that there is a zero probability that metals will ever become worthless, while companies can (and do) go out of business.

NOTE: *There are those who believe that a major disaster may result in* deflation *rather than inflation. In a deflationary scenario prices actually go* **down**. *The reasoning for this is that, during a disaster, the demand for products will decline. In this case those offering products and services for sale may find it necessary to lower prices in order to stimulate demand.*

Deflation, like inflation, can become a phenomena that begins to feed on itself and grow. This is often referred to as a 'deflationary spiral'. The demonstrated tendency of modern governments to resort to "printing money" out of thin air during difficult times suggests that a deflationary scenario is unlikely, however in today's unstable financial world nothing is certain.

NOTE: THIRD PREPPER RULE OF INVESTING IN METALS: *Consult with your metals dealer about any state laws and taxes that apply to the buying of precious metals. You may find that purchasing in larger quantities brings some good advantages.*

C.3. How and When the Prepper Benefits from Metals

In the aftermath of a major disaster the prices for food and important basic supplies may literally skyrocket, however the dollar value of precious metals will skyrocket as well. So, one important way in which the prepper can and will benefit from holding precious metals is in bartering for food and other supplies during a prolonged recovery period when their stored provisions begin to dwindle.

Additionally, and just as importantly, a prepper with debt that is denominated in dollars (or any national currency) may find that they are able pay off such debts (or simply continue to make normal debt payments) with the value of the precious metals they have stored away. This may enable them to keep a roof over their heads in a time when others are being evicted for inability to pay a mortgage (there was apparently plenty of precedent set for such evictions during America's Great Depression).

C.4. Silver vs Gold?

As of this writing an ounce of silver has a spot price of about $20.00 per troy ounce, and gold has a spot price of about $1283.00 per troy ounce. Obviously in a disaster situation in which you wanted to barter precious metals for relatively low cost supplies there would be a good advantage to having silver. However, gold does have the advantage of consolidating much more value into much less space and weight. The prepper's decision with regard to allocating their metal reserves between gold and silver should be guided by the uses they anticipate having for metals in the aftermath. If the prepper is reasonably certain that they will involved in some larger transactions (purchasing more costly weapons, land, large equipment, or possibly paying off a mortgage), then a case can be made for putting back gold. If the prepper plans on needing to use metal exclusively for smaller transactions (e.g. food, fuel and ammunition) then they may plan on having silver only. (Keep in mind that there will probably be opportunities to barter one metal for another in the aftermath of a disaster, and that in some cases larger sums may be paid "on account" in advance of actually taking possession of goods and services.)

NOTE: FORTH PREPPER RULE OF INVESTING IN METALS: *Always pay for your metals with* **real cash***, and not with a credit card, debit card or any sort of electronic transaction. This helps to maintain your privacy and security.*

C.5. Coins vs. Bullion

Many novices to investing in metals are understandably confused about the "face value" of coins that contain precious metals vs. the value of coins as collectables (the "numismatic value") vs. the "meltdown value" value of the raw metal they contain.

NOTE: FIFTH PREPPER RULE OF INVESTING IN METALS: *Don't let anyone know that you are holding precious metals unless there is an absolute need and you trust that person completely.*

During times of plenty it is easy to imagine that wealthy collectors of rare items emerge, and that the collectible value of items (including coins) may greatly surpass their material value. Conversely, during difficult times it is easy to imagine that collectors disappear and items start to become more valued for their metal content. As a result, the prepper should be concerned with purchasing metals as a raw commodity rather than as collectibles. In other words, the prepper should be looking at the *meltdown value* of metals.

This suggests that he prepper might be more interested in bars of gold and silver bullion, for example, than collecting gold or silver coins. The reality, however, is that this decision is not quite so straightforward for the following reasons:

- Most (if not all) coins from private mints *("rounds")* are just "pretty bullion". Any detailed engraving on these rounds can be considered as a strong indication of authenticity if and when you need to barter with them later.

- The prices of coins per ounce of metal are not substantially higher than the prices of raw bullion and rounds.

- Coins circulated by governments carry with them an additional assurance of authenticity, as governments tend to pursue, prosecute and imprison those who counterfeit their currencies. As a result the prepper should expect to pay slightly higher premiums for coins vs. privately-minted rounds.

AUTHOR'S NOTE: *A quick check on the prices of gold and silver bullion and coins today shows that, at the time of this writing, the price of privately minted silver rounds is 8.05% over the spot price, while the price of circulated silver coins minted by government is marked up 10.2% over the spot price.*

Interestingly, a similar check on gold revealed a 6.2% markup for privately minted gold rounds over spot and a 3.8% markup for 1 oz. Canadian Gold Maple coins over the spot price (which, in this case, is surprisingly less than the cost of the privately minted 1 oz. gold rounds!).

When it comes to precious metal coins circulated by governments the "face value" of such coins can pretty well be ignored. That value is going to be far less than the *'meltdown value'* of the coin due to the raw metal it contains. You certainly **could** use such a coin to make a purchase but you would essentially be giving away much of its true value! **The face value on a precious metal coin is important only in that it indicates that it is issued as currency and its integrity will be protected by the law enforcement agencies of the government of the issuing country.**

> **NOTE: SIXTH PREPPER RULE OF INVESTING IN METALS:** *Give careful consideration with regard to how and where you will be storing your metals. Consider that there are laws on the books that allow governments to inspect safe-deposit boxes and seize their contents under special circumstances. Consider that many wealthy investors in metals have actually resorted to carefully packaging and burying their own precious metals.*

C.6. The Problem of Metal Counterfeiting

In recent years there have been incidents of both gold and silver being counterfeited.[392] In fact, if you conduct an Internet search on the words "gold" and "tungsten" you'll discover many articles that describe how bars of gold-plated tungsten (tungsten has a weight and density extremely close to that of gold) have been discovered on the open market. A search on the words "silver" and "molybdenum" will reveal similar stories about counterfeit silver.

While this counterfeiting has been known to happen, the stories of it are not pervasive. Both modern assaying techniques and reasonable human inspection should expose attempts to counterfeit metals (particularly in smaller physical sizes such as 1 oz. bars and coins). It has been said that one easy way to quickly distinguish between gold and silver counterfeit coins (and small bullion bars) is to simply listen to the distinctive clinking sound they make when shaken in one's hand (the counterfeits produce a noticeably different sound). So, it is advisable for the prepper who plans on investing in metals to own a pair of calipers and a good scale for weighting and measuring, as well as to become familiar with the distinctive sounds made by legitimate coins when they are clinked together.

C.7. Popular Metal Products

Because gold is a soft metal, a coin that is made of almost pure gold is subject to wear if handled excessively. As a result many gold coins are alloyed with other less valuable metals to make them more durable for frequent handling. The more popular coins favored by investors, however, are extremely close to being 100% pure metal (because those investors plan on packaging and handling those coins carefully). A generic "pure" gold or silver coin is typically 99.9% pure. Higher quality coins have a purity of 99.99%, and some runs of the Canadian "Maple Leaf" coins advertise a purity of 99.999%. Many metals investors are perfectly happy to have coins of the 99.9% purity, and these "generic rounds" are purchased very regularly by collectors.

The original modern-day investment-quality gold coin is the Krugerrand, which was first minted by South Africa in 1967. The Krugerrand contains 1 troy ounce of gold, and is actually an alloy of gold and copper (it is 91.67% gold). Other countries made note of the Krugerrand's success and began minting their own gold and silver coins. Today popular gold coins include the Canadian "Gold Maple Leaf" (99.99% - 99.999% gold content), the Chinese "Gold Panda" (99.9% gold content), the American "Gold Eagle" (91.67% gold content) and the British "Britannia" (99.99% gold content - 91.7% gold content prior to 2013). These are among the most popular gold coins among investors today.[394]

The more popular silver coins include the "American Silver Eagle" (99.9% silver content), the "Silver Brittania" (99.9% silver content - 95.9% silver content prior to 2013) and the Canadian "Silver Maple Leaf" (99.99% silver content).

In addition to gold and silver, coins, rounds and bullion are often produced in other precious metals such as platinum and palladium. Such metals should be of much less interest to the prepper simply because they will not be as readily recognized or accepted as gold and silver in a post-disaster economy.

C.8. Securely Trading and Storing Metals

If buying metals from a dealer, check the reputation of the dealer before conducting business with them. Also, determine if the dealer buys metals as well as selling them, and understand the terms under which they purchase metals (because you may need to turn your metals back into cash some day, and if you're going to build a relationship with a metals merchant you want to build that relationship with someone who offers reasonable terms for both buying **and** selling).

RECOMMENDATION: Ask a potential dealer what the terms would be if you were to sell some metals today.

Securely Buying and Selling Metals

Those who trade in physical metals have a tendency to be sensitive about keeping their transactions private. A listen to the nightly news on any given day provides plenty of rationalization for such caution. The pages of history are also filled with cautionary tales in this regard. While the security-related measures described here may seem a little excessive ... *"better safe than sorry"*!

The following are best practices that will help to assure confidentiality and personal safety when buying or selling precious metals:

- If possible, purchase metals face-to-face with a professional metals dealer that enjoys a good, well-established reputation in the community.

- If possible, purchase metals with cash so as to minimize any electronic trail that sophisticated thieves may have to follow. It is also a good idea to accumulate the cash gradually and in increasingly-large quantities before making the purchase so that even a sophisticated thief who may be able to monitor your bank account transactions may not notice deviations from normal behavior.

- When buying metals from private individuals that you do not know well, conduct the transaction in a public setting - for example the food court of a shopping mall (if you can find a shopping mall that isn't boarded up!). Also, take some time to "shop" before leaving the public area, park your vehicle in a location that is in plain view and, if meeting in a shopping mall, don't park near the entrance that is closest to your meeting location.

  You may also consider not driving directly home, and making a stop somewhere along the way. (Driving through covered parking garages can be a good place to confound anyone who may be trying to follow you.)

Storing Precious Metals

While there is much disagreement among experts as to how metals are best and most securely stored, there seems to be much agreement that the place **NOT** to store metal investments is in a bank safe-deposit box. The rationale for this belief is that many metal-buyers are not wholly optimistic about the continuity of the modern banking system, and believe that any country is susceptible to *bank closures* or *bank holidays* (In fact, it is often these very concerns that drive investors into metals.) Also, many governments (the US included) have recently expanded their legal rights to seize the contents of safe-deposit boxes without even needing a warrant.[513] With historical precedent and the economic turmoil in the world it is easy to understand why metals-buyers would have such concerns!

As a result, many metals-buyers are opting to either maintain tight secrecy and conceal their metals on property that they own and control or to store their metals with institutions that offer *'allocated storage'* that is either *'segregated'* or *'non-segregated'*. Segregated storage means that your specific items are physically packaged together and stored for you, and that when you reclaim them those exact items are returned to you. Non-segregated storage means that if you stored a certain amount of metal, that quantity of metal will be returned to you, however it may not be the specific items that you initially stored.

DISCLAIMER: *Having authored this book that is offering advice on metals storage causes me to have to make use of professional allocated storage services such as I am describing here for any metals I may own. Otherwise the simple writing of this book would make me a target. This should be a good indicator to you why it is super-critical to stay as tight-lipped as possible regarding any valuables you may personally possess.* **Even pre-disaster these are dangerous times in which we live!**

Best Practices for personally storing metals include:

- If you choose to keep your metals in a safe be certain that the safe is bolted to the floor. Also, be certain that the safe was made by a manufacturer with a good reputation. If the safe must be installed professionally, make sure it is installed by an individual and/or a company that you trust.

- If you choose to hide your metals then hide them in multiple, carefully-chosen locations. Have one location only contain a small quantity of metals (or some metals that are of relatively low-value) so that, under threat, you have the option to reveal only that location. You may also consider depositing a weapon of some sort with your metals.

- If you choose to bury your metals (you might be surprised how many metals-owners take this option), here are some best practices:

  - Enclose the items to be stored in PVC pipe (with both ends carefully sealed with PVC cement), and bury the pipe at least 4 feet below the surface (so that it cannot be detected by most metal detectors). Post hole diggers are perfect for digging such holes.

  - Consider placing a metal object of some sort over the buried pipe so that anyone searching with a metal detector may take the decoy and not dig deeper (a railroad spike would be ideal for this purpose).

  - Consider burying other metal around the property in random locations to further confound anyone using a metal detector.

  - Consider placing a plant of some sort over the top as a way of both helping to mark the location as well as concealing the purpose of your dig.

  - If you draw a map to the location, consider varying both the 'x' and 'y' scales on the map by some factor that only you know, thereby rendering the map worthless to anyone who might stumble upon it.[513]

- Consider typing the location into a text file and encrypting it with a trusted encryption program. If you are concerned with your secret surviving your own death then you might consider breaking the decryption password into two pieces and storing each piece at a different location in a sealed envelope, with instructions on each envelope that it is only to be opened on your death.

Regardless of how you choose to store your metals, keep all information about your transactions and storage as private as possible. The only thing that is important is that those you intend to benefit from your metals investment realize those benefits.

D. Guns and Ammunition - 101

Because guns play a central role in modern defense, and because it is anticipated that law enforcement personnel may be spread extremely thin in the aftermath of a major disaster, it is important that anyone planning a serious survival strategy incorporate gun defense into their planning. As the title of this appendix implies, the intent here is to provide a general introduction to guns and ammunition such that the reader will have sufficient knowledge to begin speaking with their local gun dealer and others to identify guns to to meet their own unique needs.

Thanks to the efforts of Hollywood we all have some familiarity with guns. Unfortunately, and to everyone's disadvantage, Hollywood's representation of guns does not quite conform to reality. Hollywood will depict some unfortunate movie character being "sprayed" with automatic gun fire and somehow not being hit. Or in other scenes someone who is shot is depicted as immediately falling to the ground dead. All of these unrealistic portrayals create false impressions in the viewer's mind that can lead to deadly consequences.

In the real world a poorly placed shot may ricochet off the skull of a rushing attacker, or penetrate the attacker's body only to inflict sufficient damage in the short term to cause them to increase the ferocity of their attack. In order to maximize the effectiveness of a gun used for defense it is important that the gun be a good fit for the person using it, and that the gun and ammunition be a good fit for the situation. For example, a rifle with a long barrel might be very powerful but the length of the barrel may very well be unwieldy for use indoors, or it may be so powerful it penetrates through walls and hits unintended targets.

D.1. Types of Guns

Over the years a wide variety of guns have been designed to address a wide range of needs. Guns are most broadly organized into the two categories of *handguns* and *long guns*. Handguns are guns that are designed to be held and fired from one hand. Long guns are designed to be held by both hands and braced against the shoulder. Hand guns are faster to bring to bear on a target and generally shoot lighter ammunition in contrast to long guns, which are more accurate and powerful, and have a longer effective range. Handguns and long guns each break down into further categories:

- **Handguns**

    - *Pistols* - Handguns for which the chamber is attached to the barrel.

    - *Revolvers* - Handguns that have a rotating cylinder that contains multiple chambers for bullets.

- **Long Guns**

    - *Rifles* - guns that shoot a single projectile and have *'rifled'* barrels that impart a rotation to the bullet. This rotation results in greatly increased accuracy.

    - *Shotguns* - guns that shoot a powerful spread of solid round pellets.

Rifles are further organized into:

- *Bolt-Action Rifles* - rifles that require the shooter to operate a handle between shots to eject the spent cartridge and load a new one into the chamber.

- *Lever-Action Rifles* - rifles that require the shooter to operate a lever on the underside of the gun between shots to eject the spent cartridge and load a new one into the chamber.

- *Semi-Automatic Rifles* - rifles that use the force of the bullet firing to eject the spent cartridge and load a new one. Shooters using semi-automatic rifles simply pull the trigger repetitively to shoot multiple bullets in succession.

- *Fully-Automatic Rifles* - "multiple shots fired with a single trigger pull". Like semi-automatic rifles, fully-automatic rifles use the force of the gunshot itself to eject a spent cartridge and load a new one. Unlike a semi-automatic rifle, fully-automatic rifles fire multiple shots for a single pull of the trigger. Due to their potential for causing mass casualties, possession of fully-automatic weapons is subject to strict controls in most countries. Most fully-automatic rifles feature a *'selective fire'* lever that allows the gun to be switched between semi- and fully- automatic fire (as well as, in some cases, modes which fire in which some fixed number of rounds are fired for each pull of the trigger).

Shotguns are further organized into:

- *Breech-loaders* - shotguns that are designed with the barrel of the gun hinged such that the barrel can be exposed and shells inserted manually. Breech-loaders may be single-barreled or double-barreled (double-barreled shotguns have one trigger for each barrel).

- *Pump action shotguns* - shotguns that require the shooter to operate a sliding handle below the barrel to eject a spent shell and load another.

- *Autoloading (or semi-automatic) shotguns* - shotguns that use the force of discharge to eject the spent shell and load another.

DISCLAIMER: *Throughout the history of the gun there have been virtually infinite combinations of the various features described here for all types of handguns and long guns. This book describes those features that are most commonly found in modern guns used to meet hunting and defense needs.*

Hunting Rifles vs. Assault-Style Rifles vs. Assault Rifles

In modern times the term *assault rifle* has been coined to refer to rifles that are designed primarily for military use. Lately many in the media have begun to also refer to rifles designed for personal defense as being assault rifles. More precisely, these personal defense weapons should be referred to as "assault-style" weapons because they physically resemble military assault weapons, accept the same or very similar ammunition, and can support many of the same accessories, yet lack certain advanced features (such as a fully-automatic firing option).

The characteristics that define assault rifles and assault-style weapons include pistol-style grips, flash suppressors, integrated handles for easy carry, and collapsible metal shoulder stocks to allow the gun to be adjusted for different uses. Guns that are black in color are often characterized as assault-style weapons as well, as they are thought to be easier to conceal at night.

While today it is very common for assault-style weapons to be used for hunting, classic hunting weapons tend to incorporate more wood into their construction, are more ornate and may be collected as much for art as for hunting. Some hunters may prefer the assault-style guns to the classic guns simply because they are perceived as being more rugged, portable, reliable and maintainable.

NOTE: *The term 'machine gun' refers to any fully-automatic rifle that shoots large caliber ammunition. The term 'submachine gun' refers to any fully-automatic gun that fires the smaller caliber ammunition that is normally used by handguns.*

Figure D.1.: Side-by-side comparisons of common ammunition.

D.2. Ammunition

Shotgun Shells

Ammunition for shotguns takes the form of cylindrical "shotguns shells" between 2 1/2 and 3 1/2 inches in length. Shotgun shells are packed with power and a number of metallic pellets that are discharged by the gun when it is fired. Some shells contain more numerous but smaller pellets that are more appropriate for shooting birds, while others contain larger *'buck shot'* that is more suitable for small game (with 00-buckshot - pronounced *'double-ought'* buck shot - being heavier and suitable for taking down larger game such as deer). Shotgun shells can also contain *'slugs'*; which are single, large lead projectiles that are capable of taking down larger animals (e.g. bears and lions).

Shotgun sizes are classified by *gauge*, which is an indirect measure of the size of the barrel. The gauge is actually the number of lead balls that are the diameter of the barrel that are one pound in weight. This rather strange formula results in larger shotguns actually having smaller gauge numbers. The most popular gauges available today are:

- *12 Gauge* - Recommended most by experts for home defense

- *20 Gauge* - A shotgun that receives smaller shells, shoots with less force, and produces less recoil, yet is still a reasonable gun to use for home defense.

Other gauges are available, although not nearly as popular as the 12 and 20 gauge shotguns. There are also *'.410 shotguns'* (with .410 actually being a caliber) which are very under-powered and used mainly as "starter guns" for young shooters.

Rifle and Handgun Cartridges

Ammunition for handguns and rifles takes the form of "cartridges" that are available in many sizes and are suitable for just as many uses. Some are lighter and suited for close range shooting, while others are heavy and powerful enough to provide greater range and stopping power. See Figure D.1 for a side-by-side comparison of common types of rifle and shotgun ammunition.

Rifle and handgun cartridges consist of a metal *casing* that contains powder and to which is attached a metal projectile (the *bullet*). The bullet is usually made of lead, although it may be lead-coated with a steel 'jacket' (or it may be made entirely of some other metal).

Soft-Point, Hollow-Point and Jacketed Ammunition

Normal bullets used in the cartridges of handguns and rifles are solid lead projectiles. Such ammunition is known as *ball ammunition*. There are some cases, however, in which a solid projectile is not the most effective option. Against *soft-tissue targets* such as animals or humans a solid bullet is not as effective as one that features a hollow-point. Hollow-point bullets tend to flatten out when coming into contact with softer targets and, as a result, cause more damage due to their irregular shape and altered trajectory. For purposes of better aerodynamics other *soft-point bullets* are available which have tips that are filled with a softer material that still flattens when coming into contact with the target. Several of the ammunition rounds depicted in figure D.1 are hollow-point rounds.

In other cases, such as when a target is behind a bullet-resistant barrier, it may be desirable to encase the relatively soft lead of the bullet with a harder metal for better penetration. Such bullets are referred to as *jacketed rounds*. Those which are fully encased in a harder metal are known as *full metal jacket* ('FMJ') rounds. The FMJ rounds tend to exit the gun at higher velocity, which increases both range and penetrating power.

NOTE: *For self defense purposes it is very common for preppers and survivalists to keep a supply of hollow-point rounds. However lower cost ball ammunition remains important for use in target practice.*

Bullet and Cartridge Sizes

Rifle and handgun bullets are often referred to by their *caliber*, which is basically the number of hundredths of an inch across their base. So, a 50 caliber bullet is one-half inch across, and a .308 caliber bullet is just a little less than one third of an inch across. (Suddenly you can appreciate why a 50 caliber gun is considered to represent some rather awesome firepower!)

The *30-06 round* is so named because it is a 30 caliber round (and the '06' is because it was initially released in the year 1906). Military bullets (which often have civilian counterparts) are named according to their size as expressed in millimeters. So, the 7.62x51mm NATO cartridge is 7.62 millimeters across and 51 millimeters in length.

CAUTION: *If you do the conversion you'll find that 7.62mm = .308 inches; which means that the 7.62x51mm NATO cartridge is the same size as a .308 civilian round. A .308 cartridge can be fired from any gun that is designed to take the NATO round, however the the NATO round should never be fired in a gun designed for the civilian .308 cartridge due to its more powerful charge (for which many civilian guns are not designed).*

Selecting Proper Ammunition

Galileo's famous experiment in which he dropped two balls of different mass from the Leaning Tower of Pisa demonstrated that different objects of different size and weight, when dropped together from the same height, will reach the ground at the same time.[416] This same law of physics applies to bullets. This means that for a bullet to travel further before hitting the ground it must travel faster. For two different-sized bullets fired at the same time and propelled by identical forces, the lighter bullet will have the greater range.

Of course a smaller bullet may inflict less damage on a target, however a mid-sized rifle bullet still brings plenty of stopping power. And, in a long distance self-defense situation, having the greatest range can easily be a critical factor.

The bottom line, when it comes to ammunition bigger is not always better.

NOTE: *Even bullets of the same caliber can vary with regard to their firing charge and the weight of the bullet (often expressed in 'grains'). It is incumbent on the prepper to give careful consideration to their own unique defensive situation and to choose ammunition that is the best fit. Table D.1 provides a list of the most common calibers of rifle bullets, including their weights and velocities.*

Cartridge	Bullet Weight	Velocity Range
.243 Winchester[410]	55 - 105 grain	4058 - 2986 ft/sec.
.223 [5.56mm Nato][404]	36 - 77 grain	3750 - 2750 ft/sec.
.270 Winchester [408]	90 - 130 grain	3603 - 2850 ft/sec.
7mm Magnum [411]	110 - 175 grain	3500 - 2860 ft/sec.
.300 Winchester Magnum[412]	165 - 220 grain	3260 - 2850 ft/sec.
5.45x39mm (AK 74 round)[409]	49 - 80 grian	3000 - 990 ft/sec.
.338 Winchester Mignum[413]	200 - 275 grain	2950 - 2489 ft/sec.
.30-06[407]	150 - 220 grain	2910 - 2500 ft/sec.
.308 [7.62x51mm NATO][405]	147 - 175 grain	2733 - 2480 ft/sec.
.30-30[414]	110 -170 grain	2684 - 2227 ft/sec.
7.62x39mm (AK47 round)[406]	7.9 - 10 grain	2100 - 2421 ft/sec.
.22 Long Rifle (.22LR)[415]	32 - 40 grain	1640 - 1080 ft/sec.

Table D.1.: Common Rifle Cartridges

D.3. Gun Terminology

Before discussing and researching guns be sure that you have added the following additional gun- and ammunition- related terms to your vocabulary:

- *Pistol* - A handgun for which the chamber from which the bullet is fired is part of the barrel.

- *Revolver* - A handgun that contains multiple chambers in a single rotating cylinder, with each chamber able to accept a single bullet. When the round from a chamber is fired the cylinder rotates the next bullet into position for firing.

- *Riot Shotgun* - Shotguns that are specialized for defensive use. Specializations include the addition of hand grips and the reduction of barrel length to between 18.5 and 20 inches (which allows for better use in close-quarters situations).[390]

- *Rifling* - The cutting of spiraled grooves into the inside of a rifle's barrel to impart a trajectory-stabilizing spin on bullets as they leave the barrel.

- *Rifle* - A long gun that accepts cartridges for ammunition and features a rifled barrel that is responsible for the rifle's improved accuracy.

- *JHP Ammunition* - JHP ("jacketed hollow-point") ammunition consists of hollow-point bullets that are jacketed for better penetration.

- *Centerfire Cartridges* - Cartridges that fire when struck in the center of the base of the cartridge casing by the firing pin.

Figure D.2.: Anatomy of a Rifle.

- *Rimfire Cartridges* - Cartridges that fire when the firing pin strikes the edge of cartridge base. Rimfire cartridges are less costly to manufacture and tend to be used by smaller caliber guns. Guns that use rimfire cartridges have a reputation for being less accurate and having a greater incidence of ammunition jams compared to guns that take centerfire cartridges.

- *Recoil* - The force that the gun exerts against the shooter when it is fired (colloquially this is often referred to as the 'kick').

- *Semi-automatic* - Refers to guns that fire one shot, eject the spent cartridge and load a new cartridge each time trigger is pulled.

- *Fully-automatic* - Refers to guns that fire multiple bullets for each press of the trigger.

- *Single Action* - Refers to revolvers that require the hammer to be cocked before the trigger can be pulled to fire the gun.

- *Double Action* - Refers to revolvers that can cock the trigger and fire the gun with a single pull on the trigger.

D.4. Anatomy of a Gun

All guns share the following features:

- *Ammunition* - shells or cartridges that contain the propellent and projectile(s).

- *Barrel* - the metal tube through which the bullet travels when the gun is fired. In the case of rifles and handguns this tube may be *'rifled'* to impart a spin to the bullet for increased accuracy.

- *Trigger* - the lever the shooter pulls with their finger to fire the gun.

- *Chamber* - the internal compartment at the end of the barrel from which the bullet is fired.

- *Firing Pen* - the solid contact that strikes the ammunition and causes it to fire.

- *Sights* - the markers on the barrel that allow the shooter to visually align the gun's barrel with the target.

- *Grips* - the structures on the gun that allow the shooter to properly hold the gun.

The great majority of guns also feature a *'safety'*, which is a lever or button that disables the gun's ability to fire. Quite often these safeties have bright red visual indicators when firing is enabled.

Other features shared by many guns include:

- *Receivers* - The central part of virtually all long guns that houses the moving parts and to which the barrel, shoulder stock, etc. are attached. From a legal regulatory perspective the receiver **is** the gun, and all other parts are accessories.[395]

- *Frame* - The frame is the central working part of any handgun (as the receiver is for long guns).[396]

- *Bolts* - For long guns the bolt is the mechanism inside the receiver that ejects spent ammunition, feeds in new ammunition and controls firing. For revolvers the bolt is the part to which the cylinder is attached and around which it rotates.

- *Shoulder Stocks* - The part of a long gun intended to be held against the shooter's shoulder when it is fired.

- *Scope* - An optical device mounted on a gun that provides a magnified view of the target for increased accuracy.

- *Magazine* - A small box that holds ammunition for a handgun or long gun that attaches to the gun's receiver or frame to provide ammunition to the gun. Not all guns make use of magazines. Revolvers provide a cylinder that contains several firing chambers that rotate into position to provide ammunition, while some shotguns and rifles are designed to contain ammunition internally.

D.5. Frequently-Mentioned Long Guns

The following types of rifles are common, with many rifles fitting multiple classifications:

- *Sniper Rifle* - a rifle that has the potential to hit targets accurately at very long range.

- *Battle Rifle* - a defensive rifle that shoots a heavy round and is capable of effectively engaging the enemy at ranges exceeding 200 yards.

- *Assault Rifle* - a defensive rifle that generally has the following characteristics:

    - Has a selector that selects between semi- and fully- automatic fire

    - Has a mid-length barrel (making it easier to handle and transport, particularly in times of action).

    - Accepts a mid-sized cartridge (allowing more cartridges to be carried into battle).

    - Has a typical defensive range between 0 and 200 yards.

- *Assault-Style Rifle* - an assault-style rifle has the characteristics of an assault rifle with the exception that it can only fire in semi-automatic mode.

- *Hunting Rifle* - a rifle that is optimized for hunting (since big game must often be hunted at long distance hunting rifles are often well-suited to be sniper rifles as well).

The AR-10 is a military battle rifle first developed for the US Army in the late 1950's. It shoots the NATO 7.62x51mm round, which is the military version of the .308 Winchester cartridge. As a military-use weapon the AR-10 is capable of fully-automatic fire, however a number of companies produce similar semi-automatic rifles that resemble the AR-10 in varying degrees and which accept the same ammunition.[423]

Among the assault and assault-style rifles, the Russian AK-47 and the US AR-15 and M-16 are the best known. The AK-47 is known for its ruggedness and ability to function under the harshest and most demanding circumstances. It is also known for having lower cost ammunition that tends to be highly available (because the gun is used by so many people throughout the world). The AK-47 shoots a 7.62x39mm round. Like the AR-10, there are many semi-automatic variants of the AK-47 manufactured around the world for non-military use.

The AR-15 is the predecessor to the M-16, which is the fully-automatic assault version of the AR-15 used by the US military as well as other military organizations throughout the world. It is an assault-like rifle that is **highly customizable and configurable**. This rifle shoots a 5.56x45mm NATO civilian round or the equivalent civilian .223 caliber Remington round. It is **NOT** recommended that weapons designed specifically to fire the .223 Remington round be used to fire the NATO round, as the NATO round generates significantly higher pressure in the firing chamber.

The AR-15 design is so universal and customizable that there are often references to the *'AR-15 platform'*, which simply means that a gun has been built around an AR-15 lower receiver.

The *Mosin-Nagant rifle* is a bolt-action rifle that was developed by the Imperial Russian Army in the late 1800's.[424] This vintage rifle continues to be popular among preppers because it shoots the Russian 7.62x54R round[425], which is very similar to the .308 Winchester round in terms of projectile weight and muzzle velocity. However, these rifles can be purchased at a fraction of the cost of the typical modern .308 caliber rifle, and ammunition for the Mosin-Nagant is also available at much lower cost than the more modern .308 caliber rifle cartridges (often for half the price).

The *Remington 870* and *Mossberg 500* 12-gauge shotguns both receive frequent recommendations from experts in home defense. In fact, both seem to receive virtually equal respect from numerous sources. Both provide an excellent, low-cost solution to home defense needs. The Mossberg is a little lighter weight than the Remington, and has a capacity of 5 rounds vs. the 4 round capacity of the Remington. There are numerous other high-quality 12 gauge pump-action shotguns on the market, and you are strongly encouraged to consult with your local gun dealer to select the best fit for your particular needs.

D.6. Scopes for Rifles, Shotguns and Handguns

Many shooters - particularly those who shoot rifles - will tell you that good *'optics'* is essential to accurate long-distance shooting, and that it is easy to justify spending almost as much on a good scope as on the rifle itself. While this may be somewhat of an exaggeration (or maybe not, depending on your specific need) there is no doubt that being able to place shots with precision is important.

With rifle scopes as with ammunition, **bigger is not always better**. As you look at a target with increased magnification the amount of light you see is reduced and the target becomes

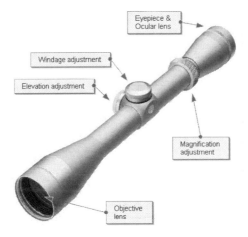

Figure D.3.: Anatomy of a Gun Scope.

more difficult to discern from the background. Additionally, as magnification increases the shooter may become disoriented because they may only be looking at some small area of the target.

Often the minimum magnification of a scope is more significant than the maximum magnification, as the minimum magnification is usually best for shooting at targets that are within typical ranges.[417] A minimum magnification of 3x or 4x is recommended. Any magnification over 9x should just be considered to be 'icing on the cake'.

The front lens on a scope (the lens at the font of the scope that collects the image) is the *'objective lens'*. The larger this lens is the more light is collected and presented to the shooter. So, a scope with a larger lens presents a clearer, more distinct picture. In addition to the size of the objective lens, the amount of light that finds its way to the shooter's eye is reduced by the other optical elements within the scope. The more costly scopes tend to present the shooter with about 10% more light than the mid-priced scope. Under difficult lighting conditions this can make the difference in being able to distinguish the target from the background. Figure D.3 depicts the main components and controls for a typical gun scope.

Scope Ratings

The capabilities of a scope are denoted by an industry standard notation that reads similar to '3-9x40' (read as "three to nine by forty"). In this case the notation describes a scope with a minimum magnification of 3x, a maximum magnification of 9x and an objective lens with a diameter of 40 millimeters. The low magnification is important because it suggests that you can use the rifle to shoot at targets that are nearer. The higher magnification indicates the maximum zoom level available for shooting targets at longer range, and the 40 millimeters lens size indicates the amount of light the scope can present to the shooter (which is essential to be able to see the target under low light conditions). If a scope has a fixed magnification of 10x with a 40 millimeter objective lens then the notation would be '10x40' (or perhaps '10x40mm').

Objective lens sizes ranging from 40 to 44 millimeters are pretty standard and practical. Larger lenses only improve shooting under particularly low lighting conditions when shooting at longer range (adjusting to higher magnifications). Much of this advantage is offset by the disadvantages of having a physically larger scope attached to the gun.[417]

NOTE: *One exception to the "9x-magnification-is-enough rule" might be the case of using a gun specifically as a 'counter-sniper' weapon. In this scenario you should expect to be utilizing a higher-magnification scope that is consistent with the longer range to target.*

While many commercial rifle scopes offer magnifications of 20:1 or greater, and provide controls that allow the shooter to adjust the level of magnification, most military snipers use rifles with scopes that are fixed at a magnification of 10:1. There are a few reasons for this, including the fact that it greatly reduces the complexity of calculations needed to compensate for wind and other factors; resulting in reduced probability of error.[417]

Red dot sights are special 1x magnification scopes produced for many shotguns and handguns. These scopes present a small red dot superimposed over the target image to indicate where the gun is pointing. Because shotguns and handguns have significantly shorter ranges than rifles there is no need for a magnification higher than 1x. However the red dot superimposed over the target allows for much faster target acquisition than taking the time to align regular front and rear sights. Red dot sights require a battery to provide the illumination of the dot, however they consume so little power that the scope may be used for thousands or tens of thousands of hours before the battery needs to be replaced.[419]

Scope Reticles

The markings visible through the scope that often appear as *'crosshairs'* are known as *'reticles'*. Recticles are created through a variety of technologies. In some cases microscopic fibers are attached to the lens to produce the fine lines, and in other cases the lines are engraved directly onto the lens. Some modern scopes even project computer-generated lines over the viewed image. A few advanced scopes feature illuminated colored reticles for easier viewing (which is especially helpful in low-light conditions or when shooting against dark backgrounds).

Some scopes feature reticles that are more elaborate than simple crosshairs.[402] These markings allow the shooter to measure distances at the target and more easily make adjustments for the drop of the bullet over the range-to-target. One of the more common reticle patterns is the *'mil-dot-reticle'*, which displays a series of horizontal and vertical dots that form the crosshair. The distance between the dots can be looked up for various ranges to allow the shooter to more quickly and easily compensate for bullet drop.[403]

D.7. Defensive Ranges of Handguns, Shotguns and Rifles

While there are precise ballistics-based formulas to calculate various ranges for guns (one of the most popular classifications is that of *effective range*), these ranges are not really applicable to situations involving real-world self-defense. This is because these ranges do not take into consideration that the shooter and target are both in motion, under duress, and possibly shooting at one-another. And, of course the prepper is interested in the ranges at which guns can be used for practical defense. This appendix will use the term *'defensive range'* to describe the ranges for which guns are most suitable for use in self-defense. The oft-cited defensive ranges for pistols, shotguns, assault-style rifles and hunting/sniper rifles are:

- *Handguns* - 0 to 25 feet.

- *Shotguns* - 25 feet to 50 yards

- *Assault-style rifles* - 50 to 100 yards

- *Hunting / Sniper Rifles* - 100 to 500 yards (and much longer in the hands of an expert)

D.8. Gun Accessories

A large number of accessories have been manufactured for all makes of handguns, shotguns and rifles. These accessories include:

- *Rails* - General purpose metal brackets that are attached to a handgun or long gun and to which other accessories such as scopes, flashlights, laser sights and night vision equipment can be attached.

- *Scopes* - As described in section D.6, scopes are mounted on guns to provide the shooter with a magnified view of the target to increase shooting accuracy.

- *Bipods and Tripods* - Retractable stands that can be attached to a long gun to provide a steady base for accurate long-distance shooting.

- *Sights* - Sights are physical structures attached to the front and rear of a gun's barrel which the shooter visually aligns with the target for increased accuracy. Some more sophisticated sights incorporate the slightly radioactive substance *tritium* to allow the shooter to align illuminated sights under reduced lighting conditions.

- *Flashlights* - Flashlights are sometimes mounted to the barrels of handguns, shotguns and rifles as a means of illuminating, blinding or disorienting a target.

- *Holsters* - Holsters are carriers for guns that are designed to be worn by a shooter. Some holsters are designed to maximize the wearer's ability to conceal the fact that they are carrying a gun. Holsters are also available for long guns to provide protection while in transit by vehicle or on horseback.

- *Shotgun Shell Holders* - To compensate for the fact that shotguns generally hold a very limited number of shells, many shotguns have extra shell holders attached to the gun's shoulder stock.

- *Adjustable Shoulder Stocks* - Sliding shoulder stocks can be purchased which adjust the gun to better fit shooters of various body types.

- *Shotgun Barrel Chokes* - These are attachments that can be placed at the end of a shotgun barrel to cause the pattern of shot directed to the target to be more closely grouped (for shooting targets at longer ranges).

- *Carrying Straps* - For a long gun, these are straps connected to the end of the barrel and the shoulder stock such that the gun can be slung over someone's shoulder for hands-free transport.

- *Muzzle Brakes* - Attached or built-in ducts that redirect some of the escaping gas from each shot so as to compensate for a gun's tendency to lift slightly between shots.

- *Flash Suppressors* - Devices attached to the barrel of a gun that reduce or eliminate the flash of light at the muzzle when a gun is fired. This reduces the probability that the shooter's position will be observed (particularly at night).

- *Sound Suppressors ('Silencers')* - Devices attached to the barrel of a gun that reduce the sound produced when the gun is fired. They are as important for protecting the hearing of those standing nearby as they are for minimizing the probability that gun-shots will be heard. The legality of owning, possessing and using a sound suppressor varies with jurisdiction, and the reader is strongly encouraged to understand the relevant laws in their own jurisdiction before considering the purchase or use of any sound suppressor.[418]

D.9. Gun Storage and Maintenance

The days of storing guns by simply leaning them against the wall of the back porch are behind us. In today's world such a practice would only lead to the theft of the gun, the gun being used against you, or possible loss of life if the gun were to reach the hands of someone who had little or no training in proper gun handling and safety. **Never store guns in an insecure fashion that would provide easy access to unauthorized individuals!**

Ideally guns should be stored in a gun safe, however this is not always possible. Failing that, other proper gun storing measures should be taken, not only for safety but to best preserve the gun as well. These measures include:

- Guns that are not intended to be used for home defense should be stored in an unloaded state with magazines and ammunition in different locations and not easily accessible.

- Trigger locks should be installed on guns to prevent unauthorized or accidental discharge.

- Storing guns in safes and/or locked boxes (many reasonably-priced gun safes and gun boxes are available with built-in fingerprint sensors that allow the safe or box to be quickly opened only if the owner places their finger(s) on pre-programmed fingerprint detectors).

- Storing guns in locked rooms.

In addition to storing guns securely and in a way that is consistent with their intended use, they should also be stored in a dry environment. This means that they should not be stored long term in foam-padded gun carriers, as the foam has a tendency to attract moisture.[421]

D.9.1. Fouling of Gun Barrels

Fouling of gun barrels is the depositing of unwanted substances on the inside of the gun's barrel when the gun is fired. Any deposits on the inside of the barrel can have adverse effects on muzzle velocity (leading to a reduction in range and impact on target) and accuracy (if the bullet has a "bumpy ride" down the barrel it can result in the bullet not traveling in as straight a trajectory).

There are four ways in which the barrel of a gun becomes fouled:

- *Corrosive Salt Deposits* - The primers of many lower cost military surplus rifle cartridges produce salts when fired. These salts go into the barrel where they can begin a chemical reaction that leads to rusting.

- *Lead Fouling* - As lead bullets travel down the barrel of the gun some of the metal from the lead that comes into contact with the barrel's rifling can be deposited in the barrel.

- *Copper Fouling* - As with lead bullets, copper-jacketed bullets traveling down the barrel can leave deposits of copper in the barrel.

- *Fouling with Powder Residue* - The 'soot' produced by the burning of gunpowder also can line a gun's barrel when it is fired.

D.9.2. Gun Cleaning

Guns should be cleaned after any appreciable use, and guns that are used seasonally (for example, hunting guns) should be given a more thorough cleaning at the end of the season. A basic gun cleaning would involve removing any magazine and ammunition from the gun and using a rod-and-patch or a '*bore snake*' to clean the barrel first with a proper solvent and then with a light gun oil. The barrel should be cleaned until the patch or bore snake is removed with no signs of dirt. A basic cleaning would also involve rubbing all exposed metal parts with light oil.

After a period of extensive use, or at the end of hunting season before a gun is stored away, the gun should be given a more detailed cleaning. Both the basic cleaning and detailed cleaning procedures are described later in this appendix.

Tools and chemicals used for gun cleaning include:

- Gun cleaning rod and patches with brass or nylon brush attachments

- Bore snake

- Oil rags

- Gun-cleaning solvents

- Gun Oil

> **AUTHOR'S NOTE:** *In researching gun cleaning I have noticed repeated positive references to Hoppe's No. 9 solvent. Hoppe's No. 9 has a good reputation for removing both powder and copper fouling from gun barrels. Other noteworthy solvents include Shooter's Choice and Sweet's 7.62. US GI Rifle Bore Cleaner is also recommended for removing salt deposits from corrosive ammunition (typically non-US-made military-surplus ammunition).[422]*
>
> *It should also be noted that some common household chemicals are used by many gun-owners for gun cleaning rather then purchasing specialized products. For example, many shooters report satisfactory results using 'Windex' window cleaner to remove salts and metal fouling, and others use high quality motor and transmission oils rather than specialized gun oils for lubrication. The reader is encouraged to consult with their local gun dealer to discuss these options as well as to identify additional gun-cleaning recommendations.*

Basic Gun Cleaning

Basic gun cleaning involves cleaning the barrel and wiping down any exposed metal surfaces with a rag that contains gun oil, such that a light coat of oil remains on all the exposed metal. An oily gun patch should then either be used to clean the barrel or an oily *bore snake* sized for the caliber of the gun being cleaned should be run through the barrel stating at the breech and exiting the muzzle. Depending on the amount of fouling observed additional patches and/or passes of the bore snake may be needed.

Detailed Gun Cleaning

Detailed cleaning of a rifle barrel should be performed in stages:

> **NOTE:** *Many shooters prefer to clean their guns using only gun oils and no solvents. This is probably acceptable if only non-corrosive ammunition has been used with the gun since the last cleaning.*

- Attach a nylon or brass brush to the end of the gun rod, immerse the brush in gun-cleaning solvent and insert the brush into the bore to scrub the inside of the barrel. If you cannot insert the brush through the breech end of the barrel then use a bore guide to insert the brush into the muzzle end to avoid creating any scratching on the muzzle end that could later affect shooting accuracy.

- Using either a gun-cleaning rod and clean patch or a bore snake, clean the barrel of any solvent and/or metal debris dislodged by the previous step.

- If the gun-cleaning solvent from the previous step is not formulated to work on copper or lead deposits (depending on whether you are firing lead or copper-jacketed ammunition) then repeat the previous brush-cleaning process using a copper or lead gun-cleaning solvent.

- If corrosive ammunition has been used with this gun, and if solvents already used are not formulated to remove salts, then pour hot, soapy water down the barrel. The hot water will dissolve and remove the salts while the soapy water will neutralize any acids the salts may have already begun to produce. Once rinsed allow the metal to dry (the hot water will dry quickly).

- Apply a thin coat of gun oil to the inside of the rifle bore using either a patch and cleaning rod or a bore snake.

Because the bullet passes through the barrel before the burned powder and any corrosive salts, some lead and copper fouling may lie below the last layer of powder residue. As a result, copper and/or lead fouling should be cleaned after the powder residue has been cleaned (some gun-cleaning solvents claim to remove both powder residue as well as copper and lead fouling).

NOTE: *There are tiny imperfections in the metal of any gun barrel, and lead and copper fouling can fill any microscopic cracks and crevices in the barrel. The cleaning of a gun's barrel will remove many of these deposits. As a gun is fired repeatedly the passage of the bullet through the barrel will, over time, smooth over these imperfections. As a result, it is a good idea to pay particular attention to cleaning the barrels of new guns before they have had an opportunity to become fully conditioned.*

After cleaning the barrel, disassemble the gun and clean all internal moving parts (revolvers do not normally require disassembly). Coat all moving parts with gun oil. Many modern gunsmiths further recommend that a light grease be applied between any major sliding metal parts (such as the frame rails of handguns and semi-automatic rifles).[420] In the case of semi-automatic, autoloading shotguns a thorough cleaning should also include a cleaning of the '*recoil spring*' in the gun's shoulder stuck. A fouled recoil spring has been demonstrated to be the cause of many problems associated with autoloading shotguns.[421]

D.10. Gun Laws

In addition to federal laws that affect gun ownership and usage, gun laws also exist at the state, county and city levels, and it is the responsibility of the gun owner to be aware of and conform to these laws. In addition to possibly controlling the purchase of guns, these laws control how guns are transported and how and where they may be used. When transporting guns inter-state there is a *'peaceable journey law'* that is (supposedly) honored by many states. This law states that as long as a gun is being transported in a way that is proper and legal in the state of origin and in the destination state, that it is legal to transport the gun in that manner through any intermediate state.

In general, gun laws control:

- If a gun must be purchased through a licensed dealer.
- If background checks must be performed for gun purchases (these background checks can require the purchaser to return to the gun store several days after the purchase to take possession of their gun).
- How a gun must be packaged and stored for transport.
- If a permit is required to purchase or own a gun.
- The maximum ammunition capacity allowed for a gun.
- If a license is required to hold the gun.
- Ability to carry a gun in plain sight *('open carry')* or concealed.
- Whether local gun laws take precedence over state gun laws.
- Proper gun use for self defense. Some states have adopted the *'castle doctrine'* which gives the gun owner greater freedom to use their gun for personal defense within their own home, and other states have adopted *'stand-your-ground laws'* that permit an individual to use their gun in self defense outside the home (California, in contrast to most states, requires you to flee or cower when confronted by a physical threat).

Often gun laws differ for handguns and long guns.

There are many easy-to-find and easy-to-understand web sites that can quickly provide you with all the information you need to legally own, transport and use a gun in your jurisdiction.

Bibliography

[1] Activated Carbon Water Filters and Purification (Granular/Granulated and Carbon Block)
   (http://www.home-water-purifiers-and-filters.com/carbon-water-filter.php)

[2] Mouse and Rat Studies on Fasting and Caloric Restruction
   (http://www.anti-aging-guide.com/31mousestudies.php\#16)

[3] Berkey Water Filter Store
   (http://www.berkeywaterfilterstore.com/)

[4] Water Filtration Systems. World's Leading Water Treatment Technologies
   (http://doultonusa.com/HTML\%20pages/water_filters_for_militaries.htm\#LP5)

[5] Where to Find Water in an Emergency
   (http://www.family-survival-planning.com/emergency-water-supply.html\#axzz2R3pXT6bd)

[6] Survival Needs - human
   (http://www.waterencyclopedia.com/St-Ts/Survival-Needs.html)

[7] Survival Skills - Wikipedia
   (http://en.wikipedia.org/wiki/Survival_skills\#Water)

[8] How To Purify Water With Household Bleach —
   (http://willowhavenoutdoor.com/featured-wilderness-survival-blog-entries/how-to-purify-water-with-household-bleach/)

[9] Drinking Swimming Pool Water in an Emergency
   (http://modernsurvivalblog.com/preps/drinking-swimming-pool-water-in-an-emergency/)

[10] Use a tennis ball to keep a pool cleaner — Digitals folder – Widget Local
   (http://tech.elecsonar.com/use-a-tennis-ball-to-keep-a-pool-cleaner/)

[11] How do you separate zinc oxide and water
   (http://wiki.answers.com/Q/How_do_you_separate_zinc_oxide_and_water)

[12] CDC - Drinking Water Wells
   (http://www.cdc.gov/healthywater/emergency/safe_water/wells/)

[13] Water Wells - What to do Before the Flood
   (http://www.env.gov.bc.ca/wsd/plan_protect_sustain/groundwater/wells/factsheets/PFRA_wells_before_flood.pdf)

[14] CDC - Emergency Disinfection of Bored or Dug Wells
   (http://www.cdc.gov/healthywater/emergency/safe_water/wells/disinfection_wells_bored.html)

[15] CDC - Emergency Disinfection of Drilled or Driven Wells
   (http://www.cdc.gov/healthywater/emergency/safe_water/wells/disinfection_wells_drilled.html)

[16] Standard coffee filter micron size? - Yahoo! Answers NZ
   (http://nz.answers.yahoo.com/question/index?qid=20120625231202AAyTEFo)

[17] Water Filtering and Purification
   (http://www.bestglide.com/emergency_equipment_highlights.html)

[18] Water Purification
   (http://www.waterfilterdude.com/water-purify.shtml)

[19] Website: American Membrane Corporation
   (http://www.americanmembrane.com/lmcs_en.asp?id=68)

[20] Water microfilters – Backcountry Drinking Water
   (http://backcountrywater.com/water-treatment-methods/water-filters-and-purifiers/water-microfilters/)

[21] sodis — Survival Shop
   (http://survivalshop.brentmart.com/?s=sodis)

[22] Water Purification - Wikipedia
   (http://en.wikipedia.org/wiki/Water_purification)

[23] Resource Development International - Cambodia
(*https : // www. engineeringforchange. org/ static/ content/ Water/ S00067/ Ceramic\ %20filter\
%20manual\ %20no-appendices. pdf*)

[24] Pool Chemical Experts With Online Water Testing and How To — Pool Geek
(*http : // www. poolgeek. com/*)

[25] DIY – How to Make Chlorine Bleach from Pool Shock
(*http : // suburbansurvivalblog. com/ diy-how-to-make-chlorine-bleach-from-pool-shock*)

[26] Calcium Hypochlorite MSDS
(*http : // www. hvchemical. com/ msds/ cahyp. htm*)

[27] Reverse Osmosis - Wikipedia
(*http : // en. wikipedia. org/ wiki/ Reverse_ osmosis*)

[28] Katadyne Products Inc.
(*http : // www. katadyn. com/ en/ katadyn-products/ products/ katadynshopconnect/
katadyn-wasserfilter-endurance-series-produkte/*)

[29] MRE Nutrition — eHow
(*http : // www. ehow. com/ facts_ 5480748_ mre-nutrition. html*)

[30] FAQ #8211; MRE Nutrition Value — The ReadyBlog
(*http : // www. thereadystore. com/ mre/ 766/ faq-mre-nutrition/*)

[31] Mylar Bags Do It Yourself Long Term Food Storage
(*http : // www. optimumpreparedness. com/ mylar_ bags_ for_ long_ term_ food_ storage. html*)

[32] Mylar Bags: Inexpensive Do-It-Yourself Long-Term Food Storage Solution
(*http://36readyblog.com/2013/03/15/
mylar-bags-inexpensive-do-it-yourself-long-term-food-storage-solution/*)

[33] Nutritional Effects of Freeze-Drying Foods — eHow
(*http : // www. ehow. com/ facts_ 5993868_ nutritional-effects-freeze_ drying-foods. html*)

[34] Nutritional Effects of Freeze-Drying Foods — eHow
(*http : // www. ehow. com/ facts_ 5993868_ nutritional-effects-freeze_ drying-foods. html*)

[35] Dehydrate Foods for Long Term Storage — Ready Nutrition
(*http : // readynutrition. com/ resources/ dehydrate-foods-for-long-term-storage_ 31032010/*)

[36] Nutrition For Dehydrated Food — LIVESTRONG.COM
(*http : // www. livestrong. com/ article/ 360320-nutrition-for-dehydrated-food/*)

[37] How Does Smoking Preserve Food? — Livestrong
(*http : // www. livestrong. com/ article/ 233286-how-does-smoking-preserve-food/*)

[38] Smoking (cooking) - Wikipedia
(*http : // en. wikipedia. org/ wiki/ Smoking_ (cooking)*)

[39] Dangers of eating smoked food
(*http : // www. helium. com/ items/ 1065023-dangers-of-eating-smoked-food*)

[40] Is Eating Smoked Foods Healthy? — LIVESTRONG.COM
(*http : // www. livestrong. com/ article/ 340131-is-eating-smoked-foods-healthy/*)

[41] Smoking Your Catch: Do it Safely
(*http : // www. foodsafety. wisc. edu/ assets/ pdf_ Files/ smokingyourcatch. pdf*)

[42] Curing
(*http : // www. wedlinydomowe. com/ sausage-making/ curing*)

[43] Curing (food preservation) - Wikipedia
(*http : // en. wikipedia. org/ wiki/ Curing_ (food_ preservation)*)

[44] Comparative assessment of drying methods, curing agents and meat-cut size on the quality and preservation of meat
under rural setting perspectives
(*http : // www. lrrd. org/ lrrd25/ 1/ ryob25010. htm*)

[45] Solar Food Drying
(*urlhttp://www.backwoodshome.com/articles/shaffer58.html*)

[46] Home Canning Basics for High Acid Foods - Yahoo Voices - voices.yahoo.com
(*http : // www. associatedcontent. com/ article/ 91397/ home_ canning_ basics_ for_ high_ acid_ foods. html*)

[47] Canning Basics For Preserving Food
(*http : // www. canning-food-recipes. com/ canning. htm*)

[48] Shelf Life of Canned Goods
(*http : // www. buzzle. com/ articles/ shelf-life-of-canned-goods. html*)

[49] foodsafety.wsu.edu
(*http : // www. foodsafety. wsu. edu/ consumers/ factsheet4. htm*)

[50]   Mountain House Product Shelf Life
       (http://www.mountainhouse.com/shelf_lif.cfm)
[51]   The Benefits of Fuel Treatment Explained
       (http://www.batterystuff.com/tutorial_fuel_storage.html)
[52]   Fuel Degradation In Storage
       (http://theepicenter.com/tow021799.html)
[53]   Methyl tert-butyl ether - Wikipedia
       (http://en.wikipedia.org/wiki/MTBE)
[54]   Diesel fuel - Wikipedia
       (http://en.wikipedia.org/wiki/Diesel_fuel)
[55]   Gasoline Expiration - Ethanol Blend Fuels Have a Short Shelf Life
       (http://www.fuel-testers.com/expiration_of_ethanol_gas.html)
[56]   Long Term Diesel Storage
       (http://amsca.com/files/Download/Fuel_news_long_term_storage_diesel.pdf)
[57]   Does Diesel Fuel Go Bad — eHow
       (http://www.ehow.com/about_6577235_diesel-fuel-go-bad.html)
[58]   Homestead Fuel Storage and Rotation
       (http://www.survivalblog.com/2008/05/homestead_fuel_storage_and_rot.html)
[59]   For safety sake, homestead fuel storage must be handled properly by Emory Warner Issue #43
       (http://www.backwoodshome.com/articles/warner43.html)
[60]   Burning Coal Vs. Wood — eHow
       (http://www.ehow.com/about_6594940_burning-coal-vs_-wood.html)
[61]   Wood Pellets Vs. Coal — eHow
       (http://www.ehow.com/about_5597091_wood-pellets-vs_-coal.html)
[62]   Lehmans Kerosene Refrigerators
       (http://www.lehmans.com/store/Appliances___Gas_Refrigerators_and_Freezers___Dometic___
       Dometic_Kerosene_Refrigerator___RK400?Args=)
[63]   The World Factbook
       (https://www.cia.gov/library/publications/the-world-factbook/geos/us.html)
[64]   Camo Hunting Clothes - Types of Camo and Brands You Should Look For — Camo Hunting Clothes
       (http://www.camohuntingclothesinfo.com/camo-hunting-clothes-types-camo-brands)
[65]   Eating Alligators: A Healthy Meat Alternative - Yahoo Voices - voices.yahoo.com
       (http://www.associatedcontent.com/article/84848/eating_alligators_a_healthy_meat_alternative.
       html)
[66]   How to Cook a Snake: 8 Steps (with Pictures) - wikiHow
       (http://www.wikihow.com/Cook-a-Snake)
[67]   This website is currently unavailable.
       (http://www.stuffedandstarved.org/drupal/node/391)
[68]   Catching Live Cockroaches - A Practical Guide for Parents
       (http://www.k12.hi.us/~rkubota/digiphoto/cockroach/roach.html)
[69]   Pinfish
       (http://floridasportfishing.com/magazine/baitfish-profiles/pinfish.html)
[70]   E. coli Outbreak Associated with Lettuce Prompts Call for Better Sanitation
       (http://www.reuters.com/article/2008/06/10/idUS19471+10-Jun-2008+BW20080610)
[71]   Cockroach Disease - Planet Cockroach
       (http://www.planetcockroach.com/cockroach-disease.html)
[72]   Cholera - Wikipedia
       (http://en.wikipedia.org/wiki/Cholera)
[73]   Typhoid fever - Wikipedia
       (http://en.wikipedia.org/wiki/Typhoid)
[74]   New York State Department of Health - Typhoid Fever
       (http://www.health.state.ny.us/diseases/communicable/typhoid_fever/fact_sheet.htm)
[75]   Centers for Disease Control and Prevention - Typhoid Fever
       (http://www.cdc.gov/nczved/divisions/dfbmd/diseases/typhoid_fever/)
[76]   Typhoid Mary - The Sad Story of Typhoid Mary
       (http://history1900s.about.com/od/1900s/a/typhoidmary.htm)
[77]   Gastroenteritis - Wikipedia
       (http://en.wikipedia.org/wiki/Gastroenteritis)

Bibliography

[78] Gastroenteritis Symptoms, Treatment, Contagious, Children, Infants - eMedicineHealth
(http://www.emedicinehealth.com/gastroenteritis/article_em.htm)

[79] Escherichia coli - Wikipedia
(http://en.wikipedia.org/wiki/E.coli)

[80] Pathogenic Escherichia coli - Wikipedia
(http://en.wikipedia.org/wiki/Pathogenic_Escherichia_coli)

[81] Thailand finds E. coli in European cabbage - NZ Herald News
(http://www.nzherald.co.nz/world/news/article.cfm?c_id=2&objectid=10731689)

[82] Diarrhea - Wikipedia
(http://en.wikipedia.org/wiki/Diarrhea)

[83] Why do babies get jaundice? - Answerbag
(http://www.answerbag.com/q_view/1901281)

[84] Jaundice - Wikipedia
(http://en.wikipedia.org/wiki/Jaundice)

[85] Methicillin-resistant Staphylococcus aureus - Wikipedia
(http://en.wikipedia.org/wiki/Methicillin-resistant_Staphylococcus_aureus)

[86] Clorox Bleach Facts - MRSA Infection Control Information
(http://www.factsaboutbleach.com/mrsa.html\#school_disinfection)

[87] CDC - Patient information about CRE - HAI
(http://www.cdc.gov/hai/organisms/cre/cre-patients.html)

[88] Flesh Eating Bacterial Infection Causes, Symptoms, Treatment - MedicineNet
(http://www.medicinenet.com/script/main/art.asp?articlekey=61933)

[89] How to Recognize Signs of Infection — eHow
(http://www.ehow.com/how_2066084_recognize-signs-infection.html)

[90] Bacterial Infection or Virus? - DukeHealth.org
(http://www.dukehealth.org/health_library/advice_from_doctors/your_childs_health/bacterial_infections)

[91] Antibiotics for bacterial meningitis
(http://www.webmd.com/brain/antibiotics-for-bacterial-meningitis)

[92] Meningitis: MedlinePlus Medical Encyclopedia
(http://www.nlm.nih.gov/medlineplus/ency/article/000680.htm)

[93] The Importance of Probiotics after Antibiotics
(http://www.naturalnews.com/037005_antibiotics_probiotics_gut_flora.html)

[94] Antibiotic Guidelines - Emergency Preparedness - KIO3.com
(http://www.kio3.com/prep/ant-guide.htm)

[95] List of Antibiotics - eMedExpert.com
(http://www.emedexpert.com/lists/antibiotics.shtml)

[96] Aminoglycoside - Wikipedia
(http://en.wikipedia.org/wiki/Aminoglycosides)

[97] Carbapenem - Wikipedia
(http://en.wikipedia.org/wiki/Carbapenems)

[98] Penicillin Allergy - Amoxicillin Allergy - Cephalosporin Allergy
(http://allergies.about.com/od/medicationallergy/a/penicillin.htm)

[99] Penicillin Information from Drugs.com
(http://www.drugs.com/penicillin.html)

[100] Antibiotics Types and Side Effects
(http://www.emedexpert.com/classes/antibiotics.shtml)

[101] Types of Antibiotics
(http://www.buzzle.com/articles/types-of-antibiotics.html)

[102] Povidone-iodine - Wikipedia
(http://en.wikipedia.org/wiki/Povidone-iodine)

[103] CDC - News (March 1, 2010): Assessing Haitian Patients, Immigrants, and Refugees for Rabies - Rabies
(http://www.cdc.gov/rabies/resources/news/2010-03-01.html)

[104] Rabies Symptoms, Causes, Treatment - OnHealth
(http://www.medicinenet.com/rabies/page6.htm\#how_soon_after_an_exposure_should_a_person_seek_medical_attention)

[105] Rabies - Wikipedia
(http://en.wikipedia.org/wiki/Rabies)

[106] Rabies Symptoms, Vaccine, Treatment, Transmission, Prevention - OnHealth
(*http: // www. medicinenet. com/ rabies/ article. htm*)

[107] CDC - Pet Risks - Rabies
(*http: // www. cdc. gov/ rabies/ pets/ index. html*)

[108] Treating Asthma Without Medication? - EverydayHealth.com
(*http: // www. everydayhealth. com/ specialists/ allergies-asthma/ feldweg/ qa/ asthma_ without_ medication/ index. aspx*)

[109] How to Treat a Broken Bone - Broken Bones
(*http: // firstaid. about. com/ od/ breaksandsprains/ ht/ 06_ FxTx. htm*)

[110] Skin Burns: Recognizing First, Second, and Third Degree Burns - Yahoo Voices - voices.yahoo.com
(*http: // voices. yahoo. com/ skin-burns-recognizing-first-second-third-degree-35763. html*)

[111] Separated Shoulder - Wikipedia
(*http: // en. wikipedia. org/ wiki/ Separated_ shoulder*)

[112] Shoulder Dislocation - Wikipedia
(*http: // en. wikipedia. org/ wiki/ Shoulder_ dislocation*)

[113] Posterior Shoulder Dislocation
(*http: // lifeinthefastlane. com/ 2009/ 06/ posterior-shoulder-dislocation/*)

[114] Shoulder Relocation Techniques
(*http: // www. shoulderdoc. co. uk/ article. asp? article= 1267*)

[115] Videos of various techniques — ShoulderDislocation.net
(*http: // shoulderdislocation. net/ videos*)

[116] ISK Knowledge Center: Patient information about orthopedic disorders
(*http: // www. iskinstitute. com/ kc/ shoulder/ shoulder_ dislocation/ t1. html*)

[117] Frostbite - Wikipedia
(*http: // en. wikipedia. org/ wiki/ Frostbite*)

[118] Dizziness: Causes - MayoClinic.com
(*http: // www. mayoclinic. com/ health/ dizziness/ DS00435/ DSECTION= causes*)

[119] Heat exhaustion — University of Maryland Medical Center
(*http: // www. umm. edu/ altmed/ articles/ heat-exhaustion-000075. htm*)

[120] Heat Stroke - Wikipedia
(*http: // en. wikipedia. org/ wiki/ Heat_ stroke*)

[121] Hypothermia Treatment: First Aid Information for Hypothermia
(*http: // firstaid. webmd. com/ hypothermia-treatment*)

[122] Headache Symptoms, Causes, Treatment - MedicineNet
(*http: // www. medicinenet. com/ headache/ tension-headache-treatment/ article. htm*)

[123] Rattlesnake basics
(*http: // www. alongtheway. org/ rattlesnakes/ basics. html*)

[124] Seven Home Remedies for a Toothache - Yahoo Voices - voices.yahoo.com
(*http: // voices. yahoo. com/ seven-home-remedies-toothache-101326. html? cat=5*)

[125] Benzocaine vs. Clove oil – On two approaches to tooth pain – John McDonald
(*http: // johnmcdonald. info/ benzocaine-or-clove-oil/*)

[126] How to Attend to a Stab Wound: 11 Steps (with Pictures) - wikiHow
(*http: // www. wikihow. com/ Attend-to-a-Stab-Wound*)

[127] Oligodynamic Effect - Wikipedia
(*http: // en. wikipedia. org/ wiki/ Oligodynamic_ effect*)

[128] Colloidal Silver Is Toxic - The Dark Side of a New Health Craze
(*http: // www. cqs. com/ silver. htm*)

[129] Blisters - Causes, Symptoms, Treatment, First Aid
(*http: // www. everydayhealth. com/ health-center/ blisters. aspx*)

[130] Azithromycin - Wikipedia
(*http: // en. wikipedia. org/ wiki/ Azithromycin\ #Adverse_ effects*)

[131] Ampicillin - Wikipedia
(*http: // en. wikipedia. org/ wiki/ Ampicillin*)

[132] Ciprofloxacin - Wikipedia
(*http: // en. wikipedia. org/ wiki/ Ciprofloxacin\ #Adverse_ effects*)

[133] Amoxicillin - Wikipedia
(*http: // en. wikipedia. org/ wiki/ Amoxicillin\ #Adverse_ effects*)

[134] Doxycycline - Wikipedia
(*http: // en. wikipedia. org/ wiki/ Doxycycline\ #Adverse_ effects*)

[135] Clindamycin - Wikipedia
(http://en.wikipedia.org/wiki/Clindamycin\#Adverse_effects)

[136] Metronidazole - Wikipedia
(http://en.wikipedia.org/wiki/Metronidazole\#Adverse_effects)

[137] Trimethoprim/sulfamethoxazole - Wikipedia
(http://en.wikipedia.org/wiki/Trimethoprim-sulfamethoxazole\#Side_effects)

[138] Quinolone - Wikipedia
(http://en.wikipedia.org/wiki/Quinolone)

[139] Using Bleach to Destroy Anthrax and Other Microbes
(http://www.ehso.com/bleach.htm\#bkmrk8)

[140] Anthrax Spore Decontamination using Bleach (Sodium Hypochlorite) — Pesticides — US EPA
(http://www.epa.gov/pesticides/factsheets/chemicals/bleachfactsheet.htm)

[141] Vinegar Increases Killing Power of Bleach
(http://www.eurekalert.org/pub_releases/2006-02/asfm-vik021306.php)

[142] How to Disinfect, Clean and Kill MRSA and Staph
(http://www.staph-infection-resources.com/prevention/infection-control/)

[143] Influenza - Wikipedia
(http://en.wikipedia.org/wiki/Influenza)

[144] Medical Quarantine — Protecting Your Family from Infection, by Dr. Cynthia Koelker - SurvivalBlog.com
(http://survivalblog.com/2011/01/medical-quarantine----protecti.html)

[145] Management of Dead Bodies After Disasters: A Field Manual for First Responders

[146] Vitamin D
(http://throughwoods.com/3systems-of-the-body/endocrine-system/vitamin/)

[147] Rickets - Wikipedia
(http://en.wikipedia.org/wiki/Rickets)

[148] Beriberi - Wikipedia
(http://en.wikipedia.org/wiki/Beriberi)

[149] Scurvy - Wikipedia
(http://en.wikipedia.org/wiki/Scurvy)

[150] Aerobic exercise - Ask.com Encyclopedia
(http://www.ask.com/wiki/Aerobic_exercise?oo=0\#Aerobic_versus_anaerobic_exercise)

[151] Flag semaphore - Wikipedia
(http://en.wikipedia.org/wiki/Flag_semaphore)

[152] TriSquare - 2-way Radio - Beyond FRS Beyond GMRS eXRS (TM) eXtreme Radio Service
(http://www.trisquare.us/index.html)

[153] Family Radio Service - Wikipedia
(http://en.wikipedia.org/wiki/Family_Radio_Service)

[154] General Mobile Radio Service - Wikipedia
(http://en.wikipedia.org/wiki/General_Mobile_Radio_Service)

[155] What Is the Average CB Radio Range?
(http://www.wisegeek.org/what-is-the-average-cb-radio-range.htm)

[156] Marine VHF Radio - Wikipedia
(http://en.wikipedia.org/wiki/Marine_VHF_radio)

[157] Niacin - Wikipedia
(http://en.wikipedia.org/wiki/Niacin)

[158] Vitamin B5 - Wikipedia
(http://en.wikipedia.org/wiki/Vitamin_B5)

[159] Vitamin B6 - Wikipedia
(http://en.wikipedia.org/wiki/Vitamin_B6)

[160] Vitamin B7 - Wikipedia
(http://en.wikipedia.org/wiki/Vitamin_B7)

[161] Vitamin B9 - Wikipedia
(http://en.wikipedia.org/wiki/Vitamin_B9)

[162] Vitamin B12 - Wikipedia
(http://en.wikipedia.org/wiki/Vitamin_B12)

[163] Vitamin C - Wikipedia
(http://en.wikipedia.org/wiki/Vitamin_C)

[164] Vitamin E - Wikipedia
(http://en.wikipedia.org/wiki/Vitamin_E)

[165] Vitamin K - Wikipedia
   (http://en.wikipedia.org/wiki/Vitamin_K)
[166] Medscape: Medscape Access
   (http://www.medscape.com/viewarticle/758650)
[167] What Is Vitamin D? What Are The Benefits Of Vitamin D?
   (http://www.medicalnewstoday.com/articles/161618.php)
[168] Immune-enhancing role of vitamin C and zinc a... [Ann Nutr Metab. 2006] - PubMed - NCBI
   (http://www.ncbi.nlm.nih.gov/pubmed/16373990)
[169] Age Gender Calorie Chart
   (http://www.indiacurry.com/pyramids/caloriechart.htm)
[170] What percent of calories should be from fat, protein and carbs?
   (http://caloriecount.about.com/percent-calories-fat-protein-carbs-q184)
[171] Food energy - Ask.com Encyclopedia
   (http://www.ask.com/wiki/Food_energy)
[172] Goitre - Wikipedia
   (http://en.wikipedia.org/wiki/Goiter)
[173] GoatCamp™ at Onion Creek Ranch™
   (http://www.tennesseemeatgoats.com/GoatCamp/index.html)
[174] Raising Goats for Dummies
   (http://www.dummies.com/how-to/content/raising-goats-for-dummies-cheat-sheet.html)
[175] Raising Goats My Way
   (http://www.motherearthnews.com/Sustainable-Farming/1983-07-01/
   Raising-Goats-My-Way-If-I-Could-Do-It-Over-Again-Part-One.aspx)
[176] Raising Goats
   (http://www.farminfo.org/livestock/goats.htm)
[177] Goat birthing and raising kids by Jackie Clay
   (http://www.backwoodshome.com/articles2/clay112.html)
[178] Dry sheep equivalents - DSE - for Goats « Informed Farmers
   (http://informedfarmers.com/dry-sheep-equivalents/)
[179] Fias Co Farm- Feeding your goats
   (http://fiascofarm.com/goats/feeding.htm)
[180] Providing Shelter for Your Goats
   (http://www.dummies.com/how-to/content/providing-shelter-for-your-goats.html)
[181] Raising Guinea Fowl
   (http://www.guineafowl.com/fritsfarm/guineas/)
[182] Raising Chickens
   (http://how-to-raise--chickens.blogspot.com/)
[183] Raising Poultry on Pasture
   (http://www.cias.wisc.edu/crops-and-livestock/raising-poultry-on-pasture/)
[184] All About Raising Chickens
   (http://www.southernstates.com/articles/raising-chickens.aspx)
[185] 9 steps for raising chicks — Living the Country Life
   (http://www.livingthecountrylife.com/animals/poultry/9-steps-for-raising-chicks/)
[186] Raising Chicks
   (http://www.motherearthnews.com/Modern-Homesteading/Raising-Chicks.aspx)
[187] Raising Chickens 2.0: No More Coop and Run!
   (http://www.richsoil.com/raising-chickens.jsp)
[188] How to Raise Chickens Cheaply
   (http://www.dummies.com/how-to/content/how-to-raise-chickens-cheaply.html)
[189] Raising Baby Chicks - How to Raise Chickens from Day-Old Chicks
   (http://smallfarm.about.com/od/farmanimals/a/htraisechicks.htm)
[190] How to Raise Chickens for Meat - How to Raise Meat Birds
   (http://smallfarm.about.com/od/chickens/tp/How-To-Raise-Chickens-For-Meat.htm)
[191] Raise Pastured Poultry - How to Raised Pastured Poultry
   (http://smallfarm.about.com/od/farmanimals/a/electrictractor.htm)
[192] Let Chickens Power a Chicken Tractor Around Your Garden or Farm
   (http://ezinearticles.com/?Let-Chickens-Power-a-Chicken-Tractor-Around-Your-Garden-Or-Farm)
[193] Are Eggs From Hens on Pasture More Nutritious?
   (http://smallfarm.about.com/od/faqs/f/pasturedeggs.htm)

Bibliography

[194] Chicken and Poultry Health Problems and Diseases
(http://smallfarm.about.com/od/chickens/a/Chicken-And-Poultry-Health-Problems-And-Diseases.htm)

[195] poultryOne Guide to Raising Backyard Chickens — Your Guide to the World of Chickens
(http://poultryone.com/)

[196] Farm Animals
(http://smallfarm.about.com/od/farmanimals/a/5tipsnestboxes.html)

[197] How to butcher a chicken in 20 minutes or less by Dr. Roger W. Grim, D.C.
(http://www.backwoodshome.com/articles2/grim79.html)

[198] Constructing a Dust Bath
(http://communitychickens.blogspot.com/2011/10/constructing-dust-bath.html\#.UEOemn3UXrE)

[199] Blogger: Sign in
(http://www.cultivatinghome.com/2008/10/how-to-butcher-chicken-easy-way.html)

[200] Cannibalism Cause and Prevention in Poultry in Eggs to Hatch and Beyond Forum
(http://backyardchickens.yuku.com/topic/4943/Cannibalism-Cause-and-Prevention-in-Poultry\#.UOm6UX3UV3M)

[201] Raising Rabbits for Food
(http://www.zombiesurvivalwiki.com/page/Raising+Rabbits+for+Food)

[202] Some Tips and Tricks on Raising Meat Rabbits
(http://www.survivalblog.com/2010/05/some_tips_and_tricks_on_raisin.html)

[203] Raising Rabbits for Meat
(http://www.survivalblog.com/2011/05/raising_rabbits_for_meat_by_ll.html)

[204] How to feed rabbits right
(http://www.breedingbunnies.com/article/feeding-rabbits.html)

[205] Advice on how and what to feed rabbits from happyhopper.co.uk
(http://happyhopper.co.uk/feeding.htm)

[206] What should you feed a pet rabbit
(http://wiki.answers.com/Q/What_should_you_feed_a_pet_rabbit\&altQ=What_should_you_feed_a_rabbit)

[207] Spaying/Neutering Your Rabbit
(http://www.mybunny.org/info/spayneuter.htm)

[208] How to Sex Your Rabbits
(http://www.rabbitnetwork.org/articles/sexing.shtml)

[209] Spaying/Neutering Your Rabbit
(http://www.mybunny.org/info/spayneuter.htm)

[210] Detecting Illness in Rabbits Before it's an Emergency
(http://www.bio.miami.edu/hare/sickbun.html)

[211] Winter Rabbit Care - Rabbit Hutches in Winter
(http://www.therabbithouse.com/outdoor/rabbitwinter.asp)

[212] Butchering Rabbits
(http://rabbittalk.com/blogs/24carrot/2011/08/24/butchering-rabbits-graphic-descriptions/)

[213] Sweet Potato Ranks Number 1 In Nutrition of All Vegetables
(http://www.foodreference.com/html/sweet-pot-nutrition.html)

[214] Sweet Potatoes
(http://www.sweetpotatoplant.com/potatoes.html)

[215] Growing Sweet Potatoes
(http://robbwolf.com/2011/04/20/growing-sweet-potatoes/)

[216] How To Grow Sweet Potatoes? Growing Sweet Potatoes The Easy Way
(http://www.tropicalpermaculture.com/growing-sweet-potatoes.html)

[217] Nutritional Value of Sweet Potatoes — How To Make Sweet Potato Fries
(http://howtomakesweetpotatofries.org/nutritional-value-of-sweet-potatoes/)

[218] Sweet Potato Facts, Selection, and Storage
(http://homecooking.about.com/cs/productreviews/p/sweetpotato_pro.htm)

[219] How to Water Sweet Potato Vines - Yahoo Voices - voices.yahoo.com
(http://voices.yahoo.com/how-water-sweet-potato-vines-7936890.html)

[220] Storing potatoes and sweet potatoes
(http://www.justbelowthesurface.com/index.php?option=com_content\&view=article\&id=71:storing-potatoes-and-sweet-potatoes\&catid=39:growing-garden-vegetables\&Itemid=58)

[221] How to Grow Carrots
(http: // www. motherearthnews. com/ Organic-Gardening/ 2008-08-01/ How-To-Grow-Carrots. aspx)

[222] Growing Carrots A Power House of Nutrition
(http: // www. everyday-vegetable-garden. com/ growing-carrots. html)

[223] Carrot Storage
(http: // www. carrotmuseum. co. uk/ carrotstorage. html \ #root \ %20cellar)

[224] How do Carrots Produce Seeds?
(http: // www. carrotmuseum. co. uk/ seeds. html)

[225] Food Gardening Guide :: National Gardening Association
(http: // www. garden. org/ foodguide/ browse/ veggie/ roots_ harvesting/ 623)

[226] A Basic Vegetable Garden — Suite101
(http: // suite101. com/ article/ abasicvegetablegarden-a59)

[227] Storing Seeds
(http: // www. theheartlandusa. com/ survival/ references/ storing_ seeds. htm)

[228] Nutrition Facts and Analysis for Pumpkin, Cooked, Boiled, Drained, Without Salt
(http: // nutritiondata. self. com/ facts/ vegetables-and-vegetable-products/ 2601/ 2)

[229] All About Pumpkins - Learn How to Grow Pumpkins - Basic Information
(http: // www. allaboutpumpkins. com/ growing. html)

[230] Fertilizing and Watering Pumpkins
(http: // www. backyard-vegetable-gardening. com/ watering-pumpkins. html)

[231] Growing Pumpkins - Garden Naturally
(http: // gardennaturallynow. com/ files/ pumpkin. htm)

[232] Keep Pumpkins from Taking Over Gardens: Organic Gardening
(http: // www. organicgardening. com/ learn-and-grow/ pumpkins-small-gardens)

[233] Nutrition Facts and Analysis for Kale, Raw
(http: // nutritiondata. self. com/ facts/ vegetables-and-vegetable-products/ 2461/ 2)

[234] Kale - Wikipedia
(http: // en. wikipedia. org/ wiki/ Kale)

[235] Kale - Growing Kale in the Home Vegetable Garden
(http: // gardening. about. com/ od/ vegetablevarieties/ p/ Kale. htm)

[236] Kale: An Easy Beginner's Guide to Growing
(http: // gentleworld. org/ kale-an-easy-beginners-guide-to-growing/)

[237] Purslane nutrition facts and health benefits
(http: // www. nutrition-and-you. com/ purslane. html)

[238] Growing Purslane: How To Grow Edible Purslane In The Garden
(http: // www. gardeningknowhow. com/ herb/ edible-purslane-herb. htm)

[239] Nutrition Facts and Analysis for Spinach, Raw
(http: // nutritiondata. self. com/ facts/ vegetables-and-vegetable-products/ 2626/ 2)

[240] All About Growing Spinach
(http: // www. motherearthnews. com/ Organic-Gardening/ 2008-10-01/ How-To-Grow-Spinach. aspx)

[241] How to Grow Spinach: Organic Gardening
(http: // www. organicgardening. com/ learn-and-grow/ spinach-growing-guide)

[242] Growing Spinach
(http: // gardening. about. com/ od/ vegetables/ a/ Growing_ Spinach. htm)

[243] Spinach: Planting, Growing and Harvesting Spinach Plants
(http: // www. almanac. com/ plant/ spinach)

[244] Nutrition Facts and Analysis for Cabbage, Raw
(http: // nutritiondata. self. com/ facts/ vegetables-and-vegetable-products/ 2371/ 2)

[245] Cabbage Growing Guide: Organic Gardening
(http: // www. organicgardening. com/ learn-and-grow/ cabbage)

[246] All Cabbage Types and Cabbage Facts
(http: // www. successful-diet-cabbage-soup. com/ cabbage-types. html)

[247] Learn How to Grow Cabbage - Instructions and advice for growing Cabbages in Your Vegetable Garden
(http: // www. howtogardenadvice. com/ vegetables/ grow_ cabbage. html)

[248] Nutrition Facts and Analysis for Watermelon, Raw
(http: // nutritiondata. self. com/ facts/ fruits-and-fruit-juices/ 2072/ 2)

[249] Growing Watermelons - How To Grow Watermelon Plants From Seed
(http: // www. tropicalpermaculture. com/ growing-watermelons. html)

Bibliography

[250] Watering and Fertilizing Watermelon
       (http://www.backyard-vegetable-gardening.com/fertilizing-watermelon.html)
[251] Nutrition Facts and Analysis for Melons, cantaloupe, Raw
       (http://nutritiondata.self.com/facts/fruits-and-fruit-juices/1954/2)
[252] How to Grow Cantaloupe - Backyard Gardening Blog
       (http://www.gardeningblog.net/how-to-grow/cantaloupe/)
[253] Watering and Fertilizing Cantaloupe
       (http://www.backyard-vegetable-gardening.com/fertilizing-cantaloupe.html)
[254] Harvesting Cantaloupe
       (http://www.backyard-vegetable-gardening.com/harvesting-cantaloupe.html)
[255] Winter Squash - Wikipedia
       (http://en.wikipedia.org/wiki/Winter_squash)
[256] Growing Guide for Winter Squash: Organic Gardening
       (http://www.organicgardening.com/learn-and-grow/winter-squash)
[257] Organic Gardening Guru - How to Grow Organically
       (http://www.composting101.com/)
[258] Compost Guide: Tips for Home Composting
       (http://compostguide.com/)
[259] Using Your Compost to Amend Soils
       (http://www.nyc.gov/html/nycwasteless/html/compost/edu_using_soil.shtml)
[260] Using Humus to Improve Soil Organically
       (http://compostguide.com/using-humus-to-improve-soil-organically/)
[261] Mulch - Wikipedia
       (http://en.wikipedia.org/wiki/Mulch)
[262] Using Manure to Fertilize Your Garden - Vegetable Gardener
       (http://www.vegetablegardener.com/item/2427/using-manure-to-fertilize-your-garden/page/all)
[263] Gardening Resources, Cornell University
       (http://www.gardening.cornell.edu/factsheets/orgmatter/index.html)
[264] Using Rabbit Manure
       (http://www.hobbyfarms.com/farm-pets/pet-rabbit-information/using-rabbit-manure.aspx)
[265] Green Manure - Wikipedia
       (http://en.wikipedia.org/wiki/Green_manure)
[266] How to Use Commercial Fertilizer: 11 Steps (with Pictures)
       (http://www.wikihow.com/Use-Commercial-Fertilizer)
[267] Fertilizer: advantages and disadvantages of using fertilizers, synthetic fertilizer, tissue flowers
       (http://en.allexperts.com/q/Fertilizer-717/advantages-disadvantages-using-fertilizers.htm)
[268] 5 Things to Know About Using Fertilizer in the Garden
       (http://seattletimes.com/html/homegarden/2008047227_gardenfertilizer12.html)
[269] How to Read a Fertilizer Label - wikiHow
       (http://www.wikihow.com/Read-a-Fertilizer-Label)
[270] Plant Nutrients
       (http://www.ncagr.gov/cyber/kidsurld/plant/nutrient.htm)
[271] Urban Garden Magazine — A Fish Called Fertilizer
       (http://urbangardenmagazine.com/2011/02/a-fish-called-fertilizer/)
[272] How to Make Fish Emulsion - Yahoo Voices - voices.yahoo.com
       (http://voices.yahoo.com/how-fish-emulsion-42320.html?cat=32)
[273] Crop Rotation - Wikipedia
       (http://en.wikipedia.org/wiki/Crop_rotation)
[274] Rodale Institute - Crop Rotation
       (http://www.rodaleinstitute.org/20021001/crop_rotate)
[275] GrowVeg.com - Crop Rotation for Growing Vegetables
       (http://www.growveg.com/growguides/crop-rotation.aspx)
[276] Why is Crop Rotation So Important?: Organic Gardening
       (http://www.organicgardening.com/learn-and-grow/crop-rotation)
[277] Root Cellar - Pioneer Living Survival
       (http://www.pioneerliving.net/rootcellar.htm)
[278] Green Home Building: Article about the Lost Art of Pantries and Root Cellars
       (http://www.greenhomebuilding.com/articles/pantries.htm)

[279] Nutrition Facts and Analysis for Corn, Sweet, Yellow, Raw
(http://nutritiondata.self.com/facts/vegetables-and-vegetable-products/2415/2)

[280] How to Grow Corn: Organic Gardening
(http://www.organicgardening.com/learn-and-grow/corn-growing-guide)

[281] Sweet Corn: Planting, Growing and Harvesting Sweet Corn
(http://www.almanac.com/plant/corn)

[282] AZ Master Gardener Manual: Sweet Corn
(http://ag.arizona.edu/pubs/garden/mg/vegetable/corn.html)

[283] ENT-59: Cutworm Management in Corn
(http://www.ca.uky.edu/agc/pubs/ent/ent59/ent59.htm)

[284] Corn Earworm
(http://ipm.ncsu.edu/AG271/corn_sorghum/corn_earworm.html)

[285] European Corn Borer
(http://ipm.ncsu.edu/AG271/corn_sorghum/european_corn_borer.html)

[286] Deer and Other Animal Pests: Organic Gardening
(http://www.organicgardening.com/learn-and-grow/animal-pests)

[287] Homemade Insecticidal Soap Spray — Care2 Healthy Living
(http://www.care2.com/greenliving/homemade-insecticidal-soap.html)

[288] How to Make Cutworm Collars to Protect Seedlings — eHow
(http://www.ehow.com/how_5156427_make-cutworm-collars.html)

[289] The Most Common Beneficial Insects in the Garden: Organic Gardening
(http://www.organicgardening.com/learn-and-grow/meet-beneficial-insects)

[290] Beneficial nematodes control soil dwelling garden and lawn pests
(http://www.arbico-organics.com/product/beneficial-nematodes-info/beneficial-nematodes2)

[291] Nutrition Facts and Analysis for Onions, Raw
(http://nutritiondata.self.com/facts/vegetables-and-vegetable-products/2501/2)

[292] AZ Master Gardener Manual: Onions
(http://ag.arizona.edu/pubs/garden/mg/vegetable/onions.html)

[293] How to Grow Onions: Organic Gardening
(http://www.organicgardening.com/learn-and-grow/onions-growing-guide)

[294] How to grow Onions - all you need to know about growing Onions
(http://www.gardeningpatch.com/vegetable/growing-onions.aspx)

[295] Nutrition Facts and Analysis for Tomatoes
(http://nutritiondata.self.com/facts/vegetables-and-vegetable-products/2682/2)

[296] Tomato nutrition facts and health benefits
(http://www.nutrition-and-you.com/tomato.html)

[297] Growing Tomatoes
(http://www.wvu.edu/~agexten/hortcult/homegard/tomatoes.htm)

[298] Growing Tomatoes for Home Use
(http://www.ces.ncsu.edu/depts/hort/hil/hil-8107.html)

[299] How to Grow Tomatoes: Organic Gardening
(http://www.organicgardening.com/learn-and-grow/tomatoes-growing-guide)

[300] How to grow Tomatoes - all you need to know about growing Tomatoes
(http://www.gardeningpatch.com/vegetable/growing-tomatoes.aspx)

[301] Why are my tomatoes weird?: Organic Gardening
(http://www.organicgardening.com/learn-and-grow/weird-tomatoes)

[302] 10 Tips for Growing Awesome Tomatoes: Organic Gardening
(http://www.organicgardening.com/learn-and-grow/secrets-tomato-growing-success)

[303] Harvesting Heirloom Tomato Seeds - Sunset.com
(http://www.sunset.com/garden/fruits-veggies/harvesting-tomato-seeds-slideshow-00400000012404/)

[304] Nutrition Facts and Analysis for Pepper, Banana, Raw
(http://nutritiondata.self.com/facts/vegetables-and-vegetable-products/3040/2)

[305] How to Grow Peppers - all you need to know about growing Peppers
(http://www.gardeningpatch.com/vegetable/growing-peppers.aspx)

[306] How to Grow Peppers: Organic Gardening
(http://www.organicgardening.com/learn-and-grow/peppers-growing-guide)

[307] Growing Peppers
(http://www.wvu.edu/~agexten/hortcult/homegard/peppers.htm)

Bibliography

[308] Pepper Pests - Learn About Pepper Caterpillars, Pepper Grubs And Other Pepper Worms
(http://www.gardeningknowhow.com/problems/worms-on-peppers.htm)

[309] How to harvest seeds from peppers
(http://site.cleanairgardening.com/info/how-to-harvest-seeds-from-peppers.html)

[310] Growing Peppers In The Home Garden, HYG-1618-92
(http://ohioline.osu.edu/hyg-fact/1000/1618.html)

[311] Peppers: Safe Methods to Store, Preserve, and Enjoy
(http://anrcatalog.ucdavis.edu/pdf/8004.pdf)

[312] Seed Starting 101: Growing Peppers from Seed
(http://davesgarden.com/guides/articles/view/2266/)

[313] How to Rotate Tomato Plants & Peppers — Garden Guides
(http://www.gardenguides.com/127687-rotate-tomato-plants-peppers.html)

[314] Crop Rotation in the vegetable garden
(http://www.gardeningpatch.com/vegetable/crop-rotation.aspx)

[315] Nutrition Facts and Analysis for Cucumber, with Peel, Raw
(http://nutritiondata.self.com/facts/vegetables-and-vegetable-products/2439/2)

[316] Cucumber nutrition facts and health benefits
(http://www.nutrition-and-you.com/cucumber.html)

[317] How to Grow Cucumbers: Organic Gardening
(http://www.organicgardening.com/learn-and-grow/cucumbers)

[318] Nutrition Facts and Analysis for Garlic, Raw
(http://ipm.ncsu.edu/vegetables/pamphlets/cucumber/cucumber.html)

[319] Nutrition Facts and Analysis for Garlic, Raw
(http://nutritiondata.self.com/facts/vegetables-and-vegetable-products/2446/2)

[320] Garlic: How to grow Garlic: Organic Gardening
(http://www.organicgardening.com/learn-and-grow/garlic-buried-treasure)

[321] How to Grow Garlic: Organic Gardening
(http://www.organicgardening.com/learn-and-grow/garlic-growing-guide)

[322] Growing Your Own Garlic is Easy!
(http://www.thedailygreen.com/green-homes/blogs/organic-gardening/growing-garlic-460709)

[323] Garlic Pests
(http://www.garlic-central.com/growing/pests.html)

[324] How Do You Harden Off Plants?
(http://containergardening.about.com/od/containergardening101/f/Hardeningoff.htm)

[325] Soil pH - Wikipedia
(http://en.wikipedia.org/wiki/Soil_pH)

[326] Tips for Garden Soil Preparation and Care
(http://www.lifescript.com/life/timeout/at-home/tips_for_garden_soil_preparation_and_care.aspx)

[327] First Aid Guide and Emergency Treatment Instructions
(http://firstaid.webmd.com/)

[328] First Aid - MayoClinic.com
(http://www.mayoclinic.com/health/FirstAidIndex/FirstAidIndex)

[329] How To Use an Automated External Defibrillator - NHLBI, NIH
(http://www.nhlbi.nih.gov/health/health-topics/topics/aed/howtouse.html)

[330] Ankle Fractures Causes, Symptoms, and Treatments
(http://www.webmd.com/fitness-exercise/ankle-fracture)

[331] Cardiopulmonary resuscitation - Wikipedia
(http://en.wikipedia.org/wiki/CPR)

[332] Cardiopulmonary Resuscitation (CPR) Treatment: First Aid Information for Cardiopulmonary Resuscitation (CPR)
(http://firstaid.webmd.com/cardiopulmonary-resuscitation-cpr-treatment)

[333] Cardiopulmonary Resuscitation (CPR) for Children: First Aid Information for Cardiopulmonary Resuscitation (CPR) For Children
(http://firstaid.webmd.com/cardiopulmonary-resuscitation-cpr-for-children)

[334] How to Perform Rescue Breathing
(http://library.thinkquest.org/26106/rescuebreathing.html)

[335] How to Reduce a Dislocated Shoulder - Putting a Shoulder Back Into Place
(http://orthopedics.about.com/od/instabilitydislocations/ht/milch.htm)

[336] The Trauma Professional's Blog
 (*http://regionstraumapro.com/post/10201631357*)

[337] Blood in Stool and Bleeding in the Digestive Tract: Causes and Symptoms
 (*http://www.webmd.com/digestive-disorders/bleeding-digestive-tract*)

[338] Headache Home Remedies - WebMD
 (*http://www.webmd.com/migraines-headaches/guide/treating-headaches-yourself*)

[339] How to Treat a Wound: 8 Steps (with Pictures) - wikiHow
 (*http://www.wikihow.com/Treat-a-Wound*)

[340] Strengthforcaring.com - Caring for Others - Treating Wounds
 (*http://www.strengthforcaring.com/daily-care/first-aid-and-wound-care-wound-care-and-cleansing/treating-wounds/*)

[341] Wounds and Wound Care
 (*http://www.emedicinehealth.com/wound_care/article_em.htm*)

[342] MEDICAL: Ditch Medicine – Wound and Infection Management — DEATH VALLEY MAGAZINE
 (*http://www.deathvalleymag.com/2010/03/12/medical-ditch-medicine-wound-and-infection-management/*)

[343] Sugar Speeds Wound Healing Home Remedy - The People's Pharmacy
 (*http://www.peoplespharmacy.com/2007/09/17/sugar-speeds-wo/*)

[344] Sugardyne-The Poor Man's Antibiotic
 (*http://knowledgeisthekilleroffear.blogspot.com/2010/03/sugardyne-poor-mans-antibiotic_655.html*)

[345] Reply: Tampons for wounds? — The Modern Survivalist
 (*http://www.themodernsurvivalist.com/archives/2078*)

[346] Muscle cramp - MayoClinic.com
 (*http://www.mayoclinic.com/health/muscle-cramp/DS00311*)

[347] Nocturnal Leg Cramps: Night-time Calf Muscle Pain - For Dummies
 (*http://www.dummies.com/how-to/content/nocturnal-leg-cramps-nighttime-calf-muscle-pain.html*)

[348] Diarrhea - Wikipedia
 (*http://en.wikipedia.org/wiki/Diarrhea*)

[349] Dysentery - Symptoms, Causes, Treatments - Better Medicine
 (*http://health.bettermedicine.com/article/dysentery*)

[350] Dysentery - Symptoms - Better Medicine
 (*http://www.localhealth.com/article/dysentery/symptoms*)

[351] 1918 Spanish Flu Pandemic – The Spanish Flu That Killed Millions in 1918
 (*http://history1900s.about.com/od/1910s/p/spanishflu.htm*)

[352] Does soap kill germs? — Go Ask Alice!
 (*http://www.goaskalice.columbia.edu/1897.html*)

[353] Wood Gas Generator - Wikipedia
 (*http://en.wikipedia.org/wiki/Wood_gas_generator*)

[354] How To Choose The Right Generator - Survival Blog With A Family Focus
 (*http://preparingyourfamily.com/how-to-choose-the-right-generator/*)

[355] Outhouse, Privy, or Dunny Construction & Maintenance Guide
 (*http://www.inspectapedia.com/septic/Outhouse_Latrine.htm*)

[356] SignaLink USB Interface
 (*http://www.tigertronics.com/slusbmain.htm*)

[357] Blood Pressure - Wikipedia
 (*http://en.wikipedia.org/wiki/Blood_pressure*)

[358] Blood Pressure Table for Children & Adults
 (*http://healthblog.yinteing.com/2010/03/07/blood-pressure-table-for-children-adults/*)

[359] Lower That High Blood Pressure Now : Health tips! - News - Bubblews
 (*http://www.bubblews.com/news/201135-lower-that-high-blood-pressure-now-health-tips*)

[360] Heart rate: What's normal? - MayoClinic.com
 (*http://www.mayoclinic.com/health/heart-rate/AN01906*)

[361] Bodybuilding.com - Measuring Your Heart Rate For Fitness!
 (*http://www.bodybuilding.com/fun/moser9.htm*)

[362] What Is A Normal Resting Heart Rate For Children? — LIVESTRONG.COM
 (*http://www.livestrong.com/article/102102-normal-resting-heart-rate-children/*)

[363] Fracture - Broken Bone - Diagnosis and Treatment
 (*http://sportsmedicine.about.com/od/paininjury1/a/Fractures.htm*)

Bibliography

[364] Broken Ankle Symptoms: Break or a Sprain? - Yahoo Voices - voices.yahoo.com
(http://voices.yahoo.com/broken-ankle-symptoms-break-sprain-1617851.html?cat=5)

[365] How to Tell the Difference Between an Ankle Sprain and a Break — eHow
(http://www.ehow.com/how_2050860_tell-difference-between-ankle-sprain.html)

[366] Physical Exercise - Wikipedia
(http://en.wikipedia.org/wiki/Physical_exercise)

[367] Maintaining Proper Hydration - Online Articles: National Council on Strength and Fitness Trainer's Tools
(http://www.ncsf.org/enew/articles/articles-properhydration.aspx)

[368] Avoiding Dehydration, Proper Hydration
(http://my.clevelandclinic.org/disorders/dehydration/hic_avoiding_dehydration.aspx)

[369] Dehydration - Wikipedia
(http://en.wikipedia.org/wiki/Dehydration)

[370] What Is Nutrition? Why Is Nutrition Important?
(http://www.medicalnewstoday.com/articles/160774.php)

[371] Triage - Wikipedia
(http://en.wikipedia.org/wiki/Triage)

[372] Influenza Self-Care - Taking a Temperature - Alberta Health
(http://www.health.alberta.ca/health-info/influenza-take-temperature.html)

[373] Honey - Wikipedia
(http://en.wikipedia.org/wiki/Honey)

[374] The Importance of Probiotics After Antibiotics
(http://www.naturalnews.com/037005_antibiotics_probiotics_gut_flora.html)

[375] Digestive Care, Stomach Ulcer Relief - Melita Honey Farm
(http://www.thehoneyfarm.com.au/acatalog/Digestive_Care.html)

[376] Bio Activity of Manuka Honey
(http://www.beesandtrees.com/pages/bio-activity-of-manuka-honey)

[377] Garlic As the Natural Antibiotic
(http://blessedmommy.hubpages.com/hub/Garlic--The-Natural-Antibiotic)

[378] Fight Illness Naturally with a Garlic Poultice
(http://simplehomemade.net/fight-illness-naturally-with-a-garlic-poultice/)

[379] Andrographis – 3 Health Benefits You May Not Know About
(http://altmedicine.about.com/od/herbsupplementguide/a/andrographis.htm)

[380] ANDROGRAPHIS: Uses, Side Effects, Interactions and Warnings - WebMD
(http://www.webmd.com/vitamins-supplements/ingredientmono-973-ANDROGRAPHIS.aspx? activeIngredientId=973&activeIngredientName=ANDROGRAPHIS)

[381] Goldenseal : Science and Safety - NCCAM
(http://nccam.nih.gov/health/goldenseal)

[382] Coconut Oil Offers Hope for Antibiotic-Resistant Germs — Coconut Oil
(http://coconutoil.com/coconut-oil-offers-hope-for-antibiotic-resistant-germs/)

[383] Tea Tree Oil - What Should I Know About It?
(http://altmedicine.about.com/od/herbsupplementguide/a/TeaTreeOil.htm)

[384] ECHINACEA: Uses, Side Effects, Interactions and Warnings - WebMD
(http://www.webmd.com/vitamins-supplements/ingredientmono-981-ECHINACEA.aspx? activeIngredientId=981&activeIngredientName=ECHINACEA)

[385] PAU D'ARCO: Uses, Side Effects, Interactions and Warnings - WebMD
(http://www.webmd.com/vitamins-supplements/ingredientmono-647-PAUD'ARCO.aspx? activeIngredientId=647&activeIngredientName=PAUD'ARCO)

[386] Pau d'Arco Benefits and Cautions Explained in Detail
(http://www.paudarco.org/)

[387] List Of Natural Antibiotics — LIVESTRONG.COM
(http://www.livestrong.com/article/58240-list-natural-antibiotics/)

[388] Natural Antibiotics
(http://the-health-gazette.com/293/natural-antibiotics/)

[389] Basic Bullet Guide - Gun Noob
(http://www.gunnoob.com/HandgunGuides/BasicBulletGuide.aspx)

[390] American Rifleman - Choosing a Home-Defense Gun
(http://www.americanrifleman.org/articles/best-gun-for-home-defense/)

[391] Home Defense: The Best Survival Guns
(http://www.livingreadyonline.com/gear-advice/best-survival-gun)

[392] Fake Silver Moly-Bars?
(http://www.roadtoroota.com/public/212.cfm)

[393] FDR's Gold Confiscation, 80 Years On
(http://dailyreckoning.com/fdrs-gold-confiscation-80-years-on/)

[394] Krugerrand - Wikipedia
(http://en.wikipedia.org/wiki/Kruggerrand)

[395] Definition of Receiver as it Pertains to Guns and Shooting
(http://hunting.about.com/od/guns/g/definition-of-receiver-gun-parts-rifle-shotgun.htm)

[396] Definition of Frame as it Pertains to Guns and Shooting
(http://hunting.about.com/od/guns/g/definition-of-frame-firearms-guns.htm)

[397] Definition of Bolt as it Pertains to Guns and Shooting
(http://hunting.about.com/od/guns/g/definition-of-bolt-rifle-shotgun-pistol-revolver.htm)

[398] Soft Point Bullet - Wikipedia
(http://en.wikipedia.org/wiki/Soft_point_bullet)

[399] Hollow Point Bullet - Wikipedia
(http://en.wikipedia.org/wiki/Hollow-point_bullet)

[400] Full Metal Jacket Bullet - Wikipedia
(http://en.wikipedia.org/wiki/Full_metal_jacket_bullet)

[401] The Truth About High Velocity Hunting Bullets — Field & Stream
(http://www.fieldandstream.com/articles/guns/rifles/ammunition/2009/11/why-super-speed-cartridges-dont-kill-any-faster-and-actually)

[402] Reticle - Wikipedia
(http://en.wikipedia.org/wiki/Reticle)

[403] Trijicon, Inc.
(http://www.trijicon.com/na_en/support/how_to_use_mil_dot.php)

[404] .223 Remington Rifle Cartridge - Wikipedia
(http://en.wikipedia.org/wiki/.223_Remington)

[405] .308 Winchester Rifle Cartridge - Wikipedia
(http://en.wikipedia.org/wiki/.308_Winchester\#Usage_and_performance)

[406] 7.62x39mm Cartridge - Wikipedia
(http://en.wikipedia.org/wiki/7.62x39mm)

[407] .30-06 Springfield Rifle Cartridge - Wikipedia
(http://en.wikipedia.org/wiki/.30-06_Springfield)

[408] .270 Winchester Rifle Cartridge - Wikipedia
(http://en.wikipedia.org/wiki/.270_Winchester)

[409] 5.45x39mm Cartridge - Wikipedia
(http://en.wikipedia.org/wiki/5.45mm)

[410] .243 Winchester Rifle Cartridge - Wikipedia
(http://en.wikipedia.org/wiki/.243_Winchester)

[411] 7mm Remington Magnum Rifle Cartridge - Wikipedia
(http://en.wikipedia.org/wiki/7mm_Remington_Magnum)

[412] .300 Winchester Magnum Rifle Cartridge - Wikipedia
(http://en.wikipedia.org/wiki/.300_Winchester_Magnum)

[413] .338 Winchester Magnum Cartridge - Wikipedia
(http://en.wikipedia.org/wiki/.338_Winchester_Magnum)

[414] .30-30 Rifle Cartridge - Wikipedia
(http://en.wikipedia.org/wiki/.30-30_Winchester)

[415] .22 Long Rifle Cartridge - Wikipedia
(http://en.wikipedia.org/wiki/.22LR)

[416] Galileo's Leaning Tower of Pisa Experiment - Wikipedia
(http://en.wikipedia.org/wiki/Galileo's_Leaning_Tower_of_Pisa_experiment)

[417] Riflescopes 101
(http://www.opticsplanet.com/how-to-choose-riflescope.html)

[418] Suppressor - Wikipedia
(https://en.wikipedia.org/wiki/Suppressor)

[419] Red Dot Sights - Wikipedia
(http://en.wikipedia.org/wiki/Red_dot_sight)

[420] Firearm Maintenance - Wikipedia
(http://en.wikipedia.org/wiki/Firearm_maintenance)

Bibliography

[421] Easy & Effective Gun Maintenance
(http://www.gameandfishmag.com/2010/10/08/hunting_guns-shooting_gf_aa116902a/)

[422] Some Tips on Cleaning and Lubricating Firearms
(http://home.comcast.net/~dsmjd/tux/dsmjd/tech/clean_lube.htm)

[423] The AR-10 Rifle - Wikipedia
(http://en.wikipedia.org/wiki/AR-10)

[424] Mosin Nagant - Wikipedia
(http://en.wikipedia.org/wiki/Mosin-Nagant)

[425] 7.62x4mm Caliber Rifle Cartridge - Wikipedia
(http://en.wikipedia.org/wiki/7.62x4mmR)

[426] Tanglefoot - Wikipedia
(http://en.wikipedia.org/wiki/Tanglefoot)

[427] Catfish Slime's Healing Agents - New York Times
(http://www.nytimes.com/1988/01/26/science/catfish-slime-s-healing-agents.html)

[428] How to Build a Small Game Snare — The Art of Manliness
(http://www.artofmanliness.com/2012/03/29/how-to-build-a-small-game-survival-snare/)

[429] Wilderness Survival: Food Procurement - Traps and Snares
(http://www.wilderness-survival.net/food-2.php)

[430] California Quail - Wikipedia
(http://en.wikipedia.org/wiki/California_quail)

[431] Bobwhite Quail - Wikipedia
(http://en.wikipedia.org/wiki/Bobwhite_Quail)

[432] New World Quail - Wikipedia
(http://en.wikipedia.org/wiki/New_World_quail)

[433] Quail Eggs - Wikipedia
(http://en.wikipedia.org/wiki/Quail_eggs)

[434] Hunting Quail—Quail Hunting Tips—How To Hunt Quail—Huntland.com
(http://www.huntland.com/hunting-tips/quail/)

[435] Beginner's Guide to Quail Hunting - Yahoo Voices - voices.yahoo.com
(http://voices.yahoo.com/beginners-guide-quail-hunting-3336934.html)

[436] American Bobwhite Quail Hunting – a Beginners Guide - Yahoo Voices - voices.yahoo.com
(http://voices.yahoo.com/american-bobwhite-quail-hunting-beginners-guide-3333422.html?cat=11)

[437] Florida Quail: Ecology Distribution and Status
(http://www.wec.ufl.edu/floridaquail/Ecology/Distribution.htm)

[438] Rabbit - Wikipedia
(http://en.wikipedia.org/wiki/Rabbit)

[439] Hare - Wikipedia
(http://en.wikipedia.org/wiki/Hare)

[440] Rabbit Meat Information
(http://rabbitmeat.webs.com/)

[441] Cottontail Rabbits, Cottontail Rabbit Pictures, Cottontail Rabbit Facts - National Geographic
(http://animals.nationalgeographic.com/animals/mammals/cottontail-rabbit/)

[442] European Hare - Wikipedia
(http://en.wikipedia.org/wiki/European_hare)

[443] Rabbiting - Wikipedia
(http://en.wikipedia.org/wiki/Rabbiting)

[444] 12 Tips for Rabbit Hunters
(http://www.basspro.com/webapp/wcs/stores/servlet/CFPage?catalogId=10001\&mode=article\&objectID=28528\&storeId=10151)

[445] Techniques and Tips for Rabbit Hunting Without a Dog - Yahoo Voices - voices.yahoo.com
(http://voices.yahoo.com/techniques-tips-rabbit-hunting-without-dog-689332.html?cat=11)

[446] Ten Tips for Taking Winter Rabbits
(http://www.gameandfishmag.com/2010/12/03/hunting_rabbits-hares-squirrels-hunting_gf_aa016805a/)

[447] TIPS FOR EARLY SEASON RABBIT HUNTERS — Don Gasaway's Blog
(http://dongasaway.wordpress.com/2011/10/28/tips-for-early-season-rabbit-hunters/)

[448] Pheasant - A great game for a great meal
(http://bbq.about.com/od/poultry/a/aa121005a.htm)

[449] Ring-necked Pheasant Range Map
(http://sdakotabirds.com/species/maps/ring_necked_pheasant_map.htm)

[450] The Common Pheasant - Wikipedia
(http://en.wikipedia.org/wiki/Common_Pheasant)

[451] Pheasant Hunting Basics
(http://www.dccl.org/information/pheasant/pheasant_hunting_basics.htm)

[452] Pheasant Ecology: Food & Cover Plots
(http://www.pheasantsforever.org/page/1/foodandcover.jsp)

[453] 10 Pheasant Hunting Tips - Game & Fish
(http://www.gameandfishmag.com/2007/11/01/10-pheasant-hunting-tips/)

[454] The Locavore Hunter™: Squirrel Meat: Chicken of The Tree
(http://rule-303.blogspot.com/2010/06/squirrel-meat-chicken-of-tree.html)

[455] Squirrel Hunting Tips — Field & Stream
(http://www.fieldandstream.com/articles/hunting/small-game/when-hunt-rabbits-squirrels-and-other-small-game/2009/09/stalking-squirr)

[456] Squirrel Hunting Tips for Beginner and Experienced Hunters - Yahoo Voices - voices.yahoo.com
(http://voices.yahoo.com/squirrel-hunting-tips-beginner-experienced-3888154.html?cat=11)

[457] American Hunter - Tips for Early Season Squirrel Hunting
(http://www.americanhunter.org/articles/early-fall-squirrel-hunting-tips)

[458] Squirrel - Wikipedia
(http://en.wikipedia.org/wiki/Squirrel)

[459] Squirrel Printable Page from National Geographic Animals
(http://animals.nationalgeographic.com/animals/printable/squirrel.html)

[460] Turkey (bird) - Wikipedia
(http://en.wikipedia.org/wiki/Turkey_(bird))

[461] Turkey Hunting - Wikipedia
(http://en.wikipedia.org/wiki/Turkey_hunting)

[462] Top Ten Tips for Turkey Hunting —
(http://my.kingscamo.com/2013/top-ten-tips-for-turkey-hunting/)

[463] Turkey Hunting—Wild Turkey Hunt—How To Hunt Turkey—Huntland.com
(http://www.huntland.com/hunting-tips/turkey/)

[464] Turkey Hunting: Tips and Tactics from the Masters — Outdoor Life
(http://www.outdoorlife.com/blogs/strut-zone/2013/03/hunting-tips-3-turkey-masters)

[465] Spring Turkey Tips
(http://www.dccl.org/information/turkey/turkeyhunt.htm)

[466] Wild Turkey, Sounds, All About Birds - Cornell Lab of Ornithology
(http://www.allaboutbirds.org/guide/wild_turkey/sounds)

[467] Turkey Meat - Wikipedia
(https://en.wikipedia.org/wiki/Turkey_meat)

[468] Turkey Facts
(http://biology.about.com/od/birds/a/turkey_facts.htm)

[469] Turkey Loads - The Shooter's Log
(http://cheaperthandirt.com/blog/?p=2297)

[470] How does wild boar taste? — Field & Stream
(http://www.fieldandstream.com/answers/hunting/big-game-hunting/hunting-hogs/how-does-wild-boar-taste)

[471] Wild Boar - Wikipedia
(http://en.wikipedia.org/wiki/Wild_boar)

[472] Where to Shoot a Wild Boar Hog - Boar Hogs Aren't Built Like Deer
(http://hunting.about.com/od/deerbiggame/a/wheretoshoothog.htm)

[473] Tips and Tricks — Boarmasters — Bear, Hog, Deer, and Elk Bait, Lures, Attractants, Snares, and Hunting
(http://boarmasters.com/tips-tricks/)

[474] Hunting Wild Boars & Feral Pigs - Species Facts & Differences, Using Outfitters
(http://www.outfittersrating.com/species/featured-species/wild-boars-and-feral-pigs)

[475] Tips for a Successful and Exciting Wild Boar Hunt — The Outdoors Guy
(http://www.theoutdoorsguy.com/2009/10/tips-for-a-successful-and-exciting-wild-boar-hunt/)

[476] Facts on Feral Hogs
(http://www.texasboars.com/articles/facts.html)

[477] How to Field Dress a Wild Hog
       (http://militaryhuntingandfishing.com/field_dress_a_hog)

[478] Mule Deer - Wikipedia
       (http://en.wikipedia.org/wiki/Mule_deer)

[479] White-tailed Deer - Wikipedia
       (http://en.wikipedia.org/wiki/White-tailed_deer)

[480] Deer Hunting Tips - Huntland.com
       (http://www.huntland.com/hunting-tips/deer/)

[481] 10 Tips for Whitetail Deer Bow Hunting - Yahoo Voices
       (http://voices.yahoo.com/10-tips-whitetail-deer-bow-hunting-3887396.html)

[482] 4 Ways to Go Deer Hunting - WikiHow
       (http://www.wikihow.com/Go-Deer-Hunting)

[483] Deer Hunting for Beginners
       (http://www.motherearthnews.com/homesteading-and-livestock/deer-hunting-beginners-zmaz89ndzshe.aspx)

[484] Hunting Mule Deer
       (http://www.motherearthnews.com/homesteading-and-livestock/hunting-mule-deer-zmaz89ndzshe.aspx)

[485] Deer Hunting Basics Article
       (http://www.knightandhale.com/huntingarticles/deerhunting/favoritebiggame)

[486] Is Deer Meat Dangerous? - Dr. Weil
       (http://www.drweil.com/drw/u/QAA347474/is-deer-meat-dangerous.html)

[487] Deer Meat - Broken Arrow Ranch
       (http://www.brokenarrowranch.com/Articles/deer-meat.htm)

[488] Whitetail Deer
       (http://www.norcrossws.org/Animals/Deer\%20information.htm)

[489] Foraging - Wikipedia
       (http://en.wikipedia.org/wiki/Foraging)

[490] Wilderness Survival Skills: Foraging Edible Plants
       (http://www.motherearthnews.com/nature-and-environment/foraging-edible-plants-zmaz82mjzglo.aspx\#1376013309152 1\&action=collapse_widget\&id=8314412)

[491] Tips on Wild Food Foraging, by T.B.P. - SurvivalBlog.com
       (http://www.survivalblog.com/2011/02/tips-on-wild-food-foraging-by.html)

[492] Survival Lab: Eat Out
       (http://www.backpacker.com/march-2013-survival-lab-eat-out/survival/17289)

[493] Get to Know Your Edible Berries with a Simple Mnemonic
       (http://lifehacker.com/5334055/get-to-know-your-edible-berries-with-a-simple-mnemonic)

[494] Foraging - Edible wild plants - Edible insects, by G.B. - Survival Food Gear
       (http://www.survivalfoodgear.com/2013/04/27/foraging-edible-wild-plants-edible-insects-by-g-b/)

[495] Wilderness Survival Skills
       (http://www.primitiveways.com/survival_skills2.html)

[496] Edible Insects: Field Crickets — Advanced Survival Guide.com
       (http://advancedsurvivalguide.com/2013/04/04/edible-insects-field-crickets/)

[497] Eating Insects For Survival — Field & Stream
       (http://www.fieldandstream.com/articles/survival/survival-food/2010/08/eating-insects-survival)

[498] Survival: Insects, Lunch with Crunch - Yahoo Voices - voices.yahoo.com
       (http://voices.yahoo.com/survival-insects-lunch-crunch-1570869.html?cat=16)

[499] Nuts and your heart: Eating nuts for heart health - MayoClinic.com
       (http://www.mayoclinic.com/health/nuts/HB00085)

[500] Typha - Wikipedia
       (http://en.wikipedia.org/wiki/Cattail)

[501] Theodore Tex — Texas Monthly
       (http://www.texasmonthly.com/story/theodore-tex)

[502] Electrocardiography - Wikipedia
       (http://en.wikipedia.org/wiki/EKG)

[503] Harvard Health Publications
       (http://www.health.harvard.edu/diagnostic-tests/oxygen-saturation-test.htm)

[504] About BMI for Adults
       (http: // www. cdc. gov/ healthyweight/ assessing/ bmi/ adult_ bmi/ index. html)
[505] Circulation Ultrasound — See My Heart
       (http: // www. seemyheart. org/ circulation-ultrasound/)
[506] Guidelines For Beginning an Exercise Program
       (http: // www. timinvermont. com/ fitness/ guidline. htm)
[507] Survival Fighting
       (http: // www. civiliandefenseforce. com/ survivalfighting. html)
[508] U.S. Spies: 4 Steps to Collect, Analyze and Make Intelligence Work For You : ITS Tactical
       (http://www.itstactical.com/intellicom/tradecraft/u-s-spies-4-steps-to-collect-analyze
       -and-make-intelligence-work-for-you/)
[509] Survival Intelligence – Don’t Underestimate the Power of Information
       (http: // offgridsurvival. com/ survivalintelligence/)
[510] Federation of American Societies for Experimental Biology. "Honey as an antibiotic: Scientists identify a secret
       ingredient in honey that kills bacteria." ScienceDaily, 12 Jul. 2010. Web. 17 Mar. 2013.
[511] Society for General Microbiology. "How Manuka Honey Helps Fight Infection." ScienceDaily, 10 Sep. 2009. Web. 17
       Mar. 2013.
[512] How much land does it take to be self-reliant?
       (http: // www. thesurvivalistblog. net/ how-much-land-does-it-take-to-be-self-reliant/)
[513] The Definitive Guide to Storing Gold and Silver by Doyle Shuler
[514] Basic Feeding Guide for Dogs, How Much Should I Feed My Dog?
       (http: // www. dogbreedinfo. com/ feeding. htm)
[515] Guard Dog - Wikipedia
       (http: // en. wikipedia. org/ wiki/ Guard_ dog)
[516] Underground Bunkers Now and Then
       (urlhttp://smartproducttechnology.com/articles/underground-bunkers-now-and-then-and-the-top-ten-things-to-
       consider-when-planning-a-bunker)
[517] Bomb Shelter FAQ's
       (http: // undergroundbombshelter. com/ bomb-shelter-questions. htm)

501

Index